D1565916

Sexual Cultures and Migration in the Era of AIDS

international union
for the scientific study
of population

The International Union for the Scientific Study of Population Problems was set up in 1928, with Dr Raymond Pearl as President. At that time the Union's main purpose was to promote international scientific co-operation to study the various aspects of population problems, through national committees and through its members themselves. In 1947 the International Union for the Scientific Study of Population (IUSSP) was reconstituted into its present form.

It expanded its activities to:

- stimulate research on population
- develop interest in demographic matters among governments, national and international organizations, scientific bodies, and the general public
- foster relations between people involved in population studies
- disseminate scientific knowledge on population

The principal ways through which the IUSSP currently achieves its aims are:

- organization of worldwide or regional conferences
- operations of Scientific Committees under the auspices of the Council
- organization of training courses
- publication of conference proceedings and committee reports

Demography can be defined by its field of study and its analytical methods. Accordingly, it can be regarded as the scientific study of human populations primarily with respect to their size, their structure, and their development. For reasons which are related to the history of the discipline, and demographic method is essentially inductive: progress in knowledge results from the improvement of observation, the sophistication of measurement methods, and the search for regularities and stable factors leading to the formulation of explanatory models. In conclusion, the three objectives of demographic analysis are to describe, measure, and analyse.

International Studies in Demography is the outcome of an agreement concluded by the IUSSP and the Oxford University Press. The joint series is expected to reflect the broad range of the Union's activities and, in the first instance, will be based on the seminars organized by the Union. The Editorial Board of the series is comprised of:

Sexual Cultures and Migration in the Era of AIDS

Anthropological and Demographic Perspectives

Edited by

Gilbert Herdt

CLARENDON PRESS · OXFORD

1997

Oxford University Press, Great Clarendon Street, Oxford OX2 6DP

Oxford New York
Athens Auckland Bangkok Bombay Bogota
Buenos Aires Calcutta Cape Town Dar es Salaam
Delhi Florence Hong Kong Istanbul Karachi
Kuala Lumpur Madras Madrid Melbourne
Mexico City Nairobi Paris Singapore
Taipei Tokyo Toronto

and associated companies in
Berlin Ibadan

Oxford is a trade mark of Oxford University Press

Published in the United States
by Oxford University Press Inc., New York

British Library Cataloguing in Publication Data
Data available

Library of Congress Cataloguing in Publication Data
Data available

ISBN 0-19-829230-9

1 3 5 7 9 10 8 6 4 2

Typeset by Alliance Phototypesetters
Printed in Great Britain
on acid-free paper by
Bookcraft (Bath) Ltd., Midsomer Norton, Somerset

To John H. Gagnon, scholar and friend,
grand doyen of sex research

Preface

During the last decade few topics have provoked more controversy and a larger storm of research in anthropology and demography than the analysis of sexual risk behaviour in the global spread of sexually transmitted diseases. This thematic has been of special interest to the Committee on Anthropological Demography (International Union for the Scientific Study of Population), because of the intersection of the critical demographic interest in fertility and migration, and the new-found anthropological research on AIDS and sexuality. Demographers and anthropologists alike have found themselves caught up in an explosion of international research and education campaigns to prevent the spread of the disease. This research has included study of cross-cultural migration, new sexual practices and the commercial sex trade, and the spread of HIV/AIDS across subgroups, ethnic boundaries, cultural regions, and international borders. The transnational spread of the disease has stimulated a new dialogue between the fields of anthropology and demography and that of epidemiology, where organizations such as the World Health Organization and the Center for Disease Control have carried out surveys on the impact of human movement and sexual disease on demographic behaviours. However, it remains for anthropological demography to assist in the creation of models that integrate field methodology and qualitative data with extensive data panels for the purpose of conceptualizing the larger map of issues.

The contents of this book result from a conference convened in Bangkok, Thailand, in March 1994, which was broadly concerned with the relationship between migration and sexual practices, and AIDS in developing countries. The conference was organized by the IUSSP in cooperation with the Institute of Population Studies of Chulalongkorn University. Many research scholars made presentations and a variety of observers were also present for the meetings and intensive study workshops. The definition of sexual culture and social-historical formations that result in sexual encounters and the interruption of fertility behaviour across cultural boundaries were of particular interest to the symposium. The conference was an initiative of the Committee on Anthropological Demography, a research group attached to the IUSSP.

The meeting was organized and chaired by Dr Gilbert Herdt, an anthropologist on the Committee for Human Development of the University of Chicago. Dr Alaka Basu (Chair) and Dr Kim Streatrim of the Committee on Demographic Anthropology, and the late Mr Bruno Remiche, Executive Director of the IUSSP, participated. The meeting was funded under the auspices of the IUSSP and was supported in part by the Australian Development Commission and the Population Research Institute of Thailand. For their kind help and sponsorship, we should like to thank the following persons: Charas Suwanweal, President of Chulalongkorn University; Dr Kua Wongboonsin, Director of the Population Research Institute; Penporn Tirasawat of the Institute; along with many others from the Institute and University. We are especially indebted to Penporn Tirasawat for her gracious hospitality. We are sad at the passing of Mr Remiche and wish to convey our deepest sympathy to his family and friends.

I wish to acknowledge the help of the following persons who contributed to the success of the conference; Dr Caroline Bledsoe of Northwestern University; Dr Chayan Vanhanaphuti of Chiang Mai University; Dr Han ten Brummelhuis of the University of Amsterdam; Dr Kate Bond of the Institute of Social Research, Chiang Mai University; Dr Joseph Carrier of Los Angeles; and Mr Jan-Willem van Wyngaarten of the University of Amsterdam.

Finally, I would like to exercise my prerogative as editor in dedicating this book to my dear friend and colleague, Dr John H. Gagnon, Professor of Sociology at the State University of New York, Stony Brook. John will be surprised to learn of this dedication, because it was never discussed with him, and he participated in the symposium as one senior scholar among many others. However, there is only one John Gagnon, whose knowledge and erudition in the area of international sex research is unsurpassed and has been an inspiration to me and many others for at least a generation. This book is a small token of our gratitude.

G. H.

Chicago, Illinois
June 1996

Contents

Part I

Introduction

1 Sexual Cultures and Population Movement:
Implications for AIDS/STDs

GILBERT HERDT

Introduction

The contributors to this volume have grappled with the fundamental observation that as people migrate, the rules of sexual behaviour change, opening new avenues for sexual encounter, but also exposing the person to enhanced risk of HIV and STDs. Human mobility in the era of AIDS has dramatically increased the potential for the spread of the HIV virus and other sexually transmitted diseases in populations around the world. AIDS/HIV is now the leading killer of persons between the ages of 25 and 44 in the United States and similar Western nations. It is the leading cause of adult death in many Third World countries. Since these years are crucial to fertility in humans, and are also the time of greatest aggregate human movement, there can be little doubt of the urgent need to gain an understanding of the interaction between migration and sexual risk in AIDS/STD epidemics. It is therefore not surprising that a group of anthropologists and demographers, colleagues from social epidemiology and the health sciences, should come together to discuss these urgent problems.

Three interconnected processes are relevant to current perspectives on human movement and sexual transition: first, the worldwide increase in human movement and mobility, leading people across the boundaries of their own group— from rural to urban, urban to agrarian, or across national borders—into unknown sexual cultures; second, the historical emergence of sexual cultures and subcultures which create new contexts of behaviour, codes for sexual conduct, and networks for encounters between strangers, as in the dense urban society which gives rise to commercial sex; and third, the emergence of new sexually transmitted diseases, especially HIV/AIDS, which have created sexual risks for immigrants. Unprecedented sexual education and prevention efforts are being undertaken in many of these areas to reduce the risk of infection. Nonetheless, a question of global politics and polities is arising as never before. There is a growing crisis of policies within and between countries: as refugees and migrants increase in number, and as these persons are often in their prime reproductive years, the possibility of disruption to sexual systems and reproductive behaviour increases.

Many symposia over the past few years have examined aspects of these issues and numerous books have taken up one or another of the issues embedded within them, but none has tried to put these perspectives together. We can conceptualize how movement into new sexual cultures brings unprecedented sexual risk practices, increasing the probability of infection from sexually transmitted diseases such as HIV and simultaneously lowering fertility in the migrant populations. A global epidemic of these proportions requires culturally sensitive epidemiologies (Parker, Herdt, and Carballo, 1991). Rethinking theory and methodology in these areas has disrupted what John Gagnon (1992) has called the 'practice of social studies'; that is, the very paradigms through which normal science in the fields of anthropology and demography have addressed and studied culture and population. The studies in this book open up new areas of research as well as basic initiatives in education and prevention research regarding these processes. While case studies are drawn from cultures around the world, including Western nations, the emphasis is on Third World countries that are currently in the throes of the new sexual revolution.

Demographic anthropology is a young and interdisciplinary hybrid field that negotiates differences between the two areas of study. As Georgia Kaufmann has remarked, while anthropology finds 'meanings', demography finds 'facts'. Anthropology as a complex discipline involves quantitative and qualitative assessment. But in the classical encounter with other cultures the ethnographer is wrestling with questions of profound social and cultural significance—such as the relationship between gender roles and religious ritual, or the impact of ecological change on the family system—that invite interpretation, rather than measurement in the more rigorous empirical sense of the term. In the study of fertility and reproduction, demography has often staked a position in science that favoured surveys and quantitative assessment over the field report, with the effect that the meanings of practices, such as reproductive behaviours, have largely gone by the wayside. In a timely review, Watkins (1993) has suggested that this left out the lives of women and their role in the cultures of study. Kaufmann has also commented that when demographers turned to the study of female sexuality, social control seemed to be foremost in conceptualizing the findings. John Caldwell and colleagues (Chapter 3, below) have suggested that the survey method is the key to demography; and for all its problems, the survey method reveals long-term trends, such as fertility change, better than another methodology. Thus, we in these two fields spend a great deal of time criticizing our concepts and methodologies, as well as each other's data—signs that demographic anthropology straddles the border between science and the art of discovery, more like natural history. While this might be bad news in some corners of research, it is probably what is most needed at present to advance the study and understanding of sexuality and HIV in a cross-cultural context.

Changing Paradigms: Science, Sex, and Population

That the AIDS pandemic has had a fundamental impact on all the sciences is now widely accepted by historians of science and medicine and by those who have observed the workings of health science at close hand in the context of the epidemic over the past decade (Brandt, 1988; Burridge, 1992; Patton, 1990). Some would go so far as to suggest that 'science' will never be the same again. The inclusion of Third World views, especially on poverty and health risk, has had a critical impact on scientific thinking in its own right (Farmer, 1992; Gagnon, 1992). Several factors have amounted to a new challenge facing anthropology and demography; these include the kinds of observations considered necessary and sufficient to provide an 'account' of the disease, the insistence on community or population models in explanations of the spread of disease, describing the motives of the scientific players in the marketplace of research, and the political constituencies which read them (Abramson and Herdt, 1990; Carrier and Bolton, 1991; Herdt and Lindenbaum eds., 1992).

Sexuality has played a special part in the historical challenge posed by AIDS to science. In particular, it is now widely agreed that sexuality was ignored in social science for most of this century and that the AIDS epidemic has stimulated the greatest amount of sexuality research in history (Bolton, 1994; Laumann *et al.*, 1994). A strong tendency existed in the biological and social sciences to treat sexuality as a 'natural' function whose ultimate, or teleological purpose, was restricted to procreation (Herdt, 1994). Consequently, sexuality was perceived to be outside of culture and history, as if the interactions and relationships that resulted in sexual encounters or partnerships had nothing to do with society. In classical anthropological studies from the 1940s to the 1980s, sexual behaviour was typically omitted from the ethnographies of cultures. When sexual relations were mentioned, usually as a one-liner and an aside, they were noted in the context of reproduction and spousal relations. Reproduction was regarded as a 'natural history' mechanism of the kinship and marriage system. However, whatever differed in non-Western groups from the Western norm at the time, such as the approval of childhood sexual play, premarital sexual relations or same-sex practices— mistakenly labelled 'homosexuality'—was typically ignored or treated as beyond the limits of competence of the social anthropologist, as Vance (1991) has justly observed.

Thus, sexuality study was in a kind of 'pre-scientific period' prior to the AIDS epidemic: the constructs were often flawed by false assumptions about categories and behaviours; the methods were imperfectly applied to the phenomenon; and the quality of data was poor, complicated by the fact that most sexuality research had come out of the West (Parker and Gagnon, 1995; Weeks, 1985). Since about 1985, however, social science study at home and abroad has made tremendous advances, thanks in part to the explosion of international research on sexuality; indeed, it has been difficult to keep pace with new findings. National studies of the prevalence of sexual behaviour and HIV risk, in the United States, France, and England, resulting from survey studies constructed on the basis of national probability samples, have made available powerful new evidence about the hidden sexual patterns in society. With these discoveries come new questions about, for example, the average rate of sexual intercourse in a population. At the same time that new basic knowledge has been emerging, science has faced a series of deeply divisive questions regarding what sexuality is, whether science is biased in studying it by virtue of the position of science in political culture, whether the methods currently available are adequate for the task, and what value sexual study has for society and public health.

It is possible to identify three phases of the new sexual risk research impact on HIV/AIDS. These areas encompass developments in research, training, prevention, education, and the delivery of services to those in need. Anthropologists have argued that these areas undergo change as the society itself accepts the inherent problems of public discussion about sexual disease risk on a large and open scale, often for the first time in history. First is what we might call the 'discovery' phase of the work, where scientists attempt to examine the question: What is sexuality and sexual risk? They seek answers by way of defining basic phenomena, their boundaries or perimeters, and the unit of observation. Second is what we might call the 'modelling' phase of the work. Here, investigators ask the question: How do we know what sexual risk is and how do we define it? What methods do we employ? What do we emphasize and what do we marginalize in the effort to model the phenomenon, first in the lab, or on paper, or in our heads, and then in real world contexts, through interviews, surveys, focus groups, and so on? Third is the 'action' stage, wherein having discovered a pattern of sexual risk, and then having modelled it, action scientists seek to implement the model in order to reinforce or prevent or alter the pattern, with the ultimate aim of eradicating the disease. These narratives of discovery offer much insight into the work of anthropology and demography during the last few years. In this volume, Chapter 3 by Caldwell, Anarfi, and Caldwell on Africa and, more generally, Chapter 7 by Caraël reveal the advances and setbacks wrought by successive waves of AIDS/STD epidemics. The field sciences advance, but are then forced to take a step back; and then go on; it is not a neat and tidy, linear process (Turner *et al.*, 1989).

How is the social scientist to study populations in constant movement? Neither the form of the classical household survey in demography or survey sociology, nor the one-point-in-time ethnography of anthropology, were designed to meet the challenge of studying people on the move. Such mobility complicates the study of population, forcing cross-sectional designs, opportunistic ethnography, and focus groups (Carrier *et al.*, Chapter 13 below). Human movement makes the task of describing sexual cultures and their meaning systems a problem of incredible globetrotting for field workers, who were previously unprepared for the disruptions of time and space which undermine the idea of a 'culture' situated in a particular field site. Yet it is precisely these innovations that have been necessitated by the problems of tracking and sampling categories (e.g., tourists) and mobile groups, such as the migrating commercial sex workers in Thailand and neighbouring states (see Bond and colleagues, Chapter 11 below), or the Mexican-American migrant workers in Southern California (Carrier *et al.*, Chapter 13 below) as potential sources of the spread of HIV infection. Perhaps we can understand, then, how the very nature of scientific paradigms and models for the study of such phenomena are changing, just as we proceed to document and understand the sea change of mobility.

Modernity and Migration

There is little doubt that in the time of the modern age, people have travelled to new lands for the purpose of discovery, including the discovery of exotic customs and sexual practices foreign to their own culture's standards. In the first colonial encounters between Western and non-Western in the Pacific, John Gagnon argues in Chapter 2, the sexual encounter was critical and filled with possibilities of power, exchange, cultural transformation, and the fatal spread of disease. The voyages of Captain Cook thus heralded the negative aspects of the encounters to follow for centuries, from colonial times to the present.

The transition to modernity in Western culture in an earlier historical period and the modernization taking place in many Third World countries today repres- ent similar but unequal processes: the culmination of industrial development and colonial expansion from the West and the inherent changes that internal develop- ment and mobility have brought to social and sexual life in the East. Human movement of all kinds played a critical role in both historical transformations. Transnational and internal migration are part of this, but a critical part, since the ability to move and adapt within and across groups is part of our unique species- specific adaptive mechanism, that of culture. Because of their inherent flexibility and ability to move, humans have been better able to survive by taking advantage of the changing opportunities and challenges of their environments. Historically, we have reason to believe that movement typically involves new opportunities for sexual encounters, sometimes resulting in inter-marriage and offspring between groups (Singhanetra-Renard, Chapter 5; Bond *et al.*, Chapter 11). Indeed, it might be suggested that if change is indicative of the modern period since the later seventeenth century, then change in standards of sexual culture have often proved the vanguard of transformation and modernization in society at large (Caldwell *et al.*, Chapter 3 below).

Today, however, human mobility is occurring at an unprecedented pace around the world. Its effects are far-reaching and potentially devastating in scope, includ- ing the spread of sexually transmitted diseases as studied in this book, such that scholars increasingly think of this flood of migration as a hallmark of human society in the late twentieth century (Boehnlein and Kinzie, 1995; Long, 1993). Crossing cultural boundaries may potentially change the sexual behaviour of the agent—either for the lone individual, the married couple, the small refugee group, or the tourist or traveller. The possibilities of new mass media and interactive communication technologies informing and motivating people to move around have also enhanced the globalization that is accelerating movement. Catastrophes (natural or human) sometime results in mass migration, as we have witnessed many times this century (Long, Chapter 6 below). As the actor's cultural and personal conduct and identity changes in response to these movements, the degree of qualitative change in sexual behaviour may also increase, potentially violating beliefs or norms previously thought to be sacred by the individual or the group. Thus, too, the actor may no longer be at ease about 'going home', because of the constraints of returning to traditional norms and roles. When the greatest restrictions apply to women, it is understandable that special conditions may apply to the role of women in migration, as a special case of demographic change (see also Orubuloye, Chapter 12 below). The risk to women is greatest.

Sexual practices and identities can serve as the basis for cultural stability—but also of change at the most fundamental level of individual and society. History has shown that a process of inevitable change in matters of sexual partnerships and practices arises from social movement (Gagnon, Chapter 2 below). Change in sex norms go against the grain of many traditional ways of thinking: what seems embedded in the cultural consciousness in terms of sexual thinking—that certain things are 'permanent and natural and forever', such as women's roles or the preferred sexual technique (for example, genital-to-genital sexual intercourse, 'missionary position')—are subject to revision, and sometimes to quite radical change. Indeed, the pace of change would have been unimaginable before the AIDS epidemic made populations accustomed to sex education campaigns aimed at the explicit change of behaviour and cultural attitudes, as Parker (Chapter 4 below) suggests for Brazil. Thus the boundaries between peoples, and the lines drawn between ethnic groups and tribes, nations and states, regions and market networks, are breaking down, or being constantly transgressed and built back up again, through human sexual encounters.

The traveller from one culture to another is destined to encounter potential variation in sexual norms and roles. Cultures vary enormously in how they approve or disapprove of sexual behaviour, such as sexual play in childhood, or in variations in sexual conduct that include pleasure or non-reproductive foreplay between the married couple (Ford and Beach, 1951; Carrier, 1980). Likewise, significant differences across groups occur in how they approve or disapprove of sexuality outside the context of marriage and reproduction; indeed, a society such as America has seen change within its own ideology, from an emphasis on reproduction to one of pleasure, particularly in the two sexual revolutions of this century (D'Emilio and Freedman, 1988). Temporary movement on the part of the tourist is a form of migration that must be reckoned with in the globalization of sexually transmitted diseases. That such sexual innovation and voyaging is critical to the understanding of migration and change today is apparent from Gagnon's article below (Chapter 2).

Consider for instance the differences in cultural attitudes towards the presence or absence of commercial sex and institutionalized sex workers that greet the tourist or traveller to other cultures. Historically, societies differ markedly in their tolerance of commercial sex, from the later Roman Empire—which imposed rigorous rules on sex with slaves—to the nineteenth-century United States with their Comstock Laws intended to regulate prostitution; such variation continues up to the present (see Bond *et al.*, Chapter 11 below, on Thailand; D'Emilio and Freedman, 1988). Today, groups differ in their received social attitudes and customs about commercial sex, which are often influenced by moral systems and ethical codes, particularly those of the great world religions. But it is precisely these variations in standards that lead tourists and travellers to exotic places, whether Bangkok or Amsterdam, in search of commercial sex that is either illegal or much more difficult to locate and safely enjoy in their home countries (well examined in Brummelhuis, Chapter 10 below).

Sometimes movements from cities to smaller towns or agrarian areas are important to the demographics of movement in the era of AIDS. The shift from rural to urban settings is part of the process. But there is an oscillation, a back-and-forth dialectic, often overlooked in movements that occur from the cities to the rural villages (Caraël, Chapter 7, and Larvie, Chapter 9, below). One of the lessons of the AIDS epidemic and international research on it has been to demonstrate the fallacy of believing that human movement is always a one-way street. Thus, individuals may move to the city, and after a period of life there, perhaps having succeeded financially or failed, as the case may be, they return to the village or smaller town where they expect to find a home and security. The views of commercial sex workers in Thailand, as demonstrated below in Chapter 11 by Bond and colleagues, emphasize the role of reverse migration, and temporary oscillations of movement from towns to cities, as Singhanetra-Renard argues in Chapter 5.

The HIV/AIDS pandemic has fostered a virtual revolution of social change as the education and prevention efforts against the disease have expanded into countries and regions of the world (Bolton, 1995; Green, 1994; Turner *et al.*, 1989). A vast transformation of sexual customs is occurring in the face of the epidemic, as a recent volume of cultural case studies from around the world has demonstrated (Brummelheis and Herdt, 1995). We must wonder, as the Caldwells and John Anarfi suggest in Chapter 3 below, whether AIDS is impacting negatively upon fertility levels in many areas of Africa. Sexually transmitted diseases were not the first devastations on society, as the plagues and influenza epidemics of past centuries and decades indicate (Brandt, 1988). A difference between those cataclysms and the present, however, is that AIDS/HIV is virtually always a fatal disease, whose long-dwelling virus drains the energy of the patient, increasing morbidity in high-impact populations. To better study these processes we must operationalize the study of contextual sexual conduct.

Studying 'Sexual Cultures'

Both in cross-cultural study and from a historical perspective, we are at a scientific watershed: a revolution in social research is now advancing the understanding of the geography of sexual structures, practices, roles, and ideologies throughout the world. For the first time, investigators are collecting the sexual data necessary to compare and discuss what is universal and what is local, or, if you prefer, what is relative to particular cultures and what is true for all humans as members of the same species. It is thus an exciting time for the social science study of sexuality, and anthropology has a role to play in it which is larger than that of some other fields. However, the anthropology of sexuality is impeded by several formidable barriers: theoretical, methodological, and what might be called 'political' or ethical, all of which merit attention in the study of the understanding and prevention of HIV/AIDS. It is critical to chart the formation of what I call 'sexual culture'; that is, the cultural definition of sexual conduct by social roles and norms, cultural practices, as well as the beliefs and world-view necessary to socialize and legitimize such cultural things.

A 'sexual culture' is a consensual model of cultural ideals about sexual behaviour in a group. Such a cognitive model involves a world-view of norms, values, beliefs, and meanings regarding the nature and purpose of sexual encounters. It also involves an affective model of emotional states and moral guidelines to institutionalize what is felt to be 'normal, natural, necessary, or approved' in a community of actors. The effectiveness of the cognitive and affective models is the strength with which sanctions will be levied to punish or negatively sanction against those who violate the norms. When sexual cultures are working effectively, they include and exclude, by virtue of the received traditions and norms, including gender roles, that uphold the group. Gender also mediates these norms, since customary patterns of the expression of masculinity and femininity in society, through roles, task assignment, social status and exchange systems, influence the expression of sexual practices.

Societies differ greatly in their consensus codes of sexual conduct, as well as in the range of variation they permit across the course of life in the expression of desires, needs, and sexual outcomes (Mead, 1961). Here too we can sort sexual cultures. Reproduction is one of the most important, widespread, and stable cultural ideals of human cultures, when it comes to their sexual codes. Yet procreation is not perceived to be the only, and certainly not the exclusive aim, of sexual encounters, as was once upheld in Victorian thought or by the colonial agents who sanctioned native conduct in many non-Western lands, though reproduction is essential to the sexual cultures of many areas of the world, including large regions of the Christian world and Islamic historical cultures, including within Africa and the Middle East.

The relationship between sexual culture and cultural ideals is a key point of theory in understanding cross-cultural variations in sexual behaviour. Every culture postulates a desired and admired form of human conduct, not only for the present, but indeed, across the entire course of life (Herdt, 1990). This is its morally proper theory of 'sexuality and human nature'. Likewise, every sexual culture expresses a theory of idealized human nature—specifically, of sexual nature. Such idealistic and naturalizing world-views are expressed in behaviour through attitudes, roles, and sanctions. In many Western countries, for example, a cultural ideal is monogamous marriage where the aim of sex is to produce children, and deviations from this norm may be punished, however mildly. Sexual socialization in many cultures is surrounded with idioms of sexual nature and lore, suggestive hints and moralistic notions about why things should be done in a certain way, warning of the dire consequences should sexual taboos be broken (Miller, 1993). Sexual cultures may allow for a dominant ideal to create a dialectical reaction, in covert sexual forms within the same group, as happens, for example, in the allowance of a 'double standard' of monogamy for women and extramarital relations for their husbands (Parker *et al.*, 1991).

In the ebb and flow of the modern period and population change anthropologists have had to rethink the problems of cultural study. The creation of new sexual enclaves and cultural communities has, for a variety of theoretical reasons, required that anthropology 'rediscovered sexuality' (Vance, 1991). The rediscovery has to do with three fundamental points. First, ideal culture does not predict empirical sexual behaviour in a society. And as Mead (1961) cautioned: beware of accounts that declare the absence of a certain sexual trait, such as same-gender sexuality. Second, an individual's conscious or cultural identity does not perfectly correlate with prescribed sexual behaviour, and may have nothing to do with it, as we shall study further. Third, as new sexuality research has come in from Western European and North American countries such as the United States, and from non-Western cultures, the range of sexual variation within groups has increased. Typically, anthropologists and demographers in the past often ignored the non-reproductive and non-fertility-related behaviours.

One of the milestones of this new work on sexuality is the rediscovery that sexual behaviour norms have changed across time (see Parker, Chapter 4 below, on the general point in Brazil). Thus it follows that sexual cultures are not outside of time but are historical creations which should be seen from the perspective of population ebb and flow. The modern period in the late eighteenth century introduced the possibility of the nation-state and mass culture, with its market capitalism distinguished by an emerging middle class and the norms of sedentary, urban, nuclear family life. In the United States, the events of World War II certainly brought unprecedented change in sexuality and gender roles in a variety of ways, due to the mass mobilization of the armed forces (D'Emilio and Freedman, 1988). In Southeast Asia, as well, due to the extended conflicts of the Korean War and later the struggles between France and Vietnam and then the United States and Vietnam, many critical alternations in the political economy of sexuality in states such as Thailand and Burma and Vietnam came about (ten Brummelhuis, Chapter 10; Bond *et al.*, Chapter 11, below).

Methodologically, sexuality is special among the many domains of cultural study that require diligence in sifting fact from fancy. The research here invites a firmer grasp of the veridical nature of the cultural data collected. Sexual feelings, of course, are often expressed in private, and because many cultures regard sex as a private matter (Gagnon, 1990), we have the thorny methodological problem that rarely do field workers (or other behavioural scientists) observe the sexual act. Ethics aside, the issues make the anthropologist dependent upon second-hand reports, perhaps ones that are filled with cultural idealizations (Bolton, 1994).

Here, myths may be substituted for actual observations, or covert sexual behaviours may be missed if these contradict norms (Parker *et al.*, 1991). Thus those instances of reported absence of same-sex behaviour have later been proven false, only because enquiries were denied or suppressed, people lied, behaviour was hidden, and so on, to uphold the ideal culture that denied the existence of same-sex practice, as reported to the field worker. Underreporting of such practices, such as heterosexual anal intercourse, or denials of extramarital partnerships in societies that provide for the illicit maintenance of a 'common law' household, are illustrative of the problems of this sort encountered today.

The cultural definition of sexual behaviour and identities is critical to the issues. Consider, for example, the widely misunderstood category of 'bisexuality'. The category 'bisexuality' is too vague in dealing with the research literature across cultures; for example, rarely is the meaning that one must engage concurrently in relations with both genders central to a society's concept of bisexuality (Herdt and Boxer, 1992; Weinberg, *et al.*, 1993). Typically, actors point only to the fact that someone is known to have sex on occasion with a person of the same gender. The work of Carrier and colleagues below (Chapter 13) is useful in increasing understanding of the cross-cultural dynamics involved in such cases. Some cultures go further in institutionalizing the ideal of having relations with both sexes, as, for instance, among certain New Guinea cultures; but it must be understood that in such historical societies, the duality between homosexual and heterosexual that exists in the West was generally absent (Herdt, 1994).

A key dimension of recent concern is the public/private sex dichotomy reported from a variety of AIDS/HIV studies. The traditions of Western European and North American societies classify many actions, including sexual and romantic practices, by virtue of whether they occur in the public domain or private arenas. Sometimes it has been assumed—incorrectly—that such a model is limited to Western bourgeois cultures. In many cultures around the world, however, as Margaret Mead (1961) once showed, a distinction between public and private is essential for understanding the meaning of sexual conduct, sex/gender identities, and social status. The studies in this book demonstrate the ubiquity of the public/private distinction and the importance of building this conceptual distinction into the methodological research design of sexual conduct.

Many studies of same-sex behaviour have emerged from the epidemic, and it is useful to note that the homosexual/heterosexual dyad, as typically understood to be dichotomous in Western culture, is neither universal, nor was it always understood this way in the West. Prior to the eighteenth century, same-sex and opposite-sex desires and practices were not understood to be antithetical or dichotomous, at least in certain Western European societies (Herdt, 1994). At an earlier time, same-sex practices, regarded as sinful and later diseased or criminal behaviour, were largely hidden, kept secret, and often subject to the heaviest surveillance and negative sanctions. By the later nineteenth century, then, sexuality was expected to be confined to secluded, private quarters, but its public signs and indicators referred to heterosexual relations and reproduction, explicitly limited to genital intercourse between spouses. For a century to follow, the rubric 'homosexuality' overgeneralized about and lumped together distinctive kinds of cultural identity and sexual practice, such as those of transsexuals, transvestites, closet homosexuals, drag queens, lesbians, and many other quaint forms (Herdt, 1994). If public was thus coded as heterosexual and private was restricted to its expression, then the secret sphere referred to forbidden and illegal sex, homosexuality included.

How does sexual culture make use of social space? The fear is that in certain times and places, the private or the hidden involves violations of the ideal sexual culture. The regulation of social space is thus a critical component in the general structure of sexual and gender roles and norms and in the public debate on AIDS/HIV campaigns against sexual 'risk'. The space of a bar or a bathhouse may provide the linking network between many unlikely and unrelated actors, since it may be their attraction to a practice or a kind of partner, otherwise forbidden in their daily world, that brings them to the particular social scene (Bolton, 1992). The same point applies to the social field occupied by immigrants or travellers, removed from their normal circumstances. What we find out in the urban studies of American cities is that contacts may occur among the most unlikely people, rich and poor, business and unemployed, married men and gays, in places such as baths or parks (Gagnon, 1989). Thus we might say that the space defines the sexual practice; that sexual practice defines the contingencies of the social actor at that place and time. But is it possible to create cultural identity by being involved in a practice, localized in a certain space, sometimes in violation of norms?

Sexual Lifecourse, Migration, and Risk

Since at least the time of Kinsey it has been widely appreciated that where someone grows up, and the system of sexual socialization through which they attain maturity, is of great importance in understanding the structure of their sexuality for the entire lifecourse (Laumann *et al.*, 1994). These models of sexual development and structure assume, however, a stability of population, and an absence of movement into another sexual culture. The studies in this book, of course, demonstrate something of a very different kind. For example, in cultures such as that of Bangkok we begin to coordinate what we have discovered with methodologies of implementation, and governmental agencies or NGOs who are in the field. The outcome is to seek new means of understanding how movement across time and space exposes human actors to new forms of sexual behaviour, which, in turn, may enhance their risk of infection (see Parker, Chapter 4 below, on the situation in Brazil).

In seeking to address the problems of migration and sexual culture, a pervasive argument has concerned the question of whether the emphasis should be placed on individual behaviour or on community norms in understanding the spread of the HIV virus and other STDs. It is important to realize that the issue as typically constructed is artificial; that work in demography and sociology, in particular, makes use of individuals as members of a larger unit, thanks in part to the sophisticated analyses of cohorts and networks now available. Here, age and generation are critical, and the concept of 'historical age cohorts' is especially useful in analyzing large-scale populations and complex societies (Elder, 1974). Historical cohorts indicate demographic categories of persons who are grouped analytically, not by absolute age. Instead, patterns of identity development formed in collective periods of significant social events, wars, depressions, and now the AIDS epidemic, are totalizing experiences, or, more precisely, a sequence of events that structure decisions and outcomes, such that an indelible stamp upon identity is shared. In what milieu does the actor currently live—urban or suburban?

A variety of recent studies demonstrates links between sexual behaviour, gender, and sexual socialization across cultures (Brummelhuis and Herdt eds., 1995; Parker and Gagnon, 1995). Whatever change has occurred with modernity, however, it seems likely that the epidemic is even more portentous of change. The morbidity caused by AIDS/STDs in the age range of adolescence to mid-life, now presents unprecedented challenges to the fertility of populations, stable and in movement. As human actors come of age, they enter into the social contexts and sexual cultures of their society, prepared or unprepared, as the case may be, for their initial sexual encounters, and subsequent sexual events. We may divide these into distinctive cohorts and pathways of sexual behaviour and identity development. But it is critical to recognize that, occasionally, events may precipitate unforeseen change, such as the emergence of STDs and AIDS, without prior warning or socialization. Thus, the initial deaths due to HIV were wholly undetected and could not have been prevented; later governmental and social agendas certainly influenced the spread of the disease, however. This leads to the current situation of persons coming into sexual maturity today.

In the West as well as in Eastern cultures, adolescents and young adults who enter sexual maturity find themselves in a world saturated with the presence of AIDS and sexually transmitted diseases. Particularly in cities where 'high visibility' safe-sex campaigns and AIDS-education and prevention efforts have had official endorsement (Bolton, 1994), such as Norway or Belgium, the general population has a fairly high awareness of the threat of AIDS. Compared to a decade ago, furthermore, we can no longer think of sexual disease as a problem of a 'sexual minority' on the social fringe of what is forbidden or illegal. However, studies have shown consistently that simple knowledge of AIDS is not enough to instil safe sex or self-protection from the risk of HIV infection; other factors, such as resources, personal commitment, and empowerment are involved.

The evidence regarding sexual risk behaviour from the context of what might be called the Western and Eastern 'AIDS awareness' countries is contradictory. On the one hand, adolescents are clearly entering into sexual activity at earlier ages and with greater awareness of risk; but on the other hand they do not protect themselves from risk consistently at a high level. The issues in the broader lifecourse for men are considered in the important work of Davies *et al.* (1993) and they emerge in the Thai context, as reported below by VanLandingham and Grandjean (Chapter 8).

Drawing upon the most recent sexual survey data, we can snapshot morbidity frequencies in the United States as a critical indicator of global trends. In general, AIDS is now the leading killer of Americans in the age range of 25 to 44 (Center for Disease Control, 1993; Selik *et al.*, 1993). The latest epidemiological research shows that the AIDS curve for deaths has risen dramatically since 1981, when the first statistics were recorded. An examination of the age breakdowns of other studies provides clues to explain how this curve may work. Although American young people (aged 15–19) are 15 per cent more sexually active today than they were in 1979, their use of condoms has also increased, from 21 to 58 per cent. AIDS remains a 'problem' because the age at which HIV infection occurs is becoming lower over time. New studies estimate that 25 per cent of individuals infected with HIV between 1987 and 1991 were under 21 years of age. This is apparently a substantial increase. Sexual contact between males accounts for approximately 35 per cent of AIDS cases among young people who are 13–19 years old, and some 70 per cent of the instances are among young adult men aged 20–24 (Center for Disease Control, 1993; Selik *et al.*, 1993). The Thai study of VanLandingham and Grandjean (Chapter 8 below) provides support for this trend in South-East Asia. With the heightened risk of HIV infection for hetero-sexuals greater than before, the risk to females—particularly women of colour who are economically underprivileged—is of greater concern. Thus, all adolescents—heterosexual, bisexual, and homosexual or gay—are more at risk in the time of the epidemic than before. Data presented below by Michel Caraël (Chapter 7) from a cross-country perspective raise similar conclusions regarding risk.

A demographic trend in male adolescent and young adult sexual risk-taking is evident (Paul *et al.*, 1995). The enhanced infection rate for HIV seems to be the product of greater sexual risk-taking and continued ignorance, or deliberate ignoring, of protective measures that the individual could take against the disease. This result is puzzling, due to the high visibility of AIDS campaigns and the con-tinued efforts of society and medicine in general in countries such as the United States or Holland (DeWit *et al.*, 1994). Furthermore, sexual cultures such as those of the gay and lesbian communities in many Western nations, for instance, have remained diligent in pursuing prevention and education efforts (Herdt and Boxer, 1992b). Gay populations were characterized in the late 1980s by high frequencies of sexual practice associated with risk-laden sexual practice, such as anal sex; but recent study finds that in some populations the risk is reduced by the greater pre-cautions taken to protect against infection, typically with barrier methods such as condom use. The question of these rates of increase is troubling in itself, but it raises another issue of import for other parts of the world: how effective can such campaigns be in countries with different cultures and economies, lower literacy rates, and power systems that may obstruct the rational flow of education information? In the African situation, the work of Caldwell, Anarfi, and Caldwell

(Chapter 3 below) and Orubuloye (Chapter 12) provides critical comparisons which further the possibilities of designing interventions into the contexts of sexual risk behaviour.

Cultural Risk Milieu

AIDS has exposed the difficulties of the cultural logic and institutional matrix of sex. As Vance (1991: 881) has written, 'AIDS-inspired investigations into the realities of peoples' sexual worlds have already disclosed discrepancies between ideologies about sexuality and lived experience'. A key cultural lesson from the pandemic is that sexual and cultural identity and sexual behaviour are seldom congruent. Indeed, they may contradict one another, as when, for instance, a married man who routinely engages in opportunistic same-sex acts is identified as 'heterosexual' and is never reached by prevention efforts aimed at 'homosexuals' or 'those other people' (Parker, 1987). Obviously, the hidden discrepancy poses risk of HIV infection and spread of the virus to others. Ideals and practices may clash with the everyday necessities of life, either in the dominant folk ideology of a people or in their lived experience. Anthropological HIV prevention work in many countries has shown the need to differentiate knowledge from behaviour, to understand culturally-influenced ideal-type identities and the sexual risks that co-occur with them (Brummelhuis and Herdt, 1995). What is needed is a concept of cultural risk milieu which locates real world actors and sexual acts in order to open up the qualitative and quantitative study of sexual risk.

By 'cultural risk milieu' is meant a sexual subculture circumscribed as the behavioural context for engaging in sex and sexual risk-taking; that is, it involves the social learning and attitudes of actors in specific milieus that motivate them to take risks and give meanings to the kinds of sexual risk that they take. Arising from epidemiological study, the notion of risk milieu referred to broad population vectors, and the disease patterns embedded in 'context variables', such as specific sexual practices, forms of knowledge, and belief in the efficacy of one's own agency (Turner *et al.*, 1989). Knowledge of identities and roles is here strategic to the project of correlating action with risk. Among the factors involved in defining these meanings are the nature of the encounters between the actors, their choice of partners, erotic techniques, and how and when they might protect themselves from infections. When highly habitualized in the behaviour of the actors, we can think of the sexual risk acts as part of what Gagnon calls 'scripts'. For some actors, risk-laden sex is closely linked to their very concept of sexual desire in the time of AIDS (Gagnon, 1990). But on many other occasions and probably for most social actors, only casual and intermittent sexual risk is involved. Obviously, the immigrant or traveller is of key concern when thinking through the risk and prevention efforts outlined by this modality. The trouble is that these casual instigators of sexual risk may be unaware of the dangers contingent upon their own behaviour (Moodie and Ndatshe, 1994).

We can distinguish between two kinds of social and behavioural settings that structure the perceptions, decisions, and actions of persons, and influence their risk-taking or vulnerability to AIDS. First are milieus which promote the taking of risk and diminish the capacity of individuals to avoid taking risks. The recklessness of street gangs of young people, daring each other to acts of bravado or demonstrations of their loyalty to the group, is one such risk-enhancing milieu. Second are risk-reduction milieus, in which the cultural setting or institutions and supporting groups teach safe practices, and protection against risk, thereby supporting the ability of individuals to make reasoned and empowering decisions, as well as to take actions that ensure self-protection.

Sexual cultures cannot ultimately predict a person's sexual behaviour or prevent him or her from taking risks. Risk-taking is contingent upon many factors, including cultural competence in negotiating multiple contexts or risk milieus. And the individual who migrates from one culture to another, from one community to another, or even the student who changes high school or enters into new peer networks experiences a new vulnerability through not knowing 'the rules of the game'. Thus we must make a distinction between knowledge and behaviour which comes as a lesson from the failure of the so-called 'health belief model' to predict behaviour change (Ariss, 1992; Davies *et al.*, 1993). As researchers have established for some time, when it comes to HIV/AIDS risk, knowing the correct rule or practice to protect oneself from risk is insufficient. Several additional elements are required: a sense of identity; an ability to believe in the validity of one's own actions; and the interpersonal skills and self-confidence necessary to resist pressure from peers or from authorities, within the risk milieu, that are detrimental to personal well being. In short, what is at stake is power in a general sense, and the empowerment of the agent to make informed choices in a cultural risk milieu.

Endpoint—Empowerment and Risk

The relationship between power and culture is significant in understanding how authorities legitimize a practice or brand it as illegal. In virtually all Western countries, for instance, paid sexual service or 'commercial sex work' has been regarded as illegal and often punished with fines or imprisonment. However, it has often been the sex workers, rather than the clients, who have been harassed or arrested, and the degree to which the law has been enforced has varied with the historical period and the political climate of 'morality' being exploited by political and economic agents, at least in the United States (D'Emilio and Freedman, 1988). Larvie suggests (Chapter 9 below) that in Brazil authorities such as the police similarly utilize commercial sex as a practice by which to manipulate and a rhetoric through which to express ideals of morality and nationalism. Brummelhuis argues (Chapter 10) that both historically and in the changing context of Thai society sex work has not been regarded as a 'moral problem' but as a social solution to a number of cultural contradictions in male identity and female/male relations, especially in traditional marriage in Thailand.

Homophobia and the general persistence of hatred and violence against gays and lesbians must surely be counted as one of the main sources of the AIDS statistics. The great effort of the gay and lesbian movement has been to reform basic civil rights and gain acceptance of same-sex desire in a heterosexist tradition, one that initially responded to the AIDS epidemic by wrongly thinking of it as a 'gay disease'. The opposition of the politicians and the governmental medical bureaucracies of the 1980s, as dramatized in Randy Shilts's *And The Band Played On*, only changed when the wider epidemiological threat to the population drew a clamour for AIDS-prevention funding. The obstructionism of the politicians has continued in a variety of ways, as witnessed in the heavily political selection of the Director-General of WHO and the recent controversy over the comment favourable about masturbation made by the former Surgeon General of the United States. In general, the risk of HIV is a function of the cultural and socioeconomic context. We believe it needs to be seen as a function of the cultural milieu; that is, of the political, social, and economic barriers and contexts that help or hinder the spread of the disease throughout any sector of the population.

Research evidence confirms this trend in one specific area. A more fully developed and socially acknowledged gay or lesbian identity tends to reduce the risk of infection with HIV/AIDS, both at the level of subjective perception of risk and of objective behaviour. The narratives of American adolescents reflect how AIDS permeated their sexual identity formation process (Herdt and Boxer, 1992). AIDS education significantly affected the sexual practice of more than half of the young people interviewed, in the direction of reduced risk-taking. In general, however, these adolescents had a high level of HIV/AIDS knowledge and a consistent and accurate understanding of what makes a sexual encounter 'safer'. The overall effect was that the greater degree of involvement and identification with the gay and lesbian culture at the time, the greater the self-protection on the part of those concerned, and the lesser the risk they incurred. Such a finding is not totally surprising; twenty years ago, a cross-country study demonstrated that positive mental health among gays and lesbians was associated with involvement in the gay community (Weinberg and Williams, 1974). A new study from Holland shows that when a gay man is comfortable with his sexual identity and behaviour (such as enjoying anal sex), he will be more capable of taking the necessary steps to protect himself (DeWit *et al.* 1994).

A critical point about empowerment from studies such as these and others coming out of Africa (Oppong, 1993; Schoepf, 1992) concerns the creation of a new context, or cultural milieu, for a safe, agency-enhancing sexual/gender identity formation. All transitions engender the possibilities of risk. The migration into a new context, a new sexual culture, is a situation fraught with many of the economic, social, and sexual vulnerabilities studied in this book. But the coping skills of people can be enhanced through teaching and support that build confidence in making decisions relevant to sexuality. People's behaviour may be resistant to change as well (VanLandingham and Grandjean, Chapter 8 below). The possibilities of sexual violence, especially in contexts of social upheaval, require special attention (Long, Chapter 6). Where sexuality is shaped by structures of social control and surveillance of sexual practice, including village authorities, kinship roles and extended family, the person probably has a greater support system in time of need. Hence the terrible price paid by refugees in times of war and conflict, as Long so eloquently describes in her discussion of the issues.

Protection and disease prevention are only the first step in the process of amelioration. More basic, it has been argued, is the issue of empowerment; of enabling persons to make informed and adaptive choices. At issue is not merely the protection of the actor, but of their social and psychological empowerment. Empowerment presupposes the provision of resources sufficient to express and articulate desires and dislikes; the process of allowing an adolescent, for example, to understand how she or he may become the agent of their own desires (Fine, 1992). Among the youth, including sex workers, lesbians, gays, and bisexuals in their teens, their psychological and cultural knowledge is a decisive factor in their ability to protect themselves (Larvie, Chapter 9 below), to gain knowledge, and to form a network with others who are helpful in the negotiation of violence on the streets, homophobia in everyday life and in the classroom, and risk-taking in the context of sexual encounters. The withholding of these resources is a danger and a liability to the self- and social development of all people, but especially the young who are entering sexuality. Both adults and adolescents who engage in sexual behaviour are less vulnerable to risk-taking and recklessness that may lead to infection if they are secure in their own identities. Economic and social support is critical, just as the absence of a community of peers or a network of friends makes the person more susceptible to greater risk-taking behaviour.

The change to modernity and new sexual forms documented in this book are a call to examine more closely all factors that lead people to migrate or stay in the same place. The trend of interdisciplinary research initiated by demographers and anthropologists suggests the value that is to be reaped from both fields. In the era of AIDS and STDs, this cooperative effort will lead, we hope, to the prevention and education necessary to cope with the epidemic in the coming years.

REFERENCES

Abramson, Paul and Gilbert Herdt. 1990. 'The Assessment of Sexual Practices Relevant to the Transmission of AIDS: A Global Perspective', in *Journal of Sex Research*, 27: 215–232.

Ariss, Robert. 1992. 'Against Death', Unpublished dissertation, University of Sydney, Australia.

Boehnlein, James K. and J. David Kinzie. 1991. 'Refugee Trauma', in *Transcultural Psychiatric Research Review*, 32: 223–52.

Bolton, Ralph. 1992. 'Mapping Terra Incognita: Sex Research for AIDS Prevention—An Urgent Agenda for the 1990s', in Herdt, G. and S. Lindenbaum, eds, *The Time of AIDS*, 124–58. Newbury Park, CA: Sage Publications.

Bolton, Ralph. 1994. 'Sex, Science, and Social Responsibility: Cross-Cultural Research on Same-Sex Eroticism and Sexual Intolerance' in *Cross-Cultural Research*, 28.

—— 1995. 'Rethinking Anthropology: The Study of AIDS' in Brummelhuis, H. and G. Herdt, eds, *Culture and Sexual Risk*. New York: Gordon and Breach, Publishers.

Brandt, A. 1988. 'AIDS in Historical Perspective: Four Lessons from the History of Sexually Transmitted Diseases', in *American Journal of Public Health*, 78: 367–71.

Brummelhuis, Han ten, and Gilbert Herdt, eds. 1995. *Culture and Sexual Risk*. New York: Gordon and Breach, Publishers.

Burridge, Virginia. 1992. 'AIDS: History and Contemporary History', in Herdt G. and S. Lindenbaum, eds, *The Time of AIDS*, 41–64. Newbury Park, CA: Sage Publications.

Carrier, Joseph. 1980. 'Homosexuality in Cross-Cultural Perspective', in Marmor, J., ed., *Homosexual Behavior: A Modern Reappraisal*, 100–22. New York: Basic Books.

—— and Ralph Bolton. 1991. 'Anthropological Perspectives on Sexuality and HIV Prevention', in *Annual Review of Sex Research*, 1.

Center for Disease Control. 1993. 'Update: Mortality Attributable to HIV Infection/AIDS Among Persons Aged 25–44 Years—United States, 1990 and 1991', in *Morbidity and Mortality Weekly Reports*, July 2, 1993, 42 (25): 481–6.

D'Emilio, John and Estelle Freedman. 1988. *Intimate Matters: A History of Sexuality in America*. New York: Harper and Row.

Davies, P. M. *et al.* 1993. *Sex, Gay Men, and AIDS*. London: The Falmer Press.

DeWit, John *et al.* 1994. 'Behavioral risk reaction strategies to prevent HIV infection among homosexual men: a grounded theory approach', in DeWit J., ed., *Prevention of HIV Infection Among Homosexual Men: Behavior Change and Behavior Determinants*. Amsterdam: Thesis Publishers.

Dyson, Tim, ed. 1992. *Sexual Behavior and Networking: Anthropological and Socio-Cultural Studies on The Transmission of HIV*. Liège, Belgium: Editions Derouax–Ordina.

Elder, Glen. 1974. *Children of the Great Depression*. Chicago: University of Chicago Press.

Farmer, Paul. 1992. *AIDS and Accusation*. Berkeley: University of California Press.

Fine, Michele. 1992. *Disruptive Voices: The Possibilities of Feminist Research*. Ann Arbor: University of Michigan Press.

Ford, Clelland and Frank Beach. 1951. *Patterns of Sexual Behavior*. New York: Harper.

Gagnon, John. 1989. 'Disease and Desire', in *Daedalus* 118: 47–77.

—— 1990. 'The Explicit and Implicit Use of the Scripting Perspective in Sex Research', in *Annual Review of Sex Research* 1: 1–44.

—— 1992. 'Epidemics and Researchers: AIDS and the Practice of Social Studies', in Herdt, G. and S. Lindenbaum, eds, *The Time of AIDS*, 27–40. Newberry Park, CA: Sage Publications.

Green, Edward C. 1994. *AIDS and STDs in Africa: Bridging the Gap Between Traditional Healing and Western Medicine*. Boulder, Colorado: Westview Press.

Greenberg, David F. 1988. *The Construction of Homosexuality*. Chicago: The University of Chicago Press.

Herdt, Gilbert. 1990. 'Developmental Continuity as a Dimension of Sexual Orientation Across Cultures', in McWhirter, D., J. Reinisch, and S. Sanders, eds, *Homosexuality and Heterosexuality: The Kinsey Scale and Current Research*, 208–38. New York: Oxford University Press.

—— 1992. 'Introduction' in Herdt, G. and S. Lindenbaum, eds, *The Time of AIDS*, 3–26. Newbury Park, CA: Sage Publications.

Herdt, Gilbert. 1994. 'Introduction' in *Third Sex, Third Gender: Beyond Sexual Dimorph-ism in Culture and History*. New York: Zone Books.

—— and Andrew Boxer. 1991. 'The Ethnographic Study of AIDS', in *Journal of Sex Research*, 28: 171–89.

—— —— 1992. 'Sexual Identity Development and AIDS Sexual Risk', in Dyson, T., ed., *Sexual Behavior and Networking: Anthropological and Socio-Cultural Studies on the Transmission of HIV*. Liège, Belgium: Ordina Editions.

—— —— 1993. *Children of Horizons: How Gay and Lesbian Youth are Forging a New Way Out of the Closet*. Boston: Beacon Press.

Herdt, Gilbert and Shirley Lindenbaum, eds. 1992. *The Time of AIDS: Theory, Method, and Practice*. Newbury Park, CA: Sage Publications.

Herdt, Gilbert and Robert Stoller. 1990. *Intimate Communications: Erotics and The Study of Culture*. New York: Columbia University Press.

Kinsey, Alfred *et al*. 1948. *Sexual Behavior in the Human Male*. Philadelphia: W. B. Saunders.

Laumann, Edward O., Robert Michaels, John Gagnon, and Stuart Michaels. 1994. *The Social Organization of Sexuality: Sexual Practices in the United States*. Chicago: The University of Chicago Press.

Long, Lynellyn D. 1993. *Ban Vinai: The Refugee Camp*. New York: Columbia University Press.

Mead, Margaret. 1961. 'Cultural Determinants of Sexual Behavior', in Young, W. C., ed., *Sex and Internal Secretions*, 1433–79. Baltimore, MD: Williams and Wilkins.

Miller, Barbara. 1993. *Sex and Gender Hierarchies*. New York: Cambridge University Press.

Moodie, T. Dunbar and Vivienne Ndatshe. 1994. *Going for Gold: Men, Mines and Migra-tion*. Berkeley: University of California Press.

Oppong, Christine. 1993. 'Some Roles of Women: What Do We Know?—Conceptual and Methodological Issues in Sub-Saharan Africa', in *Women and Demographic Change in Sub-Saharan Africa*. Liège, Belgium.

Parker, Richard. 1987. 'Acquired Immunodeficiency Syndrome in Urban Brazil', in *Medical Anthropology Quarterly* 1: 155–75.

Parker, Richard and John H. Gagnon, eds. 1995. *Conceiving Sexuality*. New York: Routledge.

Parker, Richard, Gilbert Herdt, and Manuel Caballo. 1991. 'Sexual Culture, HIV Transmission, and AIDS Research', in *The Journal of Sex Research*, 28 (1): 75–96.

Patton, Cindy. 1990. *Inventing AIDS*. New York: Routlege.

Paul, Jay *et al*. 1995. 'The Impact of the HIV Epidemic on U.S. Gay Male Communities', in D'Augelli, A. R. and C. Patterson, eds, *Lesbian, Gay, and Bisexual Identities Over the Lifespan: Psychological Perspectives*, 347–96. New York: Oxford University Press.

Schoepf, Brooke G. 1992. 'Women at Risk: Case Studies from Zaire', in Herdt, G. and S. Lindenbaum, eds, *The Time of AIDS: Theory, Method, and Practice*. Newbury Park, CA: Sage Publications.

Selik, R. M. *et al*. 1993. 'HIV Infection as Leading Cause of Death among Young Adults in US Cities and States', in *Journal of the American Medical Association*, 269: 299–394.

Turner, Charles *et al*. 1989. *AIDS: Sexual Behavior and Intravenous Drug Use*. Washington, DC: National Academy Press.

Vance, Carole S. 1991. 'Anthropology Rediscovers Sexuality: A Theoretical Comment', in *Social Science and Medicine*, 33: 875–84.

Watkins, Susan Cotts. 1993. 'If All We Knew About Women Was What We Read in *Demography*, What Would We Know?', in *Demography* 30: 551–77.

Weeks, Jeffrey. 1985. *Sexuality and Its Discontents*. London: Routledge and Kegan Paul.

Weinberg, Martin S. *et al.* 1993. *Dual Attractions: Understanding Bisexuality*. New York: Oxford University Press.

Wellings, Kaye *et al.* 1994. *Sexual Behavior in Britain: The National Survey of Sexual Attitudes and Lifestyles*. London: Penguin.

2 Others Have Sex With Others:
Captain Cook and the Penetration of the Pacific

JOHN H. GAGNON

The Deadly Embrace

It is only recently in the history of an expanding Euro-American global cultural hegemony that there has been careful reflection on what the natives of other cultures, large and small, advanced and simple, must have thought when first confronted by (usually) white-faced bearers of advanced armaments, religious and commercial fervour, and genocidal impulses based on racist or evolutionary principles. Even those traditional cultures that are currently being recorded by anthropologists are ending with silence as they are erased by nation-building, entry-level positions in the global economy and the worldwide media (Wilford, 1994).

The encounter of Captain Cook with the 'Indians' of the South Seas at the end of the eighteenth century, fatal to Cook as an individual and to the 'Indians' as individuals and as cultures, represents a paradigmatic meeting of cultures that is regularly revisited for a variety of contemporary purposes. This paper, written in the era of AIDS and global human movement, had its origins in an attempt to make sense of the sexual aspects of this specific historic encounter between cultural strangers, in this case Europeans and Polynesians (primarily, Tahitians), in the late eighteenth century. It is an encounter in which the participants were not only 'other to each other' at the historical moment, but in which both sets of historic participants are 'other' to their cultural descendants. The quality of this 'otherness' between ancestors and descendants is, however, somewhat different for the cultures of these two regions.

The Tahitians, as well as other Pacific Islanders, depending on their utility to the national interests of states that were and are more advanced in the violent arts, have been subjected to either continuous or intermittent commercial, military, biological, linguistic, and religious interventions for nearly two hundred years. As a result of this process of domination the descendants of the pre-intervention populations often see their own past through a dark and refracted prism, sometimes recovering fragments of their own historic cultures through the records kept by cultural aliens.[1]

Following a different trajectory, the primary colonizing cultures of the Pacific Basin—the Netherlands, England, France, the United States, Germany, and more

---

[1] The journals of Cook and other early explorers are the only written or visual records of the state of pre-literate Pacific societies at the time of first contact.

recently, Japan—have accelerated into diverse examples of urban-industrial nation-states that are vastly different from their historic cultures. Even Spain and Portugal, who were early participants in the wave of Pacific colonization, but who have lagged behind their Northern European peers in economic development, differ dramatically from even their nineteenth century pasts. The agrarian, pre-industrial, sometimes peasant and quasi-feudal ways of life that dominated all these European societies two centuries ago have been extinguished and in many cases these social worlds now exist only in repositories of the more durable traces of the past. The living cultures that produced and used these surviving artifacts are dead and the artifacts themselves survive either in alien contexts such as museums, libraries, scholarly texts, or in monuments that are given life through historical re-enactments and the gaze of tourists (Selwyn, 1996).

However, these cultures, the subordinated and the superordinate, both separated from their pasts, remain in chronic tension in the present. The tourists, business persons, soldiers, sailors, and government administrators who land at the airports and docks at Papeete or Honolulu bear with them expectations about the South Seas that were first generated nearly two hundred years ago by European explorers in their sailing ships. At the centre of these expectations are the ghosts of sexual encounters between sailors and 'native girls' that have been re-represented for two centuries.

Trying to understand the sexual aspects of this late eighteenth century encounter from the perspective of the very late twentieth century requires a recognition of the dense assemblage of collective myth and individual fantasy that these first as well as subsequent encounters in the Pacific, particularly with Polynesians, have deposited in the Euro-American consciousness. Any contemporary observer must have internalized some portion of these myths and fantasies (sexual and otherwise) that make up the current Western view of the Pacific Islanders (as they existed then and now) as well as the contemporary counter strategies recommended by modernists and post-modernists that are believed to be able to counteract or adjust the gaze of the other on the other.

The Ur-text for English speakers for the first encounters of Europeans with Polynesians are the journals of Captain James Cook and his literate colleagues (Banks, 1962; Cook, 1955–1974). Written in the last third of the eighteenth century they are *in toto* an extraordinary document of late eighteenth-century English culture and mental life. They contain a limited record of the sexual aspects of these first encounters with Polynesia, encounters that provided the original framework for Anglo-American fantasies about the 'South Seas'. While the majority of the sexual myths and fantasies are hetero-erotic, and have been reiterated in combination with themes of innocence and corruption, discovery and loss, in Hollywood films such as *Hurricane, Rain, South Pacific*, and *Return to Paradise*, the journeys of Captain Cook continue to resonate in many other ways in modern Western societies.[2]

[2] For instance, we might consider the direct parallels between Captain James Cook and Captain James Kirk of the television programme *Startrek*. Echoes of both Cook's journeys and the attitudes of

Who was that man?

These resonances of Cook's voyages in present-day Euro-American culture, from low to high, from sex tourism to academic anthropology, suggest that transforming an everyday member of the Euro-American culture complex into an objective scientific hero of modern anthropology or sociology may be more difficult than was previously thought. Acquiring an academic doctorate from a Euro-American university after a couple of years of 'studying a people' is not a sufficient basis for membership of a new culture of 'positivistes', freed from their culture of origin and attached to no culture of destination. Since these 'disciplines' are an integral part of the expansionist Euro-American culture (as is the space of positivism), the anthropological traveller shares the subtle attachments to the cultural past that are threaded unnoticed through the cultural present. As a consequence, in the contemporary collision between cultures (a collision that includes anthropologists and their practices), myth and fantasy are fused with data and theory in the constructed space of objectivity.

Thus the current anthropological controversy over who Captain Cook was to the 'Indians' of Hawaii is also a controversy about who Captain Cook *is* to the core and peripheral cultures of the contemporary world order. The manifest content of this controversy focuses on whether Cook was believed to be a god when he and his crew encountered the indigenous peoples of the Hawaiian Islands in the late eighteenth century. As part of a complex argument about the ways in which cultures change, Marshall Sahlins (1981, 1985) has argued that Cook was believed by the Hawaiians to be an incarnation of the Hawaiian god Lono. Sahlins contends that the Hawaiians were required to fit Cook into their previously received cultural system and that their interpretations of the historical events that unfolded after first contact were primarily contingent on the interpretive resources provided to the Hawaiians by this fixed symbol system. Sahlins provides a re-reading of the events of the Hawaiian encounter, as recorded in the logs and journals of the

the Enlightenment that are associated with them can be found in this modern re-representation of Cook in the fictional Captain Kirk of the starship *Enterprise*. Each episode of the series begins with a dated entry (a Stardate rather than an Earthdate) usually in the Captain's log. Over the musical theme the following words are spoken: 'Space, the Final Frontier. These are the voyages of the starship *Enterprise*. Her five-year mission: to explore strange new worlds, to seek out new life and new civilizations, to boldly go where no man has gone before.'

In the next version of this series, *Startrek: the Next Generation*, the offending sexist terms 'her' and 'man' have been changed to 'its' and 'one'; however, the mission remains the same and so do the other parallels with the exploration of the Pacific. The only traces of these encounters with 'strange new worlds' are in the logs of the starship *Enterprise*—as they were in the logs of Cook's voyages (no log is kept by indigenous peoples or at least we don't know of them). And Kirk/Cook is bound by the 'prime directive' (taken from the Enlightenment and anthropology), not to change the new worlds which are visited by the introduction of new technical or social forms.

In the most recent version of the series, *Startrek Voyager*, there is a story that explicitly focuses on the 'prime directive'. A species of 'robots' or 'androids' built by a vanished race of humanoids will become extinct if they are not provided with technology commonplace to the crew of the starship. The moral crux of the story is whether supplying the technology will involve an unwarranted intervention in the course of another culture. The fact that the other culture is composed of artificial beings makes the conflict more piquant.

Europeans, interpreting each event as fitting the return and death myth of Lono. According to Sahlins, the killing of Cook during a melee on the beach was interpreted by the Hawaiians as fitting the correct ending of the Lono myth cycle which allowed for the apotheosis of Cook.

Countering these views, Gananath Obeysekere (1992), an academic anthropologist, but Sri Lankan in origin and Third World in allegiance, provides a detailed critique of Sahlins' readings of the events, particularly focusing on whether Cook was apotheosized by the culture-bound natives. The theoretical dispute centres on whether the Hawaiian were captives of their pre-existing cultural system (Sahlins's view) and therefore required in the opening phase of the encounter to interact with Cook and his crew in fixed symbolic terms (that is, the actual events are interpreted to fit the mythic template, therefore Cook equals Lono) or whether the Hawaiians had a pragmatic understanding that Cook was an important man, but only a man, and as a man had resources that could be taken and a body that could be killed.

If the latter interpretation is accepted, Cook's apotheosis would be the result of the continued colonization of Hawaii in the years after his death, a colonization that required a god myth as the continuation of the legitimation of the Euro-American conquest. The belief that Cook became a god to the Hawaiians would then be an example of European myth imposition, not Hawaiian myth fulfilling. There is evidence that Europeans often believed that they were viewed as gods by the natives they conquered (Todorov 1987) and this view of Cook would fit into the myth-making potential of European cultures. In these myths, Europeans (and later Americans and Japanese) come as saviours to raise the benighted heathen from their lives of degradation and error. This myth conceals the genocidal and culturocidal effects of the economic, military, religious, and disease-producing incursions of more militarily advanced cultures into less well-defended cultures.

There are two ways in which the anthropology of the late nineteenth and twentieth centuries support this concealment of the historical record. The first way is in acting as if the post-contact cultures were untainted descendants of the pre-contact cultures. Professional anthropologists arrived in many numbers in the South Seas nearly one hundred and fifty years after first contact. The decision of anthropologists to examine the social lives that they were recording for Western consumption, as if they closely represented pre-contact cultures rather than hybrids of various sorts, both allowed anthropologists to conduct 'comparative social research' and concealed the extent of European influence (e.g., churches, prisons, forced labour, modesty, clothing). In addition the anthropological treatment of natives as static products of their culture and social structure (see Douglas, 1966) while the anthropologists were members of dynamic, reflexive, and interpreting cultures continued the mythology of Captain Cook and his 'Indians'. In this mythology the behaviour of Europeans, North Americans, and Japanese is treated as practical and empirical—nearly freed from culture (or at least possessing a superior culture)—and preserving a belief in surviving indigenous cultures passively waiting to be studied, classified, and added to the collective cultural encyclopedia and the individual curriculum vitae.

Obeysekere's point is that the colonizer's side of the encounter remains un-analysed. What did these eighteenth-century Englishmen believe about 'Indians' prior to dropping anchor? How did the eighteenth-century culture of England condition the beliefs, actions, and records of the sailors ('scientists', officers, and men) during and after the encounter? And, in this case, what purpose did it and does it serve for Westerners, then and now, to believe that the natives believed Cook was a god?

Unnatural Conjunctions

Each of these questions about Cook's apotheosis is relevant to the far more mod-est question of why sexual relations developed so quickly and with such apparent ease between the Englishmen and certain 'Indian' women on the island of Tahiti. While these apparently facile sexual contacts have been core elements of popular Western fantasies about the South Seas there has been little reflection on how the members of two very different cultures could so easily get to what are now con-sidered extremely 'intimate' and affectively loaded interactions without a com-mon language or knowledge of each other's cultures. Who were these men to these women and who were these women to these men and why did each find copulation so easy to accomplish?

Usually this question is treated as a non-question. An interest in copulation with women is assumed to be a natural attribute of men as a species, and the lack of sexual 'inhibition' on the part of the women is assumed to result from the spe-cial circumstances of a Polynesian culture that was closer to nature in its lack of sexual repression. In this analysis, the conduct of the men is based in their funda-mental natures and strong sex drives even in the presence of repression (which would have been weak for sailors long deprived of sex) and (in a twentieth-century post-Freudian interpretation) the sexual desires and behaviour of women is closer to nature under these special cultural conditions. In this Western mythic state of nature, unrestrained and guiltless copulation is part of the expected order of things.

Such an analysis based on nature leaves unanswered the very questions that a social constructionist might ask about this highly unnatural state of affairs. How were these women and men culturally constituted and why did their prior cultural training in sexual practices allow for such apparently easy copulation? In the light of these questions, how sexual conduct is accomplished between members of cul-turally different peoples is of importance to larger theoretical understandings.

Social constructionism as a theoretical stance can vary along a continuum from weak to strong. Weak social construction simply means that the social practices of a naive 'people' derive from their own socio-cultural history, but these social prac-tices can be objectively understood by a 'non-member' of the culture trained in the appropriate discipline. This posture is no different from a culturally informed 'objectivism'. In contrast, holding a strong social constructionism position means that all interpretations of social life, including those which aspire to the privileged status of science, are emergent and contingent. That is, they are the transient results of struggles over meaning between differing groups and individuals and are entirely dependent on the historical and cultural circumstances in which they are announced and repeated. There are no statements or observations which are independent of the time and place in which they are made and all statements are part and parcel of the phenomena which they attempt to describe. Thus a scientific article, a news release, even an academic seminar about homosexuality or prostitution or HIV are as much part of the social construction of these phenomena as is the conduct that such intellectual exercises observe, interpret or represent.

This latter perspective, which emphasizes the rootedness of all action in local meaning systems, raises the critical problem of how shared meanings are acquired and actions are coordinated across cultural boundaries. How does a cultural stranger make sense of a new environment and coordinate his or her desires with those of others? In the particular case at hand:

- How does a person from eighteenth-century England with its specific sexual scripts have 'sex' with a person who comes from a culture with entirely or nearly entirely different sexual scripts (for a more extended discussion of sexual scripts, see Gagnon and Simon, 1973; Gagnon, 1990)?
- How are the differing elements, the who, what, when, where and why, of the sexual scripts of the differing cultures identified and coordinated?
- What are the mechanisms of identifying with whom it is appropriate to have 'sex'?
- Under what circumstances of time and place should the conduct be undertaken?
- What elements of a previously acquired 'sexual repertoire' are appropriate in these new circumstances?
- What reasons can the other party have to engage in sexuality, that is, what are the practical motives of the other and is there any need to attend to these motivations?

In sum, what are the points of contact between the systems of scripts that make a coordinated sexual encounter (including its cultural, interpersonal, and mental aspects) possible?

These specific concerns about the possibilities/difficulties of cross-cultural sexual encounters have emerged subsequent to a discussion by the author and his colleague William Simon about the cultural and historical specificity of sexual meanings and action (Gagnon and Simon, 1973). At that time, our intellectual concerns were different, but the underlying arguments remain the same. We wished to demonstrate the cultural specificity of sexual practice in order to critique the regnant naturalistic and biologistic paradigms (what has recently been labelled sexual essentialism) that dominated thought about sexuality until that time. As one part of this programme we attempted to deconstruct the category 'homosexual' by arguing that the physical acts between two men in Classical Greece (Dover, 1978), in late nineteenth-century London (Bartlett, 1988), and in the period of gay liberation in San Francisco in the pre-AIDS era (Bell and Weinberg, 1978) might be physically identical, but culturally incommensurate.[3] We argued further that even within a specific culture both processes of social and cultural change and differences in social position could create different kinds of 'homosexualities'. In our view 'homosexual men' of the 1920s and 1930s in the United States were not the same cultural creatures as 'gay men' of the 1990s, and the working class boy who prostituted himself to his 'queer' customer (here used in an older sense of queer) came to the encounter with a different set of scripts for the occasion than did his client (Chauncey, 1995).

The goal of this deconstructive exercise was to point out that the category homosexual and by implication, all other sexual categories, including the category heterosexual, were historical and cultural productions, not human universals (Katz, 1995). From this perspective the enacting of sexuality required the orchestration of a reflexive mental life, sequences of interpersonal actions in socially structured environments, and an attention to cultural instructions rather than the simple unfolding of biological imperatives. The problem of sexuality, indeed of all social life, was, for us, one of meanings and actions which emerged from specific cultures and social structures, rather than a natural sequence of bodily movements that were grounded in evolutionary or other behavioural programmes.

In such a version of the sexual, meaning as the grounds for action is found both in the mind and in the culture, but not immediately in the body. The concrete social event is understood as the confluence of the mental life of individuals as they are situated in the great social divisions of any specific culture or society. The interpretive move is from both the public world of meaning and social structure and the private world of memories, plans, fantasies, and desires toward the concrete sexual performance. This strategy of understanding clearly involves a different conception of the sexual from one that starts with coupling bodies or lubricated organs and argues that the content of the mind and the structure of the society are responses to the necessities of reproduction or an imperious sex drive.

There is however a difficulty which is created by such a robust vision of the cultural discontinuities of sexual life—this is the empirical observation that many persons from quite separate cultures manage to get their bodies together in ways that are interpretable as 'sexual' according to most Western definitions. This may not appear to be a very difficult question to those who view sex as 'doing what comes naturally'; however, for those with constructionist predilections, the problem only begins with an observation of coupling.

---

[3] If one lives long enough, it is possible to be overtaken by new terms for what one has already been doing for some period of time. To be understood in the new context one must use current nomenclature. The view that the meaning of statements is equivocal and that all talk and text (now called discourse) can be infinitely reinterpreted is part and parcel of the pragmatist tradition from Charles Pierce to John Dewey and George Herbert Mead. The work of Kenneth Burke contains many formal examples of these interpretative strategies dating from the early 1930s. Such analytic tactics are now called deconstruction. So be it.

Who were those 'Indians'?

To return to Captain Cook and Tahiti. Clearly the case is a prejudiced one, but the choice is not entirely idiosyncratic. Many of those from the European cultural area, particularly from Northern Europe and the United States, share the belief that an exemplary sexual encounter between strangers is the one between Europeans or Euro-Americans and Pacific Islanders, especially between Polynesian women and European men.[4] This exemplary symbolic sexual status is recognized by and responded to by Euro-American women as well as men (though for different reasons) and captivates both men who desire sex with men as well as those who desire sex with women. From Cook, Bougainville, and Diderot in the eighteenth century to Herman Melville and Gauguin in the nineteenth to Bronislaw Malinowski, Margaret Mead, James Mitchener, and Hollywood in the twentieth, the physical beauty of Polynesian settings and peoples, the abundance of nature, the ease of life, and the appearance of innocence have had a continuous fascination for the Euro-American imagination (Moorehead, 1966). Polynesia is either Eden before the fall or Eden corrupted, but unlike the Biblical Eden, sexuality is a Western myth of Eden's cultural core.

The presence of these secondary and tertiary cultural accretions have to be assumed in a reading of the primary and secondary literatures that chronicle the fatal impact of European contact on the cultures of the Pacific that began in the eighteenth century. The reports of the 'willingness' of certain Polynesian women to have sexual intercourse with the men on Cook's (and other explorers') ships seemed to require no further explanation either in the eighteenth century or now. Notice the cautious description of these events and the deliberate imprecision of the term 'willingness'. It is no longer possible in the late twentieth century, given the evidence of widespread sexual violence against women and the pervasiveness of gender inequality, to treat what appears to be the eager participation of women in sexual activity as evidence of desire or consent (Heise, 1995). At the same time to deny the capacity of women to 'demand' sexual relations with men may also deny women's own agency within their own culture.

In contrast to this twentieth century caution, one of the journal keepers reported that, on first contact, the gestures of the women in approaching canoes indicated 'their intentions of gratifying us in all of the pleasures the Sex (that is, women) can give' (quoted in Sahlins, 1981, from the Hawaiian encounter in 1788, p. 38).[5]

---

[4] Perhaps this paper can at least raise the question of why certain European sexual encounters with 'others' are sexualized or eroticized and others are not. It is clear that the contacts of Spanish and Portuguese conquerors and the indigenous populations of the 'new world' have produced a very large population with mixed ancestry. It would be useful to know whether these pre-Enlightenment invasions by Southern European cultures during the sixteenth and seventeenth centuries generated similar erotic mythologies.

[5] While Cook treats his arrival as a 'first', there is sure evidence that Bougainville arrived first and there is some evidence that at least one Spanish ship arrived earlier. Could the Tahitians have learned from these prior encounters ways to deal with these newcomers? As far as I know no one has attempted to locate the records of earlier arrivals that may have affected Cook's reception (Moorehead, 1966).

Another journal keeper reports: 'We now live in the greatest of luxury, and as to the choice of fine women there is hardly one among us who may not vie with the grand Turk himself' (quoted from Samwell by Sahlins, 1981: 38).

While these reports of sexual willingness seem straightforward enough, the reader removed by two centuries and half a world wonders exactly what sexual practices are meant by the phrase 'all of the pleasures' women can offer. The allusion to the seraglio and the Turk suggests the resources of comparison possessed by the European mind of the time, in which orientalism serves as the resonant symbol for organizing 'astonishing' sexual experiences. That these questions have not been asked before suggests a tendency to treat the journals as records of fact (that is, field notes) rather than as historical documents that require detailed interpretation. As narratives, the journals are documents of the time, influenced by all the cultural baggage of the educated Englishman and written in full awareness of the audiences back home. Like all travel journals the documents produced by Cook and others have many faces, looking backwards and forwards to and from home, while seeming to look only at the new world.

That the entire record of these encounters is written by a few literate men on board the European ships should give us serious pause. However, more serious is the profound silence when we try to locate the voices of the other half of the sexual encounter. If we can trust the observers, these women were young, unmarried, and not members of the ruling class (Sahlins, 1981). But how much else can be trusted? What were the sexual theories of these Englishmen and how do they determine the record? More importantly, and impossible to know, what were the sexual theories of the Polynesians, particularly the women? Did they even have theories that included something called 'the sexual' as a separate domain of meaning and action? More distantly and even less well understood, at least from the perspective of Euro-American traditions of sexual exclusivity and the property value of women, what were the sexual theories of Polynesian men?

It is clear from other sources that the sexual theories of the eighteenth-century British and French explorers may have been both alike and different. The literate on these ships were viewing the world from the last bright glow of the sunset of the Enlightenment, and reporting on a region of the world which, for that short moment, did not invite the exploitative energies of European civilization (Pagden, 1993). Very soon these men and the social worlds that they inhabited would disappear, just as surely as the eighteenth-century worlds of Tahitians, Tongans, and Hawaiians would disappear. The journal-keeping Europeans (as distinguished from the common sailors) came from the rising middle levels of a quasi-urban society that was in the opening stages of applied technological development. The worlds of the common sailor are recorded in ships' logs and public and private maritime records as well as in fictions of the time—but these records have not yet been fully explored. All of these worlds would dissolve in the acid onrush of the American Revolution, the Napoleonic Wars, the subsequent economic and political restructuring of Europe, and the opening of the steam, coal, iron, and railroad phase of the industrial revolution.

The sexual language of the journals is preindustrial, but not pre-empirical. It is the language of a sexuality that was grounded in the 'natural'. The sexual world of the late eighteenth century remains primarily a rural world in its theory, very different than the peculiar repressions and celebrations of sexuality that characterized the Victorian era.[6] The sexual conduct of men and women of the times was largely understood in terms of their natural lusts or bodily passions. The English background is the language of the gentry and the countryside; Moll Flanders and Tom Jones and Robinson Crusoe are alive and well. At no point are the astonished sailors reported to find the sexual accessibility of the women repellent, disgusting or sinful, unlike the religionists who would follow them to the Pacific Islands in only a few decades.

The French sexual tradition appears to be, at least theoretically, considerably more complex, since this was also the time of Choderlos de Laclos, Restif de la Bretonne and the Marquis de Sade. The libertine tradition of a decaying aristocracy was still present as were the intellectual speculations of the encyclopaedists, but these traditions and speculations rested on largely peasant society. Who the French common seamen might have been remains unknown, though the French maritime tradition was a vigorous one. One need only consider the French fishing fleets off the Grand Banks and the slaving activities that contributed to the wealth of Bordeaux and Nantes. Reactions to the explorers' journals suggest the differences between these two cultures; Diderot, reflecting on Bougainville, warns the Tahitians to protect themselves: 'one day they (the Christians) will come, with crucifix in one hand and dagger in the other, to cut your throats or force you to accept their customs and opinions; one day under their rule you will be almost as unhappy as they are.' In contrast, after the first rush of interest in Tahiti, emerging English cultural insularity was evident as Walpole responded that he had no interest in the behaviour of a lot of savages (both cited in Moorehead, 1966).

The 'wantonness' of the Polynesian women and the apparent indifference of the Polynesian men to the women's sexual assertiveness was puzzling to the journal-keepers, but they seemed to accept it in the spirit of unrestraint and play rather than as sexual lawlessness. Sexual irregularity was surely more acceptable to the English visitors than the tendency of the natives to take (the Europeans thought it 'stealing') all shiny baubles and trinkets. It is the struggle over property (rather than sexuality) that produces the most serious conflicts between the

---

[6] While Foucault's observations about the rising level of discourse about sexuality in the nineteenth century are an important corrective to the view that there was only silence about sexuality at that time, a silence that was ended by progressive sexual reformers in the late nineteenth and early twentieth centuries, his views are aimed at current disputes rather than attending to the historical record. Foucault was quarrelling with his contemporaries who viewed the sexual changes of the last century as evidence of human progress and human liberation from oppression. A more accurate version of the sexual transformations of the nineteenth century would take account of the actual repression of sexual cultures of differing social formations as well as the censorship of sexual materials in the public world and the formation of new sexual cultures in the expanding middle classes. The efflorescence of discourse justifying these transformations and facilitating them were only part of a new sexual practice that was in formation. Both silencing and speaking were part of the process.

Europeans and the natives.[7] Indeed it was one of these European incursions to recover stolen property that resulted in Cook's death in Hawaii. While taking immediate pleasure in the sexual arrangements, the journal-keepers do wonder why sex appears to have little to do with those great organizers of sexual life in Europe, shame, guilt, sin, privacy, social distinctions, economic exchange or marriage. The women are wanton, but not 'bawds'; 'they visited us with no other view, than to make a surrender of their persons' (quoted in Sahlins 1981). Consider the gender assumptions in the word 'surrender'.

What did these women want? Marshall Sahlins' twentieth-century answer is that there was a general cultural propensity among the Polynesians (specifically Hawaiians) of the pre-contact period to seek masters and as the chiefs submitted to the mastery of Cook, so the women submitted to the mastery of the sailors (Sahlins, 1981). My twentieth-century answer is that the women were products of a social order in which sex was an unmarked form of pleasurable sociability on the part of both women and men before marriage. This must have been impossible to understand for eighteenth-century Europeans for whom sexuality was a marked category: 'there are no people in the world who indulge themselves more in their appetites than these; indeed they carry it to a most scandalous degree.' (quoted from Ellis, 1792, by Sahlins, 1981). Sex as a unmarked pleasure is perhaps more difficult for twentieth century Euro-Americans to understand than for their eighteenth century predecessors, given the new ways in which sex has been marked in the last two centuries.

For the eighteenth-century sailor this way of framing copulatory life (there is no reference to procreation) may have been impossible to understand, given his cultural limitations, but not impossible to practise (it may be impossible to practise for the twentieth-century anthropologist—note the contemporary rules on not taking sexual advantage of the data) (Vance, 1991; Herdt and Stoller, 1990). The Polynesian women and the European men both knew about how to fit their bodies together in penile-vaginal intercourse and make movements that seemed appropriate (think how much more complicated all this would have been if either the men or the women had a cultural taste for oral sex or tongue kissing and tried to introduce these tastes into the script or if the Polynesian men wanted sex with the European men). Both parties to the activity are reported as being pleased by their actions, though there is no testimony from the women or the common seamen. Both partners probably assumed that the other (and both were 'other' to us

---

[7] Little is usually made of the amount of intimidation and violence that accompanied these first encounters. Cannon were often fired to remind the local people of the advanced technology of the Europeans, and natives were killed or injured without much concern. A native who snatched a musket away from a guard was shot down without much concern. Mr Parkinson, a Quaker, described the events: 'Giving orders to fire, they [the guards] obeyed with the greatest glee imaginable, as if they had been shooting at ducks, killing one stout man, and wounding many others ...' (Cook 1955, p. 81, fn. 2). Cook himself reports that after the killing, he sought to persuade them (the natives) 'that the man was killed for taking away the musquet (*sic*) and that we still would be friends with them'. Cook, 1955: 81). Obeysekere (1982) reports that Cook himself ordered more severe floggings than did his contemporary Captain Bligh, but this report is largely directed at discrediting Cook's sainted image among the white populations of the Pacific Islands, particularly in New Zealand and Australia.

in this case) were engaged in the acts for similar purposes to their own. It was indeed fortunate that neither party seemed to have very esoteric tastes in sexual practices and that the 'willingness' of the women, while surprising, did not challenge the gender power assumptions of the men.

However, such interactions, no matter how pleasing and simple-appearing in the beginning, could not have been undertaken between cultural strangers without evoking new meanings and possibilities. Willy-nilly, new elements were included as part of the behavioural script for sexual intercourse. In addition to the sexual encounters, the times spent with the Englishmen provided opportunities for the women to eat tabooed foods (for example, pig), to engage in tabooed actions (for example, on board the English ships they ate in the presence of men), and they were given gifts by the Englishmen with whom they had intercourse. The activity of the Polynesian and European bodies became conflated with the exchange of goods and the violation of correct relations between Tahitian women and Tahitian men. Only a short time passed before the activity of the bodies increasingly became contingent on the goods and the women appeared to be less and less under the control of the Polynesian men. Europeans were willing to pay for that which appeared to be freely given. In this process of gift-giving the sailors began the creation of the forms of prostitution of women which in later periods characterized the main ports of call in Polynesia. In scripting terms, these practices, initiated by the Europeans, commenced the transformation of the wanton into the bawd.

The changes in everyday social and sexual practice in Polynesia began to occur almost immediately as a result of the encounter with Europeans. The first effects resulted from the disease-ridden bodies (carcasses, said Diderot) of the Europeans themselves. Pox- and virus-ridden, they began the first stages of the decimation of Eden (Moorehead, 1966). The changes in social and sexual practice in Europe were more indirect and abstract. They were provoked by the representations of experience rather than by experience itself. The personal experience of these few sailors was publicized across Europe, where the idea of Eden was more important than Eden itself. An alternative sexual world to Christian shame and guilt or to a world of economic calculation became part of the counter-cultural ideals from the time of the early Romantics until the end of the twentieth century.

The Erasure of the 'Other'

How do these reflections on this historic instance of cultural contact relate to the larger purposes of a volume on migration, sexual risk, and HIV/AIDS? It was, after all, long ago and far away; not only are the sailors and the women dead, so too are their cultures. I would propose that there are a number of useful reflections that can be drawn from it.

Firstly, to return to the initial questions: how did these particular cultural strangers solve the problem of knowing what to do sexually? Fortunately the case was a simple one; indeed, this is why it is so well remembered. Neither the Europeans nor the Polynesians had particularly divergent bodily expectations, women and men had physical sex together, and by implication, it was 'sex' without the additional eroticism that were surely known to both officers and sailors at the time (remember that the erotic novel *Fanny Hill* had been published forty years before). Further, the encounters were initiated by the women, which meant that men did not engage in predatory acts of sexual violence that characterized other European encounters with other cultures. Finally, during the initial encounters the sex did not depend on significant convergences between cultural meaning systems since it did not extend into the larger networks of cultural life beyond the confines of the harbours where the ships were anchored. The eventual extension of Euro-American cultural penetration to the interiors of the islands would be carried out by the agents of commerce and religion and tourism, rather than by simple sailors.

When sexual tastes are more complex, and in later stages of the cultural encounter, identifiable zones (formal or informal) are set up in which sexual encounters are structured, often on a commercial basis. In Mexican border communities with the United States these were areas of prostitution named in some cases 'la Zona'. These are examples of what John and Ruth Useem once called 'third cultures', which are specialized locales or ways of life that are differentiated from the 'usual cultures' of both sets of participants. These zones are often as clearly marked in their instructions as a well-designed airport, so that the interpersonal organization of the sexual encounter is externally scripted. In some cases, these zones develop attractions of their own for certain groups of men. Men often find desired forms of sociability in ports of call, bright-light areas, and brothel districts (Green, 1980). These districts often serve to protect women in the rest of the society from social contact with strangers interested in sex, in the same way that tourist buses protect local drivers from untrained drivers from other cultures.

Secondly, one of the lessons of rereading these explorers' journals (as well the secondary literature) as historical texts, is that such a reading emphasizes that both sides of the sexual encounter were/are bearers of culture, as are those who interpret these encounters and their consequences. This particular encounter suggests most poignantly the ways in which Euro-American sexual cultures have come to dominate and transform those cultures that had/have alternative sexual practices. They were and we are, after all, sons (and increasingly daughters) of particular social, intellectual, and sexual cultures. In this process of cultural penetration, domination is usually confused with knowledge, since only a fool will disagree with the interpretations of a better armed and obviously dangerous intruder.[8]

---

[8] The 'ethno-theories' of local populations are always treated 'respectfully' by anthropologists when they are acquiring them. These theories are then converted into 'data' for the anthropologists' theories, but this is usually accomplished in another language and for other audiences. A native who gets his or her hands on an anthropologist's report and challenges its objectivity is probably in less danger than a native who challenges the commercial exploitation of the local work force (e.g., for road-building) by colonial administrations.

Thirdly, the Polynesian encounter is instructive in the way it has provided one element of the ideological framework for the ways in which Europeans, as visitors, tourists, researchers, have organized their sexual intrusions into other cultures during the last two centuries. The 'other' as sexual innocent or the other as sexual savage (often linked to differences in ethnicity or race) are part of the erotic life of the modern West (Schweder, 1982). The journey outside of one's own culture that has been so characteristic of nineteenth and twentieth century life often was and remains a sexual journey for both men who had sex with men and men who had sex with women.

Aftermaths

There are two further observations that are linked to the Polynesian case. The first is the worldwide decline in cultural diversity and, usually unmentioned, sexual diversity as indigenous peoples are threatened by physical destruction or cultural transformation (recall that 1993 was the Year of Indigenous People). Demographically small and culturally different cultures everywhere in the world are in danger as a result of changes in local habitats and the incursions of representatives of centralizing or expanding nation-states or economic enterprises (Wilford, 1994). In the absence of the creation of protected regions (cultural zoos?) it is clear that many small-scale experiments in human living will disappear in the next century.

But equally importantly there is a new homogenizing incursion into the cultural and sexual life of all societies, great and small, by the mass media centred primarily in the United States and Europe. Here the danger is not to bodies, but to the actual content of diverse sexual scripts in many societies (Cohen, 1994). The popularity of American soap operas and situation comedies not only creates a taste for middle-class goods, but conflates the good sexual life with the good consumer life. Perhaps we should rephrase Diderot with: 'one day they will come, with a satellite dish in one hand and a credit card in the other, to fill your minds and pockets and entice you to accept their customs and opinions; one day under their rule you will be almost as unhappy as they are.'[9]

---

[9] On Thanksgiving Day, 1994, I was channel-surfing on the television and came upon the Macy's Day Parade which is held annually to celebrate the commercial opening of the Christmas season. While I was watching the telecast of the parade in New York the venue of the broadcast was switched to Hawaii where a similar parade was being held. A high school marching band was preceded by two groups of young women, one of which was wearing the kinds of hula costumes and dancing in ways familiar to tourists in Hawaii or viewers of Hollywood movies of the South Seas. As they wended their way through downtown Honolulu, shaking their hula skirts modestly, the woman announcer gushed: 'Isn't it wonderful the way they continue to celebrate native Hawaiian culture?'

REFERENCES

Banks, Sir Joseph (1962), *The Endeavour Journal of Joseph Banks, 1768–1771*, edited by J. C. Beaglehole. Trustees of the Public Library of New South Wales in Association with Angus and Robertson.

Bartlett, Neil (1988), *Who Was that Man?: A Present for Mr. Oscar Wilde*. London: Serpent's Tail.

Bell, Alan P. and Martin Weinberg (1978), *Homosexualities*. New York: Simon and Schuster.

Chauncey, George (1995), *Gay New York*. New York: Basic Books.

Cobham, Rhonda (1992), 'Misgendering the Nation: African Nationalist Fictions and Nuruddin Farah's Maps', 42–59 in Andrew Parker, Mary Russo, Doris Sommer and Patricia Yaeger, eds, *Nationalisms and Sexualities*. New York: Routledge.

Cohen, Roger (1994), 'Aux Armes! France Rallies to Battle Sly and T. Rex'. *New York Times*, Section 2, Sunday, January 2: 1 and 22.

Cook, James. *The Journals of Captain James Cook on his Voyages of Discovery*. Edited by J. C. Beaglehole. Cambridge, Published for the Hakluyt Society at the University Press, 1955–1974.

Douglas, Mary (1970), *Purity and Danger: An Analysis of Concepts of Pollution and Taboo*. London: Pelican Books (originally published in 1966).

Dover, Kenneth J. (1978), *Greek Homosexuality*. Cambridge, MA: Harvard University Press.

Gagnon, John H. (1990), 'The Implicit and Explicit Use of the Scripting Perspective in Sex Research', in John Bancroft, ed., *Annual Review of Sex Research*, 1, 1–43.

—— and William Simon (1973), *Sexual Conduct*. Chicago: Aldine Press.

Greene, Graham (1980), *Ways of Escape*. New York: Simon and Schuster.

Herdt, Gilbert and Robert Stoller (1990), *Intimate Communications: Erotics and the Study of a Culture*. New York: Columbia University Press.

Heise, Lori (1995), 'Violence, Sexuality and Women's Lives', in Richard Parker and John H. Gagnon, eds, *Conceiving Sexuality*. New York: Routledge.

Katz, Jonathan (1995), *The Invention of Heterosexuality*. New York: Dutton.

Moorehead, Alan (1966), *The Fatal Impact: An Account of the Invasion of the South Pacific 1767–1840*. New York: Harper and Row.

Obeyesekere, Gananath (1992), *The Apotheosis of Captain Cook*. Princeton: Princeton University Press.

Pagden, Anthony (1993), *European Encounters with the New World*. New Haven: Yale University Press.

Sahlins, Marshall (1981), *Historical Metaphors and Mythical Realities: Structure in the Early History of the Sandwich Islands Kingdom*. Association for Social Anthropology in Oceania. Ann Arbor, MI: University of Michigan Press.

—— (1985), *Islands of History*. Chicago: University of Chicago Press.

Schweder, Richard (1982), 'On Savages and Other Children'. *American Anthopologist*, 84, 354–66.

Selwyn, Tom, ed. (1996), *The Tourist Image: Myths and Myth Making in Tourism*. London: Wiley.

Todorov, Tzvetan (1987), *The Conquest of America: The Question of the Other*. New York: Harper Torchbooks.

Vance, Carole S. (1991), 'Anthropology Rediscovers Sexuality: A Theoretical Comment'. *Social Science and Medicine*, 33 (8), 876–84.

Wilford, John Noble (1994), 'Among the Dying Species are Lost Tribes of Mankind'. *The New York Times*: The Week In Review. Sunday January 2, 1 and 3.

Part II

Population Movement and AIDS

3 Mobility, Migration, Sex, STDs, and AIDS:

An Essay on Sub-Saharan Africa with Other Parallels

JOHN C. CALDWELL, JOHN K. ANARFI, and PAT CALDWELL

Migration has always facilitated the spread of any infectious disease. This has been the case even with diseases transmitted by insect vectors as has been demonstrated in Nigeria (Prothero, 1965). Migration does this in two ways. First, it brings more people into contact with each other and is the means whereby diseases can be carried from one community to others over considerable distances. Second, it has been a major factor in the growth of urban areas where dense populations in close contact provide a context for epidemics. Sexually transmitted diseases are associated in yet other ways with migration, because many migrants move away from their usual sexual partners and seek new sexual outlets. Populations along the ancient trading routes of Africa and Asia have long experienced higher levels of venereal disease than more isolated settlements (David and Voas, 1981). In regard to both sexual and other behaviour, migration takes individuals away from their home places where their doings are often monitored and controlled, to distant parts where no one feels individual responsibility for exerting much influence over them.

All these tendencies have long been on the increase. The Black Death spread in a few years from China to Western Europe in a way that would have been impossible among pre-Neolithic populations. The influenza epidemic in the second decade of this century broke out almost simultaneously in widely scattered parts of the world. This has also been the case with the AIDS epidemic, and the low levels of the disease in some parts of the world can no longer be explained by their distance from an epicentre.

The Colonization and Modernization of the Third World

The European expansion brought with it infectious diseases which decimated the native population of the Americas and severely affected parts of Africa, Asia, and the Pacific. This phenomenon arose not merely from contact with new pathogens but also from a disruption of society that catalysed the spread of disease. It is almost certainly wrong to imply, as Frank (1992: 90–1) appears to do, that Africa was free of the major sexually transmitted diseases until the European forward

This paper has benefited from assistance from Wendy Cosford and Pat Goodall.

movement of the late nineteenth century. Rather, the diseases affected many more people at that time because of rapid social change.

The destructiveness of sexually transmitted disease is well illustrated by the experience of the African society that successively was known as the Congo Free State, Belgian Congo, the Democratic Republic of the Congo, and Zaire (Caldwell and Caldwell, 1983). The epidemic that began during the first years of the Free State was venereal disease rather than AIDS, but the conditions that promoted that epidemic would today have facilitated the spread of AIDS, and indeed the contemporary AIDS epidemic in Zaire probably owes something to the social disruption that originated over a century ago and something to the lingering STD outbreak that began in those years.

The Congo STD epidemic was so severe that by the mid-twentieth century around half the women in some districts of the region were rendered infertile at such an early age that they were unable to bear any children at all during their reproductive years. The cause was the imposition of a colonial system on a previously largely immobile population which had not usually been able to travel far from the local community because of physical danger in strange lands. The Free State administration not only reduced that danger, thus allowing freer movement, but also introduced conscripted labour for construction and allowed entrepreneurs to drive men into the forest in search of the immensely lucrative ivory and wild rubber. This removed men from their usual sexual partners, normally to seek solace with commercial sex workers with large numbers of clients. Conscripted labour also removed fathers from their families, with a resulting diminution in parental control of adolescent sexual activity. Almost a century later, the areas of high infertility were still those that had been developed by the alienation of land to concessionaires in the late nineteenth century.

Colonization also spread sexually transmitted diseases, and to some extent prepared the way for AIDS in a surprising way. Much of the sexual appetite of young unmarried men in many parts of traditional Africa had been appeased by sexual relations with such near relatives as wives of brothers, younger wives of fathers, and cousins (Caldwell, Orubuloye, and Caldwell, 1991; Caldwell, Caldwell, and Orubuloye, 1992). This was regarded as incest by many of the missionaries, with the result that sex was increasingly obtained by travelling outside the community, often to towns, and frequently for payment. A constant worry and puzzle to colonial regimes was why sexually transmitted diseases and infertility had increased so much under their administrations. There was also, of course, a range of other reasons including much more labour migration and the monetization of the economy. Development, migration, and an increased risk of STDs were almost synonymous in what we now call the Third World.

The Contemporary World

World systems theory, drawing the distinction in development between the centre and the periphery, has emphasized that, in the periphery, foreign companies and national elites pay rural–urban male migrants a wage just sufficient to support them alone in town so that the businesses are in effect being subsidized by the support that the traditional rural sector provides for the subsistence back in the village of the worker's wife and children. Whether this is a correct description of motivation, or whether alternatively the businesses cannot compete nationally or internationally by paying higher wages, it is true that many cities in the developing world are characterized by a surplus of adult males which generates a demand for a substantial commercial sex industry. Many of the clients are rural–urban male migrants who either are unmarried or have left wives back in the countryside.

However, this is not the whole story, because the generation of a male surplus in the towns is also influenced by the work prospects of females there and this is largely determined by the gender distinctions made by the culture. In most of coastal West Africa and Central Africa, cities have approximate parity in numbers by sex. The reason is that most of the small-scale trading is in the hands of women, and furthermore, rural populations, though somewhat apprehensive of the likely impact of urban living on the sexual morality of their daughters, are not so seized by this fear as to forbid their migration (Caldwell, 1969: 106–111). Thus there are jobs for women as well as men in the town and they migrate in roughly equal numbers.

This situation contrasts with that in most of East Africa where males impose stricter rules on their daughters or wives in relation to their sexual morality and hence to their migration, and where almost the only recognized occupation for a woman is agriculture, leaving urban commerce in the hands of male nationals or Asian men. That this is not the whole explanation for the East African AIDS epidemic is shown by the fact that near-balance in the numbers by sex in Kampala has not protected it from a severe epidemic. The imbalance in the numbers by sex in the larger urban areas of most of East Africa and much of Southern Africa has been explained by the exclusion of migrant women from some of the larger towns, especially those in mining areas, by colonial governments (Larson, 1989), but the fact remains that the imbalance exists in places where there were no such restrictions, and has persisted elsewhere during subsequent decades of rapid post-independence urban growth when the restrictions no longer applied.

The only city in West Africa with a comparable male surplus is Abidjan. For decades it was the boom city of West Africa, and drew migrants from far away in the West African savannah. They headed for Abidjan partly because they understood the French type of administration and had at least some French. The savannah people, whether Muslim or not, did not encourage their women to migrate (Painter, 1992) and this is certainly part of the explanation for Abidjan's severe AIDS epidemic. Also, the women did not have a tradition of trading, and a significant number of women in the savannah markets come from the coast.

It is not only the long-term migrants who seek sexual activity in the city, but also the seasonal migrants (Painter, 1992: 36). In one sense they present a greater danger in that they bring infections back with them regularly. Many of the males are young and very sexually active. Among married men who participate in seasonal migration, a study in Casamance, Senegal, demonstrated that the majority had extramarital relations while they were away although they claimed not to do so when back home with their wives (Enel and Pison, 1992: 261–3). Even rural–rural migrants, harvesting palm wine, had sexual relations and spent their earnings during brief visits to the town. The World Health Organization GPA surveys in Africa demonstrated a significant relationship between men living in a non-cohabiting state and having multiple sexual partners (Caraël *et al.*, Chapter 7 below). In northern Namibia a hospital STD clinic's load of patients almost trebles when the migrant labourers come home temporarily to help harvest the millet crop (Webb and Simon, 1993: 6).

In order to meet the sexual needs of the male migration stream from the savannah to Abidjan, a smaller but predominantly female migration stream has developed from southern Ghana to Abidjan (Anarfi 1992, 1993). Doubtless there is a similar movement from southern Côte d'Ivoire into Abidjan. The sources of these migratory movements are determined less by proximity to Abidjan than by the fact that the migrants come from cultures which do not place strong emphasis on male control of female sexual morality, and whose young women do not risk lifelong social obloquy as a result of their enterprise. An added incentive has been the economic difficulties faced in recent years by Ghana and many other African countries (Orubuloye, Chapter 12 below).

These are not situations unique to sub-Saharan Africa but have parallels throughout much of the world as is demonstrated by chapters in this book describing aspects of the lives of Thais, Vietnamese, Indians, and Haitians (VanLandingham and Grandjean, Chapter 8 below; Singhanetra-Renard, Chapter 5; Brummelhuis, Chapter 10; Carrier *et al.*, Chapter 13). This is the result of the formation of a global economy and society, with, as usual, the greatest strains falling on the poorer societies. This is especially the case with regard to STDs, both as painful and dangerous disorders in their own right and as cofactors for AIDS, because it is poverty which prevents the formation or use of a health system which can cope adequately with STDs.

Sexual Behaviour and Consequent Movement

In sub-Saharan Africa, as elsewhere, urban–rural differentials are marked in the case of AIDS: urban levels are typically four to ten times those of rural areas. This suggests different urban sexual regimes, although it should be noted that West African research demonstrates either that urban people do not have a markedly higher number of different sexual partners than rural dwellers (Caldwell *et al.*, 1991: 23) or that this is true at least in the case of men (Anarfi and Awusabo-Asare, 1993: 40).

What is clear is that the amount of prostitution increases with the size of the urban centre, with even small trading posts providing facilities for it not found in completely agricultural villages (Way and Stanecki, 1993: 7). The cities are seen by villagers as, above all, places of bright lights, bars, hotels, fancy clothes, dancing, and sexual temptation. They are also seen as places of anonymity where it is possible to behave differently from in the village and it is unlikely that sexual or other behaviour will be reported back to the village. Many rural young women long to participate for at least some years in such life and seem uncertain both before and later whether the experience involves providing purely commercial sex.

The reasons for the male demand for commercial sex in urban areas are more complex. Rural males are away from wives or other long-term female companions. They feel they need sex and cannot readily strike up relations with women they have long known or even ones from their particular origin. On the whole they seek commercial sex with girls from their own ethnic group, although some enjoy having close relations with women from different backgrounds as they savour the strangeness and freedom of the city. In West Africa, young male migrants often join the commercial sex workers in their rooms or houses because the cost of accommodation and food is cheaper than in specialized commercial accommodation. They are welcomed because they help meet the cost of rent and food, pay for sex, and provide the young women with additional protection. Lifelong urbanites also patronize the bars and brothels, but perhaps at no greater level than rural men commute to the nearest town for the same purpose. In most of Africa it is the rural migrants to the city who are most likely to be found in the slum and shanty town bars where the commercial sex workers are more likely to have uncured STDs and are probably more likely to have many different customers and to be HIV-positive.

In Africa, as apparently elsewhere, commercial sex work is almost synonymous with migration. In order to ensure a later life of marriage, business ownership and respectability in one's area of origin, the period spent as a commercial sex worker means living a long way away. In the provincial towns of Nigeria, the women in the hotels, bars, and brothels almost invariably come from elsewhere, commonly from another ethnic group (Orubuloye, Caldwell, and Caldwell, 1994). Even in Lagos, with five million people, most commercial sex workers (except the elite with a limited number of 'boyfriends') come from outside the city. The occupation is associated not only with the initial move but with frequent visits back home to see relatives and demonstrate urban success in a job ill-defined to the family and other villagers, and often to see to the building of a house or the establishment of a business. Even within the town, movement between occupational locations may be frequent. A similar picture emerges elsewhere in West Africa, for instance in The Gambia (Pickering and Wilkins, 1993), and the situation is close to that described in Thailand (Bond, *et al.*, Chapter 11 below). The contrast with India (Ramasubban, 1992), and probably with all the cultures extending from the Mediterranean to Bangladesh where men are the keepers of women's sexual morals, is that in the latter many commercial sex workers never return to their places of origin. A more ominous aspect to commercial sex work and migration is beginning: it is becoming clearer that the women with symptomatic AIDS quickly return to their places of origin (Anarfi, 1992), and may be encouraged to do so by the bar or hotel owners. This may explain why so few of the commercial sex workers—or their clients—in places as far apart as Chiang Mai and Lagos ever seem to have known a fellow worker with symptoms. If the returner at first hides her condition, the epidemic is spread further and faster.

Not only are commercial sex workers likely to be mobile, but so is a significant proportion of their clients. This is not merely explained by rural–urban migration. In a study of Ondo Town (really a small city) in Nigeria it was discovered that a disproportionate fraction of the clients were travellers (Orubuloye, Caldwell, and Caldwell, 1992), and in Thailand it is noted that clients preserve their anonymity by patronizing commercial sex workers only when away from their home areas (VanLandingham and Grandjean, Chapter 8 below).

It is clear that in many parts of the world, for instance the United States (Grmek, 1990) and Brazil (Parker, Chapter 4; Larvie, Chapter 9 below), there is an even stronger urge for homosexuals to flee the countryside and provincial towns for the city. They need to escape their relatives and their communities for the freer and more anonymous cities whether they go to seek non-commercial or commercial relationships. A similar phenomenon has not been described for sub-Saharan Africa, and, if it exists, its scale is very small. The cultures are so antipathetic to homosexual relationships that anal intercourse appears from clinical, demographic,[1] and social research to have played an insignificant part in promoting the African AIDS epidemic (Caldwell and Caldwell, 1993).

Specific Occupations and Consequent High-Risk Sexual Activity

Apart from commercial sex, the other occupation that has been most closely identified with high risks of AIDS infection and transmission is long-distance trucking. This may, in fact, represent an over-concentration on a single occupation because the evidence is that all travel and the whole commercial system help to spread the disease. It is clear that there are high rates of infection along many main roads with rates falling off with distance from the road. This is not solely the product of the activities of drivers because other travellers, many of them in buses or lorries, also play a role. The epidemic has also been spread by other forms of transport, and boat traffic may have played a major role in infecting populations around the shores of Lake Victoria.

Long-distance truck drivers are certainly at risk (Orubuloye, Caldwell, and Caldwell, 1993) because of their way of life. They travel great distances, spend much of their lives away from home, and are sufficiently well off to be able to buy their pleasures. In Nigeria it was found that they craved not merely sex but other home comforts and attempted to organize their schedules so that they stayed frequently for the night with the same woman at each stop and received sex, friendship, food, and a bed. The women who supply these comforts usually have a number of semi-permanent clients and often a husband as well who absents himself when required and whose existence is unknown to the drivers.

[1]   i.e. the sex ratios in the seropositive population.

But this should be seen as part of a whole commercial system. In Nigeria the highways go northward from the ports and the commercially developed south to the cities of the far north. They cut through the poorest parts of the country for hundreds of miles while traversing the 'Middle Belt'. The highways are the major potential resource and way of tapping into the national and international economies for villagers for scores of miles on either side. People from these villages commute, or move semi-permanently, to the roadside to set up stalls and build shacks. They tap the wealth of the road by offering petrol, automotive repairs, tyres, food, alcohol, soft drinks, and sex, often managing to sell several of these items during a single stop. In the larger towns and at their destinations the trucks and buses stop in lorry parks beside the markets. Itinerant vendors—girls and young women waiting to be married and to secure a stall in the adjacent market—patrol these parks offering food and other items for sale, frequently including sex (Orubuloye *et al.*, 1993). They are at risk of both other sexually transmitted diseases and AIDS and they subsequently spread these diseases into the towns.

Truck drivers and itinerant traders are not the only high-risk occupational groups but they are the easiest to study. Soldiers and police are also prone to catch and spread the disease. One reason in Africa is that they are in a position to force themselves upon women or to demand sex in return for overlooking offences in countries where soldiers are frequently used for police duties. In addition, young soldiers are often stationed in large numbers in military camps away from their homes. The atmosphere of male camaraderie encourages the seeking of commercial sex, and bars and brothels quickly grow up around new camps. A study of Namibia noted: 'The pattern of HIV spread within Owambo is closely connected to several factors: the main tarred road through the area, traffic densities on each road, the location of trading centres, and the location of military bases' (Webb and Simon, 1993: 9). The study also notes that intensity patterns suggest that other STDs and hepatitis-B have spread through the same networks.

The risk posed to and by soldiers during wartime is even more acute. During the military engagement between Tanzania and Uganda, soldiers of both armies are reported to have just assumed that they could conscript the local women into providing meals and sex as well as cleaning up the men's quarters. Most of the women and their families seemed relieved that there was this employment with the soldiers in such difficult times. Wars and refugee streams also provide the desperate conditions where the selling of sex may be the main way of survival.

A final group at high risk is prisoners. An exception to the previous evidence on anal intercourse is the clear testimony in Nigeria that male prisoners who are exclusively heterosexual in their relationships when out of prison participate in anal sex while in gaol (Orubuloye, Omoniyi, and Shokunbi, 1994).

The Spread of AIDS

In a specific sense people around the world associate AIDS with population movement. When the AIDS epidemic was identified in the US in the early 1980s, Haiti and sub-Saharan Africa were soon pointed to as possible sources. In East Africa the disease is said to have entered the continent through the port of Mombasa and so to have begun its journey westward along the Trans-African Highway. In Ghana, AIDS is seen as a foreign disease, a definition which does not point exclusively to Côte d'Ivoire (Anarfi, 1992: 243). A meeting of commercial sex workers in Lagos arrived at a resolution that they would protect themselves against AIDS by refusing all white customers. This is in keeping with the older tendency in Britain and France to refer to syphilis as the French and English disease respectively.

There still is a feeling that AIDS must have had an epicentre, especially an African one, and a recent survey of the disease suggests that the high-intensity areas of East Africa may be explained by their proximity to an epicentre (de Vincenzi and Mertens, 1994).

In most of sub-Saharan Africa, as elsewhere, HIV levels are higher in urban than rural areas. At first this pattern looked like a process of diffusion and this is probably partly true. Nevertheless, many of the differentials between urban and rural areas have altered little over a decade and seem to be achieving some stability. Apart from such rural areas as south-west Uganda and north-west Tanzania, it appears increasingly likely that the rural epidemic would not persist without population mobility. A purely heterosexual epidemic, such as is the primary source of infection in sub-Saharan Africa (with vertical transmission from mother to child and transmission through infected blood as secondary transmission) is not easily sustained because heterosexual transmission without co-factors has a low level of infectivity. It is quite possible that in most of sub-Saharan Africa the only self-sustaining epidemic occurs in the small urban groups constituted by female commercial sex workers, their boyfriends and their most frequent clients. With the exception of those areas mentioned above, the HIV levels in rural areas may be almost entirely the result of persistent reinfection brought back from the towns by returning migrants, or, more often, by those who commuted to the urban areas for sex—or for other purposes, but with a visit for sex to a bar or hotel largely taken for granted as part of the urban experience.

AIDS and Contemporary Movement

The migration streams to African cities to provide commercial sex are complex movements. They are perhaps seen best in the movement from Ghana to Abidjan in Côte d'Ivoire in that this migrant stream seems to exist almost solely for the provision of commercial sex (Anarfi 1992, 1993).[2] Around 30 per cent of this migration stream is male, almost entirely composed of men who will derive earnings

---

[2] Painter's (1992) observation lends support to this assertion. Describing where the sexual partners of Niger and Mali migrants in Abidjan come from, he says, 'Ghanaian women are of particular interest in several respects. First, they are most frequently identified by the men with easy and cheap sex, and for this reason, first time migrants are said to visit them as an initiation to sex life in Abidjan. They were frequently mentioned during our interviews with men in Bamako and Niamey' (Painter, 1992: 36).

in one way or another from the female sex trade. Some are boyfriends and other hangers-on, while others work as pimps and managers. The experience of this component of the stream is much less well documented, but it is likely that their chance of being infected with AIDS is almost as high as that of the women, and the chance that they will infect others outside the trade is probably considerably greater.

The movement of rural and provincial women into city commercial sex in sub-Saharan Africa is changing. Commercial sex workers used to be typically young widows, or deserted wives, especially those who were sterile. There is evidence from both Nigeria and Ghana that there has been a steep increase in the proportion who are single (Orubuloye *et al.*, 1994). Furthermore, their education is at least of average standard and usually above average. Part of the reason for the migration is that their schooling has made them aspire to modern-sector jobs in the city, which are relatively hard to get. Commercial sex offers city employment with net financial returns comparable with senior white-collar positions. Another part of the explanation is that their schooling has made them reluctant to turn to traditional marketing or farming which takes the form of hoe tillage in shifting cultivation. Most would prefer to work in the city bars and save money for their return, perhaps in their late twenties. The timing of this return is partly occasioned by the male clients' demand for young women, and partly by the women's aspiration to establish a business and to get married while there is still time. These businesses are usually not market stalls but small shops in such fields as hairdressing, dressmaking, or even photography. Very few of the commercial sex workers in southern Nigeria believe that they have endangered their marriage prospects, or that their pasts will catch up with them and so endanger the continuation of a marriage once established. Because of their age, and possibly because of their dubious past, they may have to become second wives, but, if their business flourishes, they will not find themselves short of respect or power.

To a surprising extent, migrant men and migrant commercial women sex workers in West Africa live in social enclaves. The men associate mostly with other men from their own areas of rural origin while the women are not encouraged to leave their work premises except for work. The women who work in bars, and especially in nightclubs, meet men behaving in an urban sophisticated way more than do those who offer sexual services in brothels. The latter, even when they meet the same men, find them behaving with less aplomb in this very different context. Where they do meet with urban sophistication is when men arrange to take them out for the night or to accompany them for longer trips. Some join the urban milieu as full-time mistresses and sometimes wives. These migrant men and women create their own urban subculture which is not only more sex-oriented than the village but also than the rest of the city. Indeed, this migrant culture does much to give the city its reputation for being sexually wide open.

There are ways in which the women change. They learn more about sexual activities from the women who have preceded them and the demands of their clients. Furthermore, the higher-class commercial sex workers and those who work in higher-class establishments come into greater contact with native urban-ites. Both their sexual activities and the attitudes of the urbanites loosen the hold of traditional rural values. The poor migrant men—and most are poor—come in less close contact with the long-term residents. What changes them is their need for sex and its availability. In this way they come in close contact with women from other ethnic groups and so achieve a certain cosmopolitanism. Furthermore, the main 'red-light' districts are places of movement and excitement, more a product of those who work there, go there or have businesses there, than of anything eman-ating from city culture. But it is only possible in the city, and to many it is the chief characteristic of the city. It leaves its mark on migrants returning home. Women commercial sex workers who return home with a little money, often to set up a small business, treat men on more equal terms than before they left. This is partly defensive but mostly arises from the intensive contacts they have had with men in the city. It owes little to the attitudes of urban women. In contrast many migrant men return to the village determined to be heavy-handed fathers and to prevent their daughters going to town.

The women working in commercial sex and their boyfriends, and other men associated with the trade, are as likely as any other migrants to return home for Christmas, Easter, and festivals, weddings, and funerals. Indeed, as they are generally believed in the village to be secure in a fairly well-paid city job, or at the very least to be club managers or waitresses, they are expected to return home as frequently as anyone else. If they are married and their mothers are looking after their small children, they may have reasons for returning even more often. These visits are certainly a way whereby the epidemic can be spread. The young women returning to the village in city clothes and with city manners often have a great allure for the young men (Anarfi, 1992: 245–6).

Returning AIDS sufferers probably pose less risk to the community because of their condition, although it should be noted that they will do their best to hide their illness and indeed they may not fully understand it. It is also possible that they will be expected to earn something towards their keep once they have returned and commercial sex may at this stage be the only way.

In much of East and Southern Africa male migration is associated with work in mining areas where commercial sex thrives. Such men may well return HIV-positive and also with other STDs, which, as cofactors, may have facilitated their HIV infection, and which they might give to their wives, thus again serving as a co-factor to facilitate the subsequent transmission of HIV to the women. Some of these men have an even more complex life than this. Lesotho miners, returning from the goldfields of South Africa to their families, frequently dally first around Maseru, where they have set up mistresses in houses, before continuing upcountry to their wives.

In West Africa there is some debate about the market women who go afield on long trading cycles or who go to the wholesalers in the cities. One study in Nigeria adduced evidence that these women tended to be older, with little interest in sex (Sudarkasa, 1973), but there is other evidence that substantial numbers of the younger long-distance traders do supplement their trading income with money from commercial sex (Omorodion, 1993: 161–8); sometimes, as with the long-distance truck drivers, mainly for the company and the accommodation.

Much is made of the role of tourists, but, at least in Africa, that role is probably not a major one in the continued internal spread of the epidemic. One reason is that tourists are fairly healthy and probably have a low rate of current STD infection (which might serve as a cofactor) because they come from backgrounds or countries where such disorders are soon treated. They usually also patronize higher-class commercial sex workers who also have STDs treated. Such women in Nairobi have been shown to have much lower STD levels, fewer partners, and almost inevitably far lower HIV levels than poorer commercial sex workers (Kreiss *et al.*, 1986: 416).

Migration and AIDS

AIDS probably has a closer relationship to migration than any other infectious disease. Apart from STDs, other infectious diseases are facilitated by migration only insofar as it causes a greater mixing of people and offers the possibility of an infected person taking the disease to places where it was previously unknown.

But AIDS is different, for migration is a primary cause of behaviour which facilitates the transmission from one person to another. Migrant men are more likely to seek new sexual partners and are more likely to find them in commercial sex than when at home. This is partly because they are no longer bound by such strong social controls as at home. But there are other factors too. They are often in the city away from their wives and girlfriends. They are sexually frustrated, lonely, and they react to the anomie of the city. They go to the bars and hotels, often not primarily seeking sex. Furthermore, these facilities are a feature of the towns and cities and are often highly visible.

For women, migration is usually essential for full-time commercial sex work. In their home areas some can provide part-time discreet paid sex with a few men, but for most women, to practise commercial sex it is necessary to migrate. There are two reasons: the first is that the necessary bars and hotels exist only in the larger centres, but the second is more important: although many of the young women are anxious to spend part of their youth in the excitement of city nightspots, and later look back on the experience with nostalgia, their chief aim is to establish themselves comfortably and respectably in later life in their home town. Their home villages usually would not yield such incomes, but, more importantly, they could not successfully and respectably retire there if they had worked there as commercial sex workers.

The spread of the AIDS epidemic in sub-Saharan Africa is related to multi-partnered sexual relations, not merely to commercial sex, although many of the extramarital relations have a transactional element. But the commercial sex is more dangerous because the women involved in it usually have a large number of partners, and because some of these partners live particularly high-risk lives. Furthermore, the commercial sex is more closely allied to migration. This is important here, not only because it is the focus of this paper, but because it is migration which spreads the disease.

Rural men increasingly go to the town to visit commercial sex workers. They can do this in places like Uganda merely by going to those larger villages which serve as trading posts, and which because of these commercial sexual activities have far higher HIV levels than the surrounding villages (Way and Stanecki, 1993: 7). In Ekiti, Nigeria, this commuting from rural areas means that rural men, unlike rural women, can no longer be distinguished from their urban counterparts by the number of different sexual partners they have (Orubuloye, Caldwell, and Caldwell, 1991). In much of sub-Saharan Africa the AIDS epidemic may not be self-sustaining in rural areas but may depend on continuous reinfection from urban centres.

The epidemic is also maintained by broader movements and indeed by the whole commercial system. It is those who travel on the roads, those they come in contact with at wayside stops, and those they contact at each end of the journey who provide the total system which spreads the epidemic.

The AIDS epidemic could not have devastated Africa a century ago. The much lower level of movement and of commercial activity, and the much lower proportion of premarital and extramarital sexual activity which found its outlet in commercial sex and in towns, would have precluded the spread of the disease. This does raise the question whether it could have smouldered for decades in some isolated population. Pandemics were probably impossible before the Neolithic revolution or even the rise of the first urban civilizations. The AIDS epidemic in sub-Saharan Africa probably could not have spread before the communications and commercial revolutions of the present century.

It is clear that an increasingly urban and mobile world is going to be an incubator for pandemics. There will undoubtedly be increasing emphasis on epidemiological early warning systems and on medical research strike forces which can strive to invent treatments and vaccines quickly. Such mobility will enlarge the possibilities for the spread of AIDS and other STDs. But, if this world of the future is also richer, it will allow more universal treatment of STDs, with an especially great impact upon those STD cofactors of AIDS which are mostly prevalent in poor societies, such as chancroid. If it is a more educated world, it may be one where sexual relations are more diverse and possibly riskier, but it should also be one where fewer married persons are forced to migrate alone, and where safe sex practices are more easily followed.

The association between AIDS and mobility has its more hopeful side. Commercial and transportational networks have their nodal points—lorry parks, markets and brothels—and their full-time workers—drivers, itinerant traders, and commercial sex workers. It is true that these are places of high risk and people at high risk, but it also means that a programme against AIDS—hopefully one without victims and obvious invidious selection—may be able to focus on these nodal points of sexual networks with a greater chance of halting the disease than a programme spread equally thinly through the whole community.

REFERENCES

Anarfi, John K. (1992), 'Sexual Networking in Selected Communities in Ghana and the Sexual Behaviour of Ghanaian Female Migrants in Abidjan, Côte d'Ivoire', in Tim Dyson (ed.), *Sexual Behaviour and Networking: Anthropological and Socio-Cultural Studies on the Transmission of HIV*, Liège: Derouaux-Ordina.

—— (1993), 'Sexuality, Migration and AIDS in Ghana—A Socio-Behavioural Study', in John C. Caldwell, Gigi Santow, I. O. Orubuloye, Pat Caldwell, and John Anarfi (eds), *Sexual Networking and HIV/AIDS in West Africa*, Supplement to *Health Transition Review*, 3, 45–67.

—— and Awusabo-Asare, Kofi (1993), 'Experimental Research in Sexual Networking in Some Selected Areas of Ghana', in John C. Caldwell *et al.* (eds), *Sexual Networking and HIV/AIDS in West Africa*, Supplement to *Health Transition Review*, 3, 29–43.

Caldwell, John C. (1969), *African Rural–Urban Migration: The Movement to Ghana's Towns*, Canberra: Australian National University Press.

—— and Caldwell, Pat (1993), 'The Nature and Limits of the Sub-Saharan African AIDS Epidemic: Evidence from Geographic and Other Patterns', *Population and Development Review*, 19(4): 817–48.

—— —— and Orubuloye, I. O. (1992), 'The Family and Sexual Networking in Sub-Saharan Africa: Historic Regional Differences and Present-Day Implications', *Population Studies*, 46(3): 385–410.

—— Orubuloye, I. O., and Caldwell, Pat (1991), 'The Destabilization of the Traditional Yoruba Sexual System', *Population and Development Review*, 17(2): 229–62.

David, Nicholas and Voas, David (1981), 'Societal Causes of Infertility and Population Decline among the Settled Fulani of North Cameroon', *Man* (n.s.), 16: 644–64.

Enel, Catherine and Pison, Gilles (1992), 'Sexual Relations in the Rural Area of Mlomp (Casamance, Senegal)', in Tim Dyson (ed.), *Sexual Behaviour and Networking: Anthropological and Socio-Cultural Studies on the Transmission of HIV*, Liège: Derouaux-Ordina, 249–67.

Frank, Odile (1992), 'Sexual Behaviour and Disease Transmission in Sub-Saharan Africa: Past Trends and Future Prospects', in Tim Dyson (ed.), *Sexual Behaviour and Networking: Anthropological and Socio-Cultural Studies on the Transmission of HIV*, Liège: Derouaux-Ordina, 89–108.

Grmek, Mirko (1990), *History of AIDS: Emergence and Origin of a Modern Pandemic*, Princeton: Princeton University Press.

Kreiss, Joan K., Koech, Davy, Plummer, Francis A., *et al.* (1986), 'AIDS Virus Infection in Nairobi Prostitutes: Spread of the Epidemic to East Africa', *New England Journal of Medicine*, 13 February: 414–18.

Larson, Ann (1989), 'Social Context of Human Immunodeficiency in Africa: Historical and Cultural Bases of East and Central African Sexual Relations', *Reviews of Infectious Diseases*, 11: 716–31.

Omorodion, Francisca Isi (1993), 'Sexual Networking among Market Women in Benin City, Bendel State, Nigeria', in John C. Caldwell *et al.* (eds), *Sexual Networking and HIV/AIDS in West Africa*, Supplement to *Health Transition Review*, 3, 159–69.

Orubuloye, I. O., Caldwell, John C., and Caldwell, Pat (1991), 'Sexual Networking in the Ekiti District of Nigeria', *Studies in Family Planning*, 22(2): 61–73.

———— ———— ———— (1992), 'Diffusion and Focus in Sexual Networking: Identifying Partners and Partners' Partners', *Studies in Family Planning*, 23(6): 343–51.

———— , Caldwell, Pat, and Caldwell, John C. (1993), 'The Role of High-risk Occupations in the spread of AIDS: Truck Drivers and Itinerant Market Women in Nigeria', *International Family Planning Perspectives*, 19(2): 43–8, 71.

———— ———— ———— (1994), 'Commercial Sex Workers in Nigeria in the Shadow of AIDS', in I. O. Orubuloye, John C. Caldwell, Pat Caldwell and Gigi Santow (eds), *Sexual Networking and AIDS in Sub-Saharan Africa: Behavioural Research and the Social Context*, Canberra: Australian National University, 101–16.

———— , Omoniyi, O. P., and Shokunbi, W. A. (1994), 'Sexual Networking, STDs, and HIV/AIDS in Four Urban Gaols in Nigeria', Paper presented to Workshop on Sexual Networking, STDs and HIV/AIDS Interventions, Ondo State University, Ado-Ekiti, Nigeria, 23–25 August.

Painter, T. M. (1992). 'Migration and AIDS in West Africa. A Study of Migrants from Niger and Mali to Côte d'Ivoire', New York: CARE.

Pickering, H. and Wilkins, H. A. (1993), 'Do Unmarried Women in African Towns Have to Sell Sex, or Is It a Choice?', in John C. Caldwell *et al.* (eds), *Sexual Networking and HIV/AIDS in West Africa*, Supplement to *Health Transition Review*, 3, 17–27.

Prothero, R. Mansell (1965), *Migrants and Malaria*, London: Longman.

Ramasubban, Radhika (1992), 'Sexual Behaviour and Conditions of Health Care: Potential Risks of HIV Transmission in India', in Tim Dyson (ed.), *Sexual Behaviour and Networking: Anthropological and Socio-Cultural Studies on the Transmission of HIV*, Liège: Derouaux-Ordina, 175–202.

Sudarkasa, Niara (1973), *Where Women Work: A Study of Yoruba Women in the Market Place and in the Home*, Ann Arbor: University of Michigan.

Vincenzi, I. de and Mertens, T. (1994), 'Male Circumcision: a Role in HIV Prevention?', *AIDS*, 8: 153–60.

Way, Peter O. and Stanecki, Karen A. (1993), 'An Epidemiological Review of HIV/AIDS in Sub-Saharan Africa', Washington DC: US Bureau of the Census.

Webb, Douglas and Simon, David (1993), 'Migrants, Money and the Military: the Social Epidemiology of HIV/AIDS in Owambo, Northern Namibia', CEDAR Research Papers 8, Egham: University of London.

4 Migration, Sexual Subcultures, and HIV/AIDS in Brazil

RICHARD G. PARKER

Introduction

By late 1993, the Brazilian Ministry of Health had recorded nearly 45,000 cases of AIDS—the highest number of cases reported in Latin America, and among the highest number anywhere in the world. Since its emergence little more than a decade earlier, the AIDS epidemic had taken shape as among the most serious public health problems in the country, and official estimates that more than 750,000 Brazilians are already infected with HIV suggest that the impact of AIDS will continue to grow dramatically in the foreseeable future. Throughout this period, the epidemic has been characterized by its apparently rampant spread—over time, across space, and beyond the boundaries that would seem to divide otherwise disparate social groups.

Yet if the spread of HIV/AIDS in Brazil has undeniably taken place rapidly, it has not in fact occurred randomly (see Parker, 1990; Daniel and Parker, 1991, 1993). On the contrary, as in other societies (see, for example, Jonsen and Stryker, 1993), the spread of HIV and AIDS in Brazil has followed clearly defined and socially determined lines. It has been shaped by the divisions of class and gender, by the processes of urbanization and modernization, by the recent history of economic and political life in Brazil. A careful examination of the ways in which the epidemic has spread in Brazil will thus uncover a range of dynamic social processes that are part and parcel of contemporary Brazilian life—and that must ultimately be more fully understood if we are to begin to make sense of the epidemic, of its profound social and economic impact, and of the possible ways in which we might fight against it (Parker *et al.*, 1994).

This chapter seeks to examine the changing shape of the HIV/AIDS epidemic in Brazil in relation to current patterns of migration and population movement,

An important part of the data discussed in this paper comes from a collaborative study of sexual behaviour and behaviour change among men who have sex with men. I am indebted to Jurandir Freire Costa, Katia Guimarães, Murilo Peixoto, Renato Quemel, and Veriano Terto Jr. for their many contributions to this work. Thanks also to Jane Galvão for conversations that have helped to clarify a number of important issues. Support for this research has been provided at different points in time by the the Wenner-Gren Foundation for Anthropological Research, the Joint Committee on Latin American Studies of the Social Science Research Council, the World Health Organization's Global Programme on AIDS, the Foundation for the Support of Research in the State of Rio de Janeiro (FAPERJ), and the Ford Foundation.

and the ways in which these patterns have affected sexual behaviour and impacted upon the spread of HIV and AIDS. The first section of the paper offers a brief overview of what might be described as the social epidemiology of AIDS in Brazil—the changing patterns of HIV transmission that seem to have character-ized the epidemic over the course of the past decade, and some of the social and cultural factors that are apparently associated with these changes. The second part of the paper provides an overview of traditional migratory patterns—particularly from the North-East to South-East of the country, from rural to urban areas, and back again—and seeks to analyse the relationship between these patterns and the spread of HIV/AIDS in Brazil. The third part of the paper focuses on what might be described more specifically as sexual migration from outlying areas to the emerging sexual subcultures, especially among men who have sex with men, in major urban centres such as Rio de Janeiro and São Paulo. The paper examines the extent to which such emerging sexual communities have served not only as a focus for the transmission of HIV and other STDs, but also as an effective point of departure for community-based prevention activities.

The Changing Epidemiology of AIDS in Brazil

Before turning to a more detailed discussion of the relationship between HIV/AIDS and population movement, it is worthwhile to situate these issues within the wider social and epidemiological context of AIDS in Brazil. What is perhaps most immediately striking is the country's remarkable diversity, and, per-haps not surprisingly, the complexity that has emerged in the epidemiology of AIDS within this context. Brazil is an immense country, with a territory of approximately 8,500,000 square kilometres, and a population estimated at more than 150 million people. It is marked by a number of important regional differ-ences, as well as by highly varied processes of modernization and social change in different parts of the country and among different sectors of the society. It was perhaps best described some years ago by Roger Bastide as a 'land of contrasts' in which the divisions of class, race, and gender are constantly apparent (Bastide, 1978).

The diverse contradictions that seem to characterize Brazilian life have become even more striking in recent decades as the result of a series of social and political changes. Rapid growth and urbanization has transformed the once largely rural society, creating a range of new social and economic divisions that have stretched the fabric of Brazilian life. The political economy of debt and dependence has produced a series of severe economic crises, resulting in a deeply rooted and apparently long-term recession by the late 1980s and early 1990s. And perhaps most important, twenty years of authoritarian military rule between 1964 and 1984, followed by a gradual return to democratic government in the mid- to late 1980s, largely undermined the legitimacy of many political institutions, facing the nation with the remarkably difficult task of having to reconstruct a tradition of citizenship within a democratic order. Together, over a number of years, these developments led to the extensive deterioriation of both the public health and social welfare systems, limiting Brazilian society's capacity to address its many, already existing health problems, and conditioning the ways in which it might respond to the emergence of a new socially, culturally, and epidemiologically explosive infectious disease (Daniel and Parker, 1991, 1993; Parker *et al.*, 1994).

It is within this context that the HIV/AIDS epidemic began to take shape in Brazil during the early 1980s, and the ways in which this epidemic has developed, as well as the ways in which Brazilian society has responded to it over the course of its first decade, have been conditioned by this particular set of circumstances. Like Brazilian society itself, AIDS in Brazil has been marked, perhaps above all else, by its complexity and diversity. By October of 1993, with 43,964 reported cases and 18,128 known deaths (see Table 4.1), AIDS had clearly emerged as one of the most serious problems in contemporary Brazilian life. While the vast majority of these cases have been in large urban centres such as São Paulo (15,007, or 34.1 per cent of the national total) and Rio de Janeiro (4,725, or 10.7 per cent), AIDS cases have now been reported from every state and region of the country (see Table 4.2). Indeed, the most rapid spread of the epidemic would now appear to be taking place not only in the heavily urbanized and industrialized South-East, but also in the less developed North and North-East.

Even greater diversity emerges in turning from its regional distribution to the specific modes of HIV transmission that have characterized the AIDS epidemic in

Table 4.1.   Cases of AIDS and number of deaths by year, 1980–1993

Year	No. of cases	No. of deaths
1980	1	1
1981	—	—
1982	7	5
1983	32	27
1984	126	105
1985	519	371
1986	1,032	700
1987	2,349	1,371
1988	3,927	2,117
1989	5,204	2,494
1990	7,072	3,154
1991	9,184	3,448
1992	10,267	3,183
1993*	4,244	1,152
TOTAL	43,964	18,128

* Preliminary data through October 1993.

Source: Data from the Ministry of Health, 1993.

Table 4.2.   Number of cases and cases per million, by Region and States or Territories (Unidades Federadas), 1980–1993*

Region, state, and territory	No.	Cases per 100,000
Brazil	43,964	32.4
North	481	5.7
Rondônia	41	5.5
Acre	24	6.7
Amazonas	97	5.5
Pará	245	5.8
Amapá	17	7.8
Tocantins	17	1.8
North-East	3,523	8.8
Maranhão	248	5.3
Piauí	110	4.5
Ceará	537	9.1
Rio Grande do Norte	202	9.4
Paraíba	177	5.2
Pernambuco	980	14.4
Alagoas	184	8.2
Sergipe	115	8.8
Bahia	970	9.0
South-East	33,901	75.2
Minas Gerais	1,683	11.5
Espírito Santo	393	17.9
Rio de Janeiro	6,208	48.3
São Paulo	25,617	85.6
South	4,294	20.7
Paraná	1,212	14.9
Santa Catarina	933	22.6
Rio Grande do Sul	2,149	25.2
Central-West	1,765	29.0
Goiás	417	9.3
Mato Grosso	268	17.9
Mato Grosso do Sul	429	26.5
Distrito Federal	651	40.9

* Through October 1993

Source: Ministry of Health, 1993.

Brazil. Whether one is looking at sexuality, the exchange of blood and blood products, or the use of intravenous drugs, the complexity that characterizes Brazilian life more generally can be found, as well, in almost all of the specific contexts in which HIV infection has become significant. While homosexual contacts have been important in the spread of HIV, for example, the social and cultural organization of such contacts in Brazil seems to be perhaps especially complex. Multiple subcultures or sexual communities have developed over the course of recent years, at least in urban Brazil, in which same-sex sexual behaviours are linked to the construction of sexual identities in a variety of diverse ways (Daniel and Parker, 1991, 1993; Parker, 1987, 1990; Parker *et al.*, 1994). A gradually emerging, largely middle-class gay community contrasts quite sharply, for example, with the subculture of transvestites and their partners, male hustlers, or even the loosely organized networks of men who have sex with men in the poorer suburban communities that surround all major urban centres in contemporary Brazil. Within these different settings, same-sex interactions do not always translate into the conscious elaboration of homosexual or even bisexual identities, and the links between specific sexual practices and perceptions of risk are mediated by diverse social structures and cultural representations (Daniel and Parker, 1991, 1993; Parker, 1987, 1988, 1990, 1991). Perhaps not surprisingly, then, although men reporting homosexual behaviour have accounted for 25.7 per cent of the cases of AIDS reported among adults in Brazil by October, 1993, men reporting bisexual contacts have accounted for another 13 per cent, while cases linked to male and female heterosexual interactions have risen to 19.4 per cent of the national total (see Table 4.3).

A similarly complex relationship between social and cultural context and epidemiological patterns can be found, as well, in the exchange of blood and blood products in Brazil, where humanitarian values have always been less important than commercial interests. Blood has traditionally circulated from the poorest sectors of Brazilian society, with the least access to adequate medical care, to the more well-to-do, and the commercialization of blood has long resulted in

Table 4.3. Percentage of cases by category of transmission and year in individuals fifteen years or older*

Category of transmission	1980–6	1987	1988	1989	1990	1991	1992	1993	1980–92
Homosexual	46.9	37.6	33.1	30.2	25.8	23.2	20.5	17.4	28.8
Bisexual	21.4	16.3	14.2	13.6	11.2	11.0	10.1	10.0	13.0
Heterosexual	5.2	7.6	11.2	14.5	17.2	19.7	23.7	27.3	19.4
IV drug use	3.0	11.4	17.5	19.6	23.5	25.6	25.6	26.1	22.3
Transfusion	4.0	7.1	5.3	4.2	3.5	3.1	3.3	3.2	3.8
Haemophilia	3.6	2.4	2.1	1.4	1.0	0.9	0.5	0.3	1.1

* Through October 1993.

Source: Ministry of Health, 1993.

relatively high incidence of illnesses such as Chagas disease. Not surprisingly, 4.9 per cent of the reported cases of AIDS in Brazil have been linked to receipt of blood and blood products on the part of haemophiliacs and blood transfusion recipients (see Table 4.3). Even though important attempts have been made recently to regulate the blood industry, these efforts have often been resisted, and, in some parts of the country, have resulted in both the creation of a kind of underground or parallel blood market, as well as in widespread uncertainty concerning the possible risks involved in both blood donation and the receipt of blood products (ABIA, 1988; Parker, 1990; see, also, Daniel and Parker, 1993).

Finally, although injecting drug use lagged behind other modes of transmission during the early years of the AIDS epidemic in Brazil, it has recently expanded rapidly, and currently accounts for 22.3 per cent of the cases reported among adults in the country as a whole (see Table 4.3). This percentage has recently increased significantly, and has been especially difficult to confront in some areas, such as parts of the state of São Paulo, where drug traffic routes have functioned for some time (and have become even more frequently used, probably in large part as the result of changing drug control policies in other parts of South America). When compared to the situation in at least some other countries, such as the United States, Spain, or Italy, injecting drug use in Brazil is perhaps less clearly defined as the focus for a unique, sharply bounded or defined underworld. Yet it seems to be characterized by a number of factors (such as the widespread injection of cocaine as opposed to heroin) that may contribute significantly to the rapid spread of HIV (see Parker *et al.*, 1994).

As a result of these different factors, the shape of the AIDS epidemic in Brazil has continued to change over the course of the past decade. Perhaps most dramatically, what once appeared to be a disease primarily of homosexual men has rapidly come to impact upon a much larger population (see Table 4.3). As a consequence of all the different factors described above, by the early 1990s heterosexual transmission had become the fastest-growing mode of transmission in the country as a whole. And in a period of fewer than 10 years, the male/female ratio in reported cases of AIDS had fallen from 125/1 in 1984 to 4/1 by 1993 (see Table 4.4). At the same time, the social and economic profile of the epidemic has rapidly changed, increasingly affecting the poorer sectors of Brazilian society—clearly the greatest mass of what is an overwhelmingly poor nation. Taken together, these developments have intensified the impact of AIDS on Brazilian society as a whole, posing among the most serious crises facing the public health system, and severely stretching the limits of already problematic legal, medical, and social services (ABIA, 1988; Daniel and Parker, 1991, 1993; Parker *et al.*, 1994).

Migration, HIV Transmission, and AIDS

What of course is unclear, on the basis of this brief overview of the social epidemiology of AIDS in Brazil, is the extent to which patterns of migration and

Table 4.4. Number of cases by sex, year of diagnosis, and male/female ratio, Brazil, 1980–93*

Year of diagnosis	Male	Female	Ratio M/F
1980	1	—	1/–
1981	—	—	—
1982	7	—	7/–
1983	31	1	31/1
1984	125	1	125/1
1985	496	17	29/1
1986	959	57	17/1
1987	2,084	223	9/1
1988	3.397	488	7/1
1989	4,551	616	7/1
1990	6,132	867	7/1
1991	7,671	1,441	5/1
1992	8,358	1,875	4/1
1993	3,350	885	4/1
Total	37,162	885	4/1

* Through October 1993.
Source: Ministry of Health, 1993.

population movement in Brazilian society may have contributed—or may contribute in the future—to the transmission of HIV. At an almost intuitive level, it is of course apparent that a variety of different migratory patterns have been linked to the spread of HIV. Indeed, virtually all of the early cases of AIDS reported in Brazil (from 1982 to 1983 or 1984) were among individuals who had lived for extensive periods outside Brazil, in the major North American and Western European cities that were early epicentres in the HIV/AIDS pandemic. More recently, the gradual spread in reported AIDS cases from the Brazilian epicentres of São Paulo and Rio de Janeiro to virtually all major urban centres throughout the country has clearly been linked to internal migration (from smaller to larger urban centres within Brazil) and, perhaps especially, remigration (back from larger urban centres to place of origin) over the course of the past decade. Yet specific observations concerning the ways in which infection has taken place and the populations most severely affected are in large part lacking.

What we can observe, on the basis of existing social and demographic data, are a number of fairly clear patterns of population movement across the country. For more than a century now, no single change in Brazilian society has been as dominant or more consistent than the process of urbanization, associated, in large part, with the processes of industrialization. While Brazil came to the close of the nineteenth century as a predominantly rural and agricultural society, in the early and mid-twentieth century, industrialization became synonymous (particularly in the discourse of economic nationalists, such as Getúlio Vargas) with progress and development. As the Brazilian economy became more industrial (and agriculture itself more mechanized), the percentage of the Brazilian population working in rural, agricultural sectors decreased steadily. The urban-centred sector of Brazil's economy (which includes industry, commerce, finance, communications, and government) increased proportionally. And, in large part, the workforce for this rapid industrial and urban expansion was supplied by a constant human movement from the rural to urban sectors. Immigration from abroad also played a role, but was less important than migration from rural areas into the cities (see Graham, 1970; Sahato, 1968).

The ongoing rural–urban migration pattern that has dominated Brazilian life throughout much of the twentieth century has been a periodic one—often in response to seasonal changes, agricultural cycles, and, particularly in the North-East, extended periods of draught. Migration has also been heavily interregional, involving human movement from the poorer North and North-Eastern regions to the richer agricultural and industrial states of the South and South-East. Census data from the mid-twentieth century reflect this shift clearly—between 1940 and 1950, for example, the urban population increased by 41.5 per cent and the sub-urban (poorer areas surrounding the major cities) by 58.3 per cent, while the rural population increased by only 17.4 per cent. By the 1970 census, in spite of general population growth, many rural areas showed actual losses in population. Although data from the most recent (1991) census are not yet available, when followed over a period of a few decades, the transformation of Brazil into a predominantly urban society is already striking (see Table 4.5). And this rapid growth rate in urban areas generally has clearly been heaviest in the major cities of the South-East, such as São Paulo, Rio de Janeiro, and Belo Horizonte, as well as the newer 'frontier cities', such as Brasília, of the Central region.

Not surprisingly, this influx of population, fleeing in large part the abject poverty of rural areas and less developed regions, has tended to concentrate in the most economically and socially marginal areas of the large urban centres. The suburbs, for example, have grown more rapidly than the cities—yet these 'suburbs' in Brazil are in many ways the reverse of North American suburbs, since they often lack even the most basic services considered essential in the city, such as water, sewerage, paved streets, and so on. And within the cities, migrants tend to

Table 4.5.   Brazil: Population Increase

Census	Urban (%)	Rural (%)	Total
1940	31	69	100
1950	36	64	100
1960	45	55	100
1970	59	41	100
1980	72	28	100

settle principally in the heavily overcrowded and undeveloped urban slums or squatter communities (know as *favelas*), as well as in the run-down and partially abandoned tenements (*cortiços*) of many inner city areas. Attracted by kinship ties, by lower housing costs, and the 'informal' job market that is often their only economic option, migrants are thus largely concentrated on the margins or periphery of urban life—and urban services. They depend heavily not only on the informal economy, but on a range of other informal sources of support—such as health care, employee benefits, and so on—which fall outside the established (even if precarious) social welfare system in Brazil.

This particular social and demographic configuration has had a number of extremely important consequences in relation to the HIV/AIDS epidemic. First, and perhaps most important, it is precisely in these marginalized regions—*subúrbios, favelas, cortiços*—that, at least by the early 1990s, the bulk of HIV infection and AIDS has become concentrated. Over the course of more than a decade, the epidemic has rapidly become centred in the poorest and most marginal sectors of Brazilian society. These populations, in turn, are themselves concentrated in precisely those areas that are the principal focus for internal migration—a process which has been documented with particular clarity in São Paulo, by far Brazil's largest and fastest-growing city (see Parker *et al.*, 1994).

This is of course no surprise; on the contrary, it is apparent, not only in Brazil, but cross-culturally, that social and economic oppression are intimately linked to vulnerability in the face of HIV. It is in the *favelas* and *cortiços*, which are largely abandoned by the police and other authorities, that drug traffic is concentrated, that marginalized and stigmatized populations such as transvestite prostitutes, drug users, or others who are simply down on their luck, can find places to live, and so on. Community health services are at best limited, where they exist at all, and a range of different infirmities (sexually transmitted and otherwise) go undetected or untreated. Access to free HIV testing or support services is altogether unknown. In short, all of the social and medical 'cofactors' associated with high levels of HIV infection are found in abundant quantity, and it is in these areas that the AIDS epidemic has taken hold most firmly.

And this same social and economic marginalization is also responsible, in large part, not only for the concentration of HIV infection and AIDS within a number of specific areas within the urban geography (Parker *et al.*, 1994), but also for its gradual spread from the major urban centre of the South-East to the Amazon frontier and, indeed, back to the North and North-East. Particularly in the 1980s and 1990s, as the so-called economic miracle during the authoritarian military regime (from 1964 to 1984) came unhinged and transformed itself into spiralling inflation, unemployment, and economic debt, these same sectors of the urban South-East served as the point of departure for re-migration, on the one hand, and frontier expansion, on the other (see, for example, Flowers, 1988).

Facing the contracting job markets and increasingly miserable conditions of major cities such as Rio and São Paulo, the 1980s witnessed a rapidly expanding search for other social and economic options. For the middle class, the road to better living conditions has often been to seek work opportunities abroad in Europe or the United States. A frequently told joke asks what the *saída* or way out of the Brazilian economic crisis is, only to answer that the best *saída* is the international airport! This international population movement has in fact been linked to patterns of HIV transmission among some populations, such as gay and bisexual men as well as female, male, and transvestite prostitutes. For the poor and uneducated, however, the only available options for escaping miserable conditions have increasingly become the search for quick and easy fortune in the gold mining (*garimpo*) regions of the frontier, or the return to their communities of origin, particularly in the North and North-East.

While the most intense days of the gold rush in the mid- to late 1980s have now passed, the frontier continues to attract a gradual flow of migrants, especially from the South and South-East, though also, in lesser quantities, from the coastal cities of the North-East. Since this population is almost exclusively male, it is perhaps not surprising that it has given rise, in some places, to a small but intense parallel market revolving around female prostitution, and that this market is itself highly mobile, moving from one place to another as the search for gold shifts its focus. At the same time, the general scarcity of women has also been linked, in some sites, to a complex homosexual subculture that perhaps resembles the structures found in some institutional settings (such as prisons or reform schools) more than anything else. And although the evidence is incomplete, and has not been publicly disseminated, information from colleagues who work with the Brazilian Ministry of Health suggests that both among female prostitutes and the male *garimpeiros*, the spread of HIV infection has taken place at an alarming rate (personal communication from an anonymous [for obvious reasons] Ministry of Health staff member).

Although not as intense, similar concern has also been raised in relation to re-migration between the major South-Eastern cities and the North and North-East (see Flowers, 1988). Again, this movement focuses heavily on single males who have left families in the North-East to seek work in the South (where the huge civil construction industry, for example, is almost entirely staffed by North-Easterners), and who return home when unable to find work or sustain themselves in some way. From the mid- to late 1980s, the gradual spread of HIV from the South to the North and North-East was heavily associated with re-migration along these lines. Interestingly, though not necessarily surprisingly, transmission in the North and North-East has continued to focus more heavily than in other parts of the country on interactions between men who have sex with men, and it is only quite recently that heterosexual transmission has begun to rise significantly in this region (Ministry of Health, 1994).

Over the course of the late twentieth century, then, Brazilian society has been marked by a number of processes that have structured both the possibility and the reality of the spread of the HIV/AIDS epidemic in several highly specific ways. On the one hand, rapid urbanization and industrialization have led to an important flow of population from rural areas and the North and North-Eastern regions in particular into the large urban centres of the South-East. Simultaneously, and particularly in recent decades as the so-called economic miracle waned and the apparent attractions of the South-East lost at least some of their lustre, a gradual flow of people out toward the perceived opportunities of the frontier and re-migration back to families of origin in the North and North-East has also occurred.

The spread of HIV infection in Brazil (as in other societies) may be mapped onto these migratory patterns, responding to the social and economic conditions within which they have taken place. Nowhere has vulnerability in the face of HIV been more pronounced than in the poor and marginalized communities and neighbourhoods in São Paulo, Rio de Janeiro, and Brasília that have been the primary focus for migrants coming into the city from rural areas and other regions of the country. This heightened vulnerability exists perhaps not so much because of the particularity of sexual culture within these contexts (though this too surely plays a complex role) as because of the array of social conditions—especially economic oppression and social marginalization. In Brazil, as in many other societies, the lack of economic opportunities, the failure to provide basic social welfare and health care benefits, and the widespread denial of rights and citizenship that are in large part the lot of the popular classes, are clearly of central importance, and combine, no doubt, with the particularities of diverse sexual subcultures—among civil construction workers or *garimpeiros*, homosexual and bisexual men, female, transvestite, or male prostitutes, injecting drug users and their partners, and so on—in forming the complex social setting in which HIV/AIDS has become, quite literally, an epidemic out of control.

Sexual Migration, Sexual Community, and AIDS Prevention

Having made these points briefly, I would also like to examine a slightly different dimension of the relationship between migration, sexual cultures, and HIV/AIDS than has generally been explored. In much of my work over the course of the past decade, I have sought to analyse the ways in which an understanding of sexual cultures and subcultures can help us to understand more fully, and, I hope, respond more effectively to the HIV/AIDS epidemic. Clearly, there are a variety of ways in which we might develop a similar analysis more fully in relation to the complex intersections between sexual subcultures, HIV/AIDS, and patterns of migration in Brazilian society. In the preceding sections, I have tried at least to point to some of the ways in which recent migratory patterns have helped to shape the AIDS epidemic in specific ways, and some of the sexual settings (though not always subcultures) that have contributed to this.

Building on this discussion, however, I would like to draw tentatively on the more recent work that I have become involved in, and to try at least partially to invert this interpretive order. I would like to suggest that while both sexual subcultures and migratory patterns in Brazil have clearly affected the changing shape of HIV and AIDS in Brazilian society, the impact of HIV and AIDS has also shaped the emergence of certain sexual subcultures and related migratory patterns. In short, I would like to argue that the relationship between the different elements of the equation between sexual subcultures, migration, and HIV/AIDS is in fact more synergistic or cybernetic (for lack of better terms) than unilateral or one-dimensional.

For more than five years now, together with a group of colleagues, I have been involved in research on the impact of HIV/AIDS in Brazilian society generally— and its role in shaping the diverse sexual experience among men who have sex with men in particular. Since 1989, we have carried out two cross-sectional studies in Rio de Janeiro (one in 1989 and another in 1993), together with ongoing in-depth interviews carried out between 1989 and 1994 (principally in Rio, though on a much smaller scale in São Paulo and Recife), and have interviewed slightly more than 1,000 informants over this five-year period. The focus of this work has been to develop a fuller understanding of the social and cultural construction of sexual meanings among men who have sex with men, of the relation between sexual meaning and sexual behaviour, and of the role of HIV/AIDS in shaping changing patterns of sexual conduct. Our primary concern has been to monitor the impact of the epidemic in order to develop more effective prevention programmes serving the gay and bisexual population. In the process, however, we have collected what we believe to be one of the most extensive data bases to be found anywhere in the developing world on the sexual experience of men who have sex with men.

What has been perhaps most striking to us, however, has been the emergence of a more clearly defined gay community that has begun to take shape in Brazilian society over the course of the past decade—at least in part as a response to the HIV/AIDS epidemic. This 'community' is highly diverse, involving a number of different (homo)sexual subcultures, but has nonetheless begun to articulate itself as a community at least in part through a dynamic process of mobilization and activism in the face of HIV infection and AIDS. AIDS activism and gay activism have also become more visible and vocal, increasingly crossing or merging into the flow of daily life. Gay institutions (ranging from commercial establishments to publications and organizations) have begun to emerge and to become more visible. In short, many of the elements that have been associated with the emergence of gay communities in other societies (especially in the developed world) have begun to emerge in Brazilian society—and to play a role in the lives of our informants. In Brazil, as in a number of other developing societies (see Altman, 1992, 1994), however, the existence of AIDS has been fundamental to this process of social change.

This is not altogether surprising, of course. Never has homosexuality been such a focus for public discussion and debate as in the wake of AIDS. Precisely because of the collective representations linking HIV/AIDS to homosexuality in many parts of the world, the representation of homosexuality—in popular culture, in scientific discourse, in the mass media, and so on—has taken on a new and profoundly different salience when compared with the situation less than a decade before. The possibilities (both imported and indigenous) of homosexual and gay identities offered up by Brazilian culture have become far more clear and evident than was true even a decade before. And a whole range of possibilities for collective organizing and action around AIDS-related issues and sexual rights have emerged that might not have been problematized (at least not in the same way) were it not for the tragedy that the epidemic has wrought both in individual lives as well as in the fabric of society itself.

This discussion of the changing shape of the homosexual subculture (or subcultures) in Brazil could be extended at some length. What is perhaps most striking in relation to the current focus, however, is the way in which it cuts across the question of migration, particularly in the data that we have collected. Interestingly, of the informants we have interviewed, and across the spectrum of age, a relatively large percentage were in fact born and reared in other cities and states, having migrated to Rio de Janeiro for explicitly sexual reasons—to escape sexual oppression in their community of origin, to have more frequent or easier access to sexual contacts, to seek a community of sexual peers, and so on.

Our data show a number of important differences over the past five years, especially among younger as opposed to older informants, in the construction and rationalization of such sexual migration. For older informants, as for many of the men of all ages whom we interviewed in 1989, the explicitly stated motivations lying behind migration were more often than not to escape the sexual oppression that they experienced in their place of origin. An image of Rio de Janeiro as a site of anonymity and, hence, sexual adventure and freedom, has clearly played a key role in their personal histories. Yet this image seemed less important in pulling them to the big city than the sense of being *abafado* or smothered in their home towns which seemed to push them away from their original communities.

As time has passed, however, and a more visible sexual subculture verging on a 'homosexual community' has become a visible part of urban Brazilian life, the explanation for migration has begun to change. Home town stigma and oppression continue to play an important role, but seem to be diminishing in the face of a more positive image of freedom and liberation in centres such as Rio and São Paulo. And, interestingly, this vision of freedom seems less and less focused on anonymity and social isolation than on the existence of a sense of shared community—an alternative social space in which it is possible to *achar a sua tribo* or, literally, find your tribe. Not altogether unlike the historical and representational construction of gay Amsterdam described by Duyves (1994), the image of homosexual space taking shape in cities such as Rio has begun to transform their meaning—within a complex (and highly postmodern!) set of social representations in which Amsterdam too, like San Francisco *and* São Paulo, is very much present. And this has taken place, quite consciously and quite articulately, in spite of the risks and dangers that are so often associated, in a range of other social representations, with HIV and AIDS and their apparent link to quite diverse homosexualities.

Sexual migration is of course a broad category that often includes young women as well as men, gay as well as straight—and that certainly responds to a wide range of influences. The point is that just as HIV/AIDS (among other factors) would seem to have had an important impact in shaping aspects of an emerging gay community in cities such as Rio de Janeiro, it has also shaped what we might describe as (homo)sexual migration from outlying areas into this community. To the extent that the gay community has itself become the key focus for AIDS prevention activities, as well as for the defence of civil and human rights, it may also offer key insights into community organizing and mobilization. Whatever else it suggests, it surely offers some sense of the extent to which the world is in fact a far more complicated place than we have been able to fully comprehend in seeking to respond to AIDS within the social sciences. To move forward in the future, we must increasingly move beyond the most obvious theoretical and methodological frameworks that have guided much of our research thus far in seeking to build upon the insights that have emerged from the first decade of AIDS research. We must begin to focus on the complex processes of social change that have not only shaped the HIV/AIDS epidemic, but that have also been shaped by the epidemic. Perhaps most important, we must explore the ways in which these processes might more effectively be harnessed to reduce the profound pain and suffering that the epidemic has produced.

REFERENCES

ABIA, 1988, 'The Face of AIDS in Brazil'. Paper presented at the IV International Conference on AIDS, Stockholm, Sweden, June.

Altman, D., 1992, 'AIDS and the Discourses on Sexuality'. In R. W. Connell and G. W. Dowsett (eds), *Rethinking Sex: Social Theory and Sexuality Research*, 32–48. Melbourne: Melbourne University Press.

—— 1994, 'Political Sexualities: Meanings and Identities in the Time of AIDS'. In R. Parker and J. Gagnon (eds), *Conceiving Sexuality: Approaches to Sex Research in a Postmodern World*. London and New York: Routledge.

Bastide, R., 1978, *Brasil, Terra de Contrastes*. Rio de Janeiro and São Paulo: Difel.

Daniel, H. and Parker, R., 1991, *AIDS: A Terceira Epidemia*. São Paulo: Iglu Editora.

—— 1993, *Sexuality, Politics and AIDS in Brazil*. London: The Falmer Press.

Duyves, M., 1994, 'Framing Preferences, Framing Differences: Inventing Amsterdam as a Gay Capital'. In R. Parker and J. Gagnon (eds), *Conceiving Sexuality: Approaches to Sex Research in a Postmodern World*. London and New York: Routledge.

Flowers, N., 1988, 'AIDS in Rural Brazil'. In R. Kulstad (ed.), *AIDS 1988: AAAS Symposia Papers*, 159–68. Washington, DC: The American Association for the Advancement of Science.

Graham, D., 1970, 'Divergent and Convergent Regional Economic Growth and Internal Migration in Brazil, 1940–1960'. *Economic Development and Cultural Change*, 18: 362–82.

Johnson, A., and Stryker J., 1993, *The Social Impact of AIDS in the United States*. Washington, DC: National Academy Press.

Ministério da Saúde (Programa Nacional de Controle de DST/AIDS), 1993, *AIDS: Boletim Epidemiológico'* 4(10).

Parker, R. G., 1987, 'Acquired Immunodeficiency Syndrome in Urban Brazil'. *Medical Anthropology Quarterly*, 1, 155–75.

—— 1988, 'Sexual Culture and AIDS Education in Urban Brazil'. In R. Kulstad (ed.), *AIDS 1988: AAAS Symposia Papers*, 169–73. Washington, DC: The American Association for the Advancement of Science.

—— 1990, 'Responding to AIDS in Brazil'. In B. Misztel and D. Moss (eds), *Action on AIDS: National Policies in Comparative Perspective*, 51–77. Westport, Conn: Greenwood Press.

—— 1991, *Bodies, Pleasures and Passions: Sexual Culture in Contemporary Brazil*. Boston: Beacon Press.

Parker, R., Bastos, C., Galvão, J., and Pedrosa, J. S. (eds), 1994, *A AIDS no Brasil (1982–1992)*. Rio de Janeiro: Editora Relume-Dumará.

Sahato, G. S., 1968, 'An Economic Analysis of Migration in Brazil'. *Journal of Political Economy* 76(2).

5 Population Movement and the AIDS Epidemic in Thailand

ANCHALEE SINGHANETRA-RENARD

Introduction

The intensity of the HIV/AIDS epidemic among highly mobile populations and in dynamic areas comprised of various mobile groups in Thailand points to the importance of population movement as a crucial factor in this epidemic. Determining the patterns of population mobility is thus critical to understanding the diffusion patterns of HIV/AIDS. Areas seemingly not linked with one another may in fact actually be closely tied through spatial mobility. Such connections are pertinent to interpreting epidemiological data, formulating policy for control intervention, and care.

Routine surveillance of and epidemiological data on HIV/AIDS in Thailand show the northern region as having the highest concentration of HIV/AIDS infection among blood donors, pregnant women, military conscripts, male STD patients, commercial sex workers, and intravenous drug users from 1990–2. This situation points to the need for a closer look at structural changes of migration and their implication on the spread of HIV/AIDS in this country.

The Nature of Population Movement in Thailand

Socioeconomic development since the beginning of the 1960s has resulted in Thailand emerging as a newly industrialized country. The growth of manufacturing, construction, service, and tourist industries and their need for labour on the one hand, and the decline in agricultural demand for labour on the other, have resulted in an ever-increasing separation between home and workplace for many rural dwellers. Labour circulation is now the dominant form of population movement in Thai society.

Daily commuting, seasonal migration, and periodic short- and long-term circulation are undertaken by both the rural and urban population for employment, trade, education, and entertainment as well as for other sociocultural reasons. These include familial rites, religious functions, services, and tours. Temporary and short-term migration has now become a part of village life. As many people live in and move between two or more places conventional population

movement categories of rural–rural and rural–urban migration are no longer adequate for explaining Thai population movement patterns. Furthermore, since
many moves are made for a combination of purposes and to more than one
destination, movement flows are far from unidirectional. While contract labour
has taken Thai workers to the Middle East and other South-East Asian and East
Asian countries, the movement of others to neighbouring countries has been
facilitated by new regional economic negotiations as well as globalization
(Singhanetra-Renard, 1992a).

The development of modern transportation and communication networks has
linked almost all rural Thai villages to urban centres and the rest of the world.
Even though the journey to work is not a new phenomenon for rural population,
its present incidence is unprecedented in terms of intensity, patterns, range and
characteristics of movers, and of factors influencing their decision-making, as
well as of reasons for movement.

Linkages between internal and international labour migration have also created
a fluid situation in which the movement of replacement labour occurs between
different regions of the country, between the uplands and the lowlands and between neighbouring countries. For example, as Thai construction or commercial
sex workers move to work overseas, the same category of workers comes to
Thailand from Burma and China. Through this process, Thailand is now both a
sending and a receiving country. The dynamics and complexity of population
movement is well reflected in the HIV/AIDS epidemic, not only in Thailand but
also in the Upper Mekong region.

Explaining the Incidence of Labour Circulation in Thailand

Before the coming of rail transport to Thailand in the late nineteenth and early
twentieth centuries, when the occupational structure of the country was predominantly agricultural, transportation constraints limited population movement
mainly to nearby communities. Although some men engaged in long-distance
caravan trading during the dry season, there were few such moves. As railroad
construction connected the north, north-east, and south to the capital city,
workers, particularly from the north-east, began moving seasonally to work in the
Bangkok area.

However, this pattern no longer characterizes labour migration in Thailand as
increasing separation between home place and workplace occur. At present, large
numbers of the Thai population, men and women, throughout the country are
engaging in labour migration. Migrants constitute a major workforce in all sectors
of the Thai economy: service, commerce, construction, manufacturing, and transportation. Many move to work overseas, starting first as contract workers in the
Middle East in mid-1970s. Now Thai migrant workers are found on every continent. The Thai migration system has evolved into even more complicated networks
of people and places when ethnic minorities from the hills of Thailand and

beyond, from Burma, China, and Laos moved to find work in Thailand. The country's porous, largely unpoliced borders have proven to be no barrier to these tribal peoples, fleeing economic or political hardships, to enter Thailand illegally.

During the past decade, as Thailand's industrial production overtook agricultural output, major changes occurred in the sectoral distribution of employment. The nationwide agricultural labour force decreased from 70.8 per cent in 1980 to 66.6 per cent in 1989, with the decrease among women (6.5 per cent) greater than men (2.0 per cent) (National Statistics Office, 1989). However, an increased labour force was found in the industrial, commercial, and service sectors during the same period (Table 5.1).

**Table 5.1.   Percentage of Labour Force
Change in Selective Sectors 1980–9**

	% in 1980	% in 1989
Industry	7.9	9.0
Commerce	8.5	9.5
Service	8.4	9.4

Source: NSO Labor Force Survey, 1989.

There were higher rates of increase among female labourers in nonagricultural sectors (Singhanetra-Renard and Prabhudhanitisarn, 1992: 166). As employment loci have shifted from farms to urban enterprises, Thai spatial mobility has changed. In the north, a high incidence of movement is found among workers in construction, manufacturing, and various service industries including commercial sex. Other circulatory moves include those by tourists, professionals, students, government officials, and business people.

The Case of Labour Migration among Construction Workers in Chiang Mai City

The case of construction industries in Chiang Mai illustrates the unprecedented demand for workers in urban areas. A survey of construction in Chiang Mai City (Singhanetra-Renard, 1982) found twenty-three sites with 1,865 workers in March 1981. These projects ranged from a one million-baht light manufacturing facility to a 240 million-baht fourteen-storey hospital. Project workforce ranged from twenty to 300 workers. Most workers were from nearby areas, 75 per cent from Chiang Mai Province, with 10 per cent from provinces in the upper north. Sixty-two per cent of the construction work force commuted to work from their home villages located in six districts bordering Chiang Mai City (Muang District). Only 4 per cent were from the north-east and none from other countries.

This situation has changed markedly during Thailand's economic boom over the past five to six years. A survey conducted by Dusit Duangsa for the AIDS

Campaign Project Among Construction Workers (personal communication) in February 1992 found fifty-one construction sites of large (over 200 workers) and medium-sized (between eighty and 199 workers) projects in Chiang Mai City with about 18,000 workers living at job sites. Large-scale projects included condominiums, hotels, housing divisions, condominium/hotels, shopping complexes, hospitals, educational institutions, and shophouses. The starting up of these projects within a few years created a labour shortage in the construction industry. Besides the many workers who continued to commute daily to work sites from districts near to the city, new flows of migrant workers started, first from the north-east, and then from the hills by ethnic minorities from Thailand and from neighbouring countries. The largest projects had over 1,000 workers at the construction camp. Duangsa estimated that about half of the construction workforce in Chiang Mai is from the north east and about a quarter hill-tribe and minority from Thailand as well as other countries. About half the minority labourers are female.

Several local labour situations influence the influx of migrant workers from the hills and from across borders. These include the sectoral shortage of local labour because of the people moving to work in the more secure and expanding service, trade, and manufacturing sectors; low regional population growth; and the sudden boom in real estate in the north.

The construction workforce in Chiang Mai, however, represents but one portion of the migrant workforce. Other sectors of Chiang Mai's growing economy—such as the commercial, manufacturing, and service sectors—also employ many migrants, often female. Migration Surveys in Bangkok and regional centres carried out by the National Statistical Office from 1986 to 1988 found more female than male migrants in cities in all regions of the country except Nakhon Ratchasima. The proportion of females among all migrants was 56 per cent in Chiang Mai, with 62 per cent, 53 per cent, 50 per cent, and 46 per cent, in Bangkok, Songkhla, Chonburi, and Nakhon Ratchasima, respectively (Singhanetra-Renard and Prabhudhanitisarn, 1992: 165). Thus, contrary to the conventional pattern of male domination, the female labour force now constitutes a majority in migration streams to Thai employment centres.

At the other end of the migration stream, the economic boom that has given urban elites a disproportionately high buying-power has also led to a rapid growth in rural land purchases. Other factors include growing population pressure on land resources, the fragmentation of agricultural land, the consolidation of land ownership, the rise of large scale cash crop agriculture, and land speculation with agents buying up large tracts of rural farmland. These have all led to villagers selling their land to outsiders. Land holdings and land ownership among the local rural population is thus decreasing very rapidly, as are the income generating opportunities in the rural areas.

This situation represents a change from the past, when the main factor leading to landlessness was when, because of population growth, family land was subdivided into small plots among the offspring. When these plots were no longer

viable, they were consolidated and sold to wealthy villagers. Now, outsiders from
the city and beyond are buying village rice land and turning it into golf courses,
resorts, and exclusive housing estates. The high price being offered for land, the
unreliable returns from cash crop production because of the high inputs and
dependency on the world market, together with the spread of consumerism and
growing perceived needs—such as for consumer durables, children's education,
and medical expenses—all make villagers more inclined to sell their agricultural
land and enter non-farm employment in urban centres. What used to be supple-
mentary seasonal or periodical work in the city has now become the primary
occupation for many villages. Non-farm employment income is now the sole support for many village families. A study of Mae Sa village, twelve kilometres north
of Chiang Mai City, demonstrates a complete change in the village occupational
structure when all the village farm land was gradually bought up by outside
investors and turned into an exclusive golf course and housing subdivision. From
an agriculturally based economy in the mid-1970s the village can now be said to
have a wage labour economy. (Singhanetra-Renard 1982, 1994).

Because of such changes arising out of increased land tenancy, agricultural
labourers have turned into wage workers. The 1987 National Labour Force Survey
found that although the decrease in the agricultural labour force has occurred at
varying rates in the country's different regions as well as between sexes, the decline
among females was higher everywhere. The survey found the highest decrease in
the agricultural labour force to be 13 per cent in the south, followed by 9 per cent
in the north. For women, the decline in the south was 16 per cent, followed by 9 per
cent in the north, with rates for women elsewhere higher than for men. These
higher rates of decrease for female farm workers have affected sex selectivity in
labour migration so that Thai women are heavily represented in the rural–urban
migration streams (Singhanetra-Renard and Prabhudhanitisarn, 1992: 164).

Thus we see a pattern of migration change arising out of changes in the village
economy. From the period existing until at least the early-1950s, when most villagers were self-sufficient, conditions have changed to where many villagers are
completely dependent on the material resources that extend beyond the community. At present, moving to work in urban centres has become basically crucial for
village survival.

Migration of the Upland Ethnic Minorities to Lowland Employment

For centuries, non-Thai speaking peoples have lived in the hills of northern
Thailand. Only in the last thirty years, however, have they been perceived as being
a 'problem' requiring special assistance. The association of many such groups
with opium production (which was legal until 1959); the relation of some hill tribes,
such as the Hmong, to the fighting in Indochina that began in about 1960; and the
growth of the lowland population to a point where it began entering the hills are
all factors which have brought attention to the 'hill tribe problem'. From the 1960s

until the present, international development projects, as well as the King's Project and other Thai organizations, have worked to help the hill-tribes.

Most of the initial work focused on replacing opium. However, it is difficult to replace opium, which grows well in poor tropical soils, is cultivated in months other than when rice is grown, produces a lucrative yield, does not easily spoil, and has a ready cash market. Furthermore, when crops, such as kidney bean, temperate fruits, or coffee are introduced, the process becomes more difficult. Market development is necessary, roads and refrigeration are required, and land tenure must be given to the hill people. To bring these and other services, such as Thai schooling, to the hills, roads were constructed in many areas.

Arising out of development projects, the social structure, economy, and ecology of the hills has been changed. Also, because of restrictions on shifting cultivation and forest use by the Royal Forest Department, which in fact were essentially unrelated to suppressing opium, the chances of earning a living in the hills have declined even more than in rural villages. Although cash cropping has provided income for some, upland population growth, increases in Thai literacy, improved communications, and the greater number of lowlanders and tourists entering the hills, have caused an unprecedented number of hill people to move into the lowland employment.

Complicating factors include the newly perceived needs and the recent rapid growth in heroin addiction in the hills. Because heroin is lighter than opium and is odourless, smuggling it is much easier. And, although the suppression of poppy cultivation has been successful, rehabilitation of users has not prevented hill tribe users from turning to heroin. Since, unlike with opium, they do not control the means of production, the greater expense of a heroin habit has caused many users to fall into debt. Many have resorted to selling their resources in order to maintain their habit—and in some cases their only assets are their daughters who are sold into commercial sex.

Commercial sex among tribal people is new. Even in the mid-1970s, when development work was well underway, there were 'no' hill tribe sex workers and 'no' commercial sex among the Shans of Burma, according to Mahadewi, wife of the former president of Burma and herself a member of the Shan royal family from Yawnghwe. However, so complete has been the breakdown of upland social system, and so great the desire for money to buy necessities as well as consumer goods, that commercial sex has become a growing occupation among the hill tribe population. Even tourists trekking in the hills are greeted by the new phenomenon of small brothels or freelancers (some from other countries).

Historical Antecedents of Regional and Global Labour Migration Systems in South-East Asia

The movement of commercial sex workers into Thailand reflects the regionalization of labour migration. Besides economic reasons, there are political, geographical, and historical factors influencing migration. Because of the de-lineation of boundaries at the turn of the twentieth century in mainland South-East Asia these once customary moves are now often clandestine. None the less, these borders sometimes do generate mobility by themselves—witness the high level of tourism to Hat Yai, Mae Sai, and Sop Ruak (the so-called 'Golden Triangle' where the Ruak River enters the Mekong).

Caravans from Chiang Mai, for example, trading with Rangoon, Luang Prabang, Chiang Rung (Jinghong), Cambodia, and Vietnam have been reported from the early 1800s, but the practice is much older. The geographical and cultural proximity of border areas, centuries-old overland and river trade routes, and the resource bases along border areas have fostered the continuation, although at a reduced level, of traditional networks and linkages between people of mainland South-East Asia until the present despite the increasingly strong control exerted by the central state governments over the once remote and autonomous border areas.

This informal but extensive trade extends beyond neighbouring countries to as far away as Nepal, India, and southern China. The trading system, involving considerable short- and long-term circular mobility by people along the borders has provided the basis for the current surge of migrant labour into Thailand (Singhanetra-Renard 1992b). The move towards increased regional cooperation has resulted in a resurgence of this movement.

Yet another factor has been the half-century of strife along Thailand's borders. Besides the conflicts in Indochina dating to at least the beginning of World War II, civil war has persisted in Burma since 1948 when the Karen minority, which con-trolled most of the Thai-Burma border, rebelled. When other ethnic groups such as the Shan rebelled, exacerbating the additional problem of battles involving opium 'warlords', fighting often spilled over into Thailand. With it have come combatants as well as refugees.

Even though the Thai government has not encouraged the United Nations High Commission on Refugees to set up camps on the Burma side, many Karens and others have fled fighting in Burma to come to Thailand. On the Cambodian border, because of the harshness of the Khmer Rouge rule, from 1975 to 1979, many sought refuge from that country in Thailand. Tens of thousands also came after the Vietnamese forced the Khmer Rouge out of power. Even earlier, Chinese nationalists sought refuge both after the 1949 Chinese Revolution and then after Burma evicted some KMT troops living there.

In an attempt to monitor border crossings, a survey was carried out by the Royal Thai Survey Department. The Department found 185 crossings from Burma, 234 from Laos, 141 from Cambodia, and 54 from Malaysia. Even though much movement occurs elsewhere, just these major routes attest to the magnitude of informal border crossings and interregional migration.

The complex patterns of labour circulation within Thailand and between South-East Asian states and southern China as demonstrated above have contributed significantly to the complex patterns of diffusion and control of

HIV/AIDS in this region. In the light of this situation, it is important first to understand the sociocultural meanings of spatial mobility behaviour, particularly from the standpoint of movers, their families, and their communities.

Migration and Sexuality: The Convergence of Spatial Mobility and Social Mobility

Studies of migration in Thailand, both by academics and by the government, tend to focus on the incidence and rate of movement and the impact of migration on destinations (Goldstein, 1978). These studies rarely go beyond the economic circumstances which are perceived as intrinsically compelling. They often miss the essence of mobility behaviour since they fail to probe the decision-making process involved in migration and its sociocultural meanings.

Conventional migration studies in Thailand relied on census data and thus have usually made inferential statements to explain the incidence of migration. Systematic studies of the process involved in population mobility have yet to be written. The most common approach so far has been a structural one, focusing on situations at places of origin or destination. Rural settings and situations often cited to influence out-migration include: population pressure on land resources, the decline in importance of agriculture and agricultural labour arising out of economic development policy which emphasizes manufacturing industries and an export-oriented economy. Capitalist penetration and dependency theories have also been used to describe the loss of opportunities to make a living in the village (Santasombat, 1992). More recently, attention has been paid to the loss of economic security and means of social mobility in the rural places of origin.

At the other end of the migration streams, interest has been placed on urban situations influencing in-migration which include: centralization of development in education, employment, service, and communication/information networks; increasing demand for cheap labour in trade, service, and manufacturing industries; the growth of tourism, urbanization, and the related growth of commercial and non-commercial sex industries; and opportunities for economic security and social mobility through connections and employment.

Apart from the above explanations, few studies have tried to differentiate between the incidence of movement by different groups of people or to different areas. Nor have there been attempts to explain conditions leading to the decision to migrate within the socio-cultural contexts of the place of origin, except the work of Fuller *et al.*, 1983.

Of particular importance is how those situations are perceived and acted upon by the rural population striving for economic security and upward social mobility. There is a need to go beyond the structural approach in migration studies in the Thai context. It is of relevance in understanding the epidemiology of HIV/AIDS in northern Thailand to conceptualize population mobility as a social action. Spatial mobility on the part of northern Thai villagers is an escape from poverty, an attempt to gain economic security or to gain social mobility or a combination thereof. The urban-oriented bias of modern development policy suggests that rural people perceive the opportunity for upward social mobility as involving migration to an urban place.

For the villagers, ways to social mobility include:

- secure salaried employment in government, service, manufacturing, or business enterprises even at the low end of the hierarchy such as janitor, cleaner, or gardener, for it means being connected with city folks who have position, politically, financially, or socially;
- professional employment as a policeman/woman, soldier, nurse, or secretary or in any other jobs—including some in the informal sector—in which employees wear uniform;
- employment in enterprises which symbolize modernity or Western influence such as golf courses, discos, coffee shops, cocktail lounges, and karaoke bars; and
- marriage to government officials, Chinese, or others who have position, wealth, or connections.

Routes to social mobility, however, differ between men and women. For example, formal education up to university level as a means to social mobility, is open to all men of any economic status through the monkhood. Joining the monkhood for a lifetime in itself is one of the highest forms of social mobility. There is no such equivalent for women (Phongpaichit, 1982).

Rural women take several routes to social mobility: through urban employment, marriage, and education. Less fortunate women, however, often take a 'short cut' through commercial sex work. Some 'short cuts' are highly acceptable, such as entering beauty contests, arranged at occasions such as winter fairs or fruit festivals. Others take up work in restaurants, bars, coffee shops, golf courses, discos, massage parlours, and brothels. Although such movement is not new—a 1949 guidebook to Bangkok mentions houses on Si Phraya Road with women from Lampang, Lamphun, and Chiang Mai (Dream Lover, 1949: 19–21)— recent developments have resulted in a higher intensity of movement for commercial sex work. Today many, if not most, commercial sex workers (CSW) in Thailand are from the north. Others come from the north-east, the highlands, and neighbouring countries (Boonchalaksi and Guest, 1992).

The demonstration of their success (by either themselves or their family) through contributions to the village temples or house building has also been accepted in rural villages. These donations now raise their social status 'equal to that of the others' and then facilitate chain migration out of the village (see, for example, the works of Phongpaichit, 1982, and Santasombat, 1992). At present the migration fields of northern Thai CSWs have expanded to other countries. Migration patterns have also become more complex, with their demographic characteristics growing more varied. Whereas CSWs previously were mainly widows or divorcees, they now include single and married women. The age of some has dropped to as low as twelve or thirteen years. Their educational background ranges from having only the four-to-six years of compulsory education to as high as vocational or university degrees. While most voluntary CSWs seek this occupation, others are 'sold' by their parents or are deceived and forced into the business by proprietors and agents. The extent to which CSWs acknowledge the work they do varies from complete openness to concealment. To most CSWs, this work is seen as a temporary pathway that may lead to upward social mobility just like any other job.

This out-migration, however, does not necessarily lead to social mobility. Earlier in this century, working in the city led many villagers, men and women, to find good marriage partners, connections with influential people, or advancement in work, all of which were their major routes to upward social mobility. Now, because of the spread of the HIV virus and other recent changes, it leads many to AIDS.

The relationship between three factors in the HIV/AIDS epidemic—spatial mobility, social mobility, and sexuality—can be understood within the framework of the social field and the social network of circulation. By departing from one social field and social network in the home community and entering others in the new location, power relationships, particularly gender power relationships, become major determinants of successful social mobility. Coming from upcountry with no training except for sixth grade education, rural labourers in the city rely solely on several sets of personal relationships to gain access to information about job availability, rates of pay, and welfare, and to enhance their chances of successful job applications, pay rises, promotion, or training.

Often only cultural factors are taken into account in investigations of why many women end up as CSWs. In reality, the factors leading to the growth of commercial sex are complex and dynamic. At one time, poverty and the payment of one's debt of gratitude to one's parents may have been sufficient factors in explaining the phenomenon. As Phongpaichit (1982, 70) explains the situation, 'The growing dependence of certain families on this trade has encouraged the growth of a breed of agents, talent scouts, and middle-men. Parents can, in fact, mortgage their daughters, and there are brokers who are ready at hand to carry out this service.' Now that sex is being expanded into an industry and a business, the question of power relations, particularly gender power relation deserves a closer look. When a young girl moves into commercial sex work for example, to what extent can conventional explanations of the spatial allocation of family labour resources or the mobility options available to her or to any particular member of the family be applied?

It is important to consider power relations in the rural areas between various groups of people including men and women, husbands and wives, parents and children, and locals and non-locals. In these, men, husbands, parents, patrons, and locals often exploit the others for their own benefit. They may be the main decision-makers or at least act as an important influence in determining whether women (or men) migrate to the city to engage in employment, particularly commercial sex. In the destination areas, migrants often find themselves in new power relations, which influence their welfare in the city. Power has an important part to play in the relations between, for example, employer and employee, legal and illegal residents, citizen and alien, adult and minor, lowlander Thai and hill tribe member, resident and migrant, and official and ordinary citizen.

The worst situations occur when a migrant finds him/herself in a complex set of several of these relationships. A common example of such an exploitative situation occurs in the case of an illegal young female hill-tribe migrant.

The increase of casual and premarital sex among mobile workers can partly be explained by the functional decline of the northern Thai spirit cult, a mechanism that traditionally served to limit extramarital and premarital sex. As villagers move away from home, not only do they break free from traditional constraints that had been imposed by the spirit cults, but these moves also weaken the functioning of the cult itself in the home community (Singhanetra-Renard, 1993).

Other factors leading to increased casual sex are participation in urban employment and formal education, both of which undermine parental control over children. Also, informal rural wage workers in the cities are often exploited by their employers through low wages, poor working conditions and housing, and the lack of welfare and other benefits, such as recreational facilities. The only outlets for much of the village youth resident in the city are alcohol, sex, and drugs. Available and accessible, these have become ordinary forms of pleasure for poor migrants.

Opportunities for casual sex have also been facilitated by the growth of dormitories and makeshift work sites, where many young workers and students live. Young workers and students have access to cash that is often associated with casual sex. However, how such casual sex entails the risk of HIV/AIDS transmission is not correctly understood by most migrants. The same is true of intravenous drug use (NDU).

The Relationship Between Population Movement and the HIV/AIDS Epidemic in Northern Thailand

Northern Thailand is the area of highest HIV/AIDS concentration in the country. Between October 1984 and October 1994 it had an average of 201 AIDS cases per 100,000 people, compared to 32.8 cases per 100,000 for the whole country (Table 5.2).

Besides northern Thailand being the source of the largest number of commercial sex workers, the rapid transmission and high concentration of HIV/AIDS here has occurred because of this region's dynamism. As an area of origin, destination as well as transit for migrants, it gives rise to situations in which movers interact among themselves and with the local population. Much of interaction involves sexual contacts (and IVDU to a lesser degree) which carry a high risk of HIV transmission.

These interactions are facilitated by the high concentration of enterprises directly or indirectly associated with high risk activities. In addition, along the

Table 5.2.   AIDS Cases in Upper Northern Provinces, 1984–94

Province	Full blown cases	Symptomatic cases	Total no. of cases	AIDS cases per 100,000 population
Chiang Mai	2,606	757	3,363	228.2
Chiang Rai	1,929	900	2,829	233.4
Lamphun	413	430	861	213.8
Lampang	830	219	1,049	131.5
Payao	625	346	971	190.1
Mae Hong Son	105	97	202	95.9
Total, six provinces	6,526	2,749	9,275	201.3
Whole country	13,246	5,775	19,021	32.8

Source: Northern Communicable Disease Control Unit.

roads radiating out of the city centres similar enterprises are spatially distributed in all directions. They can be easily reached at all times, (some also bring services to residences or work sites), providing a range of services to suit all tastes and budgets. No longer located in discrete, secluded areas, sex enterprises are passed by urban residents daily on their journeys to work, to the temple, or to school. In such an environment, particularly for visitors, having casual sex and multiple sexual partners has become little more than an ordinary fact of life.

Having moved out of home environments, where the family and community exercise social control over their behaviour, movers can act differently from how they would at home. Free of social controls in the new location, migrants enter new social networks where they can easily engage in casual sex or IVDU. By bringing infected and uninfected persons into contact with each other, migration has become an important factor in the spread of HIV/AIDS in northern Thailand. Circulation, whether by government officials, business people, tourists, or students, thus influences the spread of HIV/AIDS, both within and between regions.

The high intensity of HIV/AIDS transmission in northern Thailand will prevail so long as this region remains a node for IVDU and sexual contacts between highly mobile populations of infected and non-infected individuals. Through circular mobility, the disease has now spread to provinces of origin and to the general population. The association between HIV/AIDS in northern Thailand and subsets of mobile populations and their families in this region shows that we must understand the sociocultural meanings of mobility behaviour regarding sexuality and conditions that predispose certain population subsets to engage in behaviour that entails the risk of contracting the HIV virus.

Three important interrelated issues arise: medical, moral, and developmental factors associated with migration and HIV/AIDS epidemic in northern Thailand. Since these factors interact and affect each other dynamically, they must be understood as a complex system. Stated differently, the convergence of health, sexuality, and migration constitutes the essence of the accelerated rate of HIV/AIDS transmission in this region.

Discussion: Research Questions in the Thai Context

In this era of globalization one can expect an increasing incidence of population mobility which occurs in ever more complex forms. The relationship between population movement and the HIV/AIDS epidemic raises many points of concern, three of which regarding the Thai situation are: culture and sexuality; gender–power relations; and, ethical and human rights issues.

Culture, sexuality, and sexual culture

It has been observed that mobile people tend to engage in extramarital sexual relationships or have multiple sexual partners at their places of destination. Traditionally, Thai women were cautioned about mobile men, *'rotfai, rua mae, yike, tamruat'* (on the railroads, ships, in travelling folk opera, or the police). But since most occupations now require people to be mobile, the list of such occupations is as long as the list of those at risk of HIV.

Questions can be asked about sexual culture and the sexuality of mobile populations. To what extent does Thai society face a sexual behaviour transition in relation to its mobility transition? Besides the traditional custom of *'liang du, pu sua'* ('entertain a visitor and treat him to a sexual partner afterwards'), practised by all strata of society, what other social, cultural, or economic circumstances lead students, traders, factory workers, construction workers, and tourists to engage in high-risk sexual behaviour?

How have the traditional moral values among rural families and communities changed? What factors relate to changing village mores? To what extent do changing values and social controls relate to the older generation losing its village livelihood? To what degree and at what cost has this generation lost its socioeconomic control over the younger generation now that many depend largely or solely on the financial support of migrant children?

Issues related indirectly to questions of sexual behaviour and the AIDS epidemic include the question of how spatial mobility (i.e. to work as a CSW) leads to social mobility. Will poor, uneducated, female illegal aliens, who now constitute the majority of migrants—many of whom are now exploited sexually and as cheap labour—continue to see migration as the means to social mobility? Will the AIDS epidemic, now spreading alarmingly among CSWs, change this conception? How will their chances of meeting a well-to-do future husband who leads them to social mobility be changed? As long as AIDS remains incurable, the working life of a CSW is likely to be short. Is the only way out down the social ladder?

Casual sex, and premarital or extramarital relationships with multiple partners among labour migrants, conscripts, tourists, government officials, traders, and students, are well known. What is not is the sexual culture of specific groups and their sexual networks which seem to operate in discrete ways and link groups of people who otherwise would appear to have no connections with one another in terms of HIV risk. As particular groups of men and women coalesce in urban settings, new social networks emerge with their own culture and norms.

Because of the growing problem of HIV/AIDS, Thai culture is at a crossroads in its development. Should we try—and is it possible—to control casual sex among mobile groups? If not, we must decide whether to continue regarding sexuality as a moral issue, or whether to change our perception of sexuality to that of a health issue? Can we accept that knowledge about sexuality is a basic human right for our adolescents? Are we denying them the right to know about the consequences of sexuality, or are we withholding information about sexuality and thus sex education from them? Is giving knowledge about sexuality an empowerment? Can Thais talk about sex in terms of 'users'' interests? What is the best and most acceptable approach in Thai culture? If we are not serious about how to escape this dilemma, then many of the mobile people who fall outside the formal control programmes can be expected to remain at risk of contracting HIV/AIDS and spreading it to their families.

Gender-power relations in migration and access to resources

The fact that women constitute more than half of migrant labour, that child labourers are mostly girls, that women are losing the chance to earn a livelihood in rural areas, and that girls are sold or tricked into prostitution suggests that gender-power and other power relationships are critical aspects of female migration. If power means 'the process whereby individuals or groups gain or maintain the capacity to impose their will upon others, to have their way recurrently, despite implicit or explicit opposition, through invoking or threatening punishment, as well as offering or withholding rewards' (Lipman-Blumen 1984), one can identify several power relationships that migrants encounter which facilitate HIV transmission.

Given the dynamic multifaceted phenomenon of migration, no solutions are proposed. However, power relationships that are transformed by mobility must be explored against the backdrop of labour migration to gain an adequate understanding of HIV transmission. Since women migrants almost invariably possess less bargaining power and fewer legal rights than locals and particularly local men, the role of migration in the victimization of women, and thus, the spread of HIV infection, cannot be ignored.

The first set of power relations is within a mover's family. To what extent do familial gender-power relations—between mother and daughter, father and daughter, or husband and wife—influence a daughter's migration? We need to assess in-depth data on family situations, in particular about which individuals have decision-making authority relating to movement decisions and to other economic and cultural issues.

Other sets of power relations that should receive attention include those between CSW migrants and recruitment agents, pimps, policemen, and clients. Evidence suggests that women belonging to different CSW groups have different levels of bargaining power. The parents of Shan girls usually collect a sum of money while Akha or Lahu parents do not; pricing differentials in brothels between the two also exist. What factors and which individuals have the capacity or authority to affect their bargaining power? Ethnicity, beauty, social network, or something else? Or does it depend only on market demands and personal taste?

Basic to problems relating to migration and the AIDS epidemic are power relationships and gender-power relations. One can ask why most studies on sexual behaviour ignore male client behaviour. Is it the double standard of Thai society or the fact that researchers are biased either consciously or unconsciously against women because of their orientation towards male-dominated society?

Another question is how HIV-positive men and women are treated by their families and employers. There have been cases where a woman with an HIV infection has been dismissed from her job and evicted by her in-laws with her baby while the husband has moved to work elsewhere. To what extent are such cases related to gender-power relation? Women and children suffer more from gender-related issues.

How do gender-power relations and other power relationships relate to the availability and accessibility of resources to women at each destination point? Information on dynamic situations is critical to the implementation of effective prevention, support, and care programmes among migrants, particularly females.

Ethical and human rights issues

Many migrants are female, poor, uneducated, from minority groups, illegal aliens, or some combination thereof. They leave a tradition-based agricultural world of patrons and clients, and personal relationships, and come into a more objective, capitalistic world of employers and employees, and impersonal relationships. Their marginality, arising from their socioeconomic and legal status, often puts them in vulnerable situations in the new locations.

One important shift from traditional working relations is that the patron–client is being replaced by the employer–employee relationship in the capitalist mode of production. Although employers continue to be viewed as patrons, in practice this is no longer the case, with employers often abusing their employees. The informal nature of employment coupled with the migrants' marginal status often exclude them from legal protection, health and welfare services, and human rights enjoyed by the locals.

Health research has been conducted among migrants without rigorous ethical safeguards. Similarly, hill-tribe girls have been kidnapped in their rice fields and sold into commercial sex work, ending no wages. Who monitors their welfare and health? Furthermore, we can no longer assume that these people will remain isolated from the general population since they are interacting with local people in several ways. With the growth of AIDS cases has come a problem of resource allocation for both prevention and care. Should these 'aliens' be ignored? How should mobile people be dealt with when resources are allocated?

As CSWs move, they come into contact with different client groups at different places, all under different conditions. Should programmes be adapted to deal with such variations so that CSWs can understand and cope with new situations in order to be protected from HIV? Should CSWs' coping capacities be enhanced so that they can understand the situation even if they are always victimized?

Is the policy of periodically raiding brothels to stop child prostitution the best policy? Should other means for dealing with this problem be devised since arrest only makes the CSWs more likely to move to a different province, or to go underground, which in turn makes it more difficult to monitor their welfare?

The places of employment for many migrants are usually not legally recognized. Should illegal migrant workers, whether they work in a brothel, a family-run business such as a restaurant, or in informal sector work, such as in the construction industry, be excluded from legal protection in terms of working conditions, wages, welfare benefits, basic human rights, and access to resources? Should they be left vulnerable to health hazards and high-risk behaviour just because they are migrants?

REFERENCES

Boonchalaksi, W. and Philip Guest. 1994. *Prostitution in Thailand*. Mahidol University IPSR Publication 171.

Dream Lover. 1949. *Black Shadow*. Bangkok: Central.

Fuller, Theodore D. *et al.* 1983. *Migration and Development in Modern Thailand*. Bangkok: Social Association of Thailand.

Geddes, William. 1976. *Migrants of the Mountains*. Oxford: Clarendon.

Goldstein, S. 1978. *Circulation in the Context of Total Mobility in Southeast Asia*. Paper of the East–West Population Institute, 83.

Lipman-Blumen, Jean. 1984. *Gender Roles and Power*. Englewood Cliffs, N. J.: Prentice-Hall.

National Statistics Office. 1989. Bangkok.

Phongpaichit, Pasuk. 1982. *From Peasant Girls to Bangkok Masseuses*. Geneva: International Labour Organization.

Prothero, R. Mansell and Murray Chapman. 1985. *Circulation in Third World Countries*. London: Routledge and Kegan Paul.

Santasombat, Yos. 1992. *Mae Ying Si Khai Tua, Choomchon Lae Karn Kha Prawenee Nai Sangkhom Thai* (Why Women Sell Their Bodies: Community and Prostitution in Thai Society). Bangkok: Institute of Local Community Development.

Singhanetra-Renard, Anchalee. 1982. *Commuting and Fertility of Construction Workers in Chiang Mai City*. Singapore: SEAPRAP.

—— 1992a. 'The Mobilization of Labour Migrants: Personal Links and Facilitating Networks in Sending Countries', in Mary Kritz, Lin Lean Lim, and Hania Zlotnik, eds, *Global Interactions: International Migration Systems in an Interdependent World*. Oxford: Clarendon, 190–204.

—— 1992b. 'Malaria and Migration as a Regional Problem'. Paper presented at the Forest/Border Workshop, Mae Hong Son.

Singhanetra-Renard, Anchalee. 1994. 'Complex Relationship Between Production and Reproduction: The Case of Ancestor Spirit Cults and Reproductive Choice in the Contexts of Changing Socio-economic Conditions in Northern Thailand', in Thomas Kjellqvist, ed., *The Challenge of Complexity: Third World Perspectives on Population Research*. Stockholm: SAREC.

—— and Nitaya Prabhudhanitisarn, 1992. 'Changing Socio-Economic Roles of Thai Women and their Migration', in Sylvia Chant, ed., *Gender and Migration in Developing Countries*. London: Belhaven, 154–73.

United Nations, ESCAP. 1991. *Proceedings of the Meeting of Senior Officials on Drug Abuse Issues in Asia and the Pacific*. Bangkok: ESCAP.

6 Refugee Women, Violence, and HIV

LYNELLYN D. LONG

Introduction

Seroprevalence studies among refugees migrating to the US suggest that they have relatively low HIV rates, equal to or lower than their countries of origin (Black, 1993; Tawil, 1990; Refugee Policy Group, 1989). These data, however, may not be representative of the majority of refugees who do not immigrate to a third country but remain in some of the poorest countries in the world and in regions that continue to be beset by conflict. While such studies are critical for dispelling myths of refugees as a special risk group, they do not portend the future for those in situations of conflict. The full health and psychological consequences of recent conflicts in Liberia, Somalia, Sudan, the Gulf, and Bosnia—'in the time of AIDS'—cannot yet be comprehended, much less quantified (Herdt and Lindenbaum, 1992).

Treating refugees and displaced persons as special risk groups would only further enhance their marginal status and stigmatize refugee women, in particular. Anthropologists have also pointed out the fallacy of the concept of 'risk groups', based on common social or geographical characteristics; they argue for studies of risk behaviour or practices (Bolton, 1992; Farmer, 1992). However, in the case of refugee women, I would argue that even risk behaviour or practices are not salient. Because many refugee women are not in a secure enough position to negotiate sexual relations, their own behaviour or practices do not influence their relative risk. Instead, as refugee women they face certain risk factors specific to women in situations of violence and uncertainty.

The concept of a sexual subculture must also be reconsidered when applied to refugee women. The category of 'refugee' itself reflects both a juridical and political status in a sovereign state. However, the international system—despite various universal human rights and refugee declarations—cannot guarantee that the refugees' status will be equally honoured and/or recognized. Refugees' access to

The author wishes to thank Dr Maxine Ankrah and Ms Julie Denison of AIDSCAP, Dr Mohammed Dualeh of UNHCR/Geneva, Ms Heather Courtney of UNHCR/WDC, Dr Barbara de Zalduondo of Johns Hopkins School of Public Health, and Mr Bill Brady of the Center for Disease Control for their insights and help in locating scarce materials. My own work in different refugee settings has been funded by Johns Hopkins University, the Agency for International Development, the United Nations High Commissioner for Refugees, the Catholic Organization for Relief and Refugees, and the Wenner-Gren and MacArthur Foundations. Any errors in this work are my own. This paper is dedicated to Dale Rezabek for his work with refugees.

UN protection varies widely from those refugees who have no legal recourse to a privileged minority who has access to the best legal counsel across any international boundary. As in many situations, economic circumstances create different classes and class-based refugee situations. Many women also suffer the effects of uprooting and conflict within their own homes and homelands but are not considered refugees. However, their experiences as displaced and/or dislocated women are entirely relevant to an understanding of a refugee women's sexual subculture.

The concept of a refugee women's sexual subculture is useful for (1) identifying potential changes in women's sexual experiences in periods of conflict and unrest; (2) elaborating a diversity of sexual practices across different refugee situations and within a particular situation, across different stages of the refugee experience; and (3) increasing sensitivity to the conditions which circumscribe refugee women's sexual autonomy and choices within a nexus of familial and communal relationships. Because conditions of violence, uprooting, and conflict are often so stark, until recently, many public health interventions seemed to assume that refugees did not practise sex and that sexuality was irrelevant in a conflict situation. The recent conflict in Bosnia and reported mass rapes highlighted a particular vulnerability that refugee women face in conflict, although this was certainly not the first or last time that rape had become a weapon of war. The notion of a sexual subculture, however, itself goes another step to explain how sexual experiences arising out of conditions of conflict may affect and pattern refugee women's sexual practices and post-war sexual relationships. For the purposes of this volume, the concept of a refugee women's sexual subculture is considered theoretically problematic but potentially illuminating as a partial description of a process of change and changing relationships.

In this chapter, I examine the risk factors faced by refugee and displaced women in conflict situations. In the first section, I discuss the socioeconomic factors that heighten refugee and displaced women's risks, including health, nutritional, and economic status, and social relations. In the second section, I describe the specific physical protection issues faced by refugee and displaced women at various stages of the refugee experience. These stages include: (1) conflict and uprooting; (2) flight and asylum; and (3) repatriation, local settlement, or immigration to a third country. In the third section, I present four brief histories of refugee women's sexual experiences derived from interviews with: (1) Laotian Hmong women in Ban Vinai Refugee Camp, Thailand (1982, 1986–7, 1989, 1990); (2) Ugandan refugee women in Nairobi (1990); (3) Bosnian Muslim women in Croatia, Montenegro, and Serbia (1993), and (4) lowland Lao women in San Francisco (1984, 1989, 1990). The purpose of this third section is to provide a more detailed description of the risks that these women face in their daily lives and more of an insider's perspective on their situation.

Whether refugee women's sexual experiences increase their risk of AIDS remains to be seen. In this chapter, I hypothesize some possible risk factors faced by refugee and displaced women based on knowledge of how HIV/AIDS has affected women in other settings (de Zalduondo, 1991; Gupta and Weiss, 1993; Long, 1993a; Schoepf, 1992). However, conducting research in refugee situations poses different problems from those in many other situations and one should not expect the same level of certainty in research efforts. Refugee situations themselves are highly uncertain. Unlike many other research settings, war zones involve physical and security risks for all concerned, and research may be completely inappropriate in life-threatening situations. Issues of confidentiality are also critical in all refugee situations and often it is just too dangerous to discuss certain events or experiences (particularly when the perpetrators may later be tried for their actions). The perpetrators may take revenge on refugee women who speak out about their plight. Women who speak out have also been beaten or killed by their husbands and sons, who themselves feel humiliated and shamed. Finally, the physical and mental well-being of the refugee/displaced person should always be paramount. Recall of traumatic events is often difficult and not productive for those still living these events in their daily lives (Herman, 1992; Anthony *et al.*, 1993). Researchers also have a responsibility to recommend appropriate health and counselling services for those who need help and to testify against state-sanctioned forms of violence.

Given these considerations, the data for this paper come from a variety of sources. In no case was I specifically researching refugee and displaced women's sexual practices, the prevalence and incidence of HIV, or their knowledge of the disease. In Thailand, I conducted long-term ethnographic research (including participant observation and interviews) of the daily lives of five refugee households (1993b). I also analysed a large-scale socioeconomic and demographic survey carried out by refugee parasocial workers in a camp. In Kenya, I conducted interviews and collaborated in a demographic survey with Kenyan researchers. This study was part of a multicountry study for the United Nations High Commissioner for Refugees to assess the situation of refugee women (Long *et al.*, 1991). In the former Yugoslavia, I conducted interviews during three visits to the region to assess the trauma and humanitarian assistance needs of refugees and displaced persons for the US Government (Anthony *et al.*, 1993; United States Department of State, 1993). I also include data from interviews and assessments conducted in the Sudan, Guinea, and Malawi, where relevant. What follows is the beginning of a discussion on the possible longer-term HIV consequences of these conflicts and some of the concerns of women refugees facing increasing sexual risk.

Socioeconomic Risk Factors

Of some 20 million refugees in the world, it is estimated that 75–80 per cent are women and children, which parallels the population structures of many developing countries (Long, 1993b). In some refugee situations, women and children constitute as much as 90 per cent of the population (UNHCR, 1991a). In addition, there are an estimated 15–25 million displaced persons (UNHCR, 1991a:

51–2): internal refugees within their own countries. More significantly than these figures, often cited by donors to justify programmes for women, is the rising proportion of female-headed households (in comparison to countries of origin). In Malawi, 25 per cent of Mozambican refugee households were female-headed, in Kenya, 23% of refugee households (including Ugandan, Rwandan, Mozambican, and South African refugees), and in Thailand, 25% of Hmong (Long *et al.*, 1991, 1993b). These percentages are not surprising for the poorest groups in many developing countries, but rather, they reflect a broad structural and historical trend. In many cases, these refugees also came from rural areas and now live in more urban settings.

The refugee female-headed households in one study in Malawi were found to be significantly poorer than the male (Agar and Agar, 1991; Long *et al.*, 1991). This has been observed in other refugee settings as well. Refugee women work longer hours that men but because much of their work is to maintain the household (for example, provision of child care, fuel, water, and food), they receive less income. Another reason that refugee female-headed households are poorer is that women are more likely to be short-changed on food supplies. Often, a portion of food assistance is resold to supplement household income. There is also a secondary market in many refugee settings in which refugees pay tippers and others controlling the distribution to obtain their share. Thus, the richer households are more likely to command their share and receive more, while the poor get poorer and go hungrier.

Women, however, are not only disadvantaged by their relative poverty (either within the group or as heads of households), but also by their lack of security. In some refugee situations, women and young girls report having to provide sexual favours to those distributing the food to receive their share. The household head may designate a particular daughter as the one to exchange sexual services for food rations. Experiments to put women in charge of food distribution have met with mixed success (UNHCR Field Officer, personal communication, Malawi, 1992). These women leaders in turn have been threatened and victimized. Yet, when food was provided only to women and girls, as in the case of the Cambodian relief programme in Site 2, boys dressed up as girls and men expropriated the food within the household (field interviews, 1986).

Not surprisingly, refugee women's and girls' nutritional and health status are lower than men's and boys' in many refugee settings. For example, outbreaks of pellagra in one refugee setting were higher for women than men (Long *et al.*, 1990). In another, women and girls recalled higher incidences of illnesses in the past month than men (Long *et al.*, 1991). There may also be some discrimination in treatment (in that families are more likely to have their sons than daughters treated) particularly if fees are charged, although such discrimination is also found in the refugees' countries of origin.

It is likely that sexually transmitted diseases (STDs) are also underreported in refugee settings because culturally appropriate services are not readily available. In my own field work in Ban Vinai Camp, Thailand, several Hmong and Lao women reported suspicious vaginal discharges but refused to go to the public health clinic because they would have to see a male nurse (Long, 1993). Some women also thought that the infections were caused by depo-provera administered by Thai contraceptive counsellors. Female excision and circumcision practices may also put refugee girls at risk, particularly in refugee sites where sanitation is poor (WHO, 1992). These practices also put girls at greater risk of STDs, including HIV. In one refugee camp in Malawi, a Catholic NGO provided clean razors to prevent them from being shared.

Given the high birth rates in most refugee populations—reportedly some of the highest in the world—it is clear that sexual activity also increases. In Ban Vinai refugee camp in Thailand, refugees complained that sexual activity increased because there was nothing better to do (field interviews, 1986). Both men and women who had cultivated fields in the past spent many hours in the camp sitting around and waiting for a decision about their future. In Ban Vinai, children were also seen as a form of social security. In many refugee camps, birth rates may rise to ensure the maintenance and viability of a particular ethnic minority. Genocide is a concern for certain minority groups (for example, Palestinians, Hmong, Dinka, Nuer, Bosnian Muslims, and Kurds) and high birth rates in some long-term refugee situations may reflect the communal need to preserve and defend an ethnic identity.

Having more children *per se* does not increase one's risk of HIV. Of greater concern is that the number of sexual partners may increase for refugee women and girls. Women who have lost husbands and sons in the conflict may feel obliged to remarry for their own and their children's physical protection. If practised, in the country of origin polygyny among refugees reportedly increases (for example, as found in Ban Vinai and in the Mozambican camps in Malawi) and increases the risk of HIV (Ntozi and Lubega, 1992). Although girls and women also reported opposing the practice, parents marry off daughters as second and third wives to protect them from non-consensual sex. Women in Ban Vinai worried about their daughters' perceived increased mobility and feared for their physical safety. For Hmong girls in Ban Vinai, marriage was considered so important to one's status that failed love affairs often resulted in suicides or suicide attempts. Nevertheless, young adolescent girls found many ways to have sexual relations before marriage and older men sought out increasingly younger girls for extramarital affairs. Thai madams also recruited and, in one celebrated case, forcibly abducted young ethnic minority girls for brothels in Pattaya.

In most refugee settings, reproductive health services are of poor quality, and not readily accessible. Although most refugee settings have public health services comparable to the level of the local population, such services often do not address women's reproductive health needs, including psychological needs. A British non-governmental organization (NGO), the Marie Stopes Foundation, is developing reproductive health kits for emergency situations (which include testing and treatment for STDs). Such services should be expanded to cover all refugee emergencies, and reproductive health should be included as part of emergency health services. Counselling services with trusted insiders also need to be made widely available.

Refugee women's health and nutritional status are correlated with their economic status (Long *et al.*, 1991). Where women can earn income—as in other developing country settings—they are more likely to spend it on the household and children than men. Some refugee women become the primary wage earners either through their handicrafts (as seen in Thailand, Croatia, and the Sudan) or because employers are more willing to hire them for certain low status factory and domestic jobs (as seen in the Sudan, Malawi, and Kenya). In the Sudan, displaced women in Khartoum brewed 'merisa'—a local alcohol—to earn a living but braved police harassment, arrest, and jail in doing so (Feiden *et al.*, 1990). While most refugee women find ways to earn some income (or barter services), their household earnings are less than men's and they have less control over household income (for example, men generally control the marketing and distribution of handicrafts).

Refugee women confront increasing conservatism in many refugee settings (for example, the Afghan refugees in Pakistan, Hmong in Thailand, and displaced Somali) proscribing their behaviour (Mayotte, 1992). The conservative backlash evidenced in administrative regulations, norms of behaviour, and the relegation of refugee women to domestic, private spaces may be a response to the loss of control refugees face in their daily lives. Men fear that the women will take advantage of their mobility and migration to assert new roles, while older women themselves worry that their daughters do not preserve the traditional values. Religious groups—both NGOs and indigenous leaders—sometimes further diminish women's status by ignoring women's roles in their programmes. For example, Agar and Agar (1991) found that formal training programmes for Mozambican refugees in Malawi effectively were aimed at enhancing men's income generation. In the Thai refugee camps, I observed that young men with good English speaking skills comprised the majority of the voluntary agency workers employed. Their diminished social status makes it difficult for refugee women to demand needed services or to make their concerns heard. Many camp administrators and relief workers are male, and refugee women—particularly young women and the elderly—are almost invisible. Women's groups and networks can play an important advocacy role and provide channels for information about HIV.

Refugee women worldwide face many of the same socioeconomic risks as women in their countries of origin or asylum. Indeed, 'refugee or displaced women' as categories should be suspect as they reflect international donors' and national governments' own perceptions of these people as marginalized and in need of certain forms of assistance. More insidiously, these categories function as control mechanisms to constrain these women's spheres of actions and, in the case of refugee camps, to institutionalize them (Long 1993b).

Such categories also stigmatize women at local levels—creating false dichotomies of us and them—the national versus the refugee (Said, 1979). The treatment of refugee and displaced women as the other may be manifested in local perceptions of these women as 'loose', reflecting only their mobility. Refugee women may be seen by local women as competition (for example, the Ugandan and Somali refugee women in Kenya or the Mozambican women in Malawi) and their presence may be thought to diminish local women's status. Because refugee movements at least initially place a strain on local resources and heighten these tensions, outside assistance can be critical.

Treating refugee women for HIV outside of local and national programmes, however, is likely to stigmatize them only further and create additional tensions. As UNHCR (1992) policies suggest, HIV control and prevention efforts should be incorporated into national efforts. Unfortunately, in practice, this often means that refugee and particularly displaced women are the last to receive such services. Across different refugee situations, refugee women also face certain unique risks given their common experiences of conflict and uprooting, flight, and the search for asylum. In these common experiences, the category of 'refugee' has intrinsic meaning. It denotes a common experience of suffering and endurance above and beyond the ascribed identities of international organizations and national governments determined to preserve and protect their own geographical borders and social boundaries.

The Refugee Experience and HIV Concerns

Few people choose to become refugees, contrary to official ideology in many asylum and host countries. Many refugee women, fearing for their own and their family's lives, flee direct conflict. During this stage, women report being raped, maimed, treated as slaves, and/or made to provide sexual favours for opposition forces. Wars in this century increasingly do not distinguish between soldier and civilian and, indeed, recent conflicts in Bosnia and the Sudan treat civilians as the primary targets, while protecting military and paramilitary troops.

Rape is increasingly becoming a weapon of conflict and has been used as a deliberate tactic by the Pakistani troops in Bangladesh, Renamo troops in Mozambique, Iraqi troops in Kuwait, Liberian troops in Liberia, and Bosnian Serb troops in Bosnia (to name a few well-documented cases). Rapes during conflict have also been reported in Afghanistan, Cambodia, and Vietnam.

Rapes are characteristically underreported, especially the rape of men, and rape in war is no exception. It is difficult to obtain reliable estimates since women usually do not or cannot seek services. During the war in Bangladesh, thousands of women were raped by the Pakistani forces as a deliberate tactic of terror but there are no reliable estimates of the magnitude—only memories. Similarly, rape as an instrument of torture has been used by the Iraqi regime against their own dissidents. Estimates of women raped in Bosnia and Croatia have ranged from a few hundred to 100,000 (Anthony *et al.*, 1993; Helsinki, 1992). There, the rapes are part of a larger strategy of 'ethnic cleansing' and are intended to humiliate men—husbands, brothers, and sons—as much to shame women. When a particular rape was publicized, a few women were killed by their male kin or committed suicide. Thus, it was not surprising that most rapes were vastly underreported and women did not seek services (or if they did, it was to demand abortions). At the same time, various factions in conflicts also report rapes as evidence against their opposition forces and may magnify incidence rates.

Women and men, boys and girls of all ages are at sexual risk—particularly when the purpose is to eliminate another ethnic group. The rape of men and their sexual mutilation are surprisingly common but vastly underreported. Men rarely seek direct help for such experiences, but their effects may be manifested later in post-traumatic stress syndromes. It may be that males who are molested are also more likely to be killed to prevent them from joining the opposition.

Military forces increase the demand for sex workers and brothels do well in time of war (for example, in Bangkok or Olangapo during the Vietnam War). The rapid increase in the incidence of HIV/AIDs along the Tanzanian–Ugandan border may have followed the Tanzanian invasion in 1990 (deZalduondo, personal communication 1994). In Bosnia, Serb forces have opened brothels of women prisoners. New commercial sex establishments have opened throughout Bosnia and Croatia to service the military, including the United Nations Protection Forces.

Women in conflict situations have little protection against sexual violence. Although rape can now be counted as a war crime and a crime against humanity in international law, such protection has very little meaning without means of enforcement. These laws might have more meaning if nation-states and the international community were willing to carry out war crimes trials and could provide more guarantees of witness protection. However, women are just as likely to be indicted for 'sleeping with the opposition'. Although legal and physical protection during conflicts is not likely to be forthcoming, more could be done to: educate military and peace-keeping forces about HIV; provide condoms for soldiers; and provide emergency obstetrical/gynaecological and counselling services for rape victims (male and female). These preventative measures may only provide a degree of safety, but signal the international relief community's recognition of what have been to date the invisible but enduring costs of conflict.

Flight and Asylum

During their flight across a border or to another region within the same country, refugee women may face additional danger. Many Mozambican women, for example, fled Renamo and Frelimo forces only to be raped again during their flight by one or both forces and marauding bandits. Thai, Filipino, Malay, and Khmer pirates captured, vandalized, and raped Vietnamese boat people. Refugee women are sometimes forced to provide sexual services to local officials to gain safe passage, food, shelter, and even refugee identities for their families. If imprisoned along the way, they may be raped again.

Once refugees reach their place of first asylum, they face new sexual threats. Refugee camps usually offer little protection. Many are organized by feudal-style warlords or resistance leaders who pit different factions against one another in the camp to gain wealth and power. Most security guards are male and may themselves prey on the women. Even international relief workers and Embassy personnel are predominantly male and may not be sensitive to the particular protection concerns of women. At night, bandits from nearby villages may sneak into the camps and rape, loot, and kidnap (as happened, for example, in the Khmer camps in Thailand, the Somali camps in Kenya, and the Mozambican camps in Malawi). Women who try to report such violations often 'disappear' and are killed.

In October 1993, UNHCR reported some 192 cases of rape in the Somali camps in Kenya, although the actual number was believed to be ten times higher (UNHCR, 1993). Many of the women were raped while foraging for firewood outside the camp. UNHCR's first step was to identify the victims but many women were unwilling to talk for fear of being rejected by their own people. Some rape victims were abandoned by their husbands and had to be resettled in a third country because they would never be accepted again by Somali society. Although UNHCR issued an appeal for US$1.1 million to provide stoves, fuel, and medical and psychological aid, funding for such activities is usually scarce and not traditionally considered part of critical emergency assistance.

Camps throughout the world are generally crowded and lack privacy. Single women, elderly women, and female household heads without male protection are often vulnerable to attack and abuse. Although many women within the international community (UNHCR, bilateral donors, and NGOs, such as the Refugee Women's Commission) have advocated increased attention and protection for vulnerable groups of women, such concerns remain at the periphery of emergency assistance and little is done until they become headline news. Refugee women themselves are rarely given a forum to voice their own concerns and those who do are sometimes ostracized, or worse still, harmed.

Refugee women outside of refugee camp settings predominantly settle in urban centres (examples are the Dinka and the Nuer in Khartoum, Mozambicans in Nairobi and Mombasa, and Bosnians and Croatians displaced in Zagreb), where they can find some marginal employment and where there are more services. Less often they settle in rural villages—usually those which share common linguistic and cultural features (as in the case of the Liberians in Sierra Leone and Ivory Coast and the Mozambicans in Southern Malawi). 'Self-settled' refugees have less access to international legal protection afforded by UNHCR but are better integrated into the local setting. In the urban areas of Nairobi, however, they became part of the peri-urban poor. These refugees had little or no access to public services, could be expelled or imprisoned at any time, and became visible only as scapegoats to explain a deteriorating economic and political environment. The Kenyan women—as women in many other invisible refugee communities—could also be preyed upon by local men, and their own male kin were often powerless to protect them. In refugee communities outside of formal camp settings, indigenous community groups and NGOs may have access to and knowledge of self-settled refugee communities that the larger international NGOs may not have.

Indigenous organizations often play a critical role in providing services and publicizing the situation of otherwise invisible refugee communities.

Whether in refugee camps or integrated locally, refugee women rarely feel completely secure. They know that their situation is temporary and that at any time, they can be forced to repatriate or to flee again. Their prolonged liminality is a convenient mechanism for reinforcing the boundaries of the nation-state by distinguishing between the national and the alien (Turner, 1974). Although there is little reason not to afford refugees national status, it serves the interests of the state to create its own imagined communities (Anderson, 1991). When the state is itself economically and politically threatened, refugees become pariah groups vulnerable to all kinds of physical harassment, and the least protected are often the most vulnerable.

Repatriation and Resettlement

UNHCR and other international organizations prioritize solutions to most refugee conflicts in the following order: (1) repatriation to the home country; (2) local integration in a neighbouring country; and (3) resettlement in a third country following asylum in a second country. Once the fighting has subsided enough for refugees to return home, the international organizations (primarily UNHCR, ICRC, and IOM) will often provide transport or bus or plane ticket home and food aid, seeds, and tools until the first harvest. Although the international community maintains the fiction of planned repatriation, as their first priority, in reality, most repatriations are largely spontaneous and occur with little support from the international community. Planned repatriations, such as the one along the Cambodian border, are extremely costly and mean that there are fewer resources to assist refugees in their eventual reintegration. The alternatives—local settlement or third country resettlement—are afforded to fewer refugees, and for many refugees, temporary asylum becomes a long-term way of life.

In some refugee situations, refugees who repatriate face reprobation for having failed to obtain a better life in a wealthy third country. Their kin left behind may resent having to share resources and may feel that the refugees escaped the suffering and deprivation during the war. Those who return are often treated as the enemy, particularly when they fled the very same regime (for example, Vietnam, Laos, and Mozambique). Refugee settlements are likely to receive fewer resources and poorer lands than those who remained (see, for example, Luche, 1991, on the Hmong in Laos).

Women, in particular, may be considered polluted by their contacts with others—those living across the border and international relief workers—or the fast life in the city. If they have been away for many years, the refugees themselves may not have a home to return to or the needed skills to earn a living in their home country. For example, young Mozambican refugees and their elders reported that the young ones no longer knew how to farm or raise livestock.

Local integration or third country resettlement poses similar problems. Refugees are often unprepared for life in the new country and there is very little assistance to ease their transition. Young refugee women must cope with new dating practices, which create tensions between them and their elders. Many young adolescent South-East Asian girls and boys who resettled in Western countries, for example, had no one to provide advice about social situations. Some rebelled against their parents and practised unsafe sex (field interviews in the Lao community in San Francisco). Whatever sex education messages they did receive, they felt did not apply to them. Others tried to maintain traditional practices and felt out of place and depressed. Teenage suicides are not uncommon—both among those who try to maintain a former way of life and those who rebel. In the Hmong community in the US, misunderstandings have also arisen about rape, extramarital affairs, and traditional marriage by capture practices, which have been compounded by the courts (Hammond, 1992).

Countries of resettlement and repatriation have also demanded that refugees be tested for HIV and have tried to use positive test results to deny immigrant or national status. Merely requiring an HIV/AIDS test suggests that governments, employing a 'geography of blame', treat refugees as a special risk group (for example, the Haitian refugees in the US or the Vietnamese returnees in Vietnam) (Farmer, 1992). Although UNHCR has drafted policy guidelines to protect HIV positive refugees from being denied immigrant or national status, fears of such discrimination have also led to a general unwillingness to recognize the risks of HIV faced by many refugees (Dualeh, personal communication, 1994).

At each stage of their journey, refugee women confront situations in which they can be raped, coerced into non-consensual sex, and/or forced into prostitution. Even as they gain increasing control over their lives in the journey from conflict to safe haven and a homeland, their spheres of action are often limited by a lack of access to reproductive health care, counselling, and information, and by others' perceptions of them as 'refugees'. Yet, their experiences are individually specific and the risk factors are situationally specific, as will be shown in the sexual histories of four refugee women.

Sexual Histories

Xiong Mee

Xiong Mee, a Laotian Hmong girl of fourteen, lived with her father and mother (a second wife) in Ban Vinai Refugee Camp, Thailand. Unlike many other girls her age, she was not interested in boys or marriage but preferred the company of other girls and women. When asked about marriage, she explained that she never wanted to become a second wife as her mother and that she hoped some day to be a doctor or teacher.

The Hmong have a celebrated New Year's Ceremony in which boys and girls toss a ball back and forth to show their interest in the opposite sex. As they grow older, the game is played more seriously and becomes a courtship ceremony. Although many girls of Xiong Mee's age played the game seriously, she refused to get involved and, if she played at all, she continued to play with other girls or younger children. However, her father bought her some new clothes and encouraged her to find a suitor.

Xiong Mee was extremely beautiful by all accounts and many young and old Hmong men were interested in her. She ignored them all and spoke instead of how sad it was that so many other young Hmong girls committed or attempted suicide over failed love affairs. 'I don't need a man,' she said once. 'If I can get an education, I could earn my own way and take care of my family.' When Xiong Mee reached her sixteenth birthday, her father, frustrated at her obvious indifference, arranged her marriage to a well-known resistance leader, a man of forty-five with two other wives and several children. A traditional marriage by capture ceremony took place and Xiong Mee found herself wed to a man who coerced her into sex and whose wives resented their husband's newest attraction.

The sexual relationship between Xiong Mee and her husband did not last long and the resistance leader went back to his mistresses in the camp and in the nearby Thai villages. Being a wealthy man, he could have whom he pleased. Meanwhile, Xiong Mee became pregnant. However, before her first child was born, the resistance leader died of unknown causes and, according to tradition, Xiong Mee was then married off to his younger brother, where this time she became a second wife.

Elisabeth

Elisabeth, a Ugandan refugee women in her early twenties, lived in Dandora, a poor area of Nairobi, with her two children and her sister's three children. When I met her, she had just had her trading license taken away by young Kenyan paramilitary forces. The paramilitary felt entitled to harass refugees because President Moi had recently made a speech in which he complained that the refugees were taking jobs from Kenyans. When she recounted her story, Elisabeth was visiting another Ugandan refugee friend, who owned a small beauty parlour and was asking her advice about what to do next.

Elisabeth married a soldier who joined Idi Amin's army and was killed in the war. When the war came to her village, the soldiers dragged her out of her home and raped her in front of her two young children. After the soldiers left, her parents rescued her and put her on the next lorry to Nairobi. Her children stayed behind with her parents. En route to Nairobi, she slept with one of the drivers and became pregnant with her third child. Once there, she joined up with friends from her village. They provided a room but work was scarce and it was difficult to obtain a vendor's license as an unregistered refugee woman. To support herself and her child, Elisabeth became a prostitute. Ugandan women were said to be very beautiful and are much sought after by men in Nairobi. She had many customers.

Eventually, one of the Kenyan Catholic NGOs was able to help her register with UNHCR and she obtained an official refugee identity card. This allowed her after several months to obtain a vendor's licence. By this time, she had had another child.

Shortly after she obtained her license, Elisabeth's 'sister'—another woman from her village in the same household—died of the 'disease'. Elisabeth now had four children to look after, her own and her sister's two as well. And now she told her friend, the hairdresser, that she needed to find customers again. When I asked Elisabeth whether she feared that she, too, would get the 'disease', she responded, 'Yes, but what choice do I have?'

Mira

Mira fled to Slavonsky Brod in Croatia when she was released by the Bosnian Serb forces. There, she joined her parents. She was a young Bosnian Muslim woman of twenty years. Her mother recounted their family's flight, while Mira watched. She sat, wordless, staring straight ahead with little expression, as her mother spoke. Yet, Mira was the only one who spoke fluent English.

The mother said that they knew for two weeks the Serbs were coming as they heard the sound of artillery fire approaching. The day and time of the attack were also announced on the radio. Mira was in another town attending university. She and her husband loaded what they could into their car and drove across the bridge to the Croatian town on the other side of the river. Later they heard that those who remained were herded into the high school stadium. The Bosnian Serb forces separated people first by ethnic group and then by sex. They herded Bosnian Muslim girls and women into the high school and raped them repeatedly day after day. Some were eventually released. Most of the Muslim boys and men who were taken prisoner have not been heard of since that time. Two days later Serbian planes came and bombed the bridge between Bosnia and Croatia.

For the next two months, the family had no word of Mira. They heard that the town in which she attended university had also been taken over by the Bosnian Serb forces. Finally, an exchange of prisoners was negotiated and Mira was bussed to the border. She was one of the lucky ones. However, she refuses to speak about what happened, is very withdrawn, and has aged far beyond her twenty years. Her mother wants her to study at another university in Croatia or elsewhere in Europe, but Mira says nothing. 'She was such a good student,' her mother says.

Damdy

Damdy was the second daughter in a lowland Lao family that lived in the Tenderloin District of San Francisco. Her family came to the US in 1982 from the refugee camps in Thailand. Damdy was a small, thin girl who initially looked much younger than her years and was in second grade when we first met. A year later, she began to develop as an adolescent and her elementary school teacher realized that Damdy did not belong in third grade. 'Ask them to put you in seventh grade,' I told her when she told me her real age. She did, and a week later she was attending junior high school.

Damdy did exceptionally well in school until tenth grade when she became interested in boys. She was fighting a lot with her mother, who did not want her to date anyone. However, the mother was spending all her time trying to make enough money for the family and worked two shifts. Damdy would put her younger brothers to bed and then sneak out to join her Puerto Rican American boyfriend.

This pattern continued for some time until her mother learned what was happening. They had a fight and her mother threw her out of the house. Damdy then called me from a pay phone on a street near her boyfriend's house in the Mission district. It was 11.30 pm in California, but 3.30 am on the East Coast where I lived. She asked my husband and me if she could live with us. We agreed but requested that she get permission from her mother first. Damdy said she had no intention of ever speaking to her mother again and would try to move into her boyfriend's house.

A few days later, she called and said that she had temporarily moved into a girlfriend's house. She was no longer speaking to her boyfriend, although would visit his father and brothers who had also befriended her.

Damdy then asked me what I thought about premarital sex and said that she had had several boyfriends already. 'Do they use condoms?' I asked. 'No, not those disgusting things,' she replied. I asked her if she worried about AIDS and she told me that she could not get AIDS because she did not go out with gay men. When I tried to point out the risks, she replied, 'I don't worry about that.' A few months later, she called to tell me about a new 'steady boyfriend'.

Conclusions

These stories illustrate the diverse sexual risks that refugee women face. The diversity of refugee women's experiences preclude any universal prescription for HIV/AIDS control and prevention. The category of refugee itself ignores the diversity of experiences which women as refugees face. Such experiences are patterned by the woman's community of origin, the particular set of experiences of flight and uprooting, the sexual practices and traditions of the host and/or asylum communities, and individual attributes, including age, education, personality, etc.

Yet, there are certain commonalities which refugee women face which makes the category of refugee meaningful. Most refugee women do not enjoy the protection of a state, have less legal recourse than women who are not refugees, and can be threatened with state-sanctioned violence. Refugee women face similar situations to women trapped in domestic violence who may not be able to practise safe sex without some personal risk. For both victims of domestic and state-sanctioned violence, notions of empowerment are meaningless without fundamental changes in the political economic power structure and guarantees of safety.

While the category of refugee conveys a broad range of experiences and situations, the commonality is the absence of safety—both physical and psychological—that many refugee women face in their daily lives. This lack of control may mean that refugee women have little or no control over the kinds of sexual practices which place them at risk. This lack of control, however, is relative and the experience ranges from a woman being forcibly raped in conflict to a refugee girl negotiating sex in her new country of asylum. Although refugee women gain increasing control as they move towards greater safety, as shown in the case of Damdy, their lack of self-esteem and general uprootedness may lead them to employ risk rather than survival behaviors. Young women, in particular, may have little experience, and therefore, expectation, that they can affect their lives and that their decisions matter. Many young refugee women have experienced years of social upheaval and uprooting during which time their own needs and desires may have been sacrificed for the survival of their family and/or community. In the process, their own self-esteem may have been sacrificed.

The stories of individual refugee women across different stages of refugee experiences illustrate the complexities of designing effective and meaningful HIV/AIDS prevention and control programmes in most refugee situations. There are no quick and obvious solutions, nor are one-time interventions sufficient. Providing more information, for example, is useful but refugee women may not be in a position to act on that information. Providing condoms, and especially a female condom, should be a part of any emergency assistance operation but many refugee women cannot insist that soldiers—particularly those from an opposing side—utilize condoms.

These stories illustrate that notions of empowerment are meaningless in many refugee settings unless the underlying sources of conflict are directly addressed. War must be stopped and soldiers must stop using sexual violence as a weapon of war. But, since such recommendations are at best idealistic, there is a need to find ways of holding perpetrators accountable and of healing those who have suffered. In a time of AIDS these concerns are all the more compelling. While many refugee women who have been violated may never live to learn whether they have contracted AIDS, for others the discovery that they have may be the cruellest irony.

REFERENCES

Agar, A. and W. Agar (1991), 'A case study of refugee women in Malawi', Report for the United Nations High Commissioner for Refugees, Malawi.

Anderson, B. (1991), *Imagined Communities*, Verso, London.

Anthony, R. *et al.* (1993), 'Assistance for victims of atrocities in Croatia and Bosnia-Herzegovina', Report for the Europe Bureau, US Agency for International Development, Washington, DC.

Black, M. E. (1993), 'Reproductive freedom for refugees', Letter in *Lancet*, May 15, 341 (8855), 1285.

Bolton, R. (1992), 'Mapping terra incognita: sex research for AIDS prevention—an urgent agenda for the 1990s', in Herdt, G. and S. Lindenbaum (eds), *The Time of AIDS: Social Analysis, Theory, and Method*, Sage Publications, Newbury Park, 124–58.

deZalduondo, B. O. (1991), 'AIDS prevention for women in African countries: cultural appropriateness reconsidered', Paper presented to the American Public Health Association, November 1991.

Farmer, P. (1992), *AIDS and Accusation: Haiti and the Geography of Blame*, University of California Press, Berkeley.

Feiden, P., L. Long, and K. Stewart (1990), 'Khartoum displaced assessment and recommendations', Paper prepared for USAID/Sudan.

Gupta, G. R. and E. Weiss (1993), 'Women's lives and sex: implications for AIDS prevention', *Journal of Culture, Medicine and Psychiatry*, December.

Helsinki Watch (1992), *War Crimes in Bosnia-Hercegovina*, Helsinki Watch, Human Rights Watch, New York.

Herdt, G. and S. Lindenbaum (1992) (eds), *The Time of AIDS*, Sage, Newbury Park, CA.

Herman, J. L. (1992), *Trauma and Recovery*, Basic Books, New York.

Long, L. (1993a), 'The impact of AIDS on women's lives in developing countries: a life cycle perspective', Paper presented to the American Association for the Advancement of Science Annual Meeting, January 1993, Boston.

—— (1993b). *Ban Vinai, the Refugee Camp*, Columbia University Press, New York.

—— Cecsarini L. and J. Martin (1990), 'The local impact of Mozambican refugees in Malawi', Report prepared for the US Embassy, Malawi.

—— Agar, A., Khasiani, Long, D., and N. Kendall (1991), 'Case studies of African refugee women', Report for the United Nations High Commissioner for Refugees, Geneva.

Luche, J. E. (1991), 'Socio-economic analysis of the Lao/89/550 highland integrated rural development project', Report for United Nations Fund for Drug Abuse and Development, Laos.

Mayotte, J. (1992), *Disposable People? The Plight of Refugees*, Orbis Books, Maryknoll, New York.

Ntozi, J. and M. Lubega (1992), 'Patterns of sexual behavior and the spread of AIDS in Uganda', in T. Dyson (ed.), *Sexual Behavior and Networking: Anthropological and Socio-Cultural Studies on the Transmission of HIV*, International Union for the Scientific Study of Population, Liège, 315–34.

Refugee Policy Group (1989), 'Summary of discussions of meeting on refugees and AIDS', September 18, Washington, DC.

Said, E. W. (1979), *Orientalism*, Vintage Books, Random House, New York.

Schoepf, B. G. (1992), 'Women at risk: case studies from Zaire', in G. Herdt and S. Lindenbaum (eds), *The Time of AIDS: Social Analysis, Theory, and Method*, Sage Publications, Newbury Park, CA., 259–86.

Tawil, O. (1990), 'Population movement and AIDS', Draft document for Global Programme on AIDS, World Health Organization, Geneva.

Turner, V. (1974), *Dramas, Fields, and Metaphors: Symbolic action in Human Society*, Cornell University Press, Ithaca.

United Nations High Commissioner for Refugees (UNHCR) (1992), 'UNHCR policy and guidelines regarding refugee protection and assistance and Acquired Immune Deficiency Syndrome (AIDS)', UNHCR/IOM/82/92, Geneva.

—— (1993), 'UNHCR update on refugee developments in Africa', October 19, 1993, Geneva.

United States Department of State (1993), 'Survey report: humanitarian assessment team on Bosnia-Herzegovina', Report for President Clinton, Washington, DC.

Weiss, E. and G. R. Gupta (1993), 'AIDS prevention for women: issues and challenges', in *Women at the Center: Development Issues and Practices for the 1990s*, Kumarian Press, West Hartford, Connecticut.

World Health Organization (1992), 'Current and future dimensions of the HIV/AIDS pandemic: a capsule summary', January, Geneva.

Part III

From Rural to Urban Sexual Risk

7 Urban–Rural Differentials in HIV/STDs and Sexual Behaviour

MICHEL CARAËL

Introduction

Heterosexual transmission has accounted for about three quarters of the estimated 13 million human immunodeficiency virus (HIV) infections in adults worldwide. In the 1990s, this mode of transmission continues to grow in importance (WHO/GPA, 1993). The HIV/AIDS pandemic was initially centred in urban locations. Rural HIV and STD prevalences have generally been found to be much lower than urban prevalences, with some noticeable exceptions. In the developing world, except Latin America, the majority of the population is rural. In the absence of any specific data from rural areas in most countries, HIV projections so far have assumed rural rates to be five to ten times lower than urban rates (Chin, 1991; Anderson et al., 1991; Mertens et al., 1994). However, in the ten years following the recognition of the HIV epidemic, additional empirical data on the levels and dynamics of HIV transmission and sexual risk behaviours are beginning to nuance the picture. There is now a general perception that several types of HIV epidemics are probably co-occuring at different rates across different groups, in different areas of the same country, making assessment of the current dynamics problematical (Piot et al., 1990).

In the field of HIV/STD sexual prevention research, rural–urban variations are increasingly under scrutiny, although key issues in measurement are still debated. Indeed, much variation exists between countries in terms of residence classification. Some countries use population-size criteria, such as definitional locales of fewer than 1,500 inhabitants classified as rural, while others use socioeconomic characteristics denoted by the presence of electricity and water supply. Furthermore, many studies about HIV seroprevalence and sexual behaviour implicitly assume that current residence reflects the place of exposure which does not control for the recency of migration and the frequency of travel. Thus, the findings

The author thanks J. Cleland, T. Mertens, P. Sato, and T. Burton for reviewing the manuscript. He also thanks principal investigators in the selected countries/sites: Dr P. Somse (Central African Republic); Professor D. Séry and G. Tapé (Côte d'Ivoire); Dr M. Marcos (Guinea Bissau); Dr G. Awissi (Togo); Professor N. Ndimurukundo (Burundi); Dr P. Onyango and Dr P. Waliji-Moloo (Kenya); Dr A. Lawson (Lesotho); Dr E. Muhondwa (Tanzania); Professor A. Haworth and Dr K. Kalumba (Lusaka); Dr T. Tiglao (Manila); Professor Kok Lee Peng (Singapore); Dr A. J. Weeramunda (Sri Lanka); Dr W. Sittitrai (Thailand); Dr R. G. Parker (Rio de Janeiro).

presented below in part reflect the results of such methodological issues. We present examples of HIV/STD prevalence differentials between urban and rural settings and review urban/rural patterns of sexual behaviour from the WHO/GPA cross-country surveys. Finally, the urban–rural differentials in sexual behaviour are adjusted for using multivariate analysis of selected social variables and the results are thereby examined.

HIV Seroprevalence

The seroprevalence rates in selected groups of people in urban and rural areas of different countries vary enormously. Available data, mostly from sub-Saharan Africa, have tended to show a large differential in HIV infection levels between urban and rural areas of a country.

National cross-sectional surveys of HIV seroprevalence were conducted by a variety of countries in sub-Saharan Africa between the mid-1980s and the beginning of the 1990s. These studies necessarily involve serious logistical and methodological problems resulting from compromises necessary to implement them. Nevertheless, they provide an idea of HIV distribution in urban and rural areas, albeit with no indication of the trends or dynamic of the epidemic.

A nationwide survey in Rwanda in 1986 estimated that 23.6 per cent of the urban adult population are infected with HIV, compared with only 3.5 per cent of the rural adult population (Rwandan seroprevalence study group, 1989). In Burundi, based on review of the available data, including the national sero-survey (PNLS, 1991), it was estimated that in 1989 HIV prevalence was 15 per cent in the sexually active urban population and 1.5 per cent in the rural population. More females than males were HIV-infected, but the possibility of a methodological bias cannot be excluded. In Uganda, in 1988, a nationwide sero-survey documented the pattern of HIV infection by region and residence (ACP-AIDS Control Programme, 1990). In the West Nile district, urban and rural rates of HIV infection were nearly similar, whereas in the other districts urban levels were much higher than rural levels.

In Côte d'Ivoire, it is striking that urban–rural differenciation is less pronounced than in the other countries (Table 7.1). Like Côte d'Ivoire, Zimbabwe is a country with high urban–rural mobility. In 1990, it was estimated through sentinel site surveillance that the HIV prevalence was 7.5 per cent in the sexually active urban population versus 2.5 per cent in the sexually active rural population. By 1992, rates of 15–20 per cent or more in the sexually active urban population, and 5–10 per cent in rural areas, were being seen (WHO/GPA, 1993). In Thailand also, it appears that the rural levels of infection are only slightly lower than urban level. Military conscript data show that in 1991, 2.8 per cent of rural twenty-one year-old conscripts were HIV-infected, compared with 3.9 per cent of their urban counterparts (Sirisopana *et al.*, 1992). However, the interpretation of such results is difficult and caution should be exercised, as illustrated below.

Table 7.1. HIV seroprevalence in the adult population in selected countries (1986–9), by urban/rural residence (national sero-surveys)

	Urban % sero +	Rural % sero +
Rwanda	23.6	3.5
Burundi	15	1.5
Uganda[a]	18–28	6–13
Côte d'Ivoire[b]	7.3	4.9

Notes
  [a] According to main regions
  [b] HIV-1, HIV-2 and dually reactive

In 1985, in one of the first seroprevalence studies among volunteers conducted in rural areas, in the remote rural village of Rulimba, Rwanda, 147 adults representing 94 per cent of the village population aged between fourteen and thirty-five were tested for HIV; two persons (1.4 per cent) were found HIV-positive. About two hours walking distance of Rulimba, in a village with a market place, situated on a local road connecting two towns, among fifty-nine persons representing about 60 per cent of the adult population, five (8.5 per cent) were seropositive. In the unique health centre in the same rural area, out of 169 consecutive STD patients enrolled for HIV serological testing, 49 (30 per cent) were HIV-seropositive. A risk ratio for HIV seropositivity of eighteen and eleven, respectively, was associated with travel to an urban centre in the last five years and with a current incidence or a history of STD in the past two years (Van De Perre *et al.*, 1987). The participation bias was estimated to be minimal by the authors because HIV/AIDS was nearly unknown at the time. Nonetheless, these results show how sample selection and the definition of 'rural' provenence could have dramatically influenced the rates of seroprevalence.

Differences in prevalence rates within urban areas are also worth examining in detail. In Kigali, the capital city of Rwanda, a sample of women attending three prenatal clinics was tested for HIV from December 1988 to December 1990. Using the women's sector of residency, a map was drawn of the city providing an idea of the density of HIV infection in various areas. The high risk area (between 31 and 39 per cent of seropositivity in adults as compared to an overall urban mean of 25 per cent) included mainly squatter settlements on the periphery of Kigali, inhabited by a majority of new rural immigrants and urban poor working in the informal sector of the economy (Gotanegre *et al.*, 1992). By contrast, women living in areas of Kigali where the rural countryside is being invaded by the expanding town showed a 10–16 per cent prevalence. Again, the definition of 'urban' residential life and the ways the serosample is drawn from the population may influence the HIV prevalence estimate.

Factors Influencing Level and Distribution of HIV Infection

Such urban–rural patterns of HIV spread are likely to result from differences in the timing of the introduction of HIV into the population, differences in patterns of circulation or migration and, perhaps, differences in sexual behaviour between urban and rural settlements.

Timing and dynamic of the HIV epidemic

Because HIV/AIDS is a new disease transmitted by human sexual contact, time is required for the virus to spread. By contrast to other STDs, most of which have high infectivity rates, the probability of HIV infection—given a single sexual exposure to an infected partner, in the absence of cofactors and independently of the duration since infection—is estimated to be less than 0.003 (Peterman *et al.*, 1988). For an agent with such low infectivity to become epidemic, it can take a long time of silent and slow spread. Therefore the long-term dynamic of the HIV pandemic remains largely unknown.

Initially, when HIV was identified and its modes of transmission recognized, most attention was focused on specific populations with high risk behaviour. Studies of homosexual men, injecting drug users, and women sex workers initially centred in urban locations have shown that if the virus is present in some communities and the behaviours that transmit infection are sufficiently common and intense, HIV can quickly become epidemic within specific populations and further spread either slowly or quickly into the wider 'general' population. For example, estimation of HIV seroprevalence among injecting drug users seeking treatment in Bangkok increased from 0 per cent in 1985–6 to 16 per cent in 1988, and to 40–60 per cent in 1992 (WHO/GPA, 1991; 1993). Outside of high risk behaviour groups where the progression of the HIV epidemic may be extremely rapid, contrasting situations have been found in the so-called 'general' population (Caraël and Piot, 1989). Even where a stable overall HIV seroprevalence has been observed for several years, such as in Kinshasa, Zaïre, there is now recognition that this stability may be due to a transition from HIV epidemicity to endemicity and is consistent with a high HIV incidence in subsets of the population (Batter *et al.*, 1994). In other countries, such as Nigeria, the future of the epidemic is largely unknown (Olaleye *et al.*, 1993) and will depend primarily on the relative preponderance of different sexual behaviours associated with HIV transmission.

In the search for explanations of HIV differentials in urban and rural populations, to rely on HIV current levels bears the danger of looking backwards rather then addressing the dynamic of the epidemic and the future situation. High levels of seroprevalence in some areas may reflect a longer exposure to the virus and not necessarily higher risk behaviours than in other areas. Thus, countries with well-developed transportation infrastructures may experience currently more rapid spread of HIV infection to rural areas, as seen in Zimbabwe or Côte d'Ivoire. In contrast, in a remote rural area of Zaïre where circulation is restricted by a poor infrastructure, the seroprevalence rates among the general population remained stable over a ten-year period at nearly 1 per cent (Nzilambi *et al.*, 1988).

Behaviours and related factors that facilitate HIV circulation between networks

The 'sexual migration' of urban residents along roads and across networks has been suggested as a major vector in HIV heterosexual transmission—at least during the early stages of the epidemic. In this regard, commercial sex workers and their clients—many of whom are travellers such as migrants or truck drivers—have received some attention (Caraël *et al.*, 1995; Orubuloye *et al.*, 1993). High rates of turnover and migration are common in female prostitutes. In Thailand, length of time in the profession was reported as a median of six months to three years. One study estimated that these women changed worksites every three to four months (Weniger *et al.* 1991). Pasuk's survey (1982) showed that 70 per cent of the women working as prostitutes in the massage parlours had come from farming families, and 85 per cent had come in order to help feed their families. In 1993, data from the national surveillance system documented HIV infection rates among prostitutes working in brothels in the range of 20–40 per cent throughout the country.

The rural Ghana to Abidjan migration stream is relatively exceptional in Africa, as there is a predominance of women, most of them sex workers. This female migration stream is circular; according to Anarfi (1992), most of these women are single, with children whom they leave behind with their families; they return to rural Ghana after two–three years' absence. Women who succeed in accumulating some money would then use their earnings to buy land or business and marry. The implications for HIV/STD spread are obvious: in a recent intervention study (WHO Progress Report, 1993), 88 per cent of 479 sex workers in Abidjan were found to be HIV seropositive. Prevalences of gonorrhoea, syphilis, and genital ulcer disease were, respectively, 35 per cent, 22 per cent, and 23 per cent. Neequaye (1989) in Ghana, writing on HIV-positive women, observed: 'Almost all were young women who had come back to Ghana for medical treatment. From their case histories, it emerges that they had all been working in the Côte d'Ivoire as prostitutes.'

When a relatively smaller pool of prostitutes is serving male clients without high levels of condom use, STD and HIV are likely to increase very quickly, as exemplified in Kigali, Rwanda. There, a retrospective study of STD among 455 military conscripts of rural origin, for whom STD rates were ascertained by medical records, showed that, in 1981, of men recruited at the age of nineteen, 20 per cent had experienced an episode of STD after twenty-four months of service in cities, increasing to 60 per cent at five years of service. Cohorts recruited in each subsequent year took less time to achieve higher levels of infection. Thus, 60 per cent of the 1984 cohort had already been infected within twenty-four months of military service. Because there were no indications that sexual behaviour in that particular group or health care quality had changed in a five-year period, it seems likely that the proportion of prostitutes infected with STD/HIV had dramatically increased (Caraël and Piot, 1989). As early as 1984, in another city of Rwanda, 88 per cent of sex workers were already HIV-infected (Van De Perre *et al.*, 1985). Such characteristics of a sexual network with closed boundaries and high density is more typical of an urban environment, yet it can also be found in areas where migrant labour is concentrated, such as mining areas and industrial plantations.

The rates of STD incidence are generally much higher in the city than in rural areas but, because rural areas lack laboratories and qualified health personnel, it is often difficult to determine the levels of STD (Arya *et al.*, 1977). Sexually trans-mitted diseases in rural settings are usually less common, though also less easily treated than in the city. Their prevalence can thus be high, even though the reported incidence may be low. In the city the situation is often reversed—a low prevalence may be accompanied by a higher but unreported incidence. In Cameroon, for example, the prevalence rate of gonorrhoea among women of childbearing age was estimated at 14 per cent in the city of Yaounde and at 22 per cent in rural areas (Nasah *et al.*, 1980). When the interchange between city and countryside is extensive, or when circular migrations take people far from their home communities, the rural setting can itself constitute a vast reservoir of STD (Arya *et al.*, 1980; Hunt, 1989).

However, like those of migration, the mechanisms of infection may be circular and complex. In many parts of South-East Asia, young adults—men, and less commonly, women—migrate from rural areas to neighbouring cities with appeal-ing economic opportunities, only to return to their rural homes to marry. In these instances, HIV and STDs are contracted in the city through casual sexual relations or relations with prostitutes and are then introduced into the rural populations.

The circulation involves only rural locales in other cases: young Fulani men of northern Cameroon, for example, who travel abroad in order to solidify a social network, often find sexual partners among divorced or married women (David and Voas, 1978). In Casamance, Senegal, the harvesting of palm wine as a second-ary occupation for seven months of the year, involves seasonal migration for 82 per cent of men over twenty years of age. Half the migrants reported sexual inter-course with persons other than their regular partner in their village. In the same area, 80 per cent of women between fifteen and twenty-four years old are away, in search of 'service' jobs in towns. Seasonal migration was the only sociological factor associated with STDs and HIV seropositivity in Casamance (Pison, 1993).

Structural patterns in behaviours

Less attention has been given to urban–rural structural, socioeconomic, or cul-tural patterns of sexual behaviour that expose people to HIV infection, or to migration patterns that create unbalanced sex ratios in both sending and receiving geographical areas. Yet, in such circumstances, marriage patterns and sexual behaviours are permanently affected. In Tanzania's Mbeya region, in both urban and rural areas, HIV infection in pregnant women is increasing. From 1989 to

1991, HIV infection levels in rural pregnant women tripled from 4 to 12 per cent. The HIV infection levels in urban pregnant women increased from 10.3 to 16 per cent during this same period (NACP, 1992).

The urban environment has been described as a place in which behaviour is more individualistic, customary rules governing marriage are disappearing, and acculturation is intensifying due to schooling and the diffusion of Western models of behaviour (IDRC, 1989). The factors enumerated above are structural in nature and thus change at a relatively slow pace. Yet stereotypical dichotomies of 'urbanization, individualism, and modernity' versus 'village, community, and tradition' obscure the fact that far from abruptly losing their ethnic or cultural identities, urban residents often adapt them to the demands or constraints of the new environment. Cultural practices can continue to define sexual and marital options in cities (Parkin, 1966). Sexual freedom in the cities is thus not necessarily brought about by the abandonment of custom or transgression of control on their sexuality, but may represent the adaptation of customary rules to a new environment. For example, respect for a long period of postpartum female sexual abstinence, which is supported in rural settings by polygamy, may induce urban husbands to contract sexual relations outside of marriage with 'free' (unmarried) women. One study found that the longer the duration of the postpartum abstinence in Ibadan, Nigeria, the more STDs were present (Caldwell, 1981). In Guinea-Bissau, men who did not have sexual relations with their wives during lactation were more likely to have other 'casual' relationships than men who had sex with their wives (Hogsborg and Aaby, 1992). In Lusaka, Zambia, a study on congenital syphilis estimated that about a third of all infections were acquired by the pregnant woman during the later half of the pregnancy as a result of the traditional decrease of sexual activity between spouses and the subsequent extramarital sexual relations of the husband (Ratnam *et al.*, 1982).

Although part of the rise in HIV/STDs can result from adaptations to new environments, the notion of a 'crisis', of social disintegration, can be applied to critical events that sharply intensify the spread of HIV/STDs. Sudden huge migration flows and economic crises—events that rupture social structures and break norms—are often associated with an increase in sexually transmitted diseases (Hart, 1974). War or the long presence of an army may place selected rural populations at higher risk of HIV infection. For example, the Rakai district in rural Uganda has recorded HIV infection levels that equal those in the capital, Kampala. Across the border in Tanzania, the Bukoba district has a higher HIV seroprevalence than does Dar es Salaam. However, within the Bukoba district, in 1990, urban areas exhibited higher rates of infection than did rural areas (24 per cent and 5 per cent, respectively). In certain cities as well, the vast sexual market, therefore, may be less a culturally determined response by tradition among particular groups than it is the result of rupture brought about by a series of society-wide misfortunes and coping efforts.

More generally, widespread underemployment, the build-up of rural poverty resulting in an increase of migrants to cities, and the dearth of opportunities that women face when divorced or abandoned after becoming pregnant by transient partners (Robertson and Berger, 1986) can also be viewed as crisis situations leading to the spread of STDs and HIV. However, there is a need to acquire a greater knowledge of patterns of sexual behaviours in different sociocultural settings and their links with key factors such as gender, age, education, marital status, and residence.

Sexual Behaviour and Type of Residence

Survey data, by themselves, removed as they are from their social and cultural context, cannot furnish satisfactory explanations of sexual behaviour. Only when linked to other, largely anthropological, bodies of knowledge, will deeper insights be possible. However, they can highlight some global patterns that are worthwhile to identify.

The Global Programme on AIDS (GPA)-sponsored collaborative programme of large-scale surveys was designed in 1988 with the overall purpose of providing basic descriptive information about the knowledge, attitudes, and sexual behaviour of the general population as it relates to the risk of HIV/AIDS both within and across societies. This first cross-cultural attempt to examine aspects of sexual lifestyles focused on a limited number of key variables, such as age at first occasion of sexual intercourse, number of sexual partners, and condom use.

We present below selected survey findings, drawn from fourteen sample surveys of general populations, aged between fifteen and forty-nine. Eleven of these were based on nationally representative samples, while the remaining three were restricted to capital cities. Nine were located in sub-Saharan Africa, four in Asia, and one in South America. The surveys were conducted by teams of national investigators during 1989–92, in collaboration with, and with support from GPA. The choice of the fourteen studies selected for this study is partly pragmatic. Among more than forty surveys carried out in the developing world based on protocols and questionnaires developed by GPA, only fifteen met the following criteria: adherence to the design and content of the standard protocol; availability of 'clean' data files by mid-1993; and a reasonably high quality of survey implementation.

The methodology of the surveys has been described elsewhere (Caraël, 1995). All these surveys used clustered probability sample designs and face-to-face individual interviewing with selected adults. Sample sizes were small—typically in the range of 2000–3000 respondents. Key design features such as confidentiality, extensive training of interviewers, privacy, matching of respondent and interviewer for age and sex, and translation of questions into local languages were proposed as means to maximize the validity of results. Individual refusal rates were low, typically varying from 2 to 5 per cent. The emphasis was on sexual behaviour outside of marriage or other regular partnerships, restricting attention to heterosexual partnerships for methodological reasons linked to sample design and samples sizes.

Pre-marital sex

The initiation of sexual intercourse early in life is associated with enhanced risk of HIV and STDs (Dixon-Mueller and Wasserheit, 1990), usually due to prolonged sexual exposure, unless first sexual intercourse marks the beginning of a mutually monogamous relationship.

Measurement of the proportion of men and women who ever experienced sexual intercourse is highly dependent upon the definition of 'sexual experience' or 'sexual activity'. In the GPA surveys the definition used for sexual intercourse included vaginal, and oral or anal penetration between two individuals, but excluded mutual masturbation, intercrural sex, and other forms of non-penetrative sex.

Cities are generally associated with less parental control of adolescent sexual behaviour, more social mixing, and more exposure to 'Western' lifestyles (Larson, 1989; Caraël, 1987). For those surveys containing separate urban and rural domains, rural–urban comparisons of the proportions of unmarried male and female respondents aged between fifteen and nineteen reporting sexual intercourse in the last twelve months are shown in Figure 7.1. The proportions are higher in urban than in rural settings in Central African Republic, Togo, Burundi, Tanzania, and Sri Lanka. In the other surveys, however, initiation of sexual activity before marriage begins earlier in rural than in urban settings, or at the same time.

These results reflect the relative importance attached to virginity in different traditions. They also show that urban residence is not always associated with greater sexual freedom for young people. Patterns of urbanization vary between countries and, accordingly, shape sexual culture differently. However, an important finding is the high correlation between the prevalence of premarital sexual activity in urban and rural settings as shown in Figure 7.2. Where the proportion of of young people having premarital sex in rural areas is high, it is likely that the proportion in urban areas will be high as well. The pattern shows that sexual behaviour among young people in cities and towns is still closely linked to sexual behaviour in rural areas.

Sex outside of regular partnerships

In the GPA surveys, a major distinction was made between 'regular' sexual partnerships and other types of sexual relationship. The former were distinguished by their relative stability. Any sexual relationship that had lasted for at least 12 months, or was expected to last this long, was defined as 'regular', whether or not it involved cohabitation. For convenience of presentation, respondents having a regular partner at the time of the survey are described as 'married'.

In most surveys, there was a higher reported level of sex outside 'marriage' for both men and women in urban settings than in rural ones. The exception was for females in Thailand and Togo, where the levels in these two sites were very low

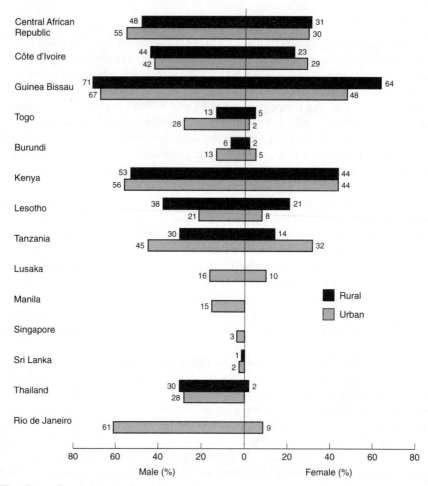

Fig. 7.1. Percentage of never-married men and women aged 15–19 years who reported sexual intercourse in the last 12 months, by residence

Source: WHO Global Programme on AIDS, 1993

(Figure 7.3). In many societies, urbanization increases opportunities for sexual encounters and provides new models of sexual behaviour. The results suggest that urbanization and modernization favour trangression of more restrictive traditions that exist in some rural areas. As more people marry late and as more relationships become informal, higher risk behaviours tend to concentrate in cities and towns. However, this difference does not mean that the extent of 'casual' sex in rural and urban areas (excluding commercial sex) is not correlated. On the contrary, the more non-regular sex in rural areas, the more there is in urban areas.

The proportion of people reporting at least one non-regular sex partner in the last twelve months varied considerably by current marital status for both sexes.

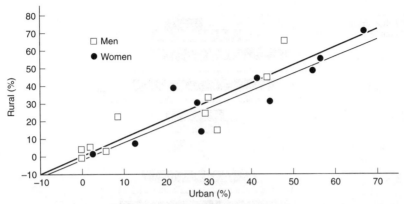

Fig. 7.2. Relationship between proportions of urban and rural never-married men and women aged 15–19 years who reported sexual intercourse in the last 12 months

Source: WHO Global Programme on AIDS, 1993

This proportion was typically highest among the 'formerly married', followed by the 'never married' and the 'currently married'. The period prevalence of non-marital sex and the number of such partners in the last twelve months were usually highest among aged between twenty and twenty-nine men and among women aged between fifteen and twenty-four. There was a significant relationship between the prevalence of premarital sex among adolescents and the level of sex outside 'marriage' among men and women (For males R-squared = 0.43, p = 0.007; for females, R-squared = 0.57, p = 0.002). This link highlights the existence of different consistent patterns of sexuality and a continuity from adolescence to adult ages.

Non-cohabiting partnerships

One of the key features affecting 'marriage' in developing countries is spousal separation due to polygamy, to migration, seasonal or permanent, especially among young males, or to separation prescribed by postpartum abstinence. The results in Table 7.2 demonstrate the importance of non-cohabitation. Non-cohabitation is most common at ages 25–34. In African surveys, impressive proportions of currently married respondents—between 11 and 43 percent- reported that they are not cohabiting. Côte d'Ivoire and Lesotho, both countries characterized by strong labor migration, exhibit the highest proportions of 'married' people not-cohabiting. In the Asian study populations, non-cohabiting partnerships are much less common, but in Rio, the level is similar to those found in Africa.

A large proportion of non-cohabiting married respondents met their regular partner only once a month or, in most cases, even less often; the proportion being invariably higher in cities when compared with rural areas and in men when

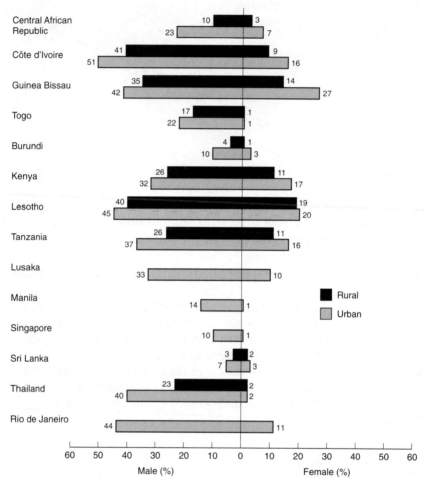

Fig. 7.3.   Percentage of all men and women who reported non-regular sex in the last 12 months, by residence

Source: WHO Global Programme on AIDS, 1993

compared with women. In countries with high levels of polygyny or multiple regular relationships, one should not expect the extent of cohabitation to be equal between men and women. In polygamous marriages, non-cohabitation is often the rule: men rotate from one spouse to the other. This pattern implies that more women than men should report non-cohabitation; this is the case to a certain extent in Tanzania but not elsewhere in Africa.

Where married men migrate away from home and find a new female partner, they might report non-cohabitation with reference to their primary marriage; more men than women would report non-cohabitation, as it occurs in Côte d'Ivoire, Lesotho, Lusaka, and Singapore. Another possible explanation is that

Table 7.2. Percentage of married men and women who were not cohabiting with principal spouse / partner, by age

	Males					Females				
	25–9	30–4	35–9	40–9	All 15–49	25–9	30–4	35–9	40–9	All 15–49
Côte d'Ivoire	47	19	8	8	43	26	19	21	16	36
Kenya	26	17	18	21	20	20	23	17	21	20
Lesotho	29	34	30	27	31	25	23	28	30	24
Tanzania	14	7	7	4	11	15	16	11	9	15
Lusaka	35	23	5	5	31	18	12	10	10	26
Manila	5	7	9	0	6	13	10	5	2	8
Singapore	29	8	3	5	12	5	2	2	2	4
Sri Lanka	7	5	4	5	5	3	6	8	5	6
Thailand	3	5	2	6	4	16	12	11	10	13
Rio de Janeiro	34	22	15	9	25	36	12	19	12	24

men and women attach different meanings to the concept of 'living together'; women may be more willing than men to report that their partner is living with them, even if co-residence is sporadic.

As expected, at the aggregate level, there is a significant association between the level of non-cohabitation and the proportion of men reporting more than one regular partner. The association is weak but significant for the ten surveys where data have been collected (R-squared: 0.55, p = 0.01). As suggested by Capron and Kohler (1975), polygyny and male emigration are mutually reinforcing in some societies. The absence of young men gives older, wealthier men, who remain at home, more opportunities for 'monopolizing' the pool of available women.

In other cultures, such as Lesotho and Rio, labour migration differentially shapes marriage systems: late marriage, increased marital disruption, and frequent extramarital sexual relationships form a series of interrelated changes that are all linked to labour migration. Not surprisingly, there is a closer association between the proportion of males in non-cohabiting partnerships and the frequency of non-regular sex within the last 12 months. For ten surveys, Figure 7.4 displays the regression of the proportion of married men who report sexual contacts outside of 'marriage' on the proportion of 'married' men reporting non-cohabitation (R-squared: 0.84, p = 0.0002). This finding is important in revealing how the nature of the marital bond as expressed through cohabitation may influence sexual behaviour outside of 'marriage'.

Commercial sex

The proportion of all adults aged between fifteen and forty-nine reporting contacts with sex workers (at least one sexual encounter in the last twelve months where money or gifts were exchanged) ranged, among men, from 1 per cent in Sri

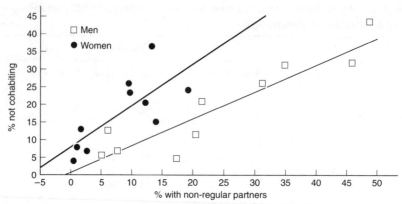

Fig. 7.4.   Relationship between percentage of men and women in non-cohabiting 'marriage' and percentage who reported non-regular patnership in the last 12 months

Source: WHO Global Programme on AIDS, 1993

Lanka to 24.7 per cent in Tanzania with a median of 9.7 per cent and, among women, from 0.1 per cent in many countries to 11.2 per cent in Tanzania, with a median of 1.3 per cent. The rather broad definition adopted in GPA/WHO surveys may have been interpreted differently by men and women. Furthermore, it is likely that women substantially involved in sex work will not be adequately represented in a household survey and/or that the few women who reported commercial sex had many male clients.

In all study sites, the proportions of men who report commercial sex is nearly the same or often higher in urban than in rural areas (Figure 7.5).

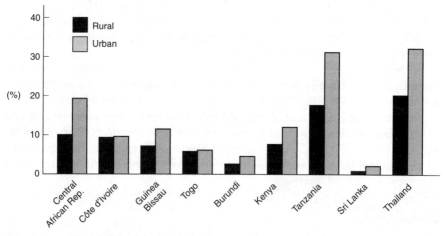

Fig. 7.5.   Percentage of male respondents who have had commercial sex in the last 12 months, by residence (urban/rural)

Source: WHO Global Programme on AIDS, 1993

In all sites, except in Lesotho, sexual behaviour levels are higher among formerly and never married. In Asian populations, commercial sex is nearly entirely concentrated among single men. There is no marked age pattern to the reporting of commercial sex, though for 'casual' sex, the proportion reporting commercial sex is usually the highest among men aged between twenty and twenty-nine.

Of particular importance for the prevention of the spread of HIV is the use of condoms during sex in exchange for money or gifts. GPA/WHO surveys (1989–92) enquired about this issue by asking a single question to respondents who reported commercial sex in the last year: '*Did you ever use a condom on these occasions? IF YES, was it each time or sometimes?*' The proportion of men who reported having always used a condom in commercial sex in the last year varied from around 10–40 per cent in urban areas to 4–15 to 4 per cent in rural areas. The urban–rural ratio was more than three in the Central African Republic, Niger, and Togo. Lesotho was the only study site where men in rural areas reported higher rates of condom use than men in urban areas, but the difference is not significant. Although the proportion of men who reported commercial sex in rural areas is lower than in urban areas, it is striking that the levels of consistent condom use in commercial sex were generally much lower in rural areas, which has huge implications in terms of HIV/STD spread.

Multivariate analysis

We have assessed the association between reported sexual behaviour and selected characteristics of respondents by logistic regression. The following predictor variables were selected for analysis: current age, level of schooling, current marital status, urban–rural residence, drinking habits (drinking alcohol at least once a week), and perceived personal risk of HIV infection. Separate logistic regressions were conducted for men and women from a subset of six surveys on the binary variable 'risk behaviour', defined as having had one or more non-regular sexual partner in the last 12 months, including commercial sex (Table 7.3).

In the four surveys, where such a distinction is possible, there is no clear link between urban/rural residence and risk behaviour. It is striking that the effect of urban/rural residence on risk behaviour, conspicuous in bivariate analysis, is so strongly attenuated or even disappears when other variables such as age, education and marital status are controlled. In Thailand and Côte d'Ivoire, unadjusted proportions of men reporting risk behaviour in urban versus rural settings were respectively 46 per cent versus 28 per cent, and 56 per cent versus 48 per cent. When adjusted, these proportions became 37 per cent versus 31 per cent, and 52 per cent versus 52 per cent. A similar finding for Thailand has been reported by VanLandingham *et al.* (1993).

Age is a net predictor of risk behaviour in eight of the twelve sex-specific study groups. In all cases where the effect age is a significant predictor, risk behaviour declines monotonically after the age of twenty-five years. Below this age, however, the pattern of association varies. Significant associations between schooling and

Table 7.3.   Net effects of residence, age, education, and marital status on proportion reporting risk behaviour in the last 12 months among sexually active men (adjusted proportions).

	CIV	BUR	LUS	MAN	THA	RIO
Residence						
Urban	0.52	0.10	—	—	0.37	—
Rural	0.52	0.12	—	—	0.31	—
Age						
15–19	0.57	0.14	0.41	ns	0.62	ns
20–24	0.60	0.14	0.59	ns	0.40	ns
25–39	0.55	0.09	0.38	ns	0.31	ns
40–49	0.42	0.03	0.21	ns	0.28	ns
Education						
None	0.41	0.05	ns	ns	0.28	ns
Primary	0.47	0.09	ns	ns	0.28	ns
Secondary +	0.61	0.16	ns	ns	0.41	ns
Marital status						
Currently married	0.47	ns	*	0.07	0.22	0.31
Never married	0.73	ns	*	0.50	0.66	0.77

Notes: * Interaction with personal vulnerability; ns: Variable not significant.

risk behaviour are less common than for age. Among men, significant net effects were found in only three out of six sites and, among women, in only two out of four sites. In all cases, there is a positive association between risk behaviour and educational background. It is uncertain, however, whether this link is a consequence of education itself or whether it reflects the higher incomes of the better educated. A further possible explanation is that educated persons experience a longer span between first sexual intercourse and first marriage or stable partnership.

The net effect of residence on ever-use of condoms is a statistically significant main or interactive influence, with higher use in urban than in rural areas.

Discussion

In the first decade of HIV/AIDS, an important feature of the dynamics of the spread of HIV in the developing world has been the diversity of HIV prevalence levels within a particular geographic area characterized by much higher infection levels in urban as compared to rural populations. However, a major uncertainty still surrounds the exact extent of the ultimate course and eventual impact of the epidemic and the degree to which HIV will spread from major foci in cities to rural populations. The increasing evidence on HIV and STD seroprevalence, although imperfect, leads to a better understanding of the transmission patterns and the recognition that a large urban–rural differential in HIV seroprevalence levels is only typical of a few countries.

Although interpretation of self-reported data on sexual behaviour must be cautiously undertaken, the main results of multisite WHO/GPA coordinated surveys presented reveal some consistent patterns that should help to improve the demographic correlates of sexual behaviour, and their relationships to the HIV pandemic. Gender, marital status, age, and a few other demographic correlates were powerful determinants of sexual behaviours in all populations, though the strength of associations varied greatly between specific locations which require further explanations.

In many fields of demography, such as fertility, nuptiality, and mortality, rural/urban differences are among the most widely studied socioeconomic variables. Empirical studies have yielded a variety of results, sometimes conflicting between them, concerning the relationship between the pattern and magnitude of such differences according to variations in types of place of residence (Singh and Casterline, 1985; Tabutin and Akoto, 1992).

A theory that has often been suggested to explain these variations relies on the differing compositions of urban and rural populations, in terms of age, education, occupation, and work status. This suggests that if the differentials are adjusted for these factors, then no significant difference between urban and rural population is observed. By contrast, another theory takes the premise that residential patterns *per se* structure the norms and beliefs of individual residents, regardless of their specific individual characteristics. Such an explanation is often referred to as the rural or urban 'subcultural' hypothesis. Finally, other complementary theories look more specifically at community-level factors or residential characteristics—such as availability of different types of services, transportation, community isolation, and family structures—to explain individual- and household-level behaviours (Anker, 1977; Casterline, 1985).

This first cross-cultural attempt to examine aspects of sexual lifestyles suggests that broad generalizations about sexual promiscuity in cities are misleading. Moreover, urban–rural disparities in sexual intercourse risking HIV/STD were less pronounced than expected in the majority of study populations and there was a strong correlation between behaviours in rural and urban areas. This result suggests that sexual behaviour among people in cities and towns is still culturally linked to sexual behaviour in rural areas and that, with a few exceptions, risk behaviour is also present in rural areas. Even urban and rural disparities in proportions of men reporting commercial sex were surprisingly low. However, among those reporting such contacts, higher numbers of sexual contacts as well as higher condom use in such relationships were typical of urban settings. Thus, the 'subcultural' claims do not seem to be borne out by the survey results: there is little evidence of a sexual lifestyle divided merely on urban or rural lines. At the aggregate level, a conceptualization of urban areas linked with modernization and sexual freedom on one hand, and rural areas incapsulated in tradition and sexual control on the other hand, would clearly be misleading.

Finally, the survey results argue for a broader definition of 'risk' behaviours and sensitivity to gender considerations. Out of the social and cultural context, without any detail about sexual networks, the isolation of 'risk' behaviours should not be considered as a basis for the extrapolation of the future course of the epidemic.

REFERENCES

ACP-AIDS Control Programme (1990). 'National serosurvey in Uganda, 1988. Report'. Ministry of Health, Entebbe.

Anarfi, J. (1992). 'Sexual networking in selected communities in Ghana and the sexual behaviour of Ghanaian female migrants in Abidjan, Côte d'Ivoire'. In Dyson, T. (ed.), *Sexual Behaviour and Networking: Anthropological and Socio-cultural Studies on the Transmission of HIV*. Ordina Press, Liège.

Anderson, R. M., May, R. M., Boily, M. C., *et al.* (1991). 'The spread of HIV-1 in Africa: sexual contact pattern and the predicted demographic impact of AIDS'. *Nature*, 352: 581–9.

Anker, R. (1977). 'The effect of group levels variables on fertility in a rural Indian sample'. *Journal of Development Studies*, 14: 63–76.

Batter, V. L., Matela, B., Nsuami, M., *et al.* (1994). 'High HIV-1 incidence in young women masked by stable overall seroprevalence among childbearing women in Kinshasa, Zaire'.

Caldwell, P. and Caldwell, J. C. (1981). 'The function of child-spacing in traditional societies, and the direction of change'. In H. J. Page and R. Lesthaeghe (eds), *Child-spacing in Tropical Africa: Tradition and Change*. Academic Press, London.

Caldwell, J. C., Caldwell, P., and Quiggin, P. (1989). 'The social context of AIDS in sub-Saharan Africa'. *Population and Development Review*, 15, 2: 185–234.

Capron, J. and Kohler, J. (1975). 'Migration de travail et pratique matrimoniale. Migration à partir du pays Mossi'. Ouagadougou. Burkina Faso. Mimeo. ORSTOM, Paris.

Caraël, M. (1987). 'Le Sida en Afrique'. In E. Hirsch (ed.), *Le Sida, Rumeurs et Faits*. Les Editions du Cerf, Paris.

—— (1993). 'Women's vulnerability to STD/HIV in sub-Saharan Africa: an increasing evidence'. Seminar on women and demographic change in sub-Saharan Africa. IUSSP, Dakar, 3–6 March.

—— (1995), 'Sexual behaviour'. In J. Cleland and B. Ferry (eds), '*Sexual behaviour and AIDS in the developing world*'. Taylor and Francis, London, 75–123.

—— and Piot, P. (1989). 'HIV infection in developing countries'. *Journal of Biological Sciences*, Suppl. 10: 35–50.

—— Cleland, J., Deheneffe, J. C., Ferry, B., and Ingham, R. (1995). 'Sexual behaviour in developing countries: implications for HIV control'. *AIDS*, 9: 1171–5.

Casterline, J. B. (ed.) (1985). *The Collection and Analysis of Community Data*. International Statistical Institute, Voorburg, Netherlands.

Chin, J. (1991). 'The epidemiology and projected mortality of AIDS'. In R. G. Feacham and D. T. Jamison (eds), *Disease and Mortality in Sub-Saharan Africa*. Oxford University Press, London.

Dixon-Mueller, R. and Wasserheit, J. (1990). 'The culture of silence: reproductive tract infections among women in the third word'. International Women's Health Coalition, New York.

Gotanegre, J. F., Bucyendore, A., Van De Perre P., *et al.* 'The social environment as a risk factor for HIV infection in African towns'. Submitted for publication. Kigali, Rwanda.

Hart, G. (1974). 'Factors influencing venereal infection in a war environment'. *British Journal of Venereal Diseases*, 50–68.

Havanon, N., Bennet, A., Knodel, J. (1993). 'Sexual networking in Provincial Thailand'. *Studies in Family Planning*, 24, 1: 1–17.

Hogsborg, M. and Aaby, P. (1992). 'Sexual relations, use of condoms and perception of AIDS in an urban area of Guinea-Bissau with a high prevalence of HIV-2'. In Tim Dyson (ed.), *Sexual Behaviour and Networking: Anthropological and Socio-cultural studies on the Transmission of HIV*. Ordina Press, Liège.

Hunt, C. W. (1989). 'Migrant labor and sexually transmitted disease: AIDS in Africa'. *Journal of Health and Social Behaviour*, 30: 353–73.

IDRC (1989). *Human Sexuality: Research Perspectives in a World Facing AIDS*, edited by A. Chouinard and J. Albert. Ottawa, 1989.

Konings, E, Anderson, R. M., Levin, A., *et al.* (1993). 'Patterns of heterosexual behaviour in a rural community in North West Tanzania'. Submitted for publication.

Larson, A. (1989). 'Social context of HIV transmission in Africa: historical and cultural bases of East and Central African sexual relations'. *Review of Infectious Diseases*, 2, 5: 716–31.

Lesthaeghe, R. J. (ed.) (1989). *Reproduction and Social Organization in Sub-Saharan Africa*. University of California Press, Berkeley.

Lindan, C., Allen, S., Caraël, M., *et al.* (1991). 'Knowledge, attitudes and perceived risk of AIDS among urban Rwandan women: relationships to HIV infection and behaviour change'. *AIDS*, 5: 993–1002.

Loodts, P. and Van De Perre, P. (1989). Une campagne d'information sur les MST et pour la promotion des préservatifs. Ann Méd Mil Belge. 3, 1: 19–20.

Mertens, T. E., Burton, T., Sato, P., Stoneburner, R., Caraël, M. (1994). 'Global estimates and epidemiology of HIV infections and AIDS'. *AIDS*, 1994.

Murray C. (1977). 'High bridewealth, migrant labour and the position of women in Lesotho'. *Journal of African Law*, 21, 1: 79–96.

National AIDS Control Programme (1992). Surveillance Report, 7, December. Dar-es-Salaam, Tanzania.

Neequaye, A., (1989). 'Prostitution in Accra'. In M. Plant (ed.), *AIDS, Drugs and Prostitution*. Tavistock/Routledge, London.

Nelson, N. (1988). 'Marital options in Mathare Valley (Nairobi). Nuptiality in Subsaharan Africa: current changes and impact on fertility', paper presented at an IUSSP meeting.

Nzilambi, N., DeCock, K. M., Forthal, D. N., *et al.* (1988). 'The prevalence of infection with HIV over a 10-year period in rural Zaïre'. *New England Journal of Medicine*, 318: 276–9.

Olaleye, O. D., Bernstein, L., Ekweozor, C. C. *et al.* (1993). 'Prevalence of HIV types 1 and 2 infections in Nigeria'. *Journal of Infectious Diseases*, 167: 710–14.

Orubuloye, I. O., Caldwell, P., and Caldwell, J. C. (1993). 'The role of high-risk occupations in the spread of AIDS: truck drivers and itinerant market women in Nigeria'. *International Family Planning Perspectives*, 19, 2: 43–8.

Parkin, D. and Nyamwaya, D. (eds) (1987). *Transformations of African Marriage*. Manchester University Press for the International African Institute, Manchester.

Peterman, T. A., Stoneburner, R. L., Allen, J. R., *et al.* (1988). 'Risk of HIV transmission from heterosexual adults with transfusion-associated infections'. *Journal of the American Medical Association*, 259: 55–58.

Phongpaichit, P. (1982). *From Peasant Girls to Bangkok Masseuses*. International Labour Organization, Geneva.

Piot, P., Laga, M., Ryder, R., *et al.* (1990). 'The global epidemiology of HIV infection: continuity, heterogeneity, and change'. *Journal of Acquired Immune Deficiency Syndromes*, 3: 403–12.

Pison, G., Le Guenno, B., Lagarde, E., *et al.* (1993). 'Seasonal migration: a risk factor for HIV infection in rural Senegal'. *Journal of Acquired Immune Deficiency Syndromes*, 6: 196–200.

PNLS (1991). 'Enquête nationale de séroprévalence au VIH. Programme national de lutte contre le Sida'. Ministère de la Santè. Document dactylographié. Burundi, Bujumbura.

Ratnam, A. V., Din, S. N., Hira, S. K., *et al.* 'Syphilis in pregnant women in Zambia'. *British Journal of Venereal Diseases*, 58: 355–8.

Rwandan seroprevalence study group (1989). 'Nationwide community-based serological survey of HIV-1 and other human retroviru infections in a Central African country'. *Lancet*, 941–3.

Singh, S. and Casterline, J. (1985). 'The socio-economic determinants of fertility'. In J. Cleland and J. Hobcrafts (eds), *Reproductive Change in Developing Countries*. Oxford University Press, London.

Sirisopana *et al.* (1992). 'The temporal trend of HIV seroprevalence among young men entering the royal Thai army: 1989–91'. Eighth International conference on AIDS. Poster PoC4084.

Sittitrai, W., Phanuphak, P., Barry, J., Brown, T. (1992). 'Thai sexual behaviour and risk of HIV infection'. Program on AIDS and Thai Red Cross, Bangkok.

Tabutin, D. and Akoto, E. (1992). 'Socio-economic and cultural differentials in the mortality of sub-Saharan Africa'. In E. van de Walle *et al.* (eds), *Mortality and Society in Sub-Saharan Africa*. Clarendon Press, Oxford.

Van De Perre, Ph., Caraël, M., Clumeck, N., *et al.* (1985). 'Female prostitutes: a risk group for infection with HTLV-III'. *Lancet*, Sept 7, 524–6.

——, Le Pollain, B., Caraël, M., *et al.* (1987) 'HIV antibodies in selected adults from a rural area in Rwanda, Central Africa'. *AIDS*, 1, 4: 212–16.

——, Caraël, M., Nzaramba, D., *et al.* (1987) 'Risk factors for HIV seropositivity in selected urban-based Rwandese adults'. *AIDS*, 1, 4: 207–11.

VanLandingham, M. J., Suprasert, S., Sittitrai, W., *et al.* (1993). 'Sexual activity among never-married men in Northern Thailand'. *Demography*, 30, 3: 297–313.

Weniger, B. C., Limpakarnjanarat, K., Ungchusak, K., *et al.* (1991). 'The epidemiology of HIV infection and AIDS in Thailand'. *AIDS*, 5 (Suppl 2): S71–S85.

WHO/GPA 1991. 'Current and future dimensions of the HIV/AIDS pandemic: a capsule summary'. WHO/GPA/RES/SFI. 91.4, Geneva.

—— 1993. 'The HIV/AIDS pandemic: 1993 overview'. WHO/GPA/CNP/EVA. 93.1, Geneva.

WHO Progress Report (1993). 'Intervention study of STD and HIV among prostitutes and clients in Abidjan, Côte d'Ivoire'. Institute of Tropical Medicine and WHO/GPA.

8   Some Cultural Underpinnings of Male Sexual Behaviour Patterns in Thailand

MARK VANLANDINGHAM and NANCY GRANDJEAN

Introduction

Many observers of Thai society have been puzzled by the persistence of unsafe sexual practices in the presence of a widening HIV epidemic.[1] Recent surveys indicate that most young Thai men have visited prostitutes, and many do so without the protection of condoms (Nopkesorn et al., 1991; Sittitrai et al., 1991; VanLandingham, 1993). The government and various nongovernmental organizations have invested heavily in educating people about the dangers of these behaviours, and this strategy has succeeded in improving the level of understanding that many Thais have about AIDS. Still, a significant proportion of men who appear to be aware of the potential consequences continue to engage in unprotected sex with prostitutes.

We argue that this behaviour is not as paradoxical as it may seem on the surface, given the long history of multiple sexual partners for men and several contemporary cultural features that are consistent with sexual risk-taking for young Thai men. To support our argument we draw upon data we collected with our Thai colleagues in a northern Thai city (Chiang Mai) and attempt to synthesize these data with other analyses of Thai sexual behaviour and Thai culture.

Our reliance on data from northern Thailand limits the degree to which our observations can be generalized to other regions of the country. The north has relatively high rates of HIV infection, and may have higher rates of prostitution and visiting of prostitutes than other regions. But other empirical data (see, for example, Knodel et al., 1994; Sittitrai et al., 1992) as well as the Thai literature and ethnographies that we draw upon focus on other regions of the country and are consistent with the cultural interpretations we make. Still, generalization to areas outside the north should be made with caution, since potential regional variations in sexual practices and norms have not been systematically investigated.

We gratefully acknowledge the study participants for their willingness to share their private lives with us. The paper benefited from discussions with Han ten Brummelhuis, Philip Guest, Gilbert Herdt, Carl Kendall, Charles Keyes, John Knodel, Anthony Pramualratana, Chanpen Saengtiechai, Werasit Sittitrai, Somboon Suprasert, and Chayan Vaddhanaphuti. Any errors of fact or interpretation, however, remain our responsibility.

[1] For discussions of the Thai AIDS epidemic, see Ford and Koetsawang (1991), Muecke (1990), and Weniger et al. (1991).

We focus on heterosexual behaviour because we wish to analyse the most dominant forms of sexual expression, and because most of the work we wish to synthesize addresses this dimension of sexuality.

AIDS Knowledge and its Effect on Male Sexual Behaviour

The 1991 Chiang Mai survey (VanLandingham, 1993), which included men from a wide spectrum of socioeconomic backgrounds, found that nearly all (98 per cent) reported some familiarity with the AIDS virus; in the national Partner Relations Survey by Sittitrai *et al.* (1992), 99 per cent reported ever hearing of the AIDS virus. However, there is substantial variation in the *extent* of AIDS knowledge by socioeconomic status among the Chiang Mai study respondents: 93 per cent of the university students versus 64 per cent of the construction workers sampled realize that there is no cure or recovery from infection. This indicates that knowledge about the consequences of infection needs to be improved among men of relatively low socioeconomic status.

Knowledge about AIDS and HIV does correlate with sexual behaviour. A multivariate factor analysis indicates that the more knowledgeable recent prostitute patrons are about the AIDS virus (especially regarding how to protect themselves against it), the more likely they are consistently to use condoms (VanLandingham *et al.*, 1994).

But knowledge about AIDS risks has not been enough to prompt widespread behavioural change. If we consider the men who report ever having sex with a prostitute (a population at risk for continuing to visit prostitutes) and who know that there is no cure or recovery from infection, 58 per cent report a recent visit to a prostitute[2], only 59 per cent of those who went used condoms consistently.

The Historical and Social Context

The tradition of extramarital sexual partners for men has varied forms and a long history in Thailand. Many traditional patterns continue in modern Thai society, although there is a fair amount of diversity in sexual behaviour among geographic and socioeconomic strata. This section will summarize the historical patterns and will attempt to outline what is known about the contemporary scene.

Visits to prostitutes

The extent of prostitution in early Thai society is not known with precision, but accounts of STDs in Thailand were made by a European traveller (La Loubère,

---

[2] 'Recently' means in the six months prior to the survey. If the population at risk is considered to be *all* sexually active men, 50 per cent report a recent visit.

1986) to Ayutthaya in the seventeenth century, in Thai chronicles of the eighteenth century, and in Thai medical texts of the nineteenth century. Many of these early accounts linked STD infections with prostitution (Bamber *et al.*, 1993). These early citations are inconsistent with Phongpaichit's (1982) view that prostitution was essentially an imported concept arriving in the late nineteenth century when international trade began to involve Thailand in earnest. In any case, this expansion of trade probably did result in the deployment of many single men (Thai and foreign) in Bangkok, as she asserts, and the spread of prostitution in Bangkok.

It is difficult to determine the extent of prostitution occurring outside the capital city in historical Thai society. Prostitution apparently expanded with the coal industry in Phuket during the first half of the nineteenth century (Boonchalaksi and Guest, 1994) and was taxed by the government in a number of provinces during the reign of King Rama V (1868–1910) (Mettarikanond, 1983). However, Zimmerman (1931) states that prostitution was limited to urban areas during the late 1920s, and Fox (1960) estimated that of the 20,000 prostitutes in the country at that time, half of those were in Bangkok, although these assertions may reflect in part the difficulty of gathering data on the subject outside of the capital. Whatever the situation was before the late 1960s, it is clear that prostitution expanded rapidly during this period (Bamber *et al.*, 1993).

The increase in prostitution beginning in the late 1960s may be attributed to several factors: the fertility decline and the resulting shift from children to income as a marker of women's status (Muecke, 1984); the conversion of Thailand to a cash economy and the concomitant increase of disposable income; urbanization and the spread of urban practices; and the presence of US servicemen seeking 'R & R' in Thailand.

Currently, there is a wide variety of commercial sex establishments, including straightforward brothels, short-time hotels, massage parlours that are fronts for prostitution, and discos and restaurants where the waitresses sell sex on the side (Rhodes, 1991). Erlanger (1991) reports that at the lower end of the commercial sex continuum are women who charge US$2.00–US$2.60 per customer and have between ten and twenty customers per day. Ford and Koetsawang's (1991) research on massage parlour workers finds that prostitutes at this level average two-three customers per day, most of whom would be upper-middle-class men. Brummelhuis (1993) points out that the variety of forms of prostitution, ranging from opportunistic and situational prostitutes to women who sell sex full time, makes the concept of prostitution in Thailand somewhat ambiguous. Women may move in and out of the field depending on their financial needs, other work opportunities, etc.

In addition to these definitional problems, prostitution has been illegal in Thailand since 1960, making it even more difficult to obtain a reliable estimate of commercial sex workers. Currently, there is a tremendous range of estimates, and many on the high end become demographically implausible. Those based on systematic data collection are in the range of 75,000 to 200,000 female prostitutes at any one time (for a discussion, see Boonchalaksi and Guest, 1994).

Establishments offering sex for sale to foreigners are concentrated in a few tourist areas—Bangkok, Pattaya, Phuket, and Hat Yai. Places providing sex for sale to Thai men, however, are ubiquitous throughout the country.

Multiple wives and mistresses

Polygyny was acceptable in Thai society until the reign of King Vijiravudh (1910–25) (Wyatt, 1984). La Loubère (1986: 52), the seventeenth-century French traveller mentioned earlier, observed:

The Siamese may have several wives, though they think it would be best to have but one; and it is only the rich that affect to have more, and that more out of pomp and grandeur, than out of debauchery.

Thai law now allows only one legal wife, but the taking of informal minor wives or mistresses (*mia noi*) continues. Though informal, the establishment of a relationship with a minor wife in Thai society implies some degree of responsibility for her welfare, and for the children that may result from this union. Of course, there is much variation in the extent of support, since these relationships are less formalized than legal marriages.

The taking of multiple wives or mistresses is by necessity an elite phenomenon, as only the well-off could afford to support more than one wife and her children. But since having more than one partner is a mark of high status, visiting prostitutes may serve as the common man's alternative to having another wife or a mistress. Of course, a prostitute would be a poor substitute for a minor wife since the client does not have exclusive access to her, but it may provide an opportunity for any man to engage in extramarital relationships, regardless of his economic status.

In the past, visiting prostitutes may have been tolerated by married women as the lesser of two evils, since the taking of a minor wife by the husband potentially had more serious consequences for the marriage relationship and the finances of the married woman's household. However, with the onset of AIDS, minor wives may now be seen by some as less of a risk, since prostitutes are more likely to be infected than are non-prostitutes.

Other trends

In addition to traditional patterns of prostitute visiting and the taking of minor wives, there are other forms of non-marital sexual relations in Thailand that do not fit easily into either of these categories. It is difficult to gauge the prevalence of premarital intercourse involving non-prostitutes in either historical or contemporary Thailand, but while casual premarital liaisons were probably not widespread, they were not unheard of, even in rural areas (Klausner, 1987a). Klausner reports in this 1972 study of village life in north-eastern Thailand that premarital intercourse was frowned upon unless plans for marriage were made, but some boys would enter into such relations in bad faith to gain access to unmarried girls. The recent rural-to-urban migrants in Ford and Saiprasert's (1993) study report that casual sexual relations are more permissible in their new urban environments than in their rural homes. Research in progress (Knodel *et al.*, 1994) suggests that new patterns of sexual relationships of neither the *mia noi*/patron nor the prostitute/ client type may be emerging in Bangkok society; these new forms seem to be characterized more by companionate relations than by pragmatic ones. It is unclear how prevalent these new types of sexual relations are, or to what extent they vary among the different segments of Thai society. Much more research is needed on these topics.

Socioeconomic differentials

We found in our Chiang Mai survey (VanLandingham, 1993; VanLandingham *et al.*, 1993b) that patterns of sexual practices among men vary quite remarkably by socioeconomic status. Less privileged men begin their sexual lives earlier, are more likely to have ever visited a prostitute, are more likely to have recently visited a prostitute, and are less likely to use condoms consistently than are more privileged men. Several researchers have speculated that sexual practices may vary by region (Nopkesorn *et al.*, 1993; Weniger *et al.*, 1991), but we are unaware of any systematic studies that investigate this hypothesis. HIV prevalence rates certainly appear to be relatively high in the north (Nopkesorn *et al.*, 1993).

Rural–urban differences are also plausible but difficult to discern given the available data. Thailand has traditionally been an agricultural and rural society, and norms and mores regarding sexual behaviour were almost certainly more strict in rural areas than in urban ones. In his 1972 study of village life in northeastern Thailand, Klausner (1987a) reports that overt expressions of physical attraction were forbidden, and, as noted above, Ford and Saiprasert's (1993) respondents report much more sexual freedom in the city than in the rural areas from which they migrated.

However, VanLandingham (1993) found that men who described their background as rural were more likely to be sexually experienced with a prostitute than were those with urban backgrounds, and VanLandingham *et al.*, (1993b) report that men with rural backgrounds were more likely to experience first intercourse before marriage. These studies are hampered by possible selection bias, since only men currently living in an urban area were interviewed. These migrants may be selected for risk-taking or boldness and therefore more likely than most rural men to have experimented with sex. However, Nopkesorn *et al.* (1993) find in their study of conscripts at a northern military base that men coming from rural areas had over double the odds of being seropositive compared with men from municipal areas. While these data should be free of the selection biases described above, they could simply reflect patterns of condom use rather than partner or initiation patterns. It may be that rural men experience first intercourse with a prostitute but then do not subsequently visit prostitutes as regularly as urban men. VanLandingham (1993) did not find men from rural areas to be likely to have *recently* visited a prostitute. Preliminary interviews in our new research (Knodel *et al.*, 1994) have indicated that many rural men will patronize prostitutes only when they are away from their home villages in order to preserve their anonymity. Obviously, much more information is needed on sexual practices in rural areas.

Contemporary Cultural Supports of Male Sexual Risk-Taking

Even though contemporary sexual practices are likely to be changing in response to numerous social forces (the AIDS epidemic being not the least of these) and information on the extent and distribution of various types of sexual patterns and relationships is less detailed than we would like, it is well known that unprotected sex with prostitutes is quite common. It is this aspect of male sexual behaviour on which we will focus in the remainder of the paper. Our contention is that risky sex with prostitutes is consistent with many features of modern Thai culture.

Gender Roles

One relevant aspect of the cultural setting can be broadly labelled as gender role expectations. Thai men and women observe distinct behavioural protocols. Thai women are expected to be reliable and reasonable, responsible for the smooth functioning of the household (Potter, 1976; Yoddumnern-Attig, 1992). Male stereotypes, on the other hand, often encompass impulsiveness and even recklessness. Even though most positions of power in Thai society are held by men, and men are almost always ostensibly in control of the public sphere, the Thai view of gender regards men as quite unstable and unreliable (Phillips, 1987). In view of this, males may feel that they are expected to have varied sexual experiences without worrying about the consequences.

The themes of male impulsiveness and female constancy are common ones in Thai folklore and literature. Mananya's short story 'The wholesome intention of Khunnaaj Saajbua' (Phillips, 1987) illustrates both of these. While the husband is nominally the head of the household, he happily defers to his wife on all matters of importance since he recognizes that he, 'as a typical Thai man', is ultimately incapable of handling the responsibility that goes along with the power to make important decisions:

If I have total freedom I'll forget myself and think I'm greater than I am. So let me be liberated only a little bit, not too much. I'm afraid of myself, quite frankly. (1987: 93)

In fact, there seems to be a consensus on gender role expectations, at least in this household:

Khunnaaj Saajbua has always ruled her husband and son peacefully, and there has never been any attempt to stage a revolution or *coup d'état*. Her government follows the axiom: 'Let them eat well and live well but have little money.' (1987: 91)

'Why do people want so much? Men and money don't get along, anyway. If you let them have a lot of money, they'd...go astray,' she used to say. (1987:91)

Another gender role feature that supports male sexual experimentation is the societal expectation regarding sexual experience before marriage. Expectations that women should be virgins at marriage are still widespread (Prasartkul *et al.*, 1987), but several respondents to the preliminary interviews for the Chiang Mai study stated that men should be sexually experienced so that they would know what to do. Demonstration of heterosexual orientation by having sex with a female prostitute may be an important rite of passage for some groups of Thai men (Erlanger, 1991), and about half of the unmarried respondents to the Chiang Mai survey indicated that they visit prostitutes to learn about sex (VanLandingham *et al.*, 1993b).

Religious teachings inform views of sexuality and gender role expectations; in Thailand, these serve to make sex problematic for male Thai Buddhists. In Buddhist thought, sex is a natural drive, but it is also an obstacle for men who wish to follow the Buddha's path (Keyes, 1986).[3] Monks are forbidden to even touch a woman since this may lead to temptation. Only the most devout of men are ultimately able to renounce their sexuality; many cite their inability to do so as the reason they do not commit their lives to the order (Keyes, 1986). As laymen, they try simply to keep the drive under control as they fulfil their worldly obligations.

The natural state of maleness—that which is undisciplined by the Buddha's precepts—is embodied by the *nag leeng*. The *nag leeng* concept is complex and multifaceted. It often depicts an unsavoury and unscrupulous character, but is also frequently used to describe exemplary personality features such as daring and fearlessness (Keyes, 1989), both of which are key aspects of stereotypical young male behaviour.

Keyes (1989) points out that *nag leeng* also incorporates the concept of 'lady killer', as sexual adroitness is an important feature of this stereotype; he argues further that potency is a key element in the Thai view of masculinity. Mulder (1990) maintains that womanizing is a vehicle for the Thai male's need for public recognition. Whatever the underlying motivations, many Thais seem to accept a norm of male sexual non-restraint. In a recent study by Deemar Corporation (1990), 80 per cent of the males and 74 per cent of the females responded that it was 'natural for men to pursue sex at every opportunity'.

Such a view may underlie a sense of entitlement to sexual variety. Male focus group respondents in the Chiang Mai study asserted they had a need to have sex with multiple partners, and over half of each respondent subgroup in the survey agreed that 'it is natural for men to visit prostitutes'. In fact, there is a popular expression that, although surely exaggerated, gives an indication of how important these behavioural patterns may be to some Thai men: '*glua oat mak gua glua aids*', or 'I'm more afraid of going without than of getting AIDS'.

[3] The most serious obstacle for women is attachment to family, especially children. See Keyes (1984).

This sense of entitlement may extend to unencumbered sexual pleasure as well. Although condom use with prostitutes appears to have increased in recent years, it is still far from universal. And in a country well known for widespread contraceptive use, condoms have never been a popular means of fertility control. Among women discontinuing contraceptive use, spousal disapproval was cited more frequently for condoms than for any other method, including withdrawal (Chayovan *et al.*, 1988). Participants in the preliminary interviews in the Chiang Mai study, when asked why they didn't use condoms with prostitutes, responded by asking, 'Why bother going [if you have to use a condom]?'

Social Interactions

We believe that another set of cultural supports for these patterns arises from a significant degree of social control over individual actions in Thai society, although there are many scholars who would disagree with this assessment. Indeed, one of the most enduring controversies in studies of Thai culture concerns the extent to which social structure (in the form of norms, social groups, etc.) influences individual behaviour. The 'loose structure' school, which was dominant in anthropological studies of Thailand during the 1950s and 1960s,[4] maintained that Thai society was characterized by individualism and a lack of strong social ties and reciprocal obligations. The most important affiliations were described as 'patron–client' relationships, where those of lower status attached themselves to powerful individuals. However, the 'loose structuralists' maintained that these relationships had no moral connotations and would last only as long as they were mutually beneficial. Individuals are basically free to pursue their own interests.

More recently, another group of scholars[5] has contested this characterization of Thai society; some have even argued that the 'loose structure' paradigm was based on atypical villages and cursory observations. This newer school maintains that social forces *do* exert strong influences on individual behaviour via norms, religious beliefs, and attachments to core groups, such as the family and close friends. Neither perspective, however, adequately addresses the dynamics of peer relationships among the Thai, although Mulder (1996) touches on the subject in his most recent work.

Mulder (1996) argues that friendship networks are a critical feature of Thai social life, in part for practical reasons: jobs are often dispensed as favours and are likely to come from close friends. But there are psychological benefits as well. He describes the Thai world view as one that sees interactions with outsiders as unpredictable and dangerous, while one's close friends provide an important sanctuary. According to this view, these friends are a primary source of physical and psychological refuge in an unstable world, and alienation from this core is greatly feared by many Thai:

[4] For examples, see Embree (1950), Hanks (1962), and Phillips (1969).
[5] For examples, see Keyes (1989), Mulder (1990), and Potter (1976).

Such [group] alliances lead to the attitude 'my group, right or wrong' (*phuakkhrai phuak-man*). These groups, from moral to functional, comprise one's moral order and are one's refuges in an unreliable world. (1996:79)

To suffer rejection means that one has to operate in a dreaded, unreliable, external world and to live by oneself. (1996:82)

Mulder postulates a relationship between this fear of the unknown and the renowned Thai capacity for compromise and appeasement. He argues that for the Thai this capacity is often a strategy to neutralize potential threats. Western observers have long been impressed by the Thai ability to negotiate even un-reasonable demands by accommodation (or the appearance of such) as opposed to direct confrontation (Embree, 1950; Klausner, 1987b). Such a strategy is not surprising in a society where smooth social interaction is so highly valued (Komin, 1990). The Thai proclivity for accommodation is found in many social encounters and is one manifestation of *kreengcaj*.

Kreengcaj is a broad concept and permeates many aspects of Thai social life. Haas (1964) translates the term 'to have consideration for; to be reluctant to impose upon.' *Kreengcaj* requires the social participant to accommodate the wishes of others, acquiesce to the needs of the social group, and graciously subordinate one's own personal agenda (Komin, 1990; Mulder, 1990). Since com-munity and social harmony are so highly valued among the Thai, it would follow from Mulder's perspective that pressures to comply with group norms are likely to be much more compelling here than in more individualistic societies. Decisions to go against the group often carry high social and psychological costs, and are thus likely to be avoided whenever possible. 'One does not so much have a "firm belief in [one's] own personality" as a belief in one's group and one's havens (*thiiphyng*)' (Mulder 1990). Thai peer groups may be especially important in the realm of sexuality. Jack Potter (1976) and Sulamith Potter (1977) report in their studies of northern Thai courting rituals that boys never go to court girls alone, but rather go in groups for mutual encouragement and support.

In the Chiang Mai study (VanLandingham *et al.*, 1993a), we found that Thai men often discuss both the visiting of prostitutes and condom use among them-selves, and that the opinion of peers does make a difference. In fact, in multivariate analysis, the perceived peer group norm regarding condom use contributed the most explanatory power to a model of actual condom use with prostitutes, and this influence did not seem to be greatly confounded by selection or covariation processes. While most of this peer influence supported condom use, there was a substantial proportion of men (13–38 per cent of each subgroup) reporting that the peer group norm held that condom use is unnecessary with prostitutes.

The mechanisms of this peer influence are difficult to discern, in part because the respondents themselves often seem to be unaware of the degree to which their own behaviour is affected by that of their friends. In both the in-depth interviews and the focus groups, many young men insisted that individuals were free to participate or not in the brothel visits; but when asked if they would go along on a trip to the brothel if encouraged by a friend, many replied that they almost certainly would. Some justified this by saying they were afraid to let their friend go alone, or simply wished to accommodate (*kreengcaj*) their friend. In the analysis of the survey data, when only those men who felt that peer norms had little or no effect on their condom use behaviour are considered, those who perceived a peer norm supporting condom use were still much more likely to use condoms than were men who perceived a negative or neutral peer norm (VanLandingham 1993).[6]

Personal independence, especially when expressed as a feature of one's masculinity, is a valued trait in Thai male culture (Mulder, 1990). Young men may not realize (or admit) the degree to which they can be influenced by their peers, since this would contradict these images of independence. But the data from the Chiang Mai study indicate that these men have a powerful influence on each other's sexual behaviour, even though this influence may not be apparent to them.

The Thai Weltanschauung

Alongside these preferences for sexual variety, unencumbered intercourse, and smooth social interactions exists a degree of existential insecurity among the Thai (Mulder, 1990). The Thai outside world is an unstable and unpredictable place and presents numerous hazards considered to be outside the individual's control. One's fate results in part from the merit obtained through previous acts. The Buddhist notion of accumulated merit or *karma* is not completely deterministic, since it allows for a fair amount of individual freedom (Keyes, 1989). But Komin (1990) finds in her national attitude survey that many (41–58 per cent) of her Thai respondents attribute good or bad events in their lives to their accumulated *kamma* (*bun wassana* or *kam*), indicating that this concept is an important aspect of the Thai world view.

The degree to which the Thai feel they have personal control over their fate is open to debate, but the widespread practice of presenting offerings to various spirits before undergoing an important task (for example, a job interview or a major examination) clearly indicates that specific outcomes are often considered to be influenced by external forces. Ford and Koetsawang (1991) argue that notions of fatalism (*siang duang*) in Thai society have hampered efforts to promote sexual precautions.

But we find that notions of fatalism or personal control vary dramatically by population subgroup. The Chiang Mai survey includes a question designed to assess the extent to which the respondents feel in control of what happens to them. The question is phrased, 'Do you believe that a person can greatly increase his personal safety by driving carefully, or is personal safety mostly a matter of fate/destiny (*chok chatha*)?' A substantial proportion (23 per cent) of men of low

[6] Subsequent analysis shows that the perceived peer norm regarding condom use is a significant predictor of actual condom use for this subset of men in multivariate analysis including controls for socioeconomic status, AIDS knowledge, risk-taking propensity, alcohol consumption, and attitudes towards condoms.

socioeconomic status (soldiers and labourers) responded that personal safety is mostly or entirely due to fate; these are also the men who are most likely to engage in sexual risk-taking with prostitutes. Men of higher socioeconomic status (students and clerks), on the other hand, are much less likely to respond that personal safety is mostly or entirely due to fate (8 per cent); these are the men least likely to engage in sexual risk-taking with prostitutes. A fatalistic view appears fairly frequently among men of low socioeconomic status, and such views are associated with risky sexual practices for these men.

The Drinking/Prostitute Visitation Ritual

Heavy drinking with friends is often a precursor to visiting a prostitute, and these peer/alcohol dynamics support patterns of sexual risk-taking among Thai men. Intoxication is a widely accepted excuse for many types of irresponsible behaviour in Thai culture (Mulder, 1990), and many of our Chiang Mai focus group respondents cite intoxication as a primary reason for visiting prostitutes. In the corresponding survey, recent heavy drinking was associated with prior and recent visits to prostitutes and inconsistent condom use with prostitutes, all in multivariate analysis (VanLandingham 1993).

Kendall, in this volume, employs Victor Turner's notions of ritual behaviour to help explain sex tourism. We find Turner's perspective useful for explaining Thai prostitute-visiting and drinking as well. Turner (1969) maintains that ritualistic behaviours often incorporate a *liminal* phase, during which the participants are temporarily released from the prevailing rules of the social order. This phase can result in a *communitas*, a new network of relations among the participants, which 'liberates [the participants] from conformity to general norms, though this is necessarily a transient condition if society is to continue to operate in an orderly fashion' (Turner, 1969: 274). Prostitute visitation and the associated heavy drinking that is often involved appear to provide such a 'moment in and out of time' (Turner, 1969: 96) for the participants to escape from the restricting conventions of everyday responsibility.

Fordham (1993) has also applied this paradigm to Thai visiting of prostitutes and to drinking. Fordham, however, sees the Thai drinking/prostitute-visiting ritual as providing an avenue for one-upmanship, competition, and demonstration of merit, even though Turner (1969) describes the ritual process as binding the participants closer together. Turner's original conception is consistent with Mulder's (1990) perception of Thai peer relations being essentially supportive in nature, as well as with our respondents' descriptions of the drinking/prostitute visiting ritual. Chiang Mai focus group respondents report that they visit prostitutes with friends because it is more fun to go with friends, they wish to accommodate their friends' wishes, they are concerned about what might happen to their friends if they don't accompany them, or their friends provide moral support if they are shy or embarrassed. There is no indication that the respondents view the drinking party or prostitute visiting ritual as a vehicle for competition.

Fordham (1993) also argues that Thai men vie for merit by drinking and describing their sexual conquests, but fails to note that such activities are *baap*, or sinful, according to Buddhist precepts. Several respondents in our qualitative study of sexual behaviour in central Thailand (Knodel *et al.*, 1994) describe such illicit activities with a fair amount of ambivalence or guilt, especially if they are married. It is our view that the drinking/prostitute visiting ritual provides an opportunity for irresponsible fun, rather than leading to a struggle for status and merit (even though the implications of the expanding AIDS epidemic may be making these activities more problematic for some Thai men).

Turner (1969) argues further that at the completion of the liminal phase there is a *reaggregation*, at which time the subject is expected to return to a stable state where he must again 'behave in accordance with certain customary norms and ethical standards...'. Viewed in this way, drinking and visiting prostitutes with friends is a singular event that provides Thai men with an opportunity to escape a restrictive social environment.

Conclusions

The persistence of risky sexual patterns in Thailand results in part from a lack of understanding of the risks involved in these practices, and efforts should be made to ensure that men are educated about the potential consequences, especially the implications of unprotected sex with prostitutes. Men of low socioeconomic status seem especially vulnerable to misinformation.

We argue that there are more embedded although perhaps less obvious features of Thai society that also tend to support unsafe sexual practices among Thai men. These cultural features are much more difficult to modify, but still require careful attention to determine their relevance to programmes seeking to promote behavioural change.

Norms supporting risk-taking and heavy alcohol consumption almost certainly hamper efforts to promote responsible sexual behaviour. Future research efforts should explore the avenues of peer influence among Thai men and should also examine how these connections might be manipulated to bring about behavioural change. Peer groups have been found to have an important influence on adolescent male sexual behaviour in the United States (DiClemente, 1990), and we have found strong evidence of significant peer effects among Thai men as well. While peers in both populations may serve as reference groups for appropriate behaviour and as important sources of information about condoms and sexuality, Thai males may depend upon their peer group to a greater degree than do US adolescents and young adults, if Mulder's proposition of relatively high levels of insecurity in the Thai world view is correct.

Peer groups may sometimes foster sexual risk-taking. Peers might discourage condom use with prostitutes by ridiculing a friend for being overcautious or fearful if he advocates condom use. Also, Mulder (1990) argues that for Thai men, the peer group provides an opportunity to escape from the constraints of everyday life; with friends, one can 'be oneself'. Alcohol consumption, which often accompanies visits to prostitutes in this population, could serve to heighten this state of relaxation and encourage irresponsibility or impulsiveness regarding sex. However, many Thai men encourage their friends to act sensibly, and programmes promoting responsible drinking and group accountability for its members' behaviour (for example, the 'friends don't let friends drive drunk' campaign in the United States) could perhaps exploit peer influence even more as a force for positive change. Sports figures and other celebrities could promote values for young men that incorporate responsible sexual behaviour.

A degree of fatalism in Thai culture does not preclude successful prevention efforts. Thai Buddhism also incorporates a strong element of ultimate personal responsibility, and Knodel *et al.* (1987) stress the importance of this cultural trait in their analysis of the rapid fertility decline in Thailand. The message to stress for AIDS prevention would seem to be that the disease is deadly but preventable through responsible individual behaviour.

Our observations have focused on general patterns of Thai male sexual behaviour and the cultural features that support these patterns. Several aspects of Thai sexual culture—for example, double standards of sexual behaviour for men and women, heavy use of alcohol before visiting a prostitute, and strong peer effects among young men—are certainly found outside Thailand, but our aim is to interpret these features within the overall Thai cultural context. Other aspects, such as group visits to prostitutes and liminal qualities of the ritual of the visit, are more culturally specific, and the unique combination of these features requires a culture-specific approach to understanding sexual behaviour in Thailand.

Even within Thailand, important differences exist among subgroups. For example, underprivileged men are more likely to engage in risky sexual practices with prostitutes than are men from more advantaged backgrounds, and fatalistic views may inform attitudes toward sexual risk-taking more for the former group than the latter. Also, regional differences may be important; systematic research should address this issue. Finally, many Thai men do not have sex with prostitutes, and many of those who do are consistent condom users. Both the number of visits to STD clinics and the number of STD-positive diagnoses among men presenting at STD clinics are falling (Thai Ministry of Health, January 1994, personal communication), suggesting that behavioural change may be taking place. It is important to explore the reasons why many Thai men do *not* fit the stereotypical patterns we have sketched, and why many have been willing and able to adapt their behaviour to the new realities posed by the HIV epidemic.

However, our recent research (Knodel *et al.*, 1994) strongly suggests that many Thai men continue to engage in risky sexual practices. Furthermore, Havanon *et al.* (1993) find that many of the men in their study who had multiple prostitute partners had non-prostitute partners as well, and many of these men who mix partners do not use condoms consistently with any of them. Thus the AIDS epidemic and efforts to combat it will undoubtedly influence many forms of sexual relations in this country for years to come.

REFERENCES

Bamber, S. D., Hewison, K. J., and Underwood, P. J. (1993), 'A history of sexually transmitted diseases in Thailand: policy and politics'. *Genitourinary Medicine*, 69, 148–57.

Boonchalaksi, W., and Guest, P. (1994), *Prostitution in Thailand*. Institute for Population and Social Research, Nakhon Pathom.

Brummelhuis, H. ten. (1993), 'The social and cultural context of the AIDS epidemic in Thailand: Do we need a Thai theory of prostitution?' Paper presented at the Fifth International Conference on Thai Studies, London.

Chayovan, N., Kamnuansilpa, P., and Knodel, J. (1988), *Thailand Demographic and Health Survey*. Institute for Resource Development, Columbia, Maryland.

Deemar Corporation (1990), *Presentations of Findings. Knowledge, attitudes and practices. Study on AIDS in Urban Thailand*. Bangkok.

DiClemente, R. J. (1990), 'The emergence of adolescents as a risk group for human immunodeficiency virus infection'. *Journal of Adolescent Research*, 5, 7–17.

Embree, J. F. (1950), 'Thailand: a loosely structured social system'. *American Anthropologist*, 52, 181–3.

Erlanger, S. (1991), 'A plague awaits'. *New York Times*, 14 July.

Ford, N., and Koetsawang, S. (1991), 'The social context of the transmission of HIV in Thailand'. *Social Science and Medicine*, 3(4), 405–14.

—— and Saiprasert, S. (1993), 'Destinations unknown: the gender construction and changing nature of the sexual lifestyles of Thai youth'. Paper presented at the Fifth International Conference on Thai Studies, London, July.

Fordham, G. (1993), 'Northern Thai male culture and the assessment of HIV risk'. Paper presented at the IUSSP Seminar on AIDS Impact and Prevention in the Developing World: The Contribution of Demography and Social Science. Annecy, France, 5–9 December, 1993.

Fox, M. G. (1960), 'Problem of prostitution in Thailand'. *Social Service in Thailand*. Department of Public Welfare, Bangkok.

Haas, M. (1964), *Thai-English Student's Dictionary*. Stanford University Press, Stanford, California.

Hanks, L. M. (1962), 'Merit and power in the Thai social order'. *American Anthropologist*, 64(6), 1,247–61.

Havanon, Napaporn, Bennett, A., and Knodel, J. (1993), 'Sexual Networking in Provincial Thailand'. *Studies in Family Planning*, 24(1), 1–17.

Keyes, C. F. (1984), 'Mother or mistress but never a monk: Buddhist notions of female gender in rural Thailand'. *American Ethnologist*, 11(1), 223–387.

—— (1986), 'Ambiguous gender: male initiation in a northern Thai Buddhist society'. In C. Bynum, S. Harrell and P. Richman (eds), *Gender and Religion: On the Complexity of Symbols*. Beacon Press, Boston, Massachusetts.

—— (1989) *Thailand: Buddhist Kingdom as Modern Nation-State*. Westview Press, Boulder, Colorado.

Klausner, W. J. (1987a), 'Sex and morality in a northeastern Thai village: ideal and practice.' In W. J. Klausner (ed.), *Reflections on Thai Culture*. Siam Society, Bangkok.

—— (1987b) 'The drunkard: challenge and response.' In W. J. Klausner (ed.), *Reflections on Thai Culture*. Siam Society, Bangkok.

Knodel, J., Chamratrithirong, A., and Debavalya, N. (1987), *Thailand's Reproductive Revolution*. University of Wisconsin Press, Madison, Wisconsin.

Knodel, J., VanLandingham, M., Saengtiechai, Chanpen, and Pramualratana, Anthony (1994), 'The social influence of primary female partners and male peers on male sexual behavior in Thailand'. Unpublished ms.

Komin, S. (1990), *Psychology of the Thai People*. National Institute of Development Administration, Bangkok.

La Loubère, S. de. (1986), *The Kingdom of Siam*. Oxford University Press, Singapore. (First published in 1693).

Mettarikanond, D. (1983), *Prostitution and Policies of Thai Government during 1868–1969*. Thesis submitted to Graduate School, Chulalongkorn University (in Thai). Cited in Boonchalaksi and Guest, 1994.

Muecke, M. A. (1984), 'Make money not babies: changing status markers of Northern Thai women'. *Asian Survey*, 24(4), 459–70.

—— (1990), 'The AIDS prevention dilemma in Thailand'. *Asian and Pacific Population Forum*, 4(4), 2–27.

Mulder, N. (1996), *Inside Thai Society: Interpretations of Everyday Life*. Amsterdam: Pepin Press.

Nopkesorn, T., Sungkorom, S., and Sornlum, R. (1991), *HIV Prevalence and Sexual Behavior among Thai Men Aged 21 in Northern Thailand*. Thai Red Cross Society, Bangkok.

Nopkesorn, T., Mastro, T. D., Sangkharomya, S., Sweat, M., Singharaj, P., Limpakarn-janarat, K., Gayle, H. D., and Weniger, B. G. (1993), 'HIV-1 infection in young men in northern Thailand'. *AIDS*, 7, 1,233–39.

Phillips, H. (1969), 'The scope and limits of the "loose structure" concept'. In H. D. Evers (ed.), *Loosely Structured Social Systems: Thailand in Comparative Perspective*. Southeast Asia Studies, Cultural Report Series 17. Yale University, New Haven, Connecticut.

—— (1987), *Modern Thai Literature*. University of Hawaii Press, Honolulu, Hawaii.

Phongpaichit, P. (1982), *From Peasant Girls to Bangkok Masseuses*. International Labour Organization, Geneva.

Potter, J. M. (1976), *Thai Peasant Social Structure*. University of Chicago Press, Chicago, Illinois.

Potter, S. H. (1977), *Family Life in a Northern Thai Village*. University of California Press, Berkeley, California.

Prasartkul, P., Chamratrithirong, A., Bennett, A., Jitwatanapataya, L., and Isarabhakdi, P. (1987), *Rural Adolescent Sexuality and the Determinants of Provincial Urban Premarital Adolescent Sex*. IPSR Publication 113. Mahidol University, Bangkok.

Rhodes, R. (1991), 'Death in the candy store.' *Rolling Stone*, 28 November 1991, 62–71.

Sittitrai, W., Phanuphak, P., Barry, J., and Brown, T. (1992), *Thai Sexual Behavior and Risk of HIV Infection*. Thai Red Cross Society, Bangkok, and Chulalongkorn University, Bangkok.

Sittitrai, W., Phanuphak, P., Barry, J., Sabalying, M., and Brown, T. (1991), *Survey of Partner Relations and Risk of HIV Infection in Thailand*. Seventh International Conference on AIDS, Florence.

Turner, V. (1969), *The Ritual Process*. Aldine Publishing Company, Chicago, Illinois.

—— (1974), *Dramas, Fields, and Metaphors*. Cornell University Press, Ithaca, New York.

VanLandingham, M. (1993), *Two Perspectives on Risky Sexual Practices among Northern*

Thai Males: The Health Belief Model and the Theory of Reasoned Action. University Microfilms, Ann Arbor, Michigan.

VanLandingham, M., Suprasert, S., Sittitrai, W., and Vaddhanaphuti, C. (1993a) 'An application of two theoretical perspectives to an analysis of condom use among prostitute patrons in northern Thailand: the health belief model and the theory of reasoned action'. Paper presented at the Annual Meeting of the Population Association of America, Cincinnati, Ohio.

——— ——— ——— ——— and Grandjean, N. (1993b), 'Sexual activity among never-married men in Northern Thailand'. *Demography*, 30(3), 297–313.

——— ——— ——— ——— ——— (1994), 'The relationship between AIDS-related knowledge and risky sexual practices among northern Thai men: a factor analysis'. Paper presented at the Annual Meeting of the American Sociological Association, Los Angeles.

Weniger, B., Limpakarnjanarat, K., Ungchusak, K., Thanprasertsuk, S., Choopanya, K., Vanichseni, S., Uneklabh, T., Thongcharoen, P., and Wasi, C. (1991), 'The epidemiology of HIV infection and AIDS in Thailand'. *AIDS*, 5, S71–S85.

Wyatt, D. K. (1984), *Thailand: A Short History*. Yale University Press, New Haven, Connecticut.

Yoddumnern-Attig, B. (1992), 'Thai family structure and organization: changing roles and duties in historical perspective'. In B. Yoddumnern-Attig, K. Richter, A. Soonthorndhada, C. Sethaput, and A. Pramualratana (eds), *Changing Roles and Statuses of Women in Thailand: A Documentary Assessment*. Mahidol University, Institute for Population and Social Research, Salaya, Thailand.

Zimmerman, C. (1931), *Siam Rural Economic Survey 1930–31*. Bangkok Times Press, Bangkok. Cited in Bamber *et al*. 1993.

9 Homophobia and the Ethnoscape of Sex Work in Rio de Janeiro

PATRICK LARVIE

Urban Ethnoscapes: The 'Red Light' Districts of Rio de Janeiro

The ethnographic 'scene' of cosmopolitan urban centres like Rio de Janeiro is perhaps characterized more by the rapidity of social change, the physical movement of people, and constant shifts in the directions and modalities of cultural, political, and ethnic affiliation than by anything else. Exactly what constitutes the object of study for ethnographers interested in 'culture', 'subcultures', or 'local' knowledge becomes increasingly difficult to define and operationalize in such contexts. The application of ethnographic methodologies to the study of populations in movement necessarily requires a redefinition of some basic concepts in anthropology (Appadurai, 1990, 1991; Abu-Lughod, 1990, 1991). Ethnographic research in urban areas must take into account the scales of distance and speed at which change occurs without losing sight of the social and cultural institutions which serve to ground these shifts in the activities of everyday life. The 'red light' districts of Rio de Janeiro are linked to globalized systems of commerce and migration and at the same time they are embedded within the institutions of urban life in Brazil. In the case of male sex workers, homophobia is one of the cultural elements which links social and physical spaces, structuring movement between and within them. Sex workers in Rio de Janeiro live and work in a space which is bounded as much by social and cultural practices that traverse national boundaries as by demarcations of neighbourhoods, cities, or countries. This essay will address the relationship of individual sex workers, male prostitutes in the cases I will examine, with a complex of cultural systems which simultaneously instigates and curtails their movement both within and across national borders.

Appadurai has used the term *ethnoscape* to refer to the '. . . landscape of persons who make up the shifting world in which we live: tourists, immigrants, refugees, exiles, guests workers, and other moving groups and persons [which] constitute an essential feature of the world. . .' (1991: 192). The sex industries of the world's major metropolitan centres, especially those which are destinations for both tourists and business travellers, present complicated and important cases for understanding the impact of global processes on local social and cultural institutions. Such theoretical work is necessary for understanding what, if any, importance these nodes of commercialized sex have with respect to the current AIDS pandemic. If ethnographic research is to be useful at all in halting the spread of HIV, exactly what is meant by 'local' knowledge and practices must be made explicit, and put into terms which relate to larger social and cultural processes (see Herdt and Boxer, 1991). This work seems particularly important given that prostitutes have been the focus of AIDS researchers' attention, often for reasons which seem to suggest that commercial sex transactions are, *per se*, generative of risk or disease (Alexander, 1987). In the case of Brazil, prostitutes have been identified as a potential source of HIV infection for the 'general public' (see Cortes, *et al.*, 1989) and blamed for tarnishing the country's already bleak image in the international tourist industry. Conclusions derived from such research presume that sex workers constitute a demographic group that is socially separate from other groups, that they pose a threat to non-sex workers' health, and that they are therefore logical targets for AIDS related interventions. These are assertions that I will attempt to challenge here, with a view to re-formulating the concept of a globalized sex industry.

Mass media technology makes cities such as Bangkok, Rio, New York, Madrid, or Miami practically as close as the nearest video store to media consumers world-wide. Such cities are not only represented as exotic or glamorous locales for media consumers to enjoy at home, they are also presented as tourist destinations for those with the means to travel. The increasing mobility of people with access to money for travel, the influx of people from rural and suburban areas into the centres of major Brazilian cities (as in other parts of the developing world), and the involvement of programme officials and social scientists concerned with the AIDS pandemic create an ethnoscape of sex work in Rio de Janeiro in which we might find, at any given moment, virtually anyone from any part of the world who has access to enough capital to be mobile. Seen in this way, the sex industry of Rio—or at least that segment of it that involves both prostitution and tourism— is not, in itself, constitutive of a singular culture or subculture. Those who particip- ate in it might be said to belong to any number of social groups which intersect in significant ways with the category 'sex worker'. The sex industry of Rio, as in other large cities throughout the world, serves as a social, cultural, and economic frame within which multiple groups interact. Commercial sex transactions pre- sume at least some degree of social distance between purchaser and provider (de Zalduondo, 1991). It is precisely this social distance which permits consumers of sex services the anonymity necessary to make such transactions possible; without it, consumers might be stigmatized as adulterers, as homosexuals, or as threats to the social order. In the case of business and tourist centres like Rio, the social dis- tance between consumer and providers of sex services is heightened in important ways. The disparities between wealthy local residents and tourists and lower class sex workers is not just a demographic feature of commercialized sex transactions, it is one of the primary logics of the sex industry of Rio. Eroticized as 'exotic', 'tropical', and 'Latin,' the lower- and working-class prostitutes' appeal to wealthy clients—foreign and domestic—depends on this social disparity, both real and imagined. The logic of commercial sex transactions in Rio, as in other global loca- tions, depends on contact between multiple and disparate groups.

I take the sex industry of Rio de Janeiro to be a geographically specific instance of a global network of people involved in multiple processes of migration, in different segments of the sex industry (whether as consumers, intermediaries, providers, researchers or managers) and with stakes in that industry that are largely determined by their social and geographic positions. Taking the sex industry of Rio de Janeiro as a local instance of a global process is important for understanding the context in which the movement of prostitutes within Brazil, and from Brazil to countries in the First World, occurs. The space of sex work in Rio is, in many ways, contiguous with the sex industries of Milan, Madrid, Paris, Miami, and New York, as well as with the social institutions of regional urban centres and rural areas of Brazil. Movement through this global space of the sex industry may include the traversal of regional and national boundaries, but may involve the crossing of relatively fewer frontiers of 'subcultural' practice.

The concept of a globalized sex industry presupposes that there is something familiar to clients, intermediaries, and prostitutes about the set of practices and beliefs—implicit or explicit—that constitute a commercial sex transaction. This also presupposes that this familiarity traverses national boundaries, incorporating certain kinds of prostitution within an increasingly globalized framework. What I wish to suggest is that there is a set of practices and beliefs that link individual actors within this globalized sex industry, making the commercial sex transactions both available and comprehensible to buyers, sellers, and intermediaries, whether they are in Rio de Janeiro, New York City, or Milan. I do not wish to argue that important differences do not exist across regional, social, or national lines; they clearly do (see deZalduondo, 1991). I do wish to foreground discussion of 'local' particularities with this concept of a globalized sex industry which targets international travellers as a primary market and exploits images of the 'exotic' sexual enticements of the Third World to attract paying customers.

Rio's prostitution districts function as a local nexus of this global network, and the movement of people through and within it is almost immediately apparent, to the casual tourist or to the trained scientist. It is also clear that the movement across this geographic space is multi-directional, though unevenly so. Rio occupies a specific and key position within this network as a point of departure for sex workers trying to get to cities in Western Europe and the United States, and as a destination for those leaving rural areas or regional capitals for Rio de Janeiro. Such movement requires access to capital, especially when it involves crossing national borders. Brazilians must meet difficult requirements to gain a visa for entry into some European countries and into the US and Canada. Even where visas are not required, Brazilians are often asked to prove their financial solvency to immigration officials upon arrival. The threat of being denied entry and sent back to Brazil is a very real one, especially for darker skinned Brazilians or for those whose gender identity is non-conventional. For those arriving in the city, Rio de Janeiro offers sex workers access to a relatively larger market than can be found in smaller cities of Brazil and also affords contact with foreigners which may facilitate travel to the US or Europe. While relatively less capital is required to move to or to live in Rio, such a move still presumes access to at least enough money to live and work, as well as contacts with networks of people involved in the local sex industry.

In a different way, Rio de Janeiro is a destination for tourists and business travellers, and as a centre of international development work. Rio de Janeiro has been promoted as a tropical paradise with a uniquely sensual population to tourist markets worldwide, and has a reputation—deserved or undeserved—for being one of the capitals of the world's sex industry. As a major urban centre in one of the so-called developing countries, Rio is also populated by a different kind of traveller, the development worker. Hundreds of development workers, including many social scientists from the First World involved in projects related to the prevention of AIDS and other sexually transmitted diseases, inhabit the city as semi-permanent residents or intermittently as representatives of agencies who send them to Brazil to monitor local projects. These programme officials and social scientists often play important roles in the sex industry, as they may be involved in the development of public health policies and interventions independent of or in collaboration with Brazilian officials and, on occasion, with sex workers themselves. The research they conduct and the services they provide affect prostitutes, clients, and intermediaries directly and indirectly. In this way, Rio is an important site for contact between the First and Third Worlds, between the cosmopolitan and the provincial, between people who are highly mobile and those whose movement is highly restricted, and between institutionally enfranchised and marginalized groups.

Homophobia is one of the cultural elements which helps to link these various social groups and institutions which traverse national borders. Homophobia plays an important role in structuring the lives of those males who engage in sex work and move from rural or suburban to urban areas of Brazil and, increasingly, to cities of Western Europe and the United States. By homophobia, I mean the set of social and cultural practices which both publicly mark as 'other' and penalize those with same-sex erotic preferences. As a term, homophobia can be somewhat slippery. It can suggest that the *phobia* of same-sex erotic preferences and social relations operates as an individual characteristic, much as other psychologically defined phobias (Blumenfeld, 1992). I wish to avoid this use of the term here, and instead focus on normative belief systems which define heterosexuality as the only publicly acceptable form of social relations and erotic preferences. In this way, homophobia functions at the collective rather than individual level, much as other forms of social stigma. Homophobia, then, targets those excluded from the category 'straight', and from the institutions related to the heterosexually defined family. By 'straight', I mean a social identity which marks the actor as *not* belonging to groups socially stigmatized for their erotic preferences and practices. The erotic preferences and practices of those who pass as straight may or may not coincide with their public presentation of self. Straightness is, in this sense, an index of social and cultural capital which retards the stigma and punishment associated with sexual marginality. Homophobia is one of the principle logics which defines sexual minorities, and as an analytic concept is indispensable in addressing the phenomenon of male prostitution. Prostitutes of all kinds and especially those who are not straight are targets for homophobia, a type of hatred closely linked to misogyny. The concept of homophobia is key to understanding how patterns of migration have developed for males involved in the sex industry in Brazil. The vast majority of paying customers for these males are also male, and the stigma associated with same sex interactions plays an important role in their negotiation of social relationships both in and outside of the sex industry (Perlongher, 1987).

Homophobia informs the institutions of surveillance, control, and punishment which affect the everyday lives of all Brazilians, whether or not they play a direct role in the sex industry. Institutions such as the church, the heterosexual family, organized medicine, and the police all exert some form of control—formal or in-formal, codified in laws, catechisms, or institutional procedures—in enforcing the existing social and cultural system which stigmatizes and punishes those publicly marked as having unacceptable or undesirable sexual identities. In this context, homophobia functions as a set of mechanisms which simultaneously minoritizes and persecutes those publicly marked as not-straight.[1] For instance, in the US, the juridical and religious institution of marriage categorically denies legal and social privileges to lesbians and gay men by locating them outside the realm of the 'family' (Weston, 1991). The set of social relations that denies the status of 'family' to non-straights also makes possible their persecution by condoning and promot-ing homophobic violence against those marked as threats to the family or as threats to a society said to be comprised of families. Examples of this from the United States include the expulsion of lesbian or gay youths from their homes and national-level campaigns to identify and imprison adult homosexuals (Boyer, 1989; Chauncey, 1993). In Brazil, homophobic violence is equally prevalent, though perhaps less well documented. Such violence has been linked to the move-ment of people from their natal homes to the centers of large cities, and to the cities of the United States (Brooke, 1993). An examination of homophobia is use-ful in linking the 'subculture' of male prostitutes to the larger societies of Brazil and the other countries to which they migrate, and in understanding how this putative subculture has come to be configured as both demographically discrete and as a threat to public health in the popular news media and in the social science literature.

During 1991 and 1992, I collaborated on two research projects in Rio de Janeiro as preliminary fieldwork for my PhD. The first project focused on the risks of 'street children' for HIV infection; the second was an evaluation study of an AIDS

---

[1] Here, the term 'straight' refers to a relationship with cultural and material power, not a set of erotic preferences. Men who have sex with other men but are able to maintain their public identities as unmarked males, for example, are clearly 'straight' in this sense. The terms 'lesbian' and 'gay' refer not only to same-sex erotic preferences, but also to cultural and political affiliations and identifications. I do not wish to combine these conceptual categories; to be marked as not-straight is clearly not the same as to be 'gay.' See Herdt (1992) for further discussion of how these identity labels relate to broader social and political processes in the United States.

prevention programme for male prostitutes. My work in Rio provided occasion for a kind of participant observation in which I played multiple roles. These included government bureaucrat, public health expert, pimp, policeman, journalist, social scientist, and gay tourist from the First World. My research provided opportunities to examine both the role of homophobia in structuring migration patterns, as well as the connections between the 'subcultures' of two marginalized groups and the governmental, non-governmental, and academic institutions which study them and make recommendations for curtailing the spread of HIV between these groups and the 'general public.' Drawing on this ethnographic research, I will show how the lives of lower-class male prostitutes are strongly affected by the homophobia that permeates the major institutions of Brazilian social and cultural life and by the homophobic violence which simultaneously instigates and curtails their movement within and across specific geographic regions. At the same time, homophobia influences some of the concepts AIDS-related research draws upon by suggesting certain interventions related to AIDS and sex work.

Media representations of prostitution in Brazil often identify sex workers as sexual 'others' who are uniquely available to public health management and control. This style of representation creates a set of linkages and boundaries between sex workers and the 'general population' of Brazil. For example, on 13 January 1993, the Brazilian newspaper *Hoje em Dia* reported the following news item:

Eighty three per cent of the hustlers in Rio de Janeiro are using condoms. Four years ago, this number did not exceed 9%. The use of condoms was such that only five cases of AIDS were reported among 'michês'[2] in Rio since 1989.

These results made 'Projeto Pegação' [an AIDS prevention programme for hustlers] the only one in Brazil to be recommended by the World Health Organization.

Lúcio Neves [of Embratur, the Brazilian National Tourist Commission] is more than happy to emphasize these data to attract tourists from all over the world and to help change the tarnished image of Rio de Janeiro.[3]

What appears as yet another news item that conflates the control of prostitutes' bodies with the management of the AIDS epidemic reveals much about the ways in which members of sexual subcultures—here represented as 'hustlers'—are configured in relation to public health officials, the 'general public', and the national symbols of Brazil. The news item describes an imaginary world whose existence depends on the readers' complicity in marking and stigmatizing sexual undesirables. The article also demonstrates an almost religious faith in science, the media, and the governmental and non-governmental agencies that work to

---

[2] The term *michê* in this context is roughly equivalent to the English term 'hustler.' As in the United States, most hustlers trade on their ability to perform 'straight' male identities for their male clients. For a study of *michês*, see Perlongher (1987); for more on gender performativity, see Butler (1991).

[3] 'Quinze Minutos: Vai pro trono', in *Hoje em Dia*, (Belo Horizonte, MG), 13 January 1993. Translation is mine. I am greatly indebted to Ranulfo Cardoso Jr. of the Institute for Higher Studies in Religion in Rio de Janeiro and to Jared Braiterman of Stanford University for passing this article along to me. My conversations with Jared Braiterman, in particular, were of great help in writing the present paper.

control the AIDS epidemic. Some of the most peculiar features of this world suggested by the news item include: the ability to identify and count the hustlers working in Rio in order to conduct a scientific survey, the discreteness of these hustlers as a demographic group, the accessibility of this group to the programme officials who ask questions about their condom use and who count their AIDS diagnoses, and a public health surveillance system capable of defining AIDS and counting the diagnoses relating to this definition, within a group that might be assumed to have relatively little access to health care. One of the most striking features of this account is that it suggests that the public relations problems that have befallen Rio's tourist industry can be corrected by informing foreigners that the bodies of the city's male prostitutes pose little risk to their health.

In this by now familiar representation of AIDS and prostitution, the sex workers themselves are visible only through the eyes of the programme officials credited with the effective management of prostitutes' bodies and only in relation to the potential threat these bodies pose to non-sex workers. That the report carries with it the authority of a quasi-official public health programme and an endorsement by the World Health Organization helps to situate this fictive sexual landscape squarely within the realm of science and common sense. That the article seemed plausible to the editors of the newspaper also attests to the prevalence of homophobia: the 'otherness' of the hustlers who are counted, diagnosed, blamed, and reformed rests in part on the assumption that their sexualities produce visible differences which leave them open to such forms of management. The stigma involving the commercial/homosexual quality of their sexual relations is represented here by the availability of prostitutes and their apparent willingness to be co-opted for scientific management techniques in the service of public health. The fictive world described by the article affords heretofore unthinkable levels of surveillance and control over sexual others and effectively links such controls to the fate of Brazil. What makes this news item even more unusual is the investment of the press, programme officials, Embratur, and representatives of the World Health Organization in the control and promotion of male prostitutes as a national resource of Brazil. In this account, the hustlers of Rio de Janeiro play a key role in the symbolics of the nation. Their bodies may pose a threat to it, contributing to the 'tarnished image' of Rio de Janeiro and scaring away foreign tourists, or they may attract those very tourists with the availability of their healthy bodies and news of their condom use and low incidence of AIDS. What goes missing in this news item are the links between the worlds of programme officials, foreign tourists, social scientists, and those who work in the sex industry as prostitutes. One crucial element in this account is the homophobia of the society which at once attempts to offer male prostitutes to foreign visitors as a kind of tourist attraction and to control those bodies through elaborate mechanisms that locate the risk that the AIDS epidemic poses to Brazil in the sex industry of the country's premiere tourist destination.

One of Rio's most famous neighbourhoods, Copacabana, is the site of a beach that is one of the city's most important tourist destinations and the centre of the segment of the sex industry that caters to tourists and to wealthier residents of the city. It is within this space that contains tourist pleasures and, at least in theory, public health dangers that the worlds of sex workers, tourists, wealthy residents of the city, and public health workers converge. As such, it was the site for much of my field work in Rio. It is to a description of this neighbourhood, and of the lives of some of the sex workers that I met there, that I now turn.

Avenida Atlântica is a spectacular avenue which separates Copacabana's most chic apartment buildings and hotels from the legendary beach. While the neighbourhood itself is socioeconomically mixed, the ostentatious apartments along the avenue and the presence of luxury hotels and foreign tourists along the beach give the impression that the neighbourhood is much wealthier than it really is. The aura of wealth and glamour associated with Copacabana as a beach, as a residential area for the privileged, and as a tourist destination for both wealthy foreigners and Brazilians is central to the context in which prostitution occurs in this part of the city. This image of Copacabana, produced and circulated through picture postcards, on television, in tourist campaigns, and in movies does not correspond to the diversity of its inhabitants, who include some of the wealthiest and most powerful as well as the poorest and most disenfranchised residents of the city. While foreign tourists comprise a significant number of prostitutes' clients in this area (and perhaps provide a disproportionate share of their earnings), the majority of clients are Brazilian, even at the peak of the tourist season. Though sex work in this neighbourhood has strong links to tourism, both foreign and national, it is not entirely dependent upon it. Many of the clients who procure the services of the prostitutes are residents of the city, and many of them reside in the middle and upper-middle class neighbourhoods located along the beach front on the city's south side.

For the purposes of this paper, I will divide male prostitution into two basic categories: that of the hyper-masculine *michês* (hustlers) and that of the ultra-feminine *travestis* (very roughly, transvestites or drag queens). This conceptual division is not the only one possible and may not even be the most useful in describing the division of gender roles among these sex workers. *Michês* may go to such great pains to display their virility that their performances cast doubt upon that very attribute. Often, their masculinity is performed with a level of theatricality that forces the observer to see it as an artifact, as a production mediated through the exaggeration of conventional symbols of masculinity. The performance of straightness can reach a level which clearly identifies the performer as something of an impostor, as an actor who is clearly not-straight. *Travestis* engage in a complex simulation of femininity rather than a mere imitation of it (Braiterman, 1992). Their exaggeration of feminine attributes while working on the streets or in nightclubs not only borders on the phallic, but depends upon it. Their clients seek them out because of their gender performance and their genitalia, not in spite of it. *Travestis* do not compete with biological female prostitutes for the same client base; their simulation of femininity is marked by their ability to perform 'male' sexual acts for their customers. For this reason, their performance of femininity is often strikingly masculine and is markedly different from that of female prostitutes.

The prostitution districts of Rio, including the geographically bounded sections of Copacabana where street prostitution and private clubs operate, provide a unique space for these types of gender performativity and the commerce associated with them. Copacabana is a site where new arrivals from provincial capitals or the rural areas seek out opportunities for moving upwards by making money, leaving the country, and finding sex with up-scale clients. This is the site where experienced erotic performers look to be hired by the owners of foreign clubs, where transvestites work to make enough money or find the right connections to go to Europe, and where tourists, businessmen, and city residents look for new and 'exotic' sexual adventures. Males working as prostitutes in Rio de Janeiro comprise a relatively small but diverse group. They may work full time, part time, or sporadically; they may work with the enthusiasm of dedicated professionals who thoroughly enjoy their work or as victims of coercive schemes that enslave those with few options for earning a living in a society that penalizes those who engage in same sex or commercial sex transactions. They may be marked as 'queer' for their gender non-conformity, or they may viewed by society as having a sexuality that is, by virtue of their involvement in sex work, essentially predatory and dangerous to the 'family' and the nation.[4] They occupy positions of relative disadvantage in multiple hierarchies of power: they may be 'provincial' newcomers to the city, adolescents who have been thrown out of their biological families for engaging in homosexual acts, or people marked as 'queer' who are sometimes able to work the streets at night but are unwelcome anywhere during the day. They are often those who have been deported from Europe or the United States either upon entry or following contact with the police. Frequently, they are from working- and lower-class suburbs or slums, engaging in micro-level processes of migration within the city to seek out opportunities for money, mobility, and sex. They almost always have less access to cultural capital than do their clients: darker skinned, less well educated, and without the kinds of resources that would insulate them from conflicts with their biological families and trouble with the police. Their positions as prostitutes are liminal, somewhere between 'legitimate citizens' and criminals[5], and to the extent that they are visible as either prostitutes or as non-straights they are targets for harassment by the institutions that are the

---

[4] The Brazilian magazines *Veja* ('O Pacto de Sangue', 13 January 1993) and *Manchete* ('Daniela Perez: Uma Tragedia de Corpo e Alma', 9 January 1993) both offered interesting explanations for the murder of a young female soap opera star by a male co-star. The actions of Guilherme de Pádua, who confessed to the killing, were 'explained', according to the magazines' reports, by the fact that he had worked as a stripper and a male prostitute. In this instance, the sexuality of a *michê* was defined in terms that related avarice and predation to lower-class homoeroticism. Such reasoning suggests that such desires are often realized through the pernicious practice of male prostitution and, as in the case of Guillherme de Pádua, cold-blooded murder.

[5] Prostitution is not a crime in Brazil, though those who engage in sex for money transactions are frequently subjected to police brutality including demands for money and free sex. They are also targets of violence from the residents of the areas in which they work or from public health authorities who equate sex work with the spread of sexually transmitted disease.

primary perpetrators of homophobic violence: the police, the church, the hetero-sexual family and, often, public health authorities. It is at this level of local, day-to-day experience that the homophobia of social and cultural institutions structures and limits occupational, geographic, and social mobility. As I learned over the course of my research, the quotidian oppression of these prostitutes, and particularly of those who are publicly marked as not-straight, reveals much about the social institutions that simultaneously isolate and link them to the larger soci-ety of Brazil and of the countries to which they migrate.

Homophobic violence in the home was the most common reason prostitutes gave me for moving to Rio. Such violence typically occurred after biological family members discovered that a son had engaged in a homosexual act. If that son was able to control the circulation of this discrediting information, the choice to remain within the natal family and town remained open. This was often the case for hustlers I met who lived in distant suburbs or neighbourhoods, but travelled to Copacabana to work the beach. They were able to return home when they wished. However, if that son was unable to control the information and had already been labelled as 'queer' within the family or within the town, the number of choices diminished significantly. One option was to continue to tolerate violence at home and endure the oppression of homophobic townspeople. The other option, for those with access to money for travel and connections with friends or relatives in cities, was to leave. Many of the prostitutes that I met left home knowing that there were neighbourhoods in São Paulo, Rio, or other large Brazilian cities where they could work as hustlers, and often arrived with connections to networks of people who helped them find such work. Frequently, these connections were brokered through slightly older peers who had been left under similar circumstances.

Ties to home and family did not disappear entirely for the vast majority of prostitutes I met who moved to Rio from distant cities or states. Many described their exit from their towns as highly motivated 'moves' rather than as irreversible expulsions. Their families frequently had knowledge of their activities in the cities, and even seemed to count on the 'red light' districts of Rio and São Paulo to pro-vide a space where their sons could capitalize on their sexual preferences. One of the ways in which both the prostitutes and the heterosexual families they leave count on the existence of these bounded geographic spaces and social networks is through the circulation of money. It is not unusual for male prostitutes working in Rio to make substantial and regular financial contributions to the very families that threw them out. Such remittances frequently figure as one of the strongest and most enduring links that sex workers are able to maintain with their biological families. Being able to send money 'home' enables some of he sex workers to con-tinue to feel a sense of belonging to the families and to the towns which they felt obliged to leave.

Over the course of my fieldwork, I formally interviewed over 60 prostitutes, and came to meet many others. There is no typical trajectory that would link all or even most of the sex workers I met; their relationships with the sex industry were highly diverse. There were, however, people whose life stories seemed particularly illustrative of the ways in which the social and cultural institutions in which they all participated impacted on the lives of those marked as not-straight. One of these people was André, who was introduced to me shortly after his arrival in Rio. André was fourteen years old when he first came to Rio from a small town in the state of Minas Gerais. His first sexual experiences were with other boys who lived in his neighbourhood, which is not unusual (Parker, 1991). What was atypical was that word got out that he enjoyed sex with other males. His father confronted him about it, but André refused to give up his sexuality to please him. At one point, his father tried to shoot him but missed. This was not the first confrontation he had had with his father, but it was the most violent, and afterwards André felt he had no choice but to leave home.

He went to Rio to look up acquaintances who were already there, and began turning tricks in Copacabana, a beach neighbourhood where he felt sure he could find wealthy tourists from the First World. André had also hoped to learn to become a *travesti*, which required considerable capital as well as contacts with people who could be of help in this process of gender transformation. Turning tricks was a way of earning money while he made these connections. When I first met André, he had only recently become 'Andrea,' and was in the early stages of the development of her feminine beauty. Life and work in Rio had not been easy, but Andrea seemed to be managing well under the circumstances. In the year since she'd come to Rio life had been exceptionally difficult. She had lived on the street, and had been kept in the home of a European man who ran a charity for 'street kids', even though that charity was housed in a building located far away from his private home. She finally ended up living in a crowded apartment where she paid exorbitant rents in exchange for sleeping space in one of the few apartment buildings in Copacabana that tolerated prostitutes. Among the worst of problems she had encountered were the recurrent confrontations with the police. Although prostitution is technically legal, she had been charged with being a 'public nuisance' and forced to pay the police for the privilege of occupying a space on the sidewalk. Such 'tolls' (*pedágios* in Portuguese) were high and her payment did not necessarily guarantee her security with respect to the police. At times, she grew tired of the police and their constant demands for money and/or free sex. Her resistance was met with violence. At times, she had been forced to stop working after the police beat her when she scoffed at their demands for free sex. Such problems were often reported to me by the sex workers I interviewed.

Her movement within the city of Rio was largely confined to the 'red light' districts of a few neighbourhoods, and even then she was able to move about only at night. At other times, she feared the routine violence that transvestite prostitutes face on the streets. She discovered that she was unwelcome in most places when dressed in feminine attire, had been thrown out of supermarkets and stores, and had been harassed on the streets during the day. Restaurants, bars, and nightclubs that routinely deny transvestites entry as customers frequently employ them to work as entertainers for their 'family' oriented audiences. Even when she did not have to fend off policemen in search of free sex at night, she had to dispute territory on the street with older transvestite prostitutes, female prostitutes, and locals who objected to the presence of transvestites, alleging that they were a nuisance, a threat to the 'family,' and a source of AIDS. When she was unable to turn enough tricks to pay her rent, she had to move to the streets, a move which frequently entailed the loss of her personal possessions, including her work clothes.

Despite the difficulties she'd had, she managed to look better than many of the tourists and local straight men who were her loyal customers during the night, but who were unwilling to be seen with her during the day. She showed considerable promise for developing her own beauty, and had managed—with very little money—to assemble a wardrobe that was the envy of many of her colleagues and admirers. She sought out my advice one night while we were hanging out in a down-scale nightclub in Copacabana. This was one of the very few gay identified nightclubs in Rio that permitted transvestites to enter through the same door as the other customers. Most gay bars in Rio cater to an up-scale crowd that club owners presume (and probably correctly) do not want to share social space with drag queens who are most frequently from the working and lower classes. Social contact between gay identified men and drag queens, while not altogether absent, is rather unusual. Social relations between gay identified men, drag queens, *michês*, and lesbians are structured in Rio, as they are in the United States among other places, along lines of social class, race, and 'respectability' to straight people. Middle-class gay men who can pass for straight may prefer not to risk their social standing by being seen in the company of drag queens or hustlers who cannot pass for straight and are considered to be less than respectable. My friendship with Andrea was something of an anomaly in this sense. We had been introduced when we were both working the street: she was looking for tricks and I was trying to conduct ethnographic research. Since few of the sex workers I met responded warmly to the idea of being interviewed by someone who was working on a study sponsored by the World Health Organization, I often ended up talking with the people I knew about other matters. It took a considerable amount of time for me to convince some of them that my objectives did not include policing the behaviour of prostitutes or writing reports that emphasized the alleged threat they posed to the 'general public.'

In the nightclub, we were watching a 'boy-show' in which muscular young men performed various kinds of strip-show drag for their gay-identified audience: fireman, soap opera hero, businessman, and surfer. Andrea told me that she hoped to find someone who might teach her to be a stage performer so that she could work in nightclubs instead of being stuck outside working the streets all the time. She was certain that she could do better than the muscle-bound boys we watched on stage. She complained that her social life was as limited as her work, and she hoped that working as a stage performer would help on both fronts. It wasn't an easy task since she was underage, lacked proper identification, and had not yet accumulated enough money to get the silicone implants she would need to acquire breasts and hips. She asked me for help in negotiating her tricks with English speaking clients, in the hope that the Earth Summit (held in Rio in June of

1992) would bring with it a lucrative foreign clientele (which it did, see below). She also told me that she wasn't sure how to negotiate the price of a trick with foreign clients. Because she was unable to read, and because inflation was running at about 30 per cent per month, she had been charging too little for her services since she wasn't able to convert the price she had set in dollars into cruzeiros.

I was happy to teach her a few phrases of English, and attempted to show her how to figure out the exchange rate so that she could maximize her earnings with foreign clients. I also referred her to my friend Mrs Gigi, a social scientist and would-be television star who tried to facilitate Andrea's employment at a popular downtown nightclub where Mrs Gigi had been appearing during the course of her research. However, she was unable to help, since Andrea lacked proper identification and was underage. Obtaining the identification she needed to work was virtually impossible; she had no access to her birth certificate or other documents which would enable her to negotiate the bureaucracy. Even if she'd had such identification, she was too young to work in nightclubs. Andrea also needed access to formal education which would give her the basic reading and maths skills she needed for her work. She had attempted to attend a publicly funded school that primarily served 'street children'. When she tried to attend class there, she was harassed by the other students and told by the teaching staff that they could not accommodate everyone. In effect, she was denied access to public education because of her gender non-conformity. This programme for 'street kids' both expected and demanded gender conformity on the part of its target population. Though she was both underage and living on the street much of the time, she did not qualify as a 'street kid' for the purposes of that public educational programme.

At the time I conducted my research in Rio, there was only one programme for 'street kids' that welcomed transvestites. That programme, however, focused on the prevention of AIDS and sexually transmitted diseases—and was clearly needed and welcomed by those it served—but was unable to offer a range of services wide enough to meet needs of young transvestites who live and work on the streets. The social service category 'street kids' was constructed in such a way as to exclude those who were homosexually identified or marked. It was clearly the homophobia of service providers, charitable organizations, and local government that maintained the heterosexuality of the social service category 'street kids' by excluding those unable to pass for straight. Many of these programmes were funded by private charitable organizations unwilling to recognize that any of the children they served had sexualities, and were particularly averse to the idea of serving transgendered and homosexually identified youths.

What Andrea was looking for was some kind of apprenticeship in feminine beauty and the art of stage performance. She was also in need of assistance in the management of her business affairs with clients and the owners of the apartment where she lived and worked. As a minor, and as a newcomer both to the city and to drag, she was at a significant disadvantage in competing for work in nightclubs as well as for customers with older, more experienced transvestite prostitutes.

Working the streets for tricks is dangerous and carries with it considerable stigma relative to other forms of prostitution, such as working in a massage parlour or in a call agency. She lacked the connections and skills she would need to work in these more protected 'closed' forms of prostitution or inside nightclubs as a stage performer. She was also unable to find work outside of prostitution because of the homophobic reactions to her gender ambiguity. Sex work and nightclub perform- ance were among the very few options available to her, and these possibilities were foreclosed by her age and lack of proper identification. And if she really wanted to make any money at all, she would have to figure out a way to get herself to Europe, where she could earn much more than in Brazil. The move to Europe would be the next logical step after she had managed to make the necessary con- nections in Rio, but also presumed access to the documents she would need to get a passport.

Despite her difficulties, Andrea seemed to be doing remarkably well. That she was able to keep herself alive, off the streets, out of jail and looking good were major accomplishments for a young transvestite with few connections in Rio upon which she could rely. Though she did not dream of a career as a prostitute, and was actively seeking other ways to make money, she was able to keep herself housed and clothed by turning tricks in Copacabana. The vast majority of her clients were closeted Brazilian men (*enrustidos* in Portuguese), but she was look- ing for ways to do business with foreigners as well. She also sent money to her mother on a regular basis, hoping that by maintaining a financial tie with her family she would one day be able to return home. Other transvestites I knew pre- ferred to wait until they had amassed significant amounts of capital before at- tempting a return home; many had managed to make enough money in Europe to buy property for their families or for themselves. The accoutrements of glamour and sophistication that come from living first in Rio de Janeiro and then cities such as Milan, Madrid, or Paris seemed to provide them with a kind of cultural capital that made them more palatable to the biological families that had rejected them. The acquisition of this cultural capital entailed years of hard work turning tricks in Brazil, and later in Europe, and enduring violent homophobia from their families, police, straight people, and the public health authorities in Europe and Brazil who equate transvestite prostitution with the spread of AIDS to 'families' (Browning and Adams, 1990; Pinel, 1989).

Many of the hustlers, or *michês*, I met were much less adept at sex work, and seemed to engage in prostitution more as a way to find sex with other men than as a way to earn a living. If they were willing and able to pass as straight and as 'male' during the day, other work options were open to them. For those I knew who came to Rio because they had been kicked out of their homes, however, sex work was often their first (though not necessarily their primary) source of income in the city. When I met Ricardo, he had only been in Rio a short time, and was living in an apartment with a drag queen with whom he was romantically involved. Under the tutelage of his mate, he managed to find his way to a hustler bar on the beach in Copacabana, where he came every night in search of clients. He had been turning tricks irregularly, and was unsure of his ability to live on what he earned from sex. Working the streets was difficult since there were so many hustlers, and because he did not like the stigma associated with prostitution. Working in nightclubs was not easy either, since many clubs advertise that they do not admit hustlers. When Ricardo did manage to get into clubs, he had to pay a hefty admission fee and buy the club's overpriced drinks or face expulsion. Like transvestites, hustlers who are identifiable as not-straight find themselves to be the objects of contempt and persecution. For him, much of that had to do with his status as a person who takes money in exchange for sex, which marked him as a social pariah, a potential source of disease, and as less than gay.[6] Ricardo found hustling to be a demeaning occupation, and resisted categorization as a prostitute:

Just because I go with men for money doesn't mean I'm a whore. I go with men because I want to, not just because they pay me. I don't give it away for free, but that doesn't mean that I don't enjoy it. I'm not in a position to give it away for free. I just think that I deserve something in exchange for my affection, as everyone does. I think that's fair.

He had hoped that his move to Rio would provide him with the opportunity to be openly bisexual (he told me that he enjoyed sex with drag queens and men) in a way that was impossible in his home town, located in the state of Minas Gerais. Being openly gay, or *entendido assumido* was nearly impossible for someone like him who lacked the necessary cultural and material capital. He did not have the resources to live independently of his family, as is true even for most middle-class Brazilians, and did not have the kind of education necessary to obtain a job where his sexual identity would not be an issue. Being openly gay, for Ricardo, was about being able to have social and sexual relations with other men without the hierarchies that he found in hustling. He wanted to be considered an equal to those with whom he had sex, rather than as a social inferior whose function was to bear the stigma that his customers were often seeking to avoid.

Prostitution was one of the very few options available to him, and the work was both difficult and seldom lucrative. Most of his clients were closeted men who were also residents of the city. They wanted sexual adventures that posed no risk to their straight identities, and a hidden encounter with a prostitute that they picked up on the street suited their needs perfectly. They did not want to have any social connections with Ricardo, because he was publicly marked as 'queer,' because he was poor, and because his primary social network consisted of other hustlers and transvestites. The social practices of homophobia that resulted in his expulsion from his 'family' were also responsible for confining his physical and social mobility in Rio de Janeiro. On one occasion, he was unable to locate the public health clinic to which he had been referred by an AIDS prevention educator, who also provided him with free condoms. He simply did not know the streets, buses, or subways that would take him out of Copacabana. In fact, he had

---

[6] In Brazil, as in the United States, the term 'gay' is highly inflected for social class, geographical place, gender role preference, and political affiliation. For a discussion of how this term relates to others used in Brazil to refer to same-sex relations, see Perlongher (1987) or MacRae (1990).

not attempted to leave Copacabana since the day he arrived in Rio. His movement had been restricted to the 'red light' district located near the beach and the tourist hotels. Unable to find employment in the formal economy or earn enough money from hustling, he was dependent on the person with whom he shared his apartment. He wanted out, not just out of Copacabana, but out of Brazil. He was trying to figure out a way to leave the country, in the hope of finding a more tolerant society elsewhere. Most of his hopes rested on finding a foreigner who would take him to the First World. He expected the Earth Summit to provide an excellent opportunity to meet such a person, who would act both as sponsor and lover.

Ricardo did not understand what I was doing in Brazil, and frequently pointed out to me that I was an oddity for moving from the First World to the Third. He understood that I was working as a researcher, that I had something to do with a university somewhere, but failed to understand why I would want to come to Brazil, a place where people like him were forced to work as prostitutes and denied access to families and jobs. He imagined life in the First World to be very different, and better, than in Brazil. The images he'd seen on television of lesbians and gays in the United States were the basis for his argument that I must have been out of my mind to come to Brazil to work. For him, my actions defied all logic:

You're crazy for coming to Brazil. What you need to do is get back on a plane and return to Chicago or New York or San Francisco, or one of those places where gays are always out in the streets demanding their rights. Every time I turn on the TV I see them out in the streets. Why would you come *here* to work? You must be crazy.

Ricardo certainly wasn't alone in feeling as he did about life in Brazil, and about the compelling reasons for leaving the country. The recent case of a gay man who was repeatedly attacked in Rio de Janeiro and moved to San Francisco is an interesting case in point (Brooke, 1993). He applied for—and was granted—political asylum based on laws that recognize as political refugees those persecuted for their membership of a social group. Violence against lesbians and gays in Brazil is not at all unusual; what is unusual is that a judge in the US actually recognized that homophobic violence is in itself generative of 'political' refugees. Ricardo was already an exile, and was looking to become a refugee somewhere in the First World.

Many of the *michês* I met in Rio shared Ricardo's desire to leave and his hope of meeting a foreigner who would facilitate their exit from the country. While it is ironic that sex tourism draws men to Brazil to experience—as tourists—the very pleasures that result in the minoritization and persecution of those who remain as resident sex workers, this situation does create certain limited possibilities for geographical and social mobility. The very media that make destinations like Rio, Bangkok, or Manila readily available to First World tourists also make the cities of Western Europe and the United States visible and attractive to residents of the Third World. The sex and tourist industries, as well as the transnational bureaucracies of public health and 'development' work, facilitate contact between these people in cities like Rio de Janeiro. I met several *michês* who had managed to get out of the country. Some of them came back after finding that life in Europe or the United States was not at all what they imagined it to be, but others stayed. Of those who managed to leave, the majority were able to do so with the help of tourists, but it was not infrequent to meet *michês* whose departure from the country was facilitated by a programme official or bureaucrat.

One of them, João, had moved to Rio from a city in North-Eastern Brazil where he had spent several years studying English. His goal was to move to the United States permanently, and he had managed first to become fluent in English and then move to Rio in order to facilitate contact with visitors from the US who could help him move there. He was an out gay man much in the style of what he had seen of gay men from the US and was quite different from either the hustlers or the transvestites with whom he competed for potential clients and patrons. He managed to distinguish himself from other service providers in the sex industry by mastering the signs of a First World gay identity, and thus attracting the kind of patron/lover who would be most likely to consider him to be their social equal and perhaps even 'sponsor' him in the United States. When I met him, he was living in the apartment of an environmentalist from the US who came to Brazil for the Earth Summit. That conference, which was simultaneously an opportunity for the city of Rio to restore its image in the foreign press (an image that had long been tarnished) and a chance for male prostitutes to find clients who would help them leave the country, proved to be lucrative for the vast majority of the hustlers I knew. Of those I knew, only one managed to find connections that would help them him the country. João found such connections after the Earth Summit had ended. When I last saw him, it was in a magazine that a colleague with whom I had worked in Brazil sent me from San Francisco. João was appearing as a model in an ad for a Los Angeles photography studio specializing in erotic art. He had managed to move across national borders, but was still (as far as I could tell) working within the sex industry.

Perhaps the most salient characteristic of the prostitutes I knew in Rio was that their lives were constantly in flux: they moved from one city to another, from one country to another, and shifted around within the bounded limits of Rio's 'red-light' districts. Their movements were both instigated and curtailed by the homophobia of the country's social and cultural institutions. Again, heterosexual families regularly expel their gay-identified children, knowing that they can always move to one of Brazil's big cities and work as prostitutes. And basic health and social services are seldom available to those who are publicly marked as sexual others. The limitations imposed on sex workers by the denial of these services structure migration both within and across national boundaries by curtailing occupational choices, limiting social mobility, and placing them at odds with legal institutions. Particularly for those whose class backgrounds preclude 'passing' in mainstream society, life chances can be limited and unappealing. Movement may be one of few viable options for a better life.

Still, many who work as providers of sex services are far from passive victims of the violence and hatred they face on a daily basis. Movement becomes essential to their survival and wellbeing, and many become masters of the signs of cultural capital that facilitate their movement. Sumptuary display becomes a strategy for survival and an art form, gender performativity an occupation, and the ability to locate, identify, and utilize the networks through which people and capital move becomes an essential tool in managing the oppression they confront every day. Even so, their mobility is problematic. As exiles, immigrants, guest workers, and refugees, male prostitutes constitute a sub-proletarian workforce that is simultaneously managed as a resource for and as a threat to Brazil in a context of transnational tourism and public health programmes. Marked as sexual others within the large cities to which they migrate, sex workers are subject to violence and curtailment of movements within these cities, restricting them to the 'red light' districts where they work and, often, live. One of the keys to understanding their position is the homophobia which structures to their lives and movements. Oddly, neither homophobia nor movement have been the focus of research on male prostitutes in Brazil.

The one service that is *sometimes* available to those who engage in same sex or commercial sex transactions is education on AIDS and sexually transmitted diseases. The sole service that is created for and targeted at them also imagines and treats them only in terms of their putative capacities to act as vectors of disease. Male prostitutes have been identified as a potential 'bridge' for spreading HIV to straight people in Brazil (Parker, 1990; Cortes, 1989; Pinel, 1989), much as in other parts of the world (see Ellifson *et al.*, 1993, for an example from the United States). *Whether* sex workers play a significant role in the transmission of anything to anyone is an open question, despite the claims of some researchers to the contrary (Coutinho *et al.*, 1988; Plummer and Ngugi, 1990). What these accounts suggest is that prostitutes are themselves constitutive of a sexual subculture that presents risks to those who are not part of it. The links between the sex workers and the 'general population' remain hazy at best. One clearly homophobic feature of these accounts is that the focus of concern of both the research and the interventions such studies suggest is the health of the 'general population' rather than the health and well-being of the sex workers themselves. What is clear in these accounts is that disease moves from sex workers to other populations, not the other way around, and therein lies the nature of the threat that prostitution is said to pose. There is nothing about the exchange of money for sex *per se* that would suggest anything but moral contagion. Even if sex work is of significance in the transmission of AIDS, it certainly does not follow that sex workers would be the vectors for its spread. High rates of seroprevalence among prostitutes may in fact be a sign of the reverse: that prostitutes are more likely to become HIV infected through contact with their customers. Governmental and non-governmental campaigns that target sex workers must be careful to not confuse the moral and social stigma associated with commercial sex with risk of HIV infection.

If it is the case that male–male commercial sex transactions tend to include practices that are less safe than non-commercial sex transactions, then that fact would seem to be relevant to AIDS prevention programmes, which could then target that set of factors related to risky sex practices. Such interventions would have to account for the fact that sex workers are an integral part of much larger social networks in which they occupy positions of relative disadvantage. As in many other parts of the world, AIDS prevention programmes in Rio were, at the time I conducted my research, targeted chiefly at sex workers (male and female) and homosexual men. Television advertisements that targeted the 'general population' (that is, not homosexual men or sex workers) of Brazil warned of the dangers of prostitutes and 'promiscuity.' This pattern of service provision fits neatly into discourses on 'risk groups' imagined to be both demographically discrete and visible to those working in the field of public health who take on the responsibility of studying and managing them (Treichler, 1989; Patton, 1990). That a subculture organized around commercial sex does not include intermediaries, clients, or other managers (such as the researchers and service providers who work 'legitimate' jobs related to the sex industry) is not consistent with my research, and certainly does not make much sense in formulating strategies to prevent the spread of HIV (deZalduondo, 1991). Sex workers are among the least likely of all participants in the sex industry to be literate, or to have access to health care and other basic social services. Targeting providers of sex services not only precludes other potentially useful forms of intervention, but places an additional set of burdens on a group that is seldom able to maintain consistent control over its working conditions. Unfortunately, such a pattern of service provision is consistent with the public health strategy adopted by the Brazilian government, which has treated AIDS as a disease of sexual and social others (Daniel, 1991). In adopting such a strategy, HIV and AIDS are treated as symptoms of marginality and moral decay facing the nation-state, rather than as expressive of long-term and deeply rooted public health problems within it (Yingling, 1991). The results of such efforts have been to further stigmatize homosexual men and sex workers by blaming them for the country's AIDS epidemic.

The idea of a sexual subculture that includes commercial sex workers must be reformulated in at least two ways. First, it must recognize the diversity of people who participate in the sex industry and the multiplicity of roles these people play in promoting, brokering, purchasing, and providing commercial sex. This means including intermediaries, managers, consumers, and providers within any such theoretical subculture. What ties these people is not their commonalities of social class, race, sexuality, or nationality, but rather the set of actions and beliefs required to participate in commercial sex transactions. A functional model of male–male commercial sex must also include those institutions that produce and perpetuate homophobic violence and sanction discrimination against non-straights. These are the institutions whose internal logics structure the sex industry both directly and indirectly. As such, they are an important part of any theoretical subculture of sex work. Drastic differences in the distribution of material and social capital, and violent homophobia that polices and stigmatizes same-sex relations, are the conditions for any theoretical 'subculture' of male prostitution in Brazil or elsewhere. Foreign and domestic consumers, sex tourists, pimps, social scientists, the heterosexual family, organized religion, and government all have important links to such a subculture.

Secondly, the fact of the physical movement of male prostitutes both within and across national borders requires a rethinking of what any 'subculture' organized around sex work might look like. In the case of Rio, that subculture includes travel agents who book tourists on trips, public relations experts who package and promote Brazil as an exotic and tropical destination, tourists, nightclub owners, taxi drivers, ethnographers, bartenders, prostitutes, heterosexual 'families', and journalists, among others. Clearly, the subculture of sex work in Rio is, perhaps more than anything else, a subculture of people in movement. The space of the sex industry in Rio extends from villages in rural states of Brazil all the way to the cities and even the universities of the First World. Interventions that attempt to delimit, contain, and eliminate transmission of HIV within specific centres of the sex industry must take into account this movement and the institutions and ideologies that structure it. Hatred of prostitutes and of homosexuals expressed through intolerance, violence, and the denial of basic social services is an integral part of this pattern of movement. The promotion of Rio as an exotic destination for travellers interested in sex relies upon these vectors of hatred to provide consumers with commercial sex services. Without these collective forms of hatred, which dislocate sexual minorities, the sex industry would take on a very different form.

Any proposed intervention to halt or slow the transmission of HIV among sex workers, or between sex workers and their clients, must necessarily take into account the demographic diversity and geographical fluidity of a globalized sex industry. Such interventions must also take into account the effects of homophobia in structuring the movement of male prostitutes within and across national boundaries. It is my belief that the sex industry of Rio has at most a minuscule relationship to the AIDS epidemic of Brazil, by far one of the worst in the world. Even so, interventions that target sex workers and others involved in the sex industry can have positive effects. When interventions are well formulated, these effects can include significant improvements in the working conditions of sex workers, increased access to health care and other social services, and a demystification of the relationships between commercial sex, homosexuality and HIV infection. Sex workers might then be seen as the logical targets of public health interventions because of their relative need for such services in general, rather than because of the threat they are said to pose to the 'general public.' But in order to achieve such positive effects, the concept of the subculture of sex work must be reformulated by those who conduct research on the AIDS epidemic and by those who make recommendations to providers of public health services. In particular, it is necessary to recognize the role of ideological constructs, such as homophobia, in the structuring of the subculture of commercial sex services. To fail to do so is to continue to scapegoat those who are already disempowered, to identify homosexuals and commercial sex workers as expendable, and to fail to take effective steps towards the containment of HIV among those who might be at risk of infection.

REFERENCES

Abu-Lughod, Lila and Catherine Lutz (1990), 'Introduction: discourse, emotion and the politics of everyday life'. In *Language and the Politics of Emotion*. New York: Cambridge University Press.

Abu-Lughod, Lila (1990), 'Shifting politics in Bedouin love poetry'. In C. Lutz and L. Abu-Lughod (eds), *Language and the Politics of Emotion*. New York: Cambridge University Press.

Abu-Lughod, Lila (1991), 'Writing against culture'. In Richard Fox (ed.), *Recapturing Anthropology*. Santa Fe, NM: School of American Research Press.

Alexander, Priscilla (1987), 'Prostitutes are being scapegoated for heterosexual AIDS'. In Delacoste and Alexander (eds), *Sex Work: Writings by Women in the Sex Industry*. Pittsburgh, PA: The Cleis Press.

Appadurai, Arjun (1990), 'Disjuncture and difference in the global cultural economy'. *Public Culture* 2 (2): 1–24.

—— (1991), 'Global ethnoscapes: Notes and queries for a transnational anthropology'. In Richard Fox (ed.), *Recapturing Anthropology*. Santa Fe, NM: School of American Research Press.

Blumenfeld, W. (1992), *Homophobia: how we all pay the price*. Boston: Beacon Press.

Boyer, Debra (1989), 'Male prostitution and homosexual identity'. In Gilbert Herdt (ed.), *Gay and Lesbian Youth*. New York: The Haworth Press.

Braiterman, Jared (1991), 'Brazilian transvestites: Fantastic identities across transnational space'. Dissertation proposal, Stanford University Department of Anthropology.

—— (1994), 'Straight masculinity: Fantastic illusion or glamour accessory?' Presentation at the Lesbian and Gay Studies lecture series, Stanford University.

Brooke, James (1993), 'In Live-and-Let-Live land, gay people are slain'. *New York Times*, 12 August.

Browning, Frank and Michael Adams (1990), 'Spectre of a vast epidemic of AIDS haunts a Latin nation', (Part 1 of 4). *San Francisco Examiner*, 28 February, A1 and A11.

Butler, Judith (1991), 'Imitation and gender insubordination'. In Diana Fuss (ed.), *Inside Out: Lesbian Theories, Gay Theories*. New York: Routledge.

Carrier, Joseph (1985), 'Mexican male bisexuality'. In F. Klein and T. Wolf (eds), *Bisexualities: Theories and Research*. New York: Haworth Press.

Carrier, Joseph (1989), 'Sexual behavior and the spread of AIDS in Mexico'. *Medical Anthropology*, 10: 129–42.

Chauncey, George (1993), 'The postwar sex crime panic'. In William Graebner (ed.), *True Stories from the American Past*. New York: MacGraw-Hill.

Cortes, Eduardo *et al.* (1989), 'HIV-1, HIV-2, and HTLV-I infection in high-risk groups in Brazil'. *New England Journal of Medicine*, 320: 953–8.

Coutinho, R. A., R. L. M. van Andel, and T. J. Rysdyk (1988), 'Role of male prostitutes in spread of sexually transmitted diseases and human immunodeficiency virus' (letter). *Genitourinary Medicine*, 64: 207–8.

Daniel, Herbert (1991), 'We are all people living with AIDS: myths and realities of AIDS in Brazil'. *International Journal of Health Services*, 22: 531–551.

deZalduondo, Barbara (1991), 'Prostitution viewed cross-culturally: toward recontextualizing sex work in AIDS intervention research'. *Journal of Sex Research*, 28: 223–48.

Ellifson, K. W., J. Boles, M. Sweat, W. W. Darrow, W. Elsea, and R. M. Green (1989),

'Seroprevalence of human immunodeficiency virus among male prostitutes'. *New England Journal of Medicine* 321: 832–3.

Ellifson, K. W., J. Boles, and M. Sweat (1993), 'Risk factors associated with HIV infection among male prostitutes'. *American Journal of Public Health*, 83: 79–83.

Herdt, Gilbert and Andrew Boxer (1991), 'Ethnographic issues in the study of AIDS'. *Journal of Sex Research*. 28 (2): 167–70.

Herdt, Gilbert (1992), *Gay Culture in America: Essays from the Field*. Boston: Beacon Press.

Lancaster, Roger (1988), 'Subject honor and object shame: The construction of male homosexuality and stigma in Nicaragua'. *Ethnology*, 27 (2): 111–26.

Larvie, P., R. Cardoso, and R. Parker (1992), 'Evaluation of Programa Pegação, an Outreach Program for Male Prostitutes in Rio de Janeiro'. Report submitted to the World Health Organization's Global Programme on AIDS.

Larvie, S. Patrick (1993), *A Construção Cultural dos Meninos de Rua no Rio de Janeiro: Implicações para a Prevenção de HIV/AIDS*. Washington DC: AIDSCOM, The Academy for Educational Development.

—— 'Nation, Science, Sex: The Transnational Bureaucracy of Male Prostitution in Rio de Janeiro'. Unpublished Master's thesis, Committee on Human Development, University of Chicago.

MacRae, Eduard (1990), *A constução da igualdade*. Campinas: Editora da Unicamp.

Parker, Richard (1987), 'Acquired immunodeficiency syndrome in Brazil'. *Medical Anthropology Quarterly*, n.s. 1 (2): 155–75.

—— (1990), 'Male prostitution, bisexual behaviour, and HIV transmission in urban Brazil'. Paper prepared for the Committee on Anthropological Demography, at the International Union for the Scientific Study of Population meeting in Copenhagen.

—— (1991), *Bodies, Pleasures, and Passions*. Boston: Beacon Press.

Patton, Cindy (1990), *Inventing AIDS*. New York: Routledge.

Perlongher, Nestor (1987), *O Negócio do Michê: A Prostituição Viril*. São Paulo: Editora Brasiliense.

Pinel, Arlette (1989), 'Sexual behavior survey of Brazilian men that are clients of transvestite prostitutes'. Fifth International Conference on AIDS, June 1989, Montreal. (Author has a copy of the paper)

Pleak R. and H. Meyer-Bahlburg (1990), 'Sexual behavior and AIDS knowledge of young male prostitutes in Manhattan'. *Journal of Sex Research*, 27: 557–87.

Plummer, F. A. and E. N. Ngugi (1990), 'Prostitutes and their clients in the epidemiology and control of sexually transmitted diseases'. In Holmes *et al.* (eds), *Sexually Transmitted Diseases*. 2nd ed. New York, NY: McGraw Hill.

Treichler, Paula (1989), 'AIDS and HIV infection in the Third World: a First World chronicle'. In Kruger and Mariani (eds), *Remaking History*. Seattle, WA: Bay Press.

Weston, Kath (1991), *Families We Choose: Lesbians, Gays, and Kinship*. New York: Columbia University Press.

Yingling, Thomas (1991), 'AIDS in America: postmodern governance, identity, and experience'. In Diana Fuss (ed.), *Inside Out: Lesbian Theories, Gay Theories*. New York: Routledge.

Part IV

Sexual Networks and Commercial Sex

10 Mobility, Marriage, and Prostitution:

Sexual Risk among Thai in the Netherlands

Until the Second World War, it was a commonly held assumption that Thai never migrate to other countries. Thai were not thought to be able to survive without rice and Buddhism. Developments since the Second World War have belied such assumptions. Now, some observers tend to presuppose a special Thai talent for mobility and survival abroad. With regard to the past, however, the statement 'Thai do not migrate' must also be qualified. Actually, processes of (im)migration and mobility were crucial to the formation and maintenance of the old Thai social fabric and polity.

These shifting patterns of mobility form a background against which recent movements of Thai to Europe should be understood. This chapter's theme is the recent formation of small Thai communities in several European countries (for example, Germany, Scandinavia, France, Switzerland, and the Netherlands). The data presented are collected in Holland and particularly reflect the situation in Amsterdam. The main perspective, however, is the question of AIDS risk and how to deal with this adequately. Although Thai form a comparatively small group among ethnic migrants in Europe, the connection between them and the AIDS epidemic is more than ephemeral. It is generally known that Thailand, especially its northern part, constitutes one of the epicentres of the epidemic in Asia (the spread of HIV in Thailand is well documented, probably better than for any Western country, see Weniger *et al.*, 1991; Brown and Werasit, 1993; Brown and Xenos, 1994; Brown *et al.*, 1994; Werasit and Brown, 1994).

In Holland, as in most European countries, a sense of reassurance that the epidemic is under control dominates the general attitude towards AIDS. There are, however, disquieting statistics about a relative increase of AIDS among women and ethnic minorities. Contact with highly endemic areas is now an officially acknowledged form of risk and some observers voice concern about the possibility of the reintroduction of HIV into the general population through the intermediary of certain ethnic groups. Although focusing on the risks posed by a specific ethnic group could provide material for blaming or stigmatizing this

I have especially to acknowledge the use of material from interviews held by Irene Stengs, Mirjam Schieveld, and Jan Willem de Lind van Wijngaarden, of archival data collected by Renée Hoogenraad, and of Dutch AIDS and Amsterdam STD figures provided by Loes Singels (NIGZ) and Frits van Griensven (GG&GD). I am grateful to Gilbert Herdt, Mirjam Schieveld, and Lisa Dondero for making comments that were helpful in the organizing and rewriting of the text.

group, it is my conviction that such a short-term consideration does not outweigh the long-term interest of an open discussion on the AIDS/HIV risk associated with Thai in Europe. A second reason to enter into such a discussion is the opportunity it offers to clarify a specific constellation of migration, marriage, and sex work. Thus Thai migration to Europe provides a case that can exemplify what could be called the cultural and social construction of prostitution. Finally, an analysis of the origin and sociocultural characteristics of Thai 'communities' in Europe is a requirement for developing effective and sensitive forms of prevention among this group.

Societies and their cultures differ in the way they require, allow, stimulate, or hinder the movement of their people. The Thai case appears quite extreme in its articulation of patterns of mobility and in providing inducements to move. The formation of Thai states in the region of contemporary Thailand has for more than ten centuries been characterized by a continuing sequence of migrations: migration from the southern parts of China to the river valleys and delta of the Chao Phraya and its tributaries; movements of people in search of new rice land from the twelfth century onwards; from the seventeenth to the twentieth century, an influx of refugees from neighbouring countries: Makassarese, Javanese, Malay, Lao, Vietnamese, Khmer, Shan, Karen, and others; the forced moving of former Malay and Lao war captives; and, especially, the periodic movements of *phraj* (retainers or clients) for the purpose of fulfilling corvée, which was Siam's main form of taxation until the great reforms at the end of the nineteenth century.

These historical patterns of mobility illustrate how migration is shaped by its social and cultural context. The Thai pattern of mobility in the past was also extremely gender-specific, since mobility was traditionally restricted to young and middle-aged males, a situation which finds its complement in female control over households. Males controlled the public sphere and women the sphere of the household, where often the wife-grandmother relationship was the crucial one (Bencha, 1992:17).

Since the Second World War, an enormous change of a twofold nature has occurred. First, mobility has been observed in almost all groups, especially among women, who now tend to dominate in rural–urban migration. This trend is related to the development of industries and urban services which often prefer women to perform various types of unskilled labour. Second, there has been an immense extension of the scale of mobility. Thai migrants have been crossing national boundaries more frequently. This became especially perceptible when, in the 1970s, thousands of Thai men went to work as labourers in the oil-producing countries of the Near East, and hundreds of Thai women journeyed to neighbouring South-East Asian countries for domestic service and factory work (see Pasuk and Samart, 1993:161–3). Third, an increasing part of Thai mobility contains a circular element. This can take several forms: as seasonal migration (for example, fulfilling corvée obligations in the past, or driving a taxi in the off-season and going back to plant the rice fields before the start of the rainy season); as incidental or frequent remittances to the family at home; as regular visits and stays in one's hometown; or as a return to the hometown after years of working and earning money in the city or abroad. Actually, this strong link between Thai migrants and their family 'at home' is what motivates many migrants, whether they have gone to Bangkok, Europe, or the Near East. The recent changes in migration patterns have resulted in a situation in which almost all rural Thai villages are connected not only with the rest of Thai society but also with societies and countries around the world. Anchalee Singhanetra-Renard (1993) has described how moving away for short or long periods of time has become part of the village way of life. These days many people have become 'bi-local' or even 'multi-local' residents.

It is only since the onset of the HIV/AIDS epidemic that the relationship between mobility and sexual behaviour has become an object of more systematic research.[1] Such behaviour is not necessarily extramarital sexual behaviour.[2] Marriage is the most important and forceful institution in shaping and regulating sexuality, but its relationship to mobility is not unidirectional. At a glance, marriage appears to be an institution that, in bringing together husband and wife, can account for some degree of mobility. But it also implies settlement, the opposite of mobility. The Thai data that I will present in this chapter even show that marriage can take the role of an important instigator or mediator of human movement. In particular, a woman's use of marriage to enhance her social independence and to improve her economic prospects can turn marriage into a vector of mobility. Before describing in detail the specific case of Thai migration to the Netherlands, I have to make some comments on the use of the general categories of marriage and prostitution in the Thai context.[3]

---

[1] Within Thai studies connections between mobility and sexual behaviour have been dealt with cursorily before the AIDS era, for instance in the *paj thiaw* (wander, go around) custom of young unmarried adolescent males taking the opportunity to leave their homes temporarily to explore the wider world. It is understood that, while away from home, they will look for sexual adventure. Given the norm of virginity in unmarried girls, it is clear that traditionally the local community did not provide any opportunity for such experience.

[2] We should, however, not overlook an often latent function of moving away—namely, creating the opportunity for sexual encounters. The physical distancing from the familiar environment can be especially consequential when, as in Thailand, the control of sexual behaviour is highly dependent on external sanctions and norms of proper sexual conduct are not heavily monitored by religion. Buddhism has strict sexual rules and taboos only for those who seek religious virtuosity, such as monks, nuns, or laymen who have pledged to 'follow the precepts' (*thyy sin*). For everyone else, the realm of sensual pleasure is not particularly condoned, but neither is it loaded with notions of sin or guilt. As long as sexual behaviour is private, it rarely has social consequences. Few people feel a need to intervene in a person's private sexual conduct. This is a situation that creates an inner link between extramarital sexual behaviour and mobility. Such behaviour is more easily kept secret or even tolerated as long as it happens 'elsewhere', in a social and cultural space which is not a part of one's own community.

[3] Thai marriage has remained a particularly under-researched theme within Thai studies (for the exceptions see Aphichat Chamratrithirong, 1984, and Sumalee, 1995; see also some of the entries in Tanabe, 1991:144 ff.). There is at least one good reason for this scholarly neglect: marriage in its present form is not, historically, an original Thai institution. The two elements that define marriage in contemporary Thailand—marriage registration at an *amphoe* (district office) and the wedding ceremony—are not deeply embedded traditions. Marriage registration is a recent government-ordered

A Thai perspective of marriage is complicated by the fact that since the Second World War, marriage and family have been focal themes in the construction of national (Western-inspired) middle-class ideologies (see Reynolds, 1991; Jiraporn, 1992). Under this cover, it is my impression that a secular, economic, pragmatic, and flexible conception of Thai marriage becomes visible. This malleable and *ad hoc* character of Thai marriage can also be seen in the past, when marriage often functioned as a mechanism for linking Thai and other ethnic groups, at a royal as well as a common level. Foreigners living in Siam had temporary Siamese wives (regarding the seventeenth century, see Smith, 1980:13). Particularly revealing is Gijsbert Heeck's description of the conditions in which about forty Dutchmen lived in the old Siamese capital of Ayutthaya *circa* 1655 (ten Brummelhuis, 1987:59–60). From his report it appears that what to the Siamese was a lawful form of a man–woman relationship (marriage) was whoredom (prostitution) in the eyes of the Dutch.[4] Here we witness an early clash of categories and perceptions which has also dominated more recent Western discourse about prostitution in Thailand. Such categories, operating within a dichotomy of 'true love' versus 'sinful' relationships, hinder the adequate description of the different forms of sexual man–wife relationships and how they were conceived.

This historical example should make us aware of the difficulty of identifying within the Thai context clear-cut equivalents for the opposed notions of 'marriage' and 'prostitution'. An essential element of the concept of prostitution as it has been developed in Western discourse is the exchange of money for sex and its opposition with true love. Here we run into problems in the Thai case. Exchange of sex for money and services exists, but it is not such a defining element. More opprobrious is not to do it for money, but (in case of a woman) to sleep around with many men indiscriminately. Getting money for it could make it more understandable and justifiable; doing it for nothing or out of pleasure would be most shameful. In general, women are encouraged to gain some benefit from making themselves sexually available to men. This logic holds for marriage, and certainly for shorter liaisons outside marriage. In the Thai case there is a wide variation among man–wife relationships, which can be documented for the past, but which still exists in more informal ways and survives in attitudes towards modern marriage. Further, there exists a continuum of forms and attitudes between prostitution and marriage. Even from the perspective of some women, the gap between 'prostitution' and 'marriage' is bridgeable.

'custom' introduced in the late 1920s; even today it is not consensually regarded as a requirement for a stable partnership. There is no Buddhist marriage ritual; the ritual used is of Brahman-Indian origin (see Bencha 1992:27). Thus we should not expect marriage to serve as the exclusive mechanism for social control of sexual conduct. Where such control exists, it is, at least partly, effected and localized within the wider family and community.

[4] Other evidence of the existence in seventeenth century Siam of a category of women that Westerners would label as 'prostitutes' is the mentioning of *jing lakhoon soopheenii* (theatre women) in the Three Seals Laws, quoted by Dararut (1983:13).

Marriage and Mobility: Siamese War Brides

We thus come to the main purpose of this chapter: to understand the origin and character of the Thai community in Holland, to asses its HIV/AIDS risk and its potential for adequate protection. In contrast to a common assumption that this community originated in the 1970s, as in some other places in Europe, it appears that more than two decades earlier, a group of Thai females followed their husbands to Holland. This group has been almost invisible within Dutch society, for they tended to be perceived as Indonesian or Eurasian. Apart from their being the pioneer group of Thai who migrated abroad and their constituting the origin of the Thai community in the Netherlands, there is an additional reason to pay attention to this group. Its history exemplifies the complex relationship between marriage and sex work.[5]

During the years 1945–7 about 2,000 Thai–Dutch marriages were registered in Thailand, between Dutch soldiers or former prisoners of war and Thai girls. Some couples stayed in Thailand, while others moved to Java or to Holland. One group of women declined to follow their husbands, and there were also reports of Thai women abandoned in Singapore or Port Said. It is remarkable, however, that more than 10 per cent of the group, comprised of Dutch who had been brought or had migrated to Siam—members of the KNIL (Royal Netherlands Indies Army) and other Dutch prisoners of war—opted for a Siamese bride. To understand the circumstances under which this occurred, it is important to remember that the Dutch and Eurasian soldiers in Siam had to wait for repatriation for a considerable period of time, often more than a year. The Dutch authorities preferred to keep them in Siam—to await developments in Indonesia, at that time still considered Dutch colonial territory.

Although Thai women marrying foreigners has been a common pattern for centuries, the greater scale in this case and the taking away of Thai women brought about some strong reactions on the Thai side. Our interviews revealed cases of strong resistance from the girls' families and Thai public opinion. In August 1946, Thai newspapers appeared with headlines such as 'Siamese Girls Who Followed Dutch Soldiers Confess their Mistake'; and sub-headlines like, 'Instead of finding happiness with their husbands as they dreamed, they became public service girls'. The Thai press did not make a point of revealing the background of some of the girls as 'taxi girls,' cabaret, or bar girls. Indignation about their bad treatment dominated; it was reported that they were forced to take up their 'old professions'. The publications even spoke of the threat that diplomatic relations between Siam and Holland would be broken off, and Dutch diplomats responded by approaching the press with letters from happily married Thai. A governmental investigation was ordered into the situation of these mixed couples

---

[5] This section is based on archival documents at the Netherlands Ministry of Foreign Affairs, The Hague (Bangkok Archive 1945–54, Nos 270–375) and on interviews with five Thai women from this group. The archival data were collected by Renée Hoogenraad and the interviews conducted by Mirjam Schieveld.

and the way Thai women were treated. The majority of the couples interviewed were living happily, though it was also reported that Siamese women were harassed by persons with 'inclinations of erotomania'. This latter term can be interpreted as the expression of an attitude towards the Siamese brides that perceived or treated them as 'former prostitutes'.

Public response to the first group of Thai migrants to Holland again reveal differences between Thai and Dutch perceptions of marriage and in the demarcation between marriage and prostitution. The women themselves were aware of a distinction between 'good' girls from well-to-do families and those who worked in bars, cabarets, or as taxi girls. In a Thai context, the distinction is especially loaded in the connotation of well-to-do versus poor families. Later success can extinguish the earlier stigma completely; in as much as there is any stigma in making a living from sex work it is, primarily, the stigma of poverty. Nevertheless, some women informants were reluctant to talk about their earlier life. They knew, of course, that in the Dutch perception, an extra dimension of moral disapproval was involved for having engaged in sex work, and thus that they had a 'sinful' past that could never be removed.

Marriage and Sex Work: The Second Wave of Migration

Although the origin of the Thai community in Holland goes back to the years following the Second World War, its growth has occurred since the late 1970s, when the second wave of Thai marriage migration sprang up. This second group differs from the first in many respects. Here I want to concentrate specifically on the connection between marriage and sex work. For some of the war brides their jobs in the entertainment sector as cabaret girls or taxi girls provided an opportunity to meet their future husband. With the exception of the few cases reported in the Thai newspapers of 1946, there is no indication that after marriage and migration they ever returned to any form of sex work. This constitutes an important difference with the second group. The further development of the tourist-oriented entertainment sector in Thailand in the 1960s and 1970s has to be taken into account to understand the background of these marriages. Further, their migration to Holland has resulted in the genesis of a recognizable Thai element within the Dutch prostitution scene.

Thai sex entertainment for tourists has an essentially double character, which has caused some authors to speak of it as 'open-ended prostitution' (Cohen, 1987; Yos, 1993). Similarly, Van Kerkwijk (1995) demonstrated how paid sex may go together with love, and that, for some Thai girls, there is often an ambiguity between strategies for pursuing romantic love and strategies for money-making. This ambiguity is an essential element which makes it problematic to interpret tourist contacts in terms of prostitution exclusively. Without an understanding of the complicated ambiguity of love and sex work with foreigners it is impossible to understand why over the last two decades in several Western countries, small but recognizable Thai communities have developed as a result of encounters at entertainment places in Thailand. It is just as inaccurate to see this cultural complex as derived exclusively from prostitution, as it is to leave the context of sex for money completely out of the picture.

Bhassorn Limanonda recently described from the perspective of a local community in northern Thailand the migrations here indicated from a European standpoint:

The first set of women in this community left to work in the sex service business in Bangkok and Pattaya about ten years ago. . . . In more recent years, many of the younger generation women who left the community to work in the city married foreign clients who happened to meet them in the work place and many of them decided to settle down in foreign countries. The practice of 'marrying out' to the foreigners (who were usually considered by the local people to be better off than Thai men in general) became a somewhat strong incentive for girls in the same community to get the same kind of job that could take them out of the poverty they had been facing, and to have a better life and be more wealthy, especially [for] the parents who were left behind in the rural village (Bhassorn, 1993: 8).

And about another, larger village she states:

For more than a decade, this community has had the reputation of having a large number of young women who went to work in the sexual service business in Bangkok, Pattaya, and in foreign countries. At present, many of them have settled down in a foreign country with a foreign husband. The women who left home to live abroad usually provided adequate financial support to their parents and to their family members who still lived in the community (Bhassorn, 12).

It is this complex of sex work, marriage, and migration that forms an important causative sequence in the formation of Thai communities abroad. Such Thai communities have come into existence all over Europe. Let us look in greater detail here at the group of Thai living in the Netherlands.

For almost two decades a visitor to the consular section of the Dutch Embassy in Bangkok stood a good chance, at any time of the day, of running into a Thai girl and a Dutch man involved in procedures regarding marriage registration. If we assume one marriage a day, this would mean 5,000 couples over the last twenty years.

There is no doubt that most marriages were and are between Dutch tourists who spend two to four weeks in Thailand and Thai girls engaged in some kind of work in the tourist-related entertainment sector; this does not necessarily mean direct sex work, but often service sector jobs as barmaids, waitresses, or guides that provide opportunities for or imply expectations of sexual service. As noted above, lumping all girls in this sector together as 'prostitutes' is not particularly illuminating ethnographically and spoils the opportunity to understand how marriages and love relationships arise out of 'payment for sex'. One of the girls interviewed protested vehemently against using a Thai phrase for prostitute (*phuujing haakin*) with regard to her work in Pattaya, while she had no problem with the term to describe her work in Amsterdam. She pointed out that in Pattaya she lived with foreigners for weeks or even for months, and that some of them became friends who returned to visit her. Such relationships are closer to what in the recent past has been called *mia chaw* (hired wife), an expression widely used for girls who lived together with American GIs during the Vietnam war.

One relevant observation is that the majority (70 per cent is my estimate) of girls who migrate through marriage, have a background of making money from short-term or long-term sexual relationships with *farang* (Western) tourists. This does not negate the fact that another type of marriage between Thai girls and *farang* occasionally takes place through a common Thai courtship pattern. Quite often these 'good' women prefer to stay away from the 'Thai community' and its activities, which to them is over-dominated by uneducated or 'bad' women. One can, however, easily overlook or underestimate this group because it remains silent, almost invisible. Finally, a third group of marriages is represented by those who have been paired off by relatives or friends.

Although women dominate the scene of Thai migrants in the Netherlands, we should include in this group of marriage-migrants those Thai who have not married but live together with a Dutch partner, or Thai men having a Dutch male partner. Then it becomes even more evident that Thai migration to Holland is largely based on marriage or sexual partnership. We must also add the group of family members who joined relatives living in Holland: children from former marriages, elder family members (mothers), or in some cases brothers and sisters recruited by women to help in small businesses or in the household. Finally, a very small group of Thai live in Holland for professional reasons or for study.

A Thai Community?

If Thai scholars are still debating the question whether Thai villages can be called communities (see Kemp, 1988), then it seems meaningless to look for a Thai community in a Western metropolis. Nevertheless I intend to use the concept here. It has to be made clear, however, that I have moved away from a concept of community that is restricted to a specific locality with clear boundaries, where people share a common identity and interact in close, face-to-face relationships. Such a concept, derivative of the old *Gemeinschaft-Gesellschaft* dichotomy and therefore easily read as 'traditional' in opposition to 'modern', is useless with regard to the group of Thai living in the Netherlands. Here I use 'community' to acknowledge not only a series of common qualities but also a specific potential for social action of the Thai in the Netherlands. Such a concept of community has to be understood within the context of—or in its opposition to—complex and differentiated societies (see Elias, 1974). It has to fulfil the following requirements:

1. *Common space with common boundaries*. This is not necessarily a territory or locality which is dominated or exclusively occupied by the members of the community. It is sufficient that they interact, in our case, as Thai, but within

Dutch territory and almost always at locations that are not exclusively Thai. Mobility, facilities for transport, and means of communication help in easing a community's dependence on a physical locality. Within the social space defined by these boundaries there is an exchange of specific information, gossip, rumour, and a potential for personal or economic conflict, especially at places such as Thai temples, Thai restaurants, or Thai shops.

2. *Objective and subjective common characteristics.* In our case these are quite obvious: Thai origin, language, food habits, culture, and common adherence to Buddhism.

3. *Some form of interdependency.* This is a crucial criterion, since it constitutes what binds a group together. It is not necessarily crude economic interdependency. In the case of the Thai community in the Netherlands we deal with more subtle forms of dependency, often not related to physical survival: emotional dependency, becoming informed about Dutch society, knowledge about how to deal with authorities, contact, and access to agencies.

My main justification for using such a broad, but nevertheless specific, concept of community is its usefulness for understanding the potential for orienting or influencing a person's behaviour that these sometimes self-chosen communities have within modern highly differentiated societies. In the Thai community in Holland we will therefore include all Thai who are open to interaction with other Thai on the basis of their 'Thainess', together with those non-Thai who participate in accordance with the same 'Thai' rules.

According to immigration police statistics, by the end of 1993 there were 226 female Thai nationals and 80 male Thai in Amsterdam with a legal, permanent or temporary, residence permit. The sex ratio becomes even more biased when one considers that among the males there is a substantial number of transvestites and transsexuals. While the figure clearly indicates the dominance of women among the Thai migrants in Amsterdam, it does not include those Thai who became Dutch nationals. For many Thai migrants, the acquisition of Dutch nationality is the fulfilment of a goal; it makes them independent from Dutch partners for support or guarantee. Further, it is obvious that these figures do not include those who entered the country illegally and are subject to deportation. My rough estimate is that about 2,000 Thai live in the greater Amsterdam area, an estimate consistent with extrapolations from figures about the weekly sale of Thai newspapers and magazines, or estimates of travel bookings by Thai. For the whole of Holland, official statistics give a number of 3,717 residents born in Thailand (persons with temporary residence permits not included). The same statistics show that 70–80 per cent of new immigrants are female. The actual figure for the number of Thai living in Holland must be substantially higher. Given these facts, the Thai community surely exceeds 10,000.

Let me make one point clear: many marriages of those who have been engaged in sex work in Thailand are stable partnerships, no different from any other Dutch marriages. Moreover, Dutch observers are often impressed by the dedication of

Thai women to their households, especially to the children and in the preparation of food. To Thai observers, Dutch husbands' willingness to deal with conflict between two divergent cultures is often moving. In this chapter I largely omit this last group, because they are less relevant to what is the ultimate objective of this research—setting up some form of adequate HIV/AIDS prevention and support among the Thai living in the Netherlands. Further, although the 'Thai community' in principle covers all Thai living in the Netherlands, the description here tends to focus on the sex work-related Thai scene in Amsterdam, where data collection took place. The engagement of Thai in sex work is, however, not restricted to Amsterdam. In several provincial capitals we also find Thai working in so-called 'window prostitution'.[6] In Amsterdam their number is estimated at 80, while in the other cities the number rarely exceeds ten. Sex workers often move around. Although the numbers can remain the same, there are indications of a high turnover rate. An important characteristic of this scene lies in the manifold connections between sex work, marriage, and other forms of partnership. What is specifically Thai in this setting thus defies easy categorization in Western terms. Marriage is used to gain legal entry into sex work; sex work can lead to marriage; and marriage and sex work are combined or alternated, according to the particulars of people and place.

No description of the Thai scene in Amsterdam is complete without reference to a group of gay-identified men, transvestites, and transsexuals. The last two categories are commonly referred to in Thai as *katheuj*. The migration of this group to Holland implies in most cases some form of connection between formal partnership and sex work. At least three subgroups can be distinguished: (a) Thai men who met a Dutch friend in the tourist entertainment sector in Thailand, and became their formal partner, which entitled them to a residence permit—a 'gay' marriage in most cases; (b) Thai men who came to Holland as the partner or friend of a Dutch man, underwent a transsexual operation (mostly in Thailand), and then entered sex work; and (c) transsexuals who came to Holland as the friend or partner of a Dutch man with the intention of engaging in sex work. Generally, in the more 'gay' relationships, long-term partnerships dominate. Among the *katheuj*, frequent partner changes take place and partnership is an instrument in achieving other goals. Occasionally marriage or formal partnerships are completely instrumental in getting a residence permit to be able to do sex work (according to Amsterdam police policy a residence permit is an absolute requirement for sex work).

The combination of sex work and marriage has dominated the origin and formation of the Thai community in Amsterdam. But it cannot be assumed that its further development has to be understood from this perspective. Firstly,

---

[6] In 'window prostitution' contacts between clients and sex workers are made at a window on a public street without any intermediary. From a customer's perspective, it is one of the cheapest forms of prostitution; from a sex worker's perspective, it is characterized by almost no control or protection by pimps, managers, or owners. In many places the only obligation is to the landlord for daily rent of the 'window'. Especially among Thai sex workers, window prostitution is often preferred to work in clubs. They value the autonomy and the possibility of higher earnings when receiving many customers a day. This form of sex work also requires some command of Dutch or English.

relationships have been developed and transformed far beyond the instrumental transactions from which they originated. Secondly, this Thai community has been transformed by the engagement of its members in many activities not in any way related to sexuality. It is however clear that the life of a substantial number of Thai living in Amsterdam (or in the Netherlands more widely) still depends more or less on regular engagement in long-term sexual relations or short-term sexual interactions with Dutch natives.

HIV/AIDS Risk

It would be naive in the extreme not to link this description of the Thai community in Amsterdam with HIV/AIDS sexual risk, and insensitive to brush aside the risk because it is such a small ethnic group that in the past has never created any problems for the Dutch authorities. HIV/AIDS risk can be postulated on account of the frequent and sometimes systematic partner change. More specifically: at both ends of the migration route, the Thai community is in touch with others whose high seroprevalence rates have already been established: homosexual or gay men in Holland and sex workers in Thailand. The circular character of almost all Thai forms of migration implies the possibility of various linkages between these populations through other so-called low-risk populations. Furthermore, our interviews indicate that as soon as a relationship is seen as a friendship or partnership, condom use outside the sphere of sex work is low. As we will see, one of the major problems lies precisely in the indistinct demarcation of sex work from the personal sphere.

There is no epidemiological data about the Thai in Amsterdam or the Netherlands that allows for reliable statements about the spread of HIV/AIDS among the Thai community. Through my own contacts, I can identify ten persons with HIV/AIDS. Five of them have died in the last few years. Two of the ten are women, one is gay, and the rest are probably best identified as *katheuj*. I have only included those cases where AIDS-related symptoms or a positive test result were reported. I have excluded several others about whom rumours of being infected circulate. As soon as a person who is engaged in sex work loses weight, suffers from unexplainable complaints and, especially, when a person travels to Thailand for plastic surgery but surgery is refused (or postponed) for medical reasons, others in their environment speculate that detection of HIV must be the cause. The general and vague Thai category of *lyad maj dii* (bad blood) is easily interpreted as 'HIV-infected' and offers a ready explanation.[7]

[7] The official registration of diagnosed AIDS cases in the Netherlands contained at 1 January 1996 fifteen persons born in Thailand; ten of them were registered in Amsterdam. It is more than probable that there is serious underreporting here. Further, given the general rule that Thai involved in sex work in Amsterdam prefer private doctors and avoid visiting the municipal STD clinics, the following (preliminary) data deserve attention. In 1993, at least twenty-three Thai nationals visited the municipal STD clinics, twenty-one women and two men (both categorized as 'homosexual'). Among the women,

The most outspoken attitude towards HIV/AIDS that we observed was among gay and *katheuj*. Our interviews revealed the existence of widespread fear. As soon as the topic was mentioned, we encountered either strong denial or strong affirmation of the severity of the problem. Several *katheuj* took the fatalistic attitude: 'Who will be the next'? There is also concern about publications that link Thai with HIV. The impact of an article in a Dutch magazine about Thai *katheuj* working in Amsterdam, which pretended to reveal the true 'identity' of the Thai 'girls' in the red light district and suggested a high rate of HIV-infection among them, is still felt and resented.

Differentiation is required to describe the attitude among the women who are regularly or incidentally involved in sex work or have frequent partner changes. The group having incidental contact with different partners tends to have the same attitude as the Dutch heterosexual population: no awareness of a specific risk in heterosexual sex. Only women who read Thai newspapers regularly or who have visited Thailand recently tend to consider HIV/AIDS a real threat. In the case of women who participate in the same circles as the *katheuj* or work with them in the red light district, there is a greater awareness. But they too tend to assume that the risk for heterosexuals is much less. Some women in this group were shocked to learn that we knew of a couple of Thai girls who were seropositive. Finally we noticed a third group of mostly young, good-looking girls who are brought to Holland with the help of persons from 'Dutch organized crime',—often under arrangements in which they have to repay huge debts. Not only are they more isolated and work with the expectation that their stay is temporary, but they work in a (Dutch) social environment where risk of HIV infection is almost completely denied. It was from this group that we found reports of consistent lack of condom use in contacts with clients and friends.

Frequent social contacts and intermingling between those engaged in sex work and other Thai groups takes place. This is not surprising since many of them have been engaged in sex work in the past and lack a middle-class contempt for *phuujing haakin* ('prostitutes'). There are also economic bonds between the groups. Those with an income from sex work are often big spenders and their patronage of shops, restaurants, and other forms of small business is highly valued.

Where partnership and love are mixed with sex work, an environment is created that makes risky sex probable. Our questioning revealed unsafe sex in most cases where customers became partners or partners frequently changed. More surprising was the discovery of two seropositive persons who had unprotected sex with their Dutch partners—even though the Dutch partner knew about the HIV-infection of his Thai friend. Both gave an explanation that consisted of a well-reasoned combination of denial and solidarity with the infected partner.

fifteen were classified as 'prostitutes'. In fourteen cases a conventional STD was diagnosed (one man with anorectal gonorrhoea, thirteen women with a vaginal STD infection).

Implications for Intervention

The situation sketched above was sufficient reason for an informal group of social scientists and others with an interest in Thailand to attempt to 'do something'. What had especially interested us for a longer time was the question of how to connect the qualitative anthropological approach of participating and interviewing with successful 'intervention'. We had the ambition to learn and put into practice experiences reported from Africa and Latin America (see ten Brummelhuis and Herdt, 1995, especially the chapters by Paiva and Schoepf).

The most critical question is that regarding 'community'. It is not primarily whether or not the Thai in the Netherlands *are* a community but especially the question of whether they have the potential to *become* a community. Here questions of theoretical concepts and practical intervention come together. The academic question of whether the Thai in the Netherlands can be called a community is connected to a series of intervention dilemmas, for instance, whether to approaching Thai sex workers as sex workers or as Thai, and the use of general HIV/AIDS services versus the development of specific services for this particular group. Needless to say, administrators and sponsors generally show a great reluctance to acknowledge the necessity of specific strategies for any particular ethnic group, especially when its magnitude is modest.

I tend to assume that addressing the Thai as members of a potential Thai community, rather than addressing some of them individually because they are 'statistical' members of established general risk groups, offers better chances for long-term sustained prevention and care. Such an approach will assign roles to many persons who would be left out in the risk group approach. For instance, some might help in identifying newcomers involved in sex work, in approaching certain persons or groups with information, in incorporating AIDS prevention into other social activities, or in giving support to HIV-infected persons.

I have to emphasize that such a community orientation does not imply any idealization of potential commonality and solidarity among Thai living abroad. The established opinion among students of Thailand is that, within Thai culture and society, association based on articulation of common interests is extremely difficult (see ten Brummelhuis, 1984). This is not, however, sufficient reason to expect that any community-oriented AIDS project among Thai has to fail. Firstly, it should be realized that a community does not necessarily depend on equality among its members; the hierarchical patron–client type relationships that dominate Thai relations are no less solid building blocks of community. Secondly, Thai living in Holland are also influenced by their new environment and especially by their Dutch partners. This accounts for a specific unpredictability, flexibility, and adaptability that is often characteristic of migrant cultures. Thirdly, AIDS is such a threat that it has created new forms of culture and community in several places, in the Western as well as in the non-Western world. Moreover, in several places, the most effective forms of prevention have been those that were rooted in local communities. The Thai response to the AIDS crisis already provides a series of

examples that indicate that Thai are prepared to question and to change established cultural patterns.

Here I have reported basically about the results of the first stage of interviewing
key persons in the Thai community (seven) plus a number of Thai involved in sex
work and living with Dutch partners (thirteen). I do not claim that the data is
representative; rather, its relevance is in helping to define important questions and
to design strategies for the next, more systematic, phase of the intervention project. Based on these first explorations the following conclusions have been drawn
regarding the format of the intervention:

1. Since members of the Thai community generally avoid involvement with
   municipal or government authorities, intervention cannot automatically
   take the form of actions initiated by health authorities directed at a specific
   group of migrants. Interventions ideally take the form of self-help, wherein
   researchers play the role of mediators who collect information, pose questions, and are instrumental in formulating or trying out certain solutions.
   None of the existing non-governmental organizations seem suitable to
   undertake such a task. They either 'specialize' in 'gays', or in 'prostitutes', or
   in migrants in general, or adhere to a concept of 'education and information'
   which in the case of these Thai is scarcely adequate.

2. Our starting point is that intervention should involve and address the wider
   Thai community, since HIV/AIDS potentially affects the whole community,
   including Dutch partners. AIDS is increasingly associated with Thai
   because of media reports about the epidemic in Thailand. Any visible or
   identifiable spread of HIV/AIDS among Thai in Amsterdam or the Netherlands may lead to an association between being Thai and having HIV/AIDS
   and thus invite stigmatizing responses. One of our research questions is to
   identify, define, and demarcate that part of the Thai community that could
   be involved in focused HIV prevention. We want to know how specific subgroups can contribute to enhancing knowledge and awareness of specific
   activities. Moreover it is important to chart not only the network of sexual
   contacts but also the network of social contacts in order to design adequate
   prevention and support.

3. The approach to follow is similar to what others have called 'action research'. Often this phrase is loosely used for all types of research that lead to
   'doing something' or that have an application. In fact, action research turns
   the traditional models of research as passive registration of 'reality' and subsequent application upside down. It starts with an active alliance between
   researcher and 'those researched'. Creating such an alliance indicates the
   magnitude of one of the first methodological problems to solve: it is not
   enough to obtain access to persons for an interview; it is important to 'convince' them of the problem, to make them aware of its magnitude, and to
   make sure that they share a concern about the HIV/AIDS risk. The processes that follow cannot suitably be described as 'data collecting'; they

require a specific commitment and involve processes of mutual learning with intermittent episodes of posing questions, finding information and answers, trying out solutions, formulating new questioning, etc.

4. The project has to address issues of prevention as well as problems related to the support of persons living with HIV/AIDS, which is crucial for a community approach. How could we approach people about the risks of becoming infected and at the same time remain indifferent to those who already suffer from the disease? Contacts with persons living with AIDS can be a constituent of effective intervention. Therefore, the possibility of involving seropositive persons in prevention work or support will be explored.

Conclusion

This study is preliminary and I am aware of its limitations. It is still unclear to what degree the data presented is representative of the whole Thai community and of their response to the HIV/AIDS epidemic. It certainly remains to become established to what degree this description of Thai in Holland is valid for other European countries. As far as I can see, only the Thai community in England possibly differs substantially, since its origin goes back to the beginning of this century and it comprises a greater percentage of Thai who migrated for educational or professional purposes. In Stockholm, Copenhagen, Hamburg, Berlin, Düsseldorf, Brussels, Zurich and many other places since the 1970s, Thai communities have developed that to a greater of lesser degree have in common a series of characteristics that makes them vulnerable to HIV/AIDS: marriage migration and involvement in sex work with an indistinct demarcation between sex work, formal marriage, and partnerships. In Amsterdam, as elsewhere, this has led to several demographic patterns that bear upon the concerns of this book: (a) shifting from sex work to living with a partner, to marriage, and back to sex work; (b) marrying a (former) customer; (c) entering (temporary) sex work in periods of emotional or financial distress; and (d) doing sex work with a 'fun loving' (*sanuk*) attitude: being selective of customers, going out with favourite customers, attempting to seduce attractive men to become customers (for a contrast, see the work ideology of London prostitutes described by Day [1990]).

A typical reaction from the side of authorities is that the Thai are too a small group to deserve specific AIDS prevention efforts or funds. We cannot, however, deny that the patterns described here recur in many places in Europe and that within these Thai communities a potential accumulation of risks exists. We have seen that its members establish a connection with a highly endemic area and that their sexual relationships often link different ethnic groups. And we can add that they often link different age groups and sometimes even groups of different sexual orientation. Needless to say, there are many other ethnic groups in Europe and elsewhere that are in similar ways strategically located on the potential routes for the spread of HIV. The focus on one specific group in this chapter had the advantage of enabling us to take into account the specific context of Thai culture and mobility patterns.

Since the collection of the data reported above, additional experience has been gained. In the middle of 1996 it is more obvious than it was at the end of 1994 that it is illusory to expect that the AIDS problem itself can be a community-creating force among Thai migrants. Possibly this reflects lessening of AIDS awareness in the general population and a process of normalization of AIDS in Thailand. Among Thai migrants there is a general reluctance to become associated with AIDS-related activities. If a community is to be established, it has to depend on other elements.

Further, some specific difficulties in setting up formal cooperation within the Thai community became obvious. Several circumstances create a potential for conflict and fission, among them the combination of a relatively low level of formal education of Thai in Holland, a Thai style that prefers smooth and pleasant relationships above cost- and time-effectiveness, and the simultaneous necessity to deal with Dutch authorities and professional organizations in the Dutch way. Few Thai are in a position to commit themselves for a longer period to community organization. Most Thai live in a situation that forces them to search permanently for chances of financial gain. This attitude almost excludes disinterested long-term commitment, for example as a volunteer or board member of a foundation. One should accept that to most Thai migrants the capacity of independently making money is an important proof of their successful adaptation. Moreover, those who have regular jobs or secure economic positions often exhibit typical middle-class attitudes that hinder good contacts with the group of Thai involved in sex work. The solution for the lack of professional expertise lies in the nearness of Dutch marriage partners who represent all sectors of Dutch society. Among those married to Thai are lawyers, doctors, lecturers, engineers, policeman, computer specialists, government officials, and journalists. The incorporation of these Dutch professionals creates, understandably, new potential for conflict, but it is obvious that in the long run this expertise is an important and essential asset. Relevant here is the persistent experience that some Thai who suffer from AIDS refuse contact with other Thai but appreciate help offered by Westerners who speak their language—a clear indication that one should not automatically assume that only Thai can help Thai.

A decade ago a paper on this topic would have represented a highly peripheral and irrelevant discourse about culture and sexuality. Now it is related to issues of life and death. In the last part of this chapter, two wider and more general issues have been addressed implicitly. Firstly, how to combine the core of the anthropological approach (as exemplified in participation, observation, and in-depth interviewing) with finding practical answers to problems posed by the AIDS crisis in the case of a small group at the margins of Holland's or Europe's 'multiethnic society.' Secondly, I have attempted to demonstrate that for adequate AIDS solutions to be found, culture has to be treated as an asset, not as a barrier that has to be removed before intervention can start. What is true for the AIDS crisis in

Thailand is in a more specific sense also valid for the Thai community in Holland: in Thailand the openness about sexuality is as much a benefit as it is constitutive of sexual risk, while within the Thai community in Holland the highly visible and varied forms of involvement with sexuality are also an advantage in addressing the issues more profoundly and with greater commitment than could be the case in heterosexual Dutch society.

REFERENCES

Anchalee Singhanetra-Renard, 1993. 'Population movement and HIV/AIDS: Some conceptual considerations'. Paper prepared for the panel on 'The social and cultural context of the AIDS epidemic in Thailand' at the Fifth International Conference on Thai Studies, London, 5–10 July.

Aphichat Chamratrithirong (ed.). 1984. *Perspectives on the Thai Marriage*. Bangkok: Institute of Population Studies and Social Research, Mahidol University.

Bencha Yoddumnern-Attig, 1992. 'Thai family structure and organization: changing roles and duties in historical perspective'. In Yoddumnern-Attig, Bencha *et al.* (eds), *Changing Roles and Statuses of Women in Thailand. A Documentary Assessment*. Bangkok: Institute of Population Studies and Social Research, Mahidol University.

Bhassorn Limanonda, 1993. 'Female commercial sex workers and AIDS: Perspectives from Thai rural communities'. Paper prepared for the panel on 'The Social and Cultural Context of the AIDS epidemic in Thailand' at the Fifth International Conference on Thai Studies, London, 5–10 July.

Brown, Tim and Werasit Sittitrai, 1993. 'Estimates of Recent HIV Infection Levels in Thailand'. Program on AIDS, Research Report 9. Bangkok: Thai Red Cross Society.

—— ——, Suphak Vanichseni, and Usa Thisayakorn, 1994. 'The recent epidemiology of HIV/AIDS in Thailand'. *AIDS*, 8 (Suppl 2): S131–S141.

Brown, Tim and Peter Xenos, 1994. 'AIDS in Asia: the gathering storm'. *Asia Pacific Issues*, 6. Honolulu: East-West Center.

Brummelhuis, Han ten, 1984. 'Abundance and avoidance. An interpretation of Thai individualism'. In H. ten Brummelhuis and J. H. Kemp (eds), *Strategies and Structures in Thai Society*. Publikatieserie Vakgroep ZZOA, 31. Amsterdam: Antropologisch Sociologisch Centrum.

—— 1987. *Merchant, Courtier, and Diplomat. A History of the Contacts between the Netherlands and Siam*. Lochem: De Tijdstroom.

—— and Gilbert Herdt (eds), 1995. *Culture and Sexual Risk: Anthropological Perspectives on AIDS*. New York: Gordon and Breach.

Cohen, E., 1987. 'Sensuality and venality in Bangkok. The dynamics of cross cultural mapping of prostitution'. *Deviant Behavior*, 8: 223–34.

Dararut Mattariganond, 1983. 'Soopheenii kab najoobaaj khoong radthabaan ph. s. 2411–2503' [Prostitution and the policy of the Thai Government, 1886–1960]. MA thesis, Department of History, Chulalongkorn University.

Day, Sophie, 1990. 'Prostitute women and the ideology of work in London'. In Douglas A. Feldman (ed.), *Culture and AIDS*. New York: Praeger.

Elias, Norbert. 'Towards a Theory of Communities'. Foreword in Colin Bell and Howard

Newby (eds), *The Sociology of the Community. A Selection of Readings*. London: Frank Cass.

Jiraporn Witayasakpan, 1992. 'Nationalism and the transformation of aesthetic concepts: theatre in Thailand during the Phibun period'. Doctoral dissertation, Cornell University.

Kemp, Jeremy, 1988. *Seductive Mirage: The Search for the Village in Southeast Asia*. Comparative Asian Studies, 3. Dordrecht: Foris.

Kerkwijk, Carla van, 1995. 'The dynamics of condom use in Thai sex work with *farang* clients'. In H. ten Brummelhuis and G. Herdt (eds), *Culture and Sexual Risk: Anthropological Perspectives on AIDS*. New York: Gordon and Breach.

Netherlands Ministry of Foreign Affairs, 1945–1954. Bangkok Archives: 270–375. The Hague, The Netherlands.

Pasuk Phongpaichit and Samart Chiasakul, 1993. 'Services'. In Peter G. Warr (ed.), *The Thai Economy in Transition*. Cambridge: Cambridge University Press.

Reynolds, C. J. (ed.), 1991. *National Identity and its Defenders. Thailand, 1939–1989*. Monash Papers on Southeast Asia, 25. Clayton: Monash University.

Smith, George Vinal, 1980. 'Princes, Nobles, and Traders. Ethnicity and Economic Activity in Seventeenth-Century Thailand'. *Contributions to Asian Studies*, 15: 6–14.

Sumalee Bumroongsook, 1995. *Love and Marriage. Mate Selection in Twentieth-Century Central Thailand*. Bangkok: Chulalongkorn University Press.

Tanabe, Shigeharu (ed.), 1991. *Religious Traditions among Tai Ethnic Groups. A selected Bibliography*. Ayutthaya: Ayutthaya Historical Studies Center.

Weniger, Bruce *et al*. 1991. 'The epidemiology of HIV infection and AIDS in Thailand'. *AIDS*, 5 (Suppl. 2): S71–S85.

Werasit Sittitrai and Tim Brown, 1994. 'Risk factors for HIV infection in Thailand'. *AIDS*, 8 (Suppl.): S143–S153.

Yos Santasombat, 1993. 'Prologue'. In *'Hello My Big Big Honey.' Love Letters to Bangkok Bar Girls and Their Revealing Interviews*, collected by D. Walker and R. Ehrlich. Bangkok: Dragon Dance Publications. Expanded edition.

11 Mobility and Migration:

Female Commercial Sex Work and the HIV
Epidemic in Northern Thailand

KATHERINE C. BOND, DAVID D. CELENTANO,
SUNKANYA PHONSOPHAKUL, and CHAYAN VADDHANAPHUTI

Introduction

The commercial sex industry in Thailand is of singular importance in the dynamics of HIV transmission. Ford and Koetsawang (1991) suggest that the sex industry developed significantly during the Vietnam war, and has been amplified recently by international tourism. The majority of female commercial sex worker (CSW) clients, especially outside of the tourist centres and Bangkok, are Thai men (DaGrossa, 1989). Female CSWs in northern Thailand are predominately young women from agrarian backgrounds, recruited by agents, brothel owners, or friends, and generally have a short (under three years) duration of work in brothels, characterized by high mobility between establishments (Ministry of Public Health, 1993). The rapid rise in HIV infection rates among brothel CSWs, and the common use of CSWs by ethnic Thai, northern Thai, Shan, and highland (Hmong, Lahu, Lisu, Akha, and Karen) men suggests that commercial sex exposure is a particularly high risk behaviour for the acquisition of HIV in Thailand. In Chiang Mai, a provincial capital in northern Thailand, an HIV infection rate of 44 per cent was detected in the first sentinel surveillance of brothel-based CSWs in June 1989. Subsequently, high incidence (over 10 per cent per month) was noted among female CSWs who were HIV-negative on the initial survey (Siraprapasiri et al., 1991).

This chapter aims to provide recent evidence of social and economic factors underlying the spread and continuation of commercial sex work in northern Thailand, with an emphasis on social and spatial mobility. First, we review the epidemiology of HIV/AIDS in Thailand before discussing mobility and migration issues in the context of socioeconomic changes that are occurring in South-East Asia. Next, we address commercial sex as a pathway to economic mobility and the individual decisions and structural factors underlying entry into commercial sex work. Recruitment and procurement processes are presented. Finally, we trace the migratory paths of a small group of female sex workers in northern Thailand.

The data that are incorporated in this chapter come from three principal sources:

1. *SOMSEX Project* (AIDSCAP/Family Health International). As part of a study of social mobility, sexual behaviour, and HIV in northern Thailand, a collaborative project between the Johns Hopkins University and Chiang Mai University's Social Research Institute, we have collected qualitative data on female commercial sex workers in northern Thailand, with foci on migration patterns, as well as on aspects of women's choices and control in the context of brothels and their implications for intervention strategies. In-depth interviews were conducted with fifty-six commercial sex workers, nine establishment owners, and public health workers in four districts of Chiang Mai Province, two districts of Mae Hong Son Province, and one district of Lamphun Province, all in the upper north of Thailand. These small-scale establishments, located in urban, peri-urban and rural areas, included fifteen brothels and three restaurants, ranging in price for service from fifty to 200 Baht in brothels to 200–1500 Baht in restaurants. The conversion rate is approximately 25 Baht for one US dollar. The ethnic backgrounds of women in these establishments were lowland northern Thai, Shan, Lahu, Akha, Lisu, and central Thai.
2. *Preparation for AIDS Vaccine Evaluation (PAVE) Project* (CSWs in three northern Provinces). The Thai PAVE cohort reflects the wide range of establishment types where sexual transactions take place. While many of the sex workers in the cohort work in brothels (44.4 per cent), many more were recruited from other types of establishments: massage parlours (17.9 per cent), restaurants (15.7 per cent), bars and pubs (10.6 per cent), night clubs (7.6 per cent), as well as traditional massage parlours, cafés, and karaoke clubs.
3. *1992 Sex Workers Survey in Chiang Mai Province.* Commercial sex establishments were nominated by Royal Thai Army and Air Force conscripts in 1991 from the north as places they most frequently visited near barracks in two Chiang Mai and Lamphun provinces. The eleven selected sex establishments were of medium size ($\geq$ ten CSWs employed). A total of 273 commercial sex workers were interviewed.

During May and June, 1992, permission was obtained from managers of brothels and other sex establishments to conduct the study. A total of seven brothels, two restaurants, one bar, and one motel were included in the sample. Each woman underwent a face-to-face interview with a trained interviewer—a nurse who was not informed of the HIV-1 status of the respondent. The questionnaire ascertained sociodemographic status, medical history, sexually transmitted diseases, drug use, frequency and types of sexual contact with husbands and boyfriends; work history as a CSW; sexual practices with clients, including condom use; and knowledge of HIV-1 and its transmission.

I. HIV/AIDS in Thailand

The epidemic of human immunodeficiency virus (HIV) infection in Thailand was first diagnosed in a bisexual male in Bangkok in 1984. While additional cases were reported, the dramatic growth in prevalence was detected among injection drug users in Bangkok beginning in 1988 (Uneklabh and Phutiprawan, 1988; Vanichseni *et al.*, 1990), and then reached epidemic proportions among female CSWs by mid-1989 (Lancet, 1989). At least 600,000 Thais were believed to be infected with HIV in mid-1994, and the principal transmission route is now heterosexual intercourse (Weniger *et al.*, 1991). Semi-annual sentinel seroprevalence surveys for HIV were established throughout the country in June 1989 for selected populations (Ungchusak *et al.*, 1989). These include intravenous drug users (IDUs), female 'direct' (brothel) CSWs, higher class 'indirect' CSWs (bars, nightclubs, karaoke, massage parlours, coffee shops and call girls/escorts), male sexually transmitted disease clinic patients, blood donors, and women attending antenatal clinics.

Of the AIDS cases reported to the Thai Ministry of Public Health (MOPH) through June 1992, 70 per cent (449 of 642) were heterosexually transmitted; IDUs comprised 10 per cent of all cases (n = 64), and homosexual/bisexual men accounted for 6 per cent (n = 39) of reported cases (Ministry of Public Health 1992). The sentinel surveys ('early warning' epidemiologic cross-sectional studies of high risk populations in each province in Thailand) have shown increases in HIV seroprevalence rates throughout the country, and with each subsequent survey, the northern provinces have consistently had the highest rates in most groups for which data are collected.

II. Mobility and Migration in the Context of Socioeconomic Changes in Thailand

During the past three decades several social and economic forces have intensified the dynamics of migration, mobility, and sexual behaviour in northern Thailand. These pressures have been discussed in terms of: changes in economic and demographic structure resulting in rural–urban migration; gender role expectations in contributing to the family household and caring for aging parents; gender differences in educational and labour opportunities, resulting in female rural–urban migration; and changes in traditional social controls over sexual behaviour. Pathways to mobility include marriage, education, and urban employment.

The economic and demographic structure of Thailand is in the midst of a major transition. The population growth rate decreased by over 100 per cent (from 3.2 per cent in 1970 to 1.3 per cent in 1991), the birth rate slowed dramatically (to 17 per 1,000 population), and the resulting demographic structure is such that the younger age strata must increasingly care for the growing aging population. Fewer children caring for older parents will be a growing problem in the coming years (Yoddamnern-Attig, 1993). Thailand's traditional agricultural base as the cornerstone of its economy and social structure is being quickly replaced by a growing industrial sector; while perhaps 60–70 per cent of the population remains in the agricultural sector, only 12.4 per cent of the 1990 GDP was contributed by farming (Komin, 1993). Further, the disparity in wealth between rural and urban households has increased, with no improvement noted in the proportion of the population living below the poverty line (Kachondham and Chunharas, 1993). In order to improve their economic and social standing, the only option available to the rural poor is to migrate to towns and cities.

Pressures on the rural poor to migrate to urban areas lead to a loss of economic security and a need for social mobility. These pressures include: population pressure on increasingly scarce land resources; a decline in the importance of agricultural work in a society which values light manufacturing and export; the decreasing importance of the village as the point of economic development; and the diminishing influence of the local community and its social control mechanisms (Singhanetra-Renard, 1994). Yoddamnern-Attig (1993) suggests that factors with important demographic and public health consequences include: declining family size and improving life expectancy; a labour shortage in the manufacturing and services industries; and high female rural–urban migration. Migration patterns in northern Thailand have been categorized as circulatory and seasonal, with labourers seeking temporary employment with the intention of returning home to rural areas. This pattern of circulatory rural–urban–rural migration has facilitated the diffusion of HIV to all regions of the country (Ford and Koetsawang, 1991, Singhanetra-Renard, 1994). Our data indicate that highland-to-lowland migration and cross-border migration patterns are also very relevant to HIV transmission in northern Thailand.

High female urban migration is linked to different familial role expectations placed on daughters and sons. Thai parents fulfil three roles: provide and raise their children to adulthood; accumulate wealth for their children to inherit; and encourage daughters to marry to allow for parental age security, so-called 'dependency reversal' (Pramualratana, 1992). Knodel *et al.*, (1984: 50), referring to parental repayment, comment that 'the expectation that children will provide comfort and support to their parents .... is shared by virtually all segments of Thai society'. *Bounkhun*, practical and moral indebtedness, reflects a sense of obligation, and serves as an impetus for women to seek employment opportunities that will allow them to accumulate wealth for the care of their (aging) parents. In contrast, sons may be viewed as having a family role associated with stability—providing local labour or participation in family economic schemes (acting as an agricultural labourers, traders of the family wares, etc.). Unlike a daughter, a son is able to repay his *bounkhun* by being ordained as a monk.

Marriage has been viewed as a woman's primary pathway to social mobility throughout Thailand, and one means by which she can provide security for her aging parents. With reference to central Thailand, Akin writes:

One of the ways by which a girl repays the parents *bounkhun* is to get married to a man who possesses resources which may be used to support her parents. He can be a wealthy man, a politically powerful man, or even a man who is hard working and able to earn money . . . It is natural, therefore, that in normal expectation, the girls are to marry up. This means that the groom should be a person of higher status than the bride (Akin, 1984: 23).

This preference for 'marrying up' existed within a system of polygamy among the upper strata. Under the *Sakdinaa* system, the feudal system of land management that preceded the nation-state, it was common for aristocrats to have several wives as an indicator of status. There are two important implications of this system. First, it was more highly valued to be the *mia noi* ('minor wife' or mistress) of a wealthy man than the *mia luang* (major wife) of a poor man with 'low mobility'. Second, the presence of many wives among the upper classes may have resulted in a shortage of women for lower class men (Hantrakul, 1983: 17). Thus, the tradition of polygamy often has been cited as a historical antecedent to the development of the commercial sex industry in Thailand (Phongpaichit, 1982; Akin, 1983; Muecke, 1992).

Educational paths to social mobility also vary according to gender. For rural men, education is universally available, through village schools, or male social institutions such as the monkhood and the military. For rural women, the pathways other than marriage to elevated social mobility are education and urban employment (Singhanetra-Renard, 1994). While educational opportunities are more commonly provided to men through the traditional institutions mentioned above (Singhanetra-Renard, 1994; Yoddamnern-Attig, 1993), a family's deliberate investment in education is preferentially female (Gray, 1994).

Daughters are considered to be a principal means of the family's economic improvement, through the provision of wages, income and other remittances, which may ultimately result in educational opportunities for younger siblings. Most occupational choices for off-farm employment are urban-based, such as office, factory, or service work. These choices are limited to village girls and families with enough resources to invest in formal education, resources beyond the grasp of many northern Thai villagers (Gray, 1990).

The choices for ethnic minorities are even more limited. The subsistence of the six predominant mountain or 'hill tribe' ethnic groups—Karen, Hmong, Lahu, Mien, Akha, and Lisu—has depended on gathering, hunting, fishing, and swidden agriculture. The majority of these groups arrived in northern Thailand in the mid- to late nineteenth century from neighbouring Burma (Myanmar), Laos, and Yunnan Province of southern China. The integration of these highland economies with the lowland has led to a greater degree of highland-lowland migration. As outlined by Kammerer *et al.*, (1993), a large part of the economic transformation has centred around the opium trade. They argue that entry into a cash economy, and eradication of their most lucrative crop, opium, have contributed to the necessity of young hill tribe women migrating to cities and—because of their limited choices—into commercial sex work.

The Thai Yai, or Shan, reside in the northern Shan States of Myanmar and border areas of Chiang Mai and Mae Hong Son Provinces. This area, also known as the 'Golden Triangle,' is regarded as the centre of opium production and trade in South-East Asia, and is the site of on-going wars for the control of opium. At the time of writing, the Myanmar military rulers, State Law and Order Restoration Council (SLORC), were involved in a massive attack on the Shan States, leading to the flight of many Shan across the border. The majority of women found in low-priced brothels were from the Shan States of Myanmar.

In summary, the social, political, and economic environment is generating the movement of populations, particularly young women, from the countryside to cities, from the hills to the lowlands, and across borders. Poverty, and lack of education and occupational choice, are the principal reasons for young women's entrance into sex work (Phongpaichit, 1982; Pramualratana, 1992; Asia Watch, 1994). The following section outlines the evolution of the commercial sex industry in Thailand.

III. Commercial Sex as a Pathway to Economic and Social Mobility

The magnitude of the Thai commercial sex industry has received considerable international attention. Estimates of the number of CSWs range from 200,000 to 700,000 (Sittitrai and Brown, 1991; Apisuk, cited in Bonacci, 1990: 28). The commercial sex industry's development corresponded with periods of economic development in Thailand's history. Entertainment tastes from each period were adopted, partially accounting for the diversity in commercial sex establishments. From the fifteenth century to the nineteenth century, women were sold by parents or husbands to serve Siamese peasants, Chinese immigrants, labourers, and Western traders. This form of slavery was not outlawed until the twentieth century. Prostitution became more urbanized after World War II, with the construction of hotels and teahouses by Chinese merchants. During the Vietnam War, internationally known areas such as Patpong in Bangkok, and Pattaya Beach, sprouted cafés, go-go bars, massage parlours, and beer bars to cater to American GIs. In the 1980s, with an increase in investment and tourism from Japan, brothels and restaurants were converted into karaoke establishments where women sit and sing with customers prior to being 'taken off'. In 1994, simple brothel structures in both urban and rural areas were closed due to the government child prostitution policy. Some establishments have re-opened in the form of restaurants and karaoke bars to avoid government crackdowns. Communication technology such as mobile telephones and page phones are also employed to get around this crackdown and facilitate new, hidden forms of commercial sex.

In addition to these socioeconomic factors, Santasombut (1991), a Thai scholar, attributes the development of the sex industry to the commodification of women's beauty. Western concepts of beauty were introduced with the first beauty pageant in 1934. Beauty pageants, a part of every festival, have since become an integral part of tourism and local development. This emphasis on physical beauty, in the presence of a growing 'monetary' culture, has undermined women's domestic authority and contributed to the acceptance of the sale of sex.

One of the earliest and widely referenced studies of pathways to commercial sex work in Thailand addressed the migration of northern and north-eastern Thai women to massage parlours in Bangkok (Phongpaichit, 1982). The initial economic transaction (more of a 'loan' than a 'sale' (Gray, 1994)) provides immediate funds for the family which can immediately effect their standard of living as well as future employment options. The fees paid by procurers in the form of a loan (with interest generally calculated at 100 per cent) may allow a family to purchase land or a homestead, to invest in 'business', to settle former debts, and to accumulate consumer goods and other symbols of prosperity (such as a television or motorcycle). The transformation of the family from landless agricultural labourers into landed farmers or traders provides a clear form of social mobility that could not exist otherwise. Further, their improved economic standing in the village may stimulate others to participate in this scheme.

Social and economic mobility through sex work extends beyond the individual woman and her family to the community in which she lives (Pongpaichit, 1982; Muecke, 1992; Limanonda, 1993; and Yoddamnern-Attig, 1993). Descriptions of previously poor villages adorned with beautiful houses and material goods due to the remissions of daughters abound in the popular media. Limandonda (1993) found that the acceptance of commercial sex work by a community often depends on the success of the households in raising their status. In some areas well-known as sources of recruitment, such as Phayao Province, women returning from the cities contribute to village development (building wells and temples), thereby raising their status in the community (Muecke, 1992).

The current political instability in Shan States, Myanmar, also contributes to the influx of ethnic Shan into sex work. Recruitment networks extend beyond Chiang Tung, the major city in Shan States. There has been evidence of ethnic minorities entering into sex work in the mid- to late 1980s. The 'illicit economy' referred to by Kammerer *et al.* (1993) highlights the trading of opium and highland women and the use of heroin. Many highland women in commercial sex work come from drug-addicted families. The demand for younger 'AIDS-free' girls has contributed to the extension of recruitment networks further into the hills (Gray, 1994; Kammerer *et al.*, 1993).

IV. Individual Decisions and Structural Factors for Entering Commercial Sex Work

The structural forces that encourage families and daughters to engage in the commercial sex industry set the stage in which individual decisions are influenced. Our interviews revealed four major reasons women gave for becoming sex workers: the need to send remittances to parents; divorce or widowhood, resulting in providing primary support for children; loss of virginity prior to marriage; and prior experience of rape or domestic abuse. The first two influences are compounded by lack of economic alternatives, while the latter two result more from personal experience and ensuing loss of a sense of identity and self-esteem. We provide examples of each of these forces using the words provided in our in-depth interviews of women in northern Thailand.

Remittances to family

Given the lucrative (by rural standards) pay associated with sex work, and the (often false or exaggerated) promises made to parents by brothel procurers, the promise of substantial economic contributions by daughters to the household economy is thought to be the principal reason for entry into sex work. Previous studies have shown that the majority of Thai sex workers send remittances to family members in their home areas. The large majority of sex workers in the PAVE study sent remittances home, with 92.7 per cent of brothel-based women doing so, and 85.7 per cent of women in so-called 'indirect' establishments. While the amounts vary, this nearly universal behaviour demonstrates the economic contribution made by daughters in the sex industry to the welfare of their parents. Information from our qualitative research on sex workers in the north substantiates the survey data.

M, a farmer's daughter from Chiang Rai Province, has been working in commercial sex establishments for over ten years. Currently, she earns 7,000–8,000 Baht per month. She has had only two years of formal education. She sends most of her earnings to her mother, with the intention of supporting her mother, father, and a daughter. Her older sister and older brother are both married. Her younger brother is also married, and is currently serving two years in the army. Since working, she has bought a house, television, and refrigerator for her family, but all have since been sold. Her older brother and sister each ask their mother for money sent home by M. When she visits home, they tell her that if she continues to work like this, she will get AIDS. She feels that as long as her siblings continue to take the earnings sent to her mother, she will be unable to stop work. Her sense of *bounkhun*, or indebtedness, prevents her from changing this situation.

Entering into sex work may be a deliberate strategy employed by women in the event of short-term emergencies and debt, particularly when they are the sole or primary contributor to the parents' household. One informant told us:

I didn't want to do it [go to work in the brothel]. I thought about it a lot. But I didn't have a choice. I have to provide for my father, mother and child. My father is seventy-five years old and in ill health. He went into the hospital, and had a bill of 7,000 Baht. I didn't know where else to work to pay off the debt. My son is four years old. I divorced my husband. I don't want to do this kind of work. I cry here every night. I miss my child. I'm ashamed to work like this.

These examples illustrate the daughter's sense of obligation (*bounkhun*) to her parents, given the few employment alternatives available to those with little education. They also raise the question of economic contributions made by other members of the household or family. In both cases, these daughters were the sole contributors to the household income. In the case of M, however, other siblings benefited from her contributions rather than sharing the responsibility to provide for parents. The family's use of remittances, in turn, determines the length a woman works and the sense of social and economic improvement she feels she has contributed to the family.

Divorce and widowhood

There are other avenues to sex work that, on the surface, appear similar to the situation described above. One of the principal reasons for older women is the loss of a stable family relationship. In a prospective study of sex workers in the north (Beyrer *et al.*, 1993), a large proportion (55 per cent) of 'indirect' CSWs (those working in establishments outside of brothels) were divorced. Many young widows were left with no means of support. Many had dependent children, and there was an economic imperative for them to become employed. With limited skills and education, sex work offered an avenue by which they were able to provide the economic needs for their parents and children. There is some familial aggregation of sex workers, with older sisters, aunts and other relatives serving as role models or procurers. One informant described this situation as follows:

T is a forty-two year-old woman from Fang district of Chiang Mai Province who entered a brothel as a means to escape her husband. She had broken up with her husband eleven times in the previous three years, each time because he drank, gambled, and had affairs. At any funeral he would play cards and dice until morning for several days on end. Each time she left him, her husband would ask for forgiveness. She finally decided to find work in a rural brothel owned by a friend in a nearby province. She left her two children in her mother's care. Our field workers visited her home, and learned that she had worked in commercial sex establishments prior to this separation.

Widowhood can also be a pathway to commercial sex work. N's father took a new wife when she was a little girl so she lived with her grandmother. N did not get along with her step-mother. When she went to visit her father, her step-mother would tell her: 'You don't have to come here. Leave now.' She stopped visiting her father. At eighteen, she married a Thai Yai (Shan) man. When her child was eight months old, her husband died of malaria; N was twenty-one. She went to work in Lamphun, collecting *lamyai* fruits in an orchard, leaving her child with an aunt. She worked in Mae Sai for ten days as a hired labourer and then went home. A friend invited her to work in Cambodia. She stayed there for five months, working with loggers during the day, and receiving customers for sex at night. Many of her customers were drivers of logging trucks. Widowed, and with no other family support, N engaged in a number of types of employment to support her son. He is now seven years old and goes to school.

These situations lead us to reflect on the husband's role in contributing to the children's welfare, and the phenomenon that many female sex workers are also mothers. Without the support of the father, or a social welfare system for single mothers, women must rely on extended family members to look after their children while they find ways to send money home and, ultimately, to advance the educational opportunities for their children.

Loss of virginity

There are discrepancies in the Thai ethnographic literature referring to the social value attached to virginity and attitudes towards premarital sexual activity. Several reports explain the existence of commercial sex work in terms of the 'double standards of sexuality' which holds premarital sexual relations as taboo for women, but acceptable and even to be encouraged for men (Ford and Koetsawang, 1991; Cash, 1993). Village-based ethnographic studies in north and north-east Thailand describe premarital sexual activity as common within the context of daily life and village social controls. In northern Thailand, social control is exerted through domestic ancestral spirit cults. Sexual misconduct is regarded as a serious offence against the spirits, *phit phii*, and results in a member of the household falling ill. Traditionally, a marriage was arranged between a young man and woman who were discovered to have engaged in premarital physical contact. For many young men and women, these marriages did not last, and once terminated, each was free to remarry (Gray, 1994; Mougne, 1981; Singhanetra-Renard, 1993). Chayan refers to multiple sexual partners among northern Thai women in terms of multiple remarriage (Chayan, 1993). A woman from a poor family may have married at a young age. Due to incompatibility or conflict between her husband and her own family, a break-up would occur. She may remarry, often several times. Chayan (1993:5) writes: 'Marriage is an institution which legitimized culturally appropriate sexual relations'.

The loss of virginity may be a catalyst for poor women to enter sex work. P is a twenty-four year-old northern Thai, also from Fang district of Chiang Mai Province. She decided to work in a brothel in a district south of Chiang Mai after she lost her virginity at the age of fourteen. She described the experience, and the shame and embarrassment that followed:

I went with a village boy. I loved and admired him so much. One day he invited me to see a movie shown at the village school. I told him I didn't have any money so he even bought my ticket. After the movie we sneaked into the school. That was my first time. I remember the blood all over my school uniform. I would have done anything for him, and I thought he really wanted me. The next day, I saw him with another girl. I felt so ashamed. I couldn't look at him in the face. I didn't know what to do. Around that time, an agent contacted my parents to work in Tung Siaw [a low-cost brothel area south of Chiang Mai City]. I thought about it and decided I had nothing to lose. So I went. My family was so poor, and my brother couldn't support us.

P eventually married a young man who was a regular customer and went to live with his family. The stigma associated with her work, along with an inability to conceive children resulted in her husband's family ostracizing her from the household. After two years, she returned to work in a brothel. The cultural belief that women with more than one sexual partner are 'bad' or 'spoiled' leads to low self-esteem among women. In P's case, she lost her virginity prior to marriage, and once married, was unable to 'redeem' herself in the role of mother.

Rape, domestic abuse, and neglect

Incidents of rape and domestic abuse are also cited by women as a reason they entered into sex work. They explain that they needed to escape their unhappy home lives, and because they have been 'spoiled' (*sia*), selling sex becomes a viable livelihood. Young girls and women with no family support are particularly vulnerable, as evident in the widespread problem of child prostitution.

S is fifteen years old, from Mae Sarieng district in Mae Hong Son, the most remote province in the north-west of Thailand. Her father died and her mother remarried. She finished the fourth grade and, at the age of thirteen, was raped by her uncle and left unconscious. Her father was still alive then and took her to the hospital. After the rape, her mother took her to 'sell her body' in Bangkok and Pattaya. She worked in establishments that catered to foreign customers. Her uncle was sent to prison and has since been released. S is afraid of her uncle, and does not dare to return home for fear of being shot.

Y's parents divorced and both remarried when she was young. She has a total of eighteen brothers and sisters. When she was nine years old, she was sent to live with her older sister who worked in a brothel. Y started sex work in a restaurant in Ayuthaya, and then moved to this Chiang Dao brothel. She learned about sex work by watching everything that went on in her sister's brothel, and has never lived outside a brothel. Hence, she regards the relationships in the brothel as normal.

We must consider the potential impact of rape or incest on women's sexual experience and development of sexuality in enduring life as a sex worker. In some establishments, the owners and other workers are regarded as fictive kin. The provision of food and shelter, the company and support shared among women, and the sweet talk of customers may provide comfort to some women whose home lives never provided them with a sense of safety or security. Most young women, however, feel a sense of despair at the lack of support and the endurement of conditions in brothels. Few shelters or other alternatives are available to these young women.

V. The Process of Recruitment or Procurement

In northern Thailand, three patterns of 'recruitment' of girls and young women into the sex industry stand out: they may be contacted by agents in their villages; they may be introduced to an establishment by friends or relatives; or they may locate an establishment and 'apply' to work there. These channels are not mutually exclusive; many women may use all three in the course of their careers.

The system of agents contacting young women in villages is well organized in northern Thailand. It is sometimes referred to by northern Thai as *tok khiew*, or 'green harvest'. The term originally meant 'pledging green paddy' for loans when farmers did not have enough to sustain themselves before harvest (Hengkietisak, 1994). It now connotes an elaborate system of village-based loans, with farmers pledging their daughters' labour in the commercial sex industry. Brothel owners approach a village and develop contacts with 'agents', villagers who may have worked in commercial sex previously, or who serve as agents to outsiders. These village-based agents know the economic or personal circumstances of each family, which may warrant the daughter's entering into sex work.

K is one example. A northern Thai woman from Chiang Rai Province, she has worked in a wide range of commercial sex establishments over a period of ten years. She described how she was recruited:

The agents who contacted me each time were different. Some were from Chiang Rai. Some were from my own village. Every time the agent got 1,500–2,000 Baht per person. It depends on how much the owners give them. I knew some of them from before, from the village. Most agents have good personalities. They'll advise us well about where there are a lot of customers, where the money is good. And when we go, it's just like they said it would be. The agent will take us to the place we work. Some of them are certain—they'll take care of us the whole way there, and are very nice.

K's perspective of these agents is not atypical, although others complain of being raped or abused by agents in transit. Many agents and owners rationalize their work as providing the girl and her family with a pathway out of poverty.

Uncle T, a brothel owner in a rural district of Chiang Mai Province, uses agents to procure new girls to work in his village-based brothel. Of the ten women currently working there, nearly half have come from Burma. The others are northern or central Thai or hill tribe. The term *nok tor*, or 'decoy', is used to describe the agents who work on behalf of the owner. This term is also used with other illegal activities. Uncle uses *nok tor* because he feels that he will not be trusted by villagers who do not know him.

I tell the agent how many girls I need and he finds them for me. He knows the girls and the villagers. It may be someone from that village. I pay the *nok tor* 2,000 Baht per person. I have to pay the girls' parents first. Like these four new girls—I paid almost 100,000 Baht—an average of 20,000 baht per family. These girls suffer from economic problems—that's why they work. If their families weren't suffering, the daughter wouldn't come. If I were them, I wouldn't do this—it ruins their health, they have to put up with the smell of alcohol. If the parents take the money first, I don't charge interest. Other places will charge 20 per cent interest. I feel sorry for them so I don't charge this money. 20 per cent is a lot.

Uncle T reflects the belief that he is helping the girls and their families. In fact, he doubles the girls' debts, as is the common practice among most owners and agents. Recently, many brothel owners have complained that they have been unable to find families willing to let their daughters work in brothels. As a result, they employ agents to recruit young women and girls farther into neighbouring countries and other regions, such as north-east Thailand.

After having worked in the commercial sex industry, many women use their friendship networks in the village or in different establishments to locate new places to work or to bring friends into the establishment. Some owners reduce the women's debt if they can recruit friends, thereby saving the agent's fee, and ensuring the women will remain longer in the establishment. Some Bangkok establishments operate almost entirely on the friendship recruitment system.

O is a seventeen-year-old northern Thai girl from Mae Sai, the northernmost town of Thailand. She has worked in a rural district restaurant for six months. She first went on a journey to Fang with her older brother. She saw a place on the way and wanted to work there because she had a friend who worked there. She earns about 1,200 Baht per month.

K also recruits friends into her establishments, reasoning: 'If I am better off, I want friends to have an opportunity to become better off. I check with those who are willing, sexually experienced, or previously married.' These categories imply that women are already 'spoiled' (*sia*) and willing to engage in commercial sex. Once women have been introduced to the sex trade via agents or friends, they learn how to contact establishments independently. Many women in sex work approach establishments in which they know someone. Others reach their city of destination and ask rickshaw drivers or local residents about establishments in which to work.

A minority of women in the industry still report having been lured or tricked into working in brothels without their knowledge (Asia Watch, 1994). This phenomenon usually occurs with ethnic minority women from within Thailand and Myanmar who have worked as itinerant labourers in one particular city in northern Thailand. Minority women and those crossing the border are particularly vulnerable to being tricked into the trade because they lack language skills, legal identity cards that allow them access to government services, and family or other support systems in the local areas.

For example, D is a young Lahu woman who had been married to a Lahu man. Her husband gambled and drank so she left him in order to find work to support her two sons. She first worked in a construction site in Mae Sai, where she earned 80 Baht per day—not enough to survive. After a short period, she was approached by a middle-aged man who told her that she would make more money in Chiang Mai. Out of desperation, she trusted him and was brought to Mae Rim, a district north of the city of Chiang Mai. They travelled at night so she was unable to discern where she was or to remember the way. She also cannot remember what the man looked like. She was never told what kind of work she would have to do.

A, another Lahu girl, was brought by an uncle at the age of five to work as domestic help for a brothel owner. When she became a young woman, *pen saaw*, she was forced to sell sex. She does not know where her home is or how to escape. In the past few years, she has tried to escape approximately twenty times. Because she does not know where to go, she travels until she runs out of money. She then contacts an establishment to find work. Each time, the network of establishment owners has been mobilized to return her to her original workplace.

Many women will not talk about the agents who brought them into the brothel, usually referring to them as *phii khon nan* ('that older brother' or older man). There have been documented cases of owners and agents who kill or threaten the women and their families in the case of disclosure or escape (Gray, 1994).

Once having been tricked into working in the commercial sex industry, women may then seek further employment on their own (Gray, 1994). O, another Lahu woman, left her husband because he was addicted to opium. After they separated, an older 'friend' (*phii khon nung*) invited her to work in Fang where he said she could wash dishes. She later discovered that this friend worked for an agent and received 2,000 Baht to trick her. She had to pay back a debt of 4,000 Baht. She described sex work as a village norm, one of the few alternatives to living, impoverished, with drug-addicted husbands.

A lot of women in the village work like this—but most of them work in Bangkok. I don't have an identity card so I didn't go. I won't stay here long. After the Thai New Year I will go home to farm. In the future, I will marry a Northern Thai man, not a Lahu man.

O's statement indicates that commercial sex work has become an accepted alternative in many hill tribes and, as with northern Thai women, a potential route to marriage. While ethnic Thai sex workers refer to mobility through marriage to a person of higher socioeconomic status, particularly a foreigner, highland women regard marriage to an ethnic Thai as 'marrying up.' This ethnic hierarchy reflects the power relations and status of men and women within and across ethnic groups. Many women see marrying a man of a different and preferably 'higher' ethnic group as an escape from existing social and economic constraints within the village, and an opportunity to gain access to a broader range of social and economic resources.

VI. Spatial and Occupational Mobility of Sex Workers in Chiang Mai, Lamphun and Mae Hong Son Provinces

While much has been written about the mobility of sex workers in general terms, little empirical data have been published concerning the actual experiences of women themselves. Mobility, as we present it here, can be characterized as spatial (or geographical) movement and occupational mobility, or movement in and out of sex work. In the Thai PAVE study, there was significant variation in education among the 396 women enrolled in the longitudinal investigation. Slightly less than one-quarter (22.7 per cent) reported no formal education, while 86.1 per cent reported primary school completion or less (seven grades in the Thai system). A further 9.1 per cent has some secondary education, with only 4.8 per cent completing a high school degree.

A breakdown of the ethnic backgrounds of this population of women from three northern Thai provinces (Lamphun, Chiang Mai, and Phayao) shows that 85.4 per cent were ethnic Thai lowlanders. Of the ethnic minorities represented, twenty-seven women (6.8 per cent) were Shan and eight (2 per cent) came from elsewhere in Myanmar, a traditional migration point for sex workers in northern Thailand. The remaining women were from ethnic minorities that have been commonly referred to as 'hill tribes'—Karen, Akha, Hmong, and Lahu.

The women in this sample had worked at an average of 1.75 different sex establishments, including the present location. Three-eighths (37.9 per cent) reported that the current establishment was their first workplace. The total number of places among those who were mobile ranged from two to eleven, with the majority having worked in a total of two locations. A review of the locations of the prior establishment demonstrated diverse geographical movement, ranging from Bangkok and the south, to locations in the same local area.

We also questioned the sex workers about their occupational history before entry into sex work. Approximately one-third (32.1 per cent) had previously worked as an agricultural labourer, and one-quarter as an employee in a small shop or as a vendor. Other common occupations were those of waitress, labourer (often in construction), or maid or domestic. Notably, two women reported that they had worked in a brothel but not as sex workers. Our in-depth interviews revealed that some women are recruited into the brothel first, as domestic labour, and later as sex workers. In addition, 18 per cent of the women reported prior long periods of unemployment.

Current income varied considerably among this population of sex workers. Their average charge per sexual service ranged from 10 Baht to 3,000 Baht. However, given the diversity of our population of women, this is not unanticipated. When stratified by establishment type (brothel versus external employment), women's income in the brothel averaged 50 Baht, as compared to nearly 500 Baht earned by women who were 'indirect' sex workers (those who sold sexual services in bars, massage parlours, etc., where a 'take-away' fee is imposed and then the charge is individually negotiated by the woman directly).

The following section outlines migratory paths of women in selected, low-priced brothels and restaurants. Our data come from in-depth interviews with fifty-six commercial sex workers, in which we asked for the temporal sequence by which they ended up in the present location and their reasons for moving. We present our data by establishment, referring to the maps of Thailand to guide the reader.

Chiang Dao—Brothel One

Brothel One of Chiang Dao district is off the main road connecting Chiang Dao to points north and south, down a dirt road entering into a mid-sized village. A number of households in the village have daughters who have 'gone south' to work, and have married foreign men. Brothel One is surrounded by a metal fence, and the gate opens out to a beautiful view of mountains and green soy fields. Beyond the dirt entry is an area with picnic tables, sheltered by a metal roof. To the left is a small bar with beer, soft drinks, stimulant drinks, and snacks for sale. Just beyond is an area with levelled benches. During the day, the young women in the brothel sit or stretch out on the benches under a ceiling fan and watch television or sleep. At night they sit under lights, waiting to be selected by customers. The customers sit at the tables at the entrance, drink, talk, play cards, and then select a woman. Behind this area is a row of cement block rooms, each supplied with a bed and a small bedside stand. To the rear of each room is a separate open area for showering, with a water urn and hose.

The women in this establishment are of diverse origins; however, several were recruited together and now comprise the core of the brothel. A, a Shan woman from Chiang Tung (Shan State, Myanmar), crossed the border at Tachilek and Mae Sai, the northernmost point in Thailand. From there she was taken to a holding-point in Chiang Khong, a border town in northeast Chiang Rai Province, where she waited three months to get her 'white card' (a transit document). She was taken to Fang where she worked in a brothel for twenty days. The brothel was forced to close, so she was moved to Chiang Dao Brothel One (where she has been for approximately four months). The brothel owner in Fang paid her family 10,000 Baht up front. She is required to pay off 20,000. When the brothel in Fang was forced to shut, the owner of Chiang Dao Brothel One paid off the debt of 20,000 Baht. She now owes this brothel 40,000 Baht. She reports a price of 100 Baht per customer, with between five and ten clients per day. A told us that her parents used the money to build a house. She has an older brother and brother-in-law who have gone to Bangkok to work as painters on construction sites. Her older sister stays at home with her mother. When asked what type of occupation she would like, she responded that she would rather go home to work in the fields than stay in the brothel.

S, H, and G are relatives from the same village near Chiang Tung. G was the first to leave the village to work in Kampaeng Din, the dirt-wall brothel district in Chiang Mai. She stayed for one year and returned to her home near Chiang Tung. She complained that when she returned, she had no friends, and there was nothing to do in the village. She left Chiang Tung with S and H, and travelled to Mae Sai, where they met A and followed the same path. As in the case of A, the brothel in Fang was forced to shut so the owner of Brothel One paid off the debts and took them in to work. S has eleven to twenty-one customers per day during the high season. She has paid off all but 5,000 Baht of her debt; however, when we asked if she planned to stay longer, she said that she would continue to work and make money.

O is from a Lisu village in Vieng Pa Pao district of Chiang Rai Province. She had been married to a man in her village. When she was pregnant, her husband took her to work in Tung Siaw, a brothel region near San Patong. She returned to her village to give birth, separated from her husband and left her child in her mother's care. She then moved to a restaurant/bar in Chiang Mai, where she served mostly foreign tourists. She then moved to Chiang Dao Brothel One, where she worked for nearly a year. At our last visit, she had escaped, and reportedly had gone home.

Y was born in the central Thai province of Saraburi. She moved to live with an older sister in a brothel in Ayuthaya when she was nine years old. She went to Mae Sai to work in a brothel for two months before coming to Chiang Dao Brothel One, where she has worked for five years. She tried to go to Hong Kong, but could not obtain a passport. She reported a price of 50 Baht per customer, although she complained of attracting very few customers. Since our last interview, she has moved to Roi Et in the north-east to work in a different brothel.

Once they enter the establishment, young women form relationships with each other, the owner, and customers, and adapt to a new set of controls. In most establishments, women of the same origin or ethnic group form close bonds which help them cope with the brothel environment. In Brothel One, the four women from Shan States have established a strong 'force' in the brothel, with S as the leader. She has adapted most quickly, formed alliances with the owner, and threatened the position of the previous 'leader'. These young women must also learn to adapt to the sexual subculture of their customers, which includes sexual practices specific to the commercial sex encounter and the relationship of client to sex worker. Some examples include 'playing positions' (*len thaa*), or customers being drunk or forceful to the point of violence (Bond, 1994).

Chiang Dao—Brothel Two

Just up the road from Brothel One in the village near Chiang Dao is a smaller brothel to the left. It is also enclosed by a fence. When we visited, there were only two women working. The owner complained that business was slow, and she was having trouble finding women to work. She had to pay for her daughter's tertiary education in the city, in addition to meeting the expenses of running the brothel and paying for the women's food and lodging. She was looking for a buyer for the brothel. Since our last visit to Chiang Dao, Brothel Two has closed. The owner has gone to live with her mother, but we do not know where the women have gone.

O is half Shan and half Khon Muang (lowland northern Thai) from Vieng Haeng district, near the border with Myanmar. She has a child of seven. She divorced her husband because he was an alcoholic. She left home at the age of twenty to work as a seamstress for two months in a factory in Sankampaeng, an area just east of Chiang Mai City with many handicraft factories. There she made 2,000–3,000 Baht per month. It was not enough to support her child. She then worked for six days making umbrellas in Bo Sang, where umbrella factories attract busloads of tourists. Again, the income was not enough to support her child, so she was taken by an agent from her village to a brothel in Had Yai, in the southern province of Songkla, where she worked for six months. She then moved to Suphanburi, north of Bangkok, and worked in a brothel for three months. She moved again to Saraburi, where she worked six months in a brothel, and took her earnings home. She returned to Saraburi for seven days, and then moved to

Lampang, where she lived for two years, working first in a brothel, then a coffee shop, and finally, a hotel. She ended up in Brothel Two in Chiang Dao. Her expenses include life insurance for her parents, self, and child at 600 Baht per adult per month and 300 per child; and payments on a debt, at 2,000 baht per month. If her parents borrow more money, she has to pay off the debt at 20–25 per cent interest per month.

L is also Shan, from Vieng Haeng, the same district as O, an area heavily populated with ethnic Shan and influenced by the Shan army. She was recruited into the brothel by the owner. She has no education and speaks very little Thai, leading us to believe that she may actually have originated from Myanmar. This is her first workplace.

Figure 11.1 presents a summary of the patterns of spatial mobility of the women in the two Chiang Dao brothels. There is strong evidence of a direct pattern of migration from border towns in the upper north and Shan State in Myanmar. The pattern follows a primary north–south autoroute connecting Chiang Rai and Chiang Mai Provinces, from the major border crossing town of Mae Sai to the town of Fang, and then down to Chiang Dao. Also seen are pathways from the north, south of Chiang Dao, to the northern capital city of Chiang Mai, with the ultimate destination being Chiang Dao. There are few deviations from this pattern. Four Shan women share a very similar pattern of migration, with short respites in eastern Chiang Rai province awaiting documentation; after this, they join the common pattern. Only two out of eight women reported any migration out of the upper north; one had originated in central Thailand (Saraburi) and made a stopover in Ayuthaya before moving to Chiang Dao. The other woman had moved to Had Yai in the south after being in a brothel in Chiang Mai for a brief period. Overall, the pattern noted for these women follows a consistent pathway, from the north to Chiang Dao, with little migration elsewhere in the country.

Mae Rim—Restaurant One

This restaurant/brothel is located off the main road past the market area of Mae Rim. It is connected to another restaurant that has since been shut down. It is a wooden structure, with tables and chairs at the front, and a small platform set up for singers. At night, the restaurant is lit with neon lights, and neon-coloured styrofoam signs. To the rear are cement block rooms where women take the customers for sexual services.

The women in this restaurant come from other areas of northern Thailand, and have used existing friendship networks to get work. S, the fifteen-year old who was raped at the age of thirteen, has been working for two years, first in Pattaya, then Bangkok and now in this Mae Rim restaurant. M is seventeen years old, from the same town of Mae Sarieng as S. She worked in two commercial establishments in Mae Sarieng before going to Mae Rim. She claims the price per service in Mae Sarieng is higher than in Mae Rim. She also worked in Lamphun in a similar kind

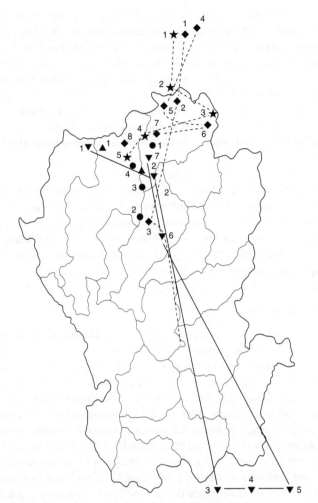

Fig. 11.1. Migration paths of Chiang Dao brothel workers

of restaurant. She stopped working in Lamphun to live with her husband, and grow garlic. In their village, many wives work as seasonal CSWs. M acted as the agent for S, telling her husband that she was going to work in Chiang Mai.

B is seventeen years old and comes from Chiang Rai. She first worked in a beer bar in Pattaya which catered to foreigners. She then moved to a teahouse in Bangkok, which entertained mostly Chinese, and moved to the south before coming to this Mae Rim restaurant, where she acquired a debt to the owner. She has worked here for two months, and earns 100 Baht per service. During our follow-up visits, we learned that B was HIV-symptomatic. Other girls in the restaurant explained that customers were disgusted by her skin disease, so she had to move.

She told our fieldworkers, 'If I get infected, I go for two injections. The cost is 2,000 Baht per needle, and it goes away.' We do not know where B has gone.

J is thirty-two years old, from Hot district in the southern part of Chiang Mai Province. She was abandoned by her husband when her child was three months old. She has one son, who has just finished the sixth grade. In order to support her son, J worked in construction in three separate locations around Chiang Mai City, in each earning only 50–60 Baht per day. She was taken by a friend to this restaurant at night to supplement her income, but became too exhausted, so she now works only in the restaurant, where she earns 100 Baht per service. Her friend has since left.

The overall migration patterns are shown in Figure 11.2. While this restaurant would be characterized by the Ministry of Public Health as an 'indirect' establishment, it is closer in nature to a brothel, with beds on the premises. Most of the women working there come from the central and western upper north. However, note that there are two women who have worked in Bangkok, the nation's capital, and Pattaya (the beach tourism area south-east of Bangkok). Nevertheless, the pattern of migration is quite tight, with few other deviations.

Mae Rim: Closed Brothel

Just north of Restaurant One, up a small dirt road, is a cluster of low-cost brothels, shops selling whisky and beer, noodle stalls and snooker tables. Some of these establishments are referred to as 'closed brothels' because the workers' movements are highly restricted (Pyne, 1992). There used to be thirteen brothels in this cluster, but after the Thai New Year, 1994, ten were closed due to a nationwide crackdown on child prostitution. One of the remaining establishments is to the west of the snooker tables. It is constructed with cement block walls, wooden poles, and a dried leaf roof. There is a small entrance with a wooden bench, which turns left into a wide open room with a few wooden benches and one stone bench. Inside is a walled square area with an opening that used to be enclosed by glass in which the women sit and wait for customers. Behind the open structure is a chicken coop; the door is usually kept closed. To the left at the back of the room is another doorway that connects the receiving area with the women's rooms through an outside space. The rooms are cement block constructions with cement floors. There are a few coloured posters of young girls posted to the walls. Most of the young women and girls in this establishment are Lahu or Shan, and most described being tricked into working.

C is a twenty-six year-old Lahu from Fang district of Chiang Mai Province. She first worked in Mae Sai, on a construction site where she made 80 Baht per day. She was tricked into selling sex at this brothel and has been held there for over one year. She has received no money for her work.

As in Chiang Dao Brothel One, many women in this establishment were recruited together from the Shan areas of Myanmar. A twenty-seven year-old Shan from Myanmar, D crossed the border into Mae Sai and worked as a domestic

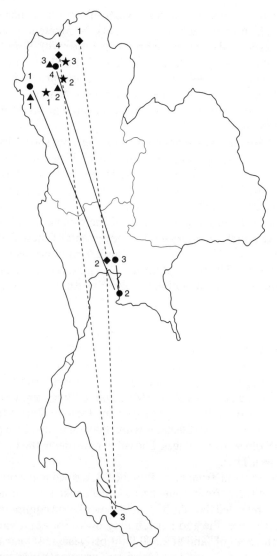

Fig. 11.2.   Migration paths of Mae-Rim restaurant workers

helper there. She was also tricked into working in this current place, where she had been for over a year. When we last visited the brothel, she had escaped to an unknown location. K is a twenty-two year-old Shan woman from Myanmar. When we first met her, she claimed to be from Fang district in Chiang Mai Province, a code for Shan women from Myanmar. She told us that she was brought to the brothel by an agent, not knowing what work she would have to do. She has been kept in the brothel, where she lost her virginity, for seven months. She has never had any formal education and does not know the price charged for this service. She has never received direct payment from the owner but claims the owner has brought money back to her parents. N, nineteen years old, is from the same village as K, and came to the brothel together with K and D. She speaks Northern Thai and says she is ethnic Northern Thai. She said the price for her virginity was 5,000 Baht, and she has worked for over a year. This is the first and only place that both have worked. Since our last visit, N and D have escaped with customers, and reportedly work in establishments in or around Chiang Mai City. Only K and L remain.

L is Lahu. She does not know her home or her age, but she looks as though she could not be older than sixteen or seventeen. She was brought to the establishment as a young girl to work as a domestic servant for the owner. Last year she was forced to 'sell her body.' She has tried to escape over twenty times, but each time has been caught and returned to the owner.

We have mapped the migration patterns of the women working in this closed brothel; Figure 11.3 shows the very limited movements of these women within the upper north. Again, note the very tight and similar paths between origin and destination of the women. There is little deviation in migration, and all is confined to minor geographical movement within the upper north.

Pai

There are only three known commercial sex establishments in this remote town on the road from Chiang Mai to Mae Hong Son. In recent years, it has become a retreat for low-budget foreign tourists, as well as for Shan itinerant labourers fleeing the frequent battles between the Myanmar military regime (State Law and Order Restoration Council) and the Shan army (Muang Tai). Most of the customers in these low-priced establishments are Shan migrants, Lisu tribesmen, and other local men from nearby villages. The women we met in the brothels are Shan, Lisu, and Northern Thai.

T is forty-two years old, from Fang Province, described in the previous sections. She came to Pai directly from home because she broke up with her husband. A visit to her village revealed that she had, in fact, worked in commercial sex prior to her marriage. At home, she and her family grow onions and garlic. They rent approximately three *rai* of land at 2,500 Baht per year. Last year the onion crop was spoiled; the loss of the crop and land rent was another reason for going to work in Pai. She has two daughters. Her first child is twenty-two years old, is married, and lives with her husband in a central Thai province. Her second child stays with her grandmother in Fang. The price of her sexual service is 60 Baht, of which T takes half. The owner provides food and board to all the women in the establishment. She works from afternoon to midnight.

N is also Northern Thai from the Fang district of Chiang Mai Province. She was described above as having lost her virginity to a village boy. After the incident she was taken to Tung Siaw, a brothel district south of Chiang Mai City. She later moved to Pai, where she worked for several years until going to live with a regular

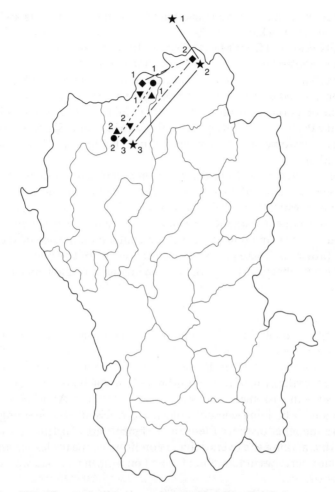

Fig. 11.3.   Migration paths of sex workers in Mae Rim Brothel

customer, whom she regarded as her husband. After two years with her husband, she went back to Pai to work. She receives the same remuneration as T. Because she entered the brothel independently, she did not incur any debts, and saves her money to purchase gold. Her family also grows onions and garlic, but because her younger brother has married, there is not enough agricultural help to support the family; hence, she continues to send remittances home.

L, twenty-three years old, worked in a department store in Chiang Mai City prior to moving to Pai. The average wage for department store employees is 2,000–3,000 Baht per month. She has one child and is separated from her husband. Her father incurred a debt of 7,000 Baht to pay a hospital bill. The money earned in the department store was not enough to pay off the debt, so she reluctantly decided to work in the Pai brothel. She had been working less than one week when we first met her, and complained bitterly about the customers and disgust she felt at having to work.

U is twenty years old from Mai Ai district, the northernmost point of Chiang Mai province. She first worked in a Bangkok hotel, where the price for her virginity was 5,000 Baht. She worked one month, and returned home to Mae Ai for a year. She then moved to Pai, where the price for service was 100 Baht.

R, sixteen years old, is from a village near Chiang Tung. She was brought recently to the Pai brothel by an agent, via the Mae Sai route. She was very reluctant to discuss her home or the agent who brought her to work. This brothel was her first location.

The overall migratory paths of these women is depicted in Figure 11.4. While their origins are more varied than those of women in other brothels, the pathways to their ultimate destination in Pai, Mae Hong Son Province, are brief, and limited to short stops in either Chiang Rai Province or in the region of Chiang Mai, the northern capital area. In no instance was there migration outside of these three contiguous provinces. These patterns are quite similar, and overlap considerably with the situation observed among the women in Mae Rim and Chiang Dao.

Lamphun

Outside of the municipality of Lamphun Province, there is a brothel district spread along a major paved road linking the industrial area of Lamphun Province to the more rural areas. Most of the establishments along this road are owned by relatives, and take the form of restaurant-brothels in which women are required to serve food, sit with customers, and provide sexual services. Attached to or near each restaurant is a building where customers are 'received' and the young women sleep. Unlike the other districts, these establishments are constructed with brick and tile floors, making the overall living conditions appear cleaner and more spacious. Our interviews in Lamphun focused on women who had worked for at least three years.

K comes from Vieng Chai district of Chiang Rai Province. Now twenty-three years old, she was taken by her father to a brothel in Chiang Kham nearly ten years ago. He received a payment of 10,000 Baht, in addition to which she owed the owner 20,000. The price for her virginity was 9,000 Baht, and she worked for over two years until the entire debt was paid. She returned home, and acquired a new debt of 6,000 Baht from an agent who sent her to a 'telephone house' in the Saphan Khwai area of Bangkok. As a 'call girl' for foreign customers, she received 600–700 Baht per service. She claims that there were many agents in her village who loaned money to her parents. Each time, she would have to pay off double the original loan. She paid off the debt after five months and returned home, again for about two weeks. Given an advance of 5,000 Baht, she was sent to a brothel southwest of Bangkok in Nakhon Pathom, where she earned only 1,500–2000 Baht per month. She paid her debt (doubled to 10,000 Baht) and returned home. Given a payment of 10,000 Baht, she then was sent by another agent to Pattani, a

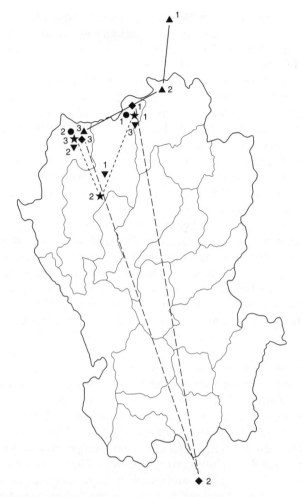

Fig. 11.4. Migration paths of sex workers in Pai Brothel

southern province, where she worked in a brothel with a glass enclosure, serving mostly Malay and Singaporean customers. She paid the 20,000 Baht (double the original amount) in five months. She returned to Bangkok for one month and then moved to a restaurant in Mahachai, Samut Sakorn Province, where most of her customers were Thai fishermen. She did not have to serve food, and the price for sexual services was 100 Baht per service. The owner took 60 Baht and she received 40 Baht. There were five women from her village in this establishment, and she stayed there for five years. During that time, she was moved back and forth by the owner to another of his restaurants in Bangkok. While in Bangkok, she was taken by a friend to another brothel in the city, but there were no customers, so she returned to the restaurant in Mahachai. If she did not send money home directly, her father would come to collect it. She did not return home for two years, but sent money home via the post office. Her mother wrote to say her father was ill, so she went home for fifteen days. She was contacted by an agent and taken to the restaurant in Lamphun, where she has worked for the past three years. She has a debt of 80,000 Baht, of which she has paid 70,000. She expects that the additional 10,000 Baht will be paid off by the end of the year, after which she may return home. She says that although there are few customers, the owner treats her well, and she is able to visit home periodically. She has since recruited several friends from home into the establishment, for which she received a 1,000–2,000 Baht agent's fee.

O is Shan, from Chiang Tung. She worked in a brothel in Chiang Rai Province when she was seventeen years old. The brothel paid her an agent's fee of 4,000 Baht. She earned 800–1000 per day. After one month she escaped, and moved to another brothel in Chiang Rai. She then moved to Had Yai and later to Singapore. She had to pay an agent 35,000 Baht to work there. She was brought to a construction site in Singapore, and earned 3,000–5,000 Baht per day. She paid the agent 1,000 Baht per day. She returned to Thailand with 85,000 Baht. She stayed in Thailand for a little over one month, and then returned to Had Yai. She waited there for her boyfriend, whom she had met while working in Singapore. She then returned to Singapore. Finally, she moved to a remote district of Lamphun Province to live with her boyfriend and work on the land. When short of money, she worked in establishments in Chiang Mai City and Lamphun. She and her boyfriend have since married, and she has stopped selling sex.

L is thirty-six years old, and has worked in the same commercial sex establishment since the age of twenty-nine. She comes from Mae Sai district of Chiang Rai Province. The owner of the restaurant exchanges women with a brothel in Phayao, so she goes back and forth to Phayao for ten days at a time.

J is a twenty-four year-old Northern Thai from Mae Ai district of Chiang Mai Province. At the age of seventeen, she first worked in Phayao as a waitress in a restaurant where she received a salary of 1,700 Baht per month. She served food for a few months and then 'went astray' (*jai taek*). The term *jai taek* is applied to young women who like to go out, and implies multiple sex partners, and is the contrasting image of a 'good woman' who stays home and has very limited contact with men. She decided to work in commercial sex establishments. She moved to Pattaya to work in a beer bar catering to foreign customers. She stayed there for three years. She said she earned good money and had lots of customers but did not know how to save. She claims the bar owner, a foreigner, cheated her out of 100,000 Baht worth of earnings, so she was left with the 300–400 Baht per day she earned in tips from customers. A friend from home also worked there, and has since married and moved to Hong Kong with her husband. Two years ago, J met a customer in Pattaya who works 'on computers for an oil field', in Bahrain. They were married in Fang over a year ago, and she anticipates moving to Bahrain in two years. His monthly salary is equivalent to 70,000 Baht, and he sends J between 10,000 and 20,000 Baht per month. Meanwhile she continues to work.

M is twenty-seven years old, born in Chiang Rai Province. She was sent by her father to a brothel in Nakhon Pathom at the age of fourteen. After receiving a virginity price of 5,000 Baht, she earned 30–40 Baht per time. She was kept in a closed brothel for three years. She returned home for fifteen days and was contacted by a village agent to work in a Bangkok brothel where she earned 50 Baht per time. She escaped to work in a hotel, where she had more freedom to come and go. During the three years in Bangkok, her father would come occasionally to collect money from the owner. Finally, he took her home to Chiang Rai. She married a man from Pichit Province, and lived with him for one year. When they broke up she moved to Phayao for two and a half months. From there, she moved to Chiang Rai, where she spent six months in a brothel. She was called home by her mother because her father was ill with tuberculosis. She then moved to a brothel in Ubon, a north-eastern province, where she stayed only three weeks. From Ubon, she travelled to Samut Sakorn, where she worked in a brothel for seven months. She then moved to Pattaya where she worked for six to seven months. There, she became pregnant by a foreign customer, but aborted the child. She moved to the Lamphun brothel-restaurant two years ago, and earns approximately 7,000–8,000 Baht per month, most of which she sends home to her mother.

The migratory routes of the women who all currently work in the Lamphun restaurant-brothel (Figure 11.5) show a much wider diversity of spatial mobility than that seen for the establishments in Mae Rim and Pai. There is significant travel outside of the upper north, with common pathways to the central region, especially the capital city of Bangkok and surrounding provinces, and to the south. One worker moved between the south and Malaysia, and another moved to the north-east at one point. Note also the frequency of movement before arrival in Lamphun. These patterns suggest a more mobile population, which also reflects village-based recruitment networks that determine the type of establishment, location, and price. The women in this restaurant-brothel reported higher earnings and Northern Thai origin, indicating greater access to resources than the Lahu and Shan women in low-paying brothels.

Discussion

There are differing patterns of spatial mobility demonstrated in the life histories of the sex workers we have interviewed, based on the type of establishment in which they currently work, as well as their ethnic and geographical origins. For the Shan women, there is a very common migration route, with a common crossing point into Thailand, and limited movement within the upper north. For most of these women, travel originated in a rural locale, with some movement into the more urban areas of Greater Chiang Mai. Hill tribe and Shan women are restricted by the Thai government to the province for which they receive 'white' or 'blue' identity cards. In addition, the patterns of recruitment determine the movement of women between brothels. It is important to note in some of the Figures that there is considerable movement between several distinct locations, which represents two or more establishments owned by one individual, or an agreement of

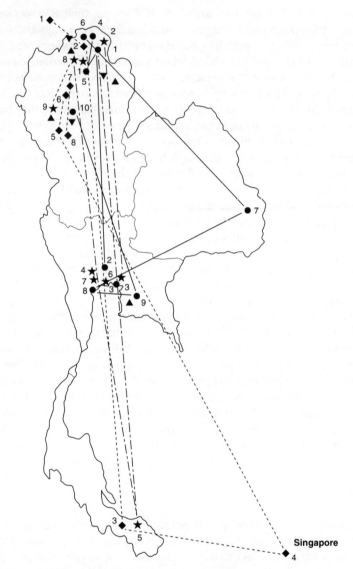

Fig. 11.5.   Migration paths of Lamphun sex workers

exchange between owners; the women are moved between the two locations. An
establishment with frequent changes of women is more likely to be patronized by
local customers. Women in closed brothels are kept for longer periods to ensure
the payment of debt. These are generally the same women whose geographical
mobility is limited by identity card restrictions.

Two principal migration patterns are found in our data. The first, represented
most closely by women recruited from Shan State (Myanmar) and women from

remote agrarian backgrounds in the upper north, is a pattern of relatively limited movement within the upper north. Most of these women work in relatively poor brothels, characterized by limited personal movement and restriction upon their behaviour (for example, the most restrictive case of the closed brothel). The second major pattern demonstrates movement throughout Thailand, with frequent moves to Bangkok and its surrounds, as well as to tourist centres in the southern coastal areas. These migratory patterns are more complex and reflect greater spatial mobility, usually on the part of women whose current work settings allow greater personal freedom and flexibility. As illustrated in the narrative, destination decisions are largely determined by local agents' networks with establishment owners in other areas.

Overall, the spatial mobility of these women reflects the transportation networks in northern Thailand, with routes mostly limited to the upgraded road network. The movement is generally north to south, with little lateral movement seen. Another pattern can be characterized as movement from areas of rural origin to rural brothels in the north. This may be a function of locally-based recruitment networks of agents and brothel owners, as well as limitations imposed by language, education, and familiarity with the locale. Highland women and Shan from Myanmar are particularly vulnerable to these restrictions. In contrast, Northern Thai women have a command of Central Thai, in addition to friendship networks throughout the country. Through these friends, they learn of other employment opportunities beyond the upper north.

These Northern Thai women, through the local agent and friendship networks, also have access into higher paying establishments from other types of low-paying work. Many of the highland and Shan women were tricked out of construction and domestic jobs into low-paying brothels. Most women in low-paying establishments aim to pay off debts and return to farming. Those in slightly higher-paying establishments have better options for marrying economically stable partners.

Social and geographical mobility are critical to the understanding of the dynamics of high risk sexual behaviour among female commercial sex workers in northern Thailand. The institution of marriage preceded the current commercial sex industry as the primary means a woman had to improve her family's social and economic standing. In recent decades, commercial sex work has emerged as one of very few pathways for rural women with little education to provide for their families. The structural and individual factors for entry into the sex industry determine, to a certain degree, the length of time a woman stays in the industry and the type of establishment in which she works. In northern Thailand, the networks of owners, agents, and villagers guide the patterns of movement of young women from home to brothel, and from establishment to establishment. Once in a brothel, a woman's ability to protect her health is largely influenced by the social controls of owners, pimps, and customers, as well as the support and friendship networks she develops in the brothel.

REFERENCES

Akin Rabibhadana (1984), 'Kinship, Marriage, and the Thai Social System', in Chamratrithirong and Apichat (eds), *Perspectives on the Thai Marriage*, Institute for Population
and Social Research.

Asia Watch and the Women's Rights Project (1994), *A Modern Form of Slavery: Trafficking
of Burmese Women and Girls into Brothels in Thailand*, Human Rights Watch, New York.

Bonacci, Mark A. (1990), *The Legacy of Colonialism: Health Care in Southeast Asia*, Asia
Resource Center, Washington.

Bond, Katherine C. (1994), 'Sexual Culture of Northern Thai Men: A Preliminary
Interpretation,' Paper presented at the Workshop on the Sociocultural Dimensions of
HIV/AIDS Control and Care in Thailand, Chiang Mai.

Beyrer, C., Khamboonruang, C., Natpratan, C., Celentano, D., and Nelson, K. E. (1994),
'Incident HIV and STDs in Direct and Indirect Commercial Sex Workers (CSWs) in
Thailand', Abstract 391C. Tenth International Conference on AIDS, Yokohama, August.

Chayan, Vaddhanaphuti (1993), 'Changing sexual behaviour in Northern Thailand',
Paper presented at the 5th International Conference on Thai Studies, London, 5–10 July.

DaGrossa, Pamela S., 'Kamphaeng Din: A Study of Prostitution in the All-Thai Brothels
of Chiang Mai City', *Crossroads*, 4: 1–7.

Ford, Nicholas and Koetsawang, Suporn (1991), 'The Socio-Cultural Context of the
Transmission of HIV in Thailand', *Social Science and Medicine*, 33, 4: 405–14.

Gray, Jennifer (1990), 'The Road to the City: Young Women and Transition in Northern
Thailand', PhD dissertation, Macquarie University, Sydney.

—— (1994), 'The Social and Sexual Mobility of Young Women in Rural Northern
Thailand—Khon Muang and Hill Tribes', Paper presented at the Workshop on the
Sociocultural Dimensions of HIV/AIDS Control and Care in Thailand, Chiang Mai.

Hantrakul, Sukanya (1993), 'Sexual Behavior of Low Socioeconomic Thai Men: A
Comment in Terms of Cultural Outlook', in Taweesak, *et al.*, *Sexual Behaviors for HIV-
Infection in Young Men in Payao*, Research Report No. 6, Thai Red Cross Society.

Havanon, Nappaporn, Knodel, John, and Bennett, Tony (1992), 'Sexual Networking in a
Provincial Thai Setting', AIDS Prevention Monograph Series, Paper 1, Family Health
International, AIDSCAP, Bangkok.

Hengkietisak, Kamol (1994), 'A green harvest of a different kind', *The Bangkok Post*,
March 20: 17.

Kachondham, Y. and Chunharas, S. (1993), 'At the Crossroads: Challenges for Thailand's
Health Development', Health Policy and Planning.

Kammerer, C. A., Hutheesing, O. K., Maneeprasert, R., and Symonds, P. V. (1993),
'Vulnerability to HIV Infection among Three Hilltribes in Northern Thailand:
Qualitative Anthropological Issues', Fifth International Conference on Thai Studies,
School of Oriental and African Studies, London.

Komin, S. (1993), 'Thailand: The National Context of Development', Paper prepared for
the RTG/UNICEF Country Programme Preparation Situation Analysis and Strategy
Development Workshop, Hua Hin, Thailand, 2–4 April.

Lancet (1989), 'AIDS: Prevention, Policies and Prostitutes', 1 (1989): 1111–13.

Limanonda, Bhassorn (1993), 'Female commercial sex workers and AIDS: Perspectives
from Thai rural communities', Paper presented at the 5th International Conference on
Thai Studies, London, 5–10 July.

Mougne, Christine (1981), 'The Social and Economic Correlates of Demographic Change in a Northern Thai Community', PhD Thesis, School of Oriental and African Studies University of London.

Muecke, Marjorie A. (1992), 'Mother Sold Food, Daughter Sells Her Body: The Cultural Continuity of Prostitution', *Social Science and Medicine*, 35 (7): 891–901.

Phongpaichit, Pasuk (1982), 'From Peasant Girls to Bangkok Masseuses', in *Women, Work and Development*, 2, International Labour Organization, Geneva.

Pramualratana, Anthony (1992), 'The Impact of Societal Change and Role of the Old in a Rural Community in Thailand', in Yoddamnern-Attig *et al.* (eds), *Changing Roles and Statuses of Women in Thailand: A Documentary Assessment*, Institute for Population and Social Research, Mahidol University, Bangkok.

Pyne, Hnin Hnin (1992), 'AIDS and Prostitution in Thailand: Case Study of Burmese Prostitutes in Ranong', Unpublished Master's Thesis, Massachusetts Institute of Technology, Boston.

Santasombut, Yot (1991), 'Mae ying si khai tua: chumchom lae kaankhaapraweni nai sangkhom thai', *Newsletter of the Thai Association of Qualitative Researchers*, 5 (1).

Singhanetra-Renard, Anchalee (1993), 'Complex Relationships Between Production and Reproduction: The Case of Ancestor Spirit Cults and Reproductive Choice in the Contexts of Changing Socio-economic Conditions in Northern Thailand', Paper presented at the conference on Population Reconsidered Empowerment, Health and Human Rights, Harare, Zimbabwe.

—— (1994), 'The Meaning of Migration in the Socio-Cultural Context of the HIV/AIDS Epidemic in Northern Thailand', Paper presented at the Workshop on the Socio-Cultural Dimensions of HIV/AIDS Control and Care in Thailand, Chiang Mai.

Siriprapasiri, T., Thanprasertsuk S., Rodklay A., *et al.* (1991), 'Risk Factors for HIV among Prostitutes in Chiang Mai, Thailand', *AIDS* 5: 579–82.

Sittitrai, Werasit and Brown, Tim (1991), 'Female Commercial Sex Workers in Thailand: A Preliminary Report', Institute of Population Studies, Chulalongkorn University and Program on AIDS, Thai Red Cross Society, Bangkok.

Uneklabh, C. and Phutiprawan, T. (1988), 'Prevalence of HIV Infection among Thai Drug Dependents', abstract 5524, Fourth International Conference on AIDS, Stockholm, June.

Ungchusak, K., Thanprasertsuk, S., Sriprapandh, S., Pinichpongse, S., and Kunasol, P. (1989), 'First National Sentinel Seroprevalence Survey for HIV-1 Infection in Thailand, June 1989', abstract FC99, Sixth International Conference on AIDS, San Francisco, June.

—— —— Chokevivat, V., Sriprapandh, S., Pinichpongse, S., Kunasol, P. (1991), 'Trends of HIV Spreading in Thailand Detected by National Sentinel Surveillance', abstract MC3246, Seventh International Conference on AIDS, Florence, June.

Vanichseni, S., Sakuntanaga, P., *et al.* (1990), 'Results of Three Seroprevalence Surveys for HIV in IVDU in Bangkok', abstract FC105, Sixth International Conference on AIDS, San Francisco, June.

Vaddhanphuti, Chayan (1993), 'Changing Sexual Behavior in Northern Thailand', Paper presented at the Fifth International Conference on Thai Studies, London.

Weniger, B. G., Limpakarnjanarat, K., Ungchusak, K., *et al.* (1991), 'The Epidemiology of HIV Infection and AIDS in Thailand', *AIDS*, 5 (Suppl 2): S71–S85.

Yoddumnern-Attig, Bencha (1993) 'Northern Thai Women and the AIDS Crisis: Family, Community and Societal Determinants', Paper presented at the Fifth International Conference on Thai Studies, London.

12 Sexual Networking, Use of Condoms, and Perception of STDs and HIV/AIDS Transmission Among Migrant Sex Workers in Lagos, Nigeria

I. O. ORUBULOYE

Across Nigeria, attitudes towards female sexuality vary among ethnic and religious groups. Some ethnic and religious groups are punitive in their pursuit of even discreet female sexual transgressions, while male sexual transgressions have always been taken for granted. In certain parts of Nigeria, women have some degree of freedom and a substantial degree of equality with men, while in some parts, especially in the north, where the majority are Muslims, the society suppresses and closets its women. Similarly, premarital chastity has traditionally been rigidly enforced among some ethnic and religious groups, while in others the society has traditionally been flexible. These differences lead to variations in sexual patterns and they are likely to cause differences in the risk of sexually transmitted diseases (STDs) and AIDS.

The nature and structure of the traditional family system are also important determinants of patterns of sexual relations within and outside marriage. Polygyny on the scale still found in Nigeria has been sustained only by the very substantial delay of male first marriage. It has inevitably produced a situation where half of adult males are single and sexually active. On the other hand, polygyny has taught men to believe that relations with only one woman are not part of man's nature, while postpartum abstinence makes women unavailable for sex for a considerable part of their reproductive life span. During the long period of postpartum abstinence men look for partners elsewhere. A significant proportion of their sex needs is met by commercial sex workers, divorced women, and widows.

The current economic difficulties arising from the collapse of high export prices for petroleum and the structural adjustment programme adopted to meet the difficulties created by the end of the oil boom have had an impact on sexual practices. The prosperous oil boom years began after the Nigerian civil war in 1970 and finally collapsed with the 1987 floating of the Naira (the Nigerian currency unit worth US$1 before the float and less than five US cents at the time of the research reported here).

The commercial sex workers' study is part of the on-going research on sexual networking, STDs, and HIV/AIDS transmission at the Ondo State University, Ado-Ekiti, Nigeria, and is supported by a grant from the Swedish Agency for Research Cooperation with Developing Countries (SAREC).

As a survival strategy, poor families encourage their young boys and girls to migrate to the major towns and commercial centres for wage employment, which is not easy to come by. The present economic situation has made it difficult for such rewards to come quickly, thereby putting pressure on the young girls to engage in commercial sex with clients who range from the new rich men to the long-distance truck drivers, commonly referred to as 'Sugar Daddies'.

The movement to the major towns and commercial centres was facilitated by the rapid growth of the educational system and of the transport network. The growth of the educational and transport systems was accelerated during the 1970s and early 1980s, as revenue from oil allowed the government to build many modern highways from south to north and west to east, linking several towns and villages. The development led to the growth of major educational, commercial, and transport centres.

The highest levels of HIV infection have been among commercial sex workers at the major nodes of communications, education, and commerce: Lagos, Ibadan, Calabar, Port-Harcourt, Enugu, and Maiduguri (Shokunbi, 1991). The growth of the commercial sex industry has long exposed women employed in it, as well as their male clients, to increased risk of STDs, and now presents the danger of infection with HIV/AIDS.

By 1990, the HIV prevalence level among Nigerian commercial sex workers was already 14 per cent (Mann, Tarantola, and Netter 1992:54). In Lagos, by 1992, the HIV level among commercial sex workers was 20 per cent (Ransome-Kuti, 1992). This implies that commercial sex in Lagos poses great dangers to the women who work in it, and that the industry constitutes the most dangerous sector of society for the spread of the disease and for creating a self-sustaining and expanding AIDS epidemic throughout the society (Orubuloye, Caldwell, and Caldwell, 1993).

This situation raises a wide range of questions which this paper will attempt to answer. Who are the commercial sex workers? Where do they come from? What facilitates commercial sex? What are their goals? Is prostitution a way of life? To what extent are the workers and their clients attempting to minimize the chances of being infected with STDs and AIDS?

The major towns in Nigeria contain a number of small and medium-sized hotels, bars, and night clubs, where young women practise commercial sex. These are entertainment centres where commercial sex workers mix with their clients, drinking, eating, and dancing with them.

The hotels and night clubs also provide accommodation for men who bring their own girlfriends for a short or longer stay, in addition to providing the environment for non-institutional commercial sex workers who usually come to solicit clients. It is now well established that these commercial sex workers in the clubs, bars, and hotels have an above average number of sexual partners. They also run an abnormally high risk of being infected by such coitally-related diseases as STDs, HIV/AIDS and of transmitting them to their clients who may in turn spread the diseases among the general population (Orubuloye, 1993).

Previous studies have shown that the commercial sex workers are mostly migrants—single, deserted, or divorced wives, and sometimes mothers. These women migrated to major towns and sometimes across national boundaries, so that they were unlikely to be recognized by people from their own area or country and thus would not jeopardize their chances of future marriage or remarriage, or of returning to respectable motherhood (Orubuloye, Caldwell, and Caldwell, 1993).

The 1992 Nigerian survey of commercial sex workers was undertaken in five major towns: Lagos, Benin, Ado-Ekiti, Port-Harcourt, and Kaduna, during the last quarter of the year as part of a larger on-going programme of research of the Ondo State University, Ado-Ekiti, Nigeria, on sexual networking, STDs, and HIV/AIDS transmission, supported by a grant from the Swedish Agency for Research Cooperation with Developing Countries (SAREC). In addition, a sixth survey with a greater concentration on condom use was carried out in Lagos, subsequently referred to as 'the Lagos Study'. The data generated from this survey form the basis of this report.

The aim of this component of the research programme was to understand the pattern of sexual networking among the commercial sex workers, as well as condom use by their clients, and perceptions of STDs and HIV/AIDS transmission. Intervention programmes at this stage of the AIDS epidemic in Nigeria need data on the perception of AIDS, whether women recognize STDs in themselves or their partners, and know or seek appropriate treatment or use condoms, and women's knowledge of the association between STDs and HIV transmission.

The Lagos Study

Lagos was until recently the federal capital of Nigeria. Despite losing the status of federal capital, it has continued to play the role of the major commercial, educational, entertainment, and tourist centre in Nigeria. Lagos has a mixture of both large migrant and native populations. However, the majority of the population are Yoruba. Because of its cosmopolitan nature, it offers a high degree of anonymity required for commercial sexual networking. It is a place where everybody minds his or her own business.

There are no accurate statistics on the number of commercial sex workers in Lagos or elsewhere in Nigeria. Hence, the commercial sex workers were contacted in a kind of snowball sample. A total of 320 respondents were contacted from Ojoo, Mainland, Surulere, Ikeja, and Agege areas of Lagos.

The subjects posed were discussed at length but respondents were also given questionnaires to complete. The cooperation of hotel managers was secured before gaining access to the premises and to the commercial sex workers who resided in the hotel or who came there to solicit for clients. The commercial sex workers were suspicious about our intention and panicked at the sight of written materials, at least at first. They took the interviewers to be journalists whose reporting could have an adverse effect on their business. However, the sex workers were persuaded that the research was urgently needed for the improvement of the welfare and the health condition of those in the trade. They were told that no attempt to record their names or identify them after the interview would occur. Those who revealed their names gave false names, usually non-Nigerian, names which they changed frequently. They usually refused to recognize the interviewers when they met later. It was difficult to ascertain their origins beyond the ethnic and state levels.

Nearly all the respondents demanded money, drinks, and cigarettes as payment for being interviewed. Their argument was that time was important to their trade and that every minute mattered. Some were paid money, ranging from 10 to 20 Naira (50 US cents to one dollar), depending on their location; the majority settled for a bottle of beer and a packet of cigarettes. Nearly all sex workers asked for a supply of free condoms, and some solicited for our fieldworkers (who were all males) as clients. Approximately four-fifths of the sex workers were interviewed in and around hotel premises, 14 per cent in bars, and 8 per cent in brothels situated mainly in the poorer sections of the city. However, brothels that offer no drink, entertainment, or company are almost unknown in Nigeria. About three-fifths were interviewed in places described as rich neighbourhoods.

Who are the Commercial Sex Workers?

The characteristics of the commercial sex workers provide clues as to the structure of the occupation. Seventy-five per cent were under twenty-five years of age, the average age being 26.2 years; 22 per cent were between twenty-five and thirty-four years of age, while about 3 per cent were thirty-five or above. It is important to note that a small proportion were below twenty years of age, the age when most of their age groups are in school or learning a trade. Well over 70 per cent had been to school, the majority having gone beyond the primary school level. Although about 21 per cent did not state their level of education, the sample was sufficiently literate by Nigerian standards. The level of education clearly shows that prostitution is no longer a product of a stream of near illiterate, rural–urban migrants obtaining the only employment for which they are qualified in the town. It is a manifestation of a general rise in the level of female education and unemployment among young female school leavers.

Only one-fourth of the sex workers were Yoruba, from outside Lagos, and the remainder were Edo, Urhobo, Ishan, Igbo, Efik, Ibiobio, and Hausa in order of importance. A small proportion was reported as non-Nigerian. This confirms our earlier finding in Ekiti and throughout the region that sex workers often work in areas and among ethnic groups other than their own (Orubuloye, Caldwell, and Caldwell, 1993). They tend to migrate in order to achieve anonymity. The dominant ethnic groups were the Igbo of eastern Nigeria and Edo of the mid-west. In the case of the Igbos this may be explained by the fact that they are an economic migrant population and their homeland was devastated by the 1967–70 Nigerian civil war. The high bridewealth and marriage costs among this group delay marriages and force the women to migrate to earn some of their marriage costs. On the question of marital status, 82 per cent reported that they were single, 15 per cent were divorced, separated, or widowed, and only 3 per cent were currently married. All the single girls reported that they had no children, and the others reported an average of 1.7 children.

The Trade

Most of the sex workers were relatively new to the trade. Of the 286 who stated the number of years of work, only 5 per cent had been in the trade for more than five years and 11 per cent had worked in it for less than twelve months, the average duration being 2.7 years. Ninety-three per cent were in the trade primarily to raise money to invest in business so as to establish themselves in respectable employment in the future. Only 8 per cent reported that they were in the trade because they were unemployed, while 3 per cent reported that they were in the trade because of frustration. The aspirations of the sex workers appear to correspond with their level of education and training. With the level of education attained before entering into their new trade, it would be a difficult task for them to secure employment in any sector of the economy, given the current high rate of unemployment in the country and the prevailing economic situation. The majority of the sex workers (88 per cent) were in the trade because they wanted to make quick money. It is indeed a lucrative business because a commercial sex worker reports about five to seven clients a day or 30 clients a week. At an average payment of about 20 Naira (US$1) for each episode, a commercial sex worker in Lagos could earn as much as between 100 and 150 Naira in one day, in addition to free drink and cigarettes and possibly a plate of food from at least one of the clients. In stable market conditions, a commercial sex worker earns well above what a university graduate would earn in the public sector of the economy. Certainly, the sex workers in Lagos are better off than their counterparts in Ondo State (Orubuloye, 1993). Nearly all the sex workers described their clients as married, and average-earning or rich young businessmen or in white collar occupations. They needed men of such good economic status to remain in business.

A small proportion of the commercial sex workers described commercial sex as immoral, and the majority would remain in the trade until they had saved enough money for their future business. Most commercial sex workers do eventually return to their home areas, or at least the nearest big town, and set themselves up in a market stall, or open a hairdressing salon, or buy a boutique selling clothes or material. Many marry or remarry at this stage. Prostitution, therefore, is a life stage rather than a way of life. However, the returnees often act as local recruiters of young girls for city managers and they receive a payment for each girl.

The desire to accumulate sufficient savings for investment in the future may have influenced the decision of just one-third who remit money home to their parents, children, brothers, and sisters. Home remittance is an important aspect of commercial sex because it assures their families that they have an office or domestic job in town. Quite often they go back home during Christmas and New Year celebrations to flaunt the wealth they have acquired through commercial sex. Parents and family members hardly knew that they practise commercial sex. Only 4 per cent had in fact told their parents about their jobs, and 12 per cent believed that others knew about their jobs. For the majority, very little discussion on this point ever takes place.

Eighty-four per cent of the single sex workers planned to get married after returning to their home areas, and, only one-fifth of this number would tell their future husbands that they had been involved in commercial sex before.

Perception of Sexually Transmitted Diseases and AIDS

The commercial sex workers were reasonably knowledgeable about STDs. Only 11 per cent reported that they were not aware or could not recognize an STD. Recognition of STDs is however, confined to gonorrhoea, and the region does not seem to be afflicted by the same high levels of syphilis and chancroid as are found commonly in East and Southern Africa.

Only two-fifths reported that they had ever contracted an STD. This is rather surprising given the high level of reporting of the knowledge of STDs. It would appear that it was a deliberate attempt to maintain their business confidence by understating their STD infections. The thought that the result of the interview could be made public, and could damage their trade, was a constant source of fear. However, all the commercial sex workers who reported that they had contracted an STD actually sought treatment from a hospital. The majority of them reported that they would seek treatment from a hospital if and when they contracted an STD.

Nearly all the respondents recognized that gonorrhoea was dangerous because it is painful and could destroy the reproductive organ, thereby leading to permanent infertility. However, the majority of the sex workers (93 per cent) reported that they were protecting themselves against STDs by taking antibiotics, mostly ampicillin, before and after sexual intercourse, testing customers before sexual episodes, and undergoing regular medical check-ups. The antibiotics are readily available and can be obtained easily from chemist shops, pharmaceutical stores, and hawkers. Their doses are much lower than the recommended courses and may be ineffective. However, the women believed that these measures were effective and reduced the danger of their becoming infected with any coitally related diseases.

Nearly all the sex workers had heard of AIDS. Their knowledge is fairly recent, mostly confined to the last two or three years. Although more than 40 per cent of the sex workers were worried about AIDS, only three respondents thought there was the chance of getting the disease, and another five believed that the disease is curable. Only 17 per cent were knowledgeable about the transmission processes. They reported indiscriminate sex, multiple sexual partners, and blood transfusion as major sources of transmission of HIV. The electronic media (radio and television), friends, and school mates, in that order, were reported as the major sources of information on AIDS.

Use of Condoms

Condoms, if properly stored and used, could give adequate protection against STDs and HIV and, in addition, prevent unwanted pregnancy. Until recently, condoms have not proved popular as a means of contraception in Nigeria primarily because of their association with prostitution and extramarital relationships and because of the fear that a condom can disappear into the womb and thereby cause sterility. Husbands do not like to suggest the use of condoms to their wives because it will imply that they themselves have been using them in extramarital affairs. However, recent research findings in the Ekiti district of Nigeria indicate that condoms are now being accepted by single girls to prevent unwanted pregnancy that could drive them into premature marriage (Caldwell, Orubuloye, and Caldwell, 1992). This may well have implications for the rate of transmission of STDs and possibly of HIV and other coitally related diseases in the region.

The situation regarding the commercial sex workers appears to be different in that 82 per cent of them had employed condoms in some kind of relationships. Of this group, 34 per cent used them always, while the remaining 48 per cent had used them sometimes. The usage has been fairly recent, mostly occurring in the last two years, a period which corresponds with a massive campaign about the use of condoms as protection against AIDS. The major sources of information were boyfriends and co-workers, while only 3 per cent were informed by their clients. Forty-eight per cent of the supplies came from the chemist and pharmaceutical stores, while 42 per cent received supplies from their customers.

Protection against STDs was the main motive offered for using condoms by the sex workers; 67 per cent had employed condoms for this purpose, 22 per cent to prevent unwanted pregnancy, 7 per cent because the customers specifically asked for it, and 2 per cent specifically as protection against AIDS. The reasons given for using condoms are not unreasonable in Nigeria. AIDS is not yet a disease to be feared, mostly because not many people have had personal contact with the victims, and because of the general belief among sex workers that the disease is a white man's disease. The sex workers believed that they are safe if they refuse European customers. The situation in respect of STDs is different. STDs are widely recognized among commercial sex workers. Many had probably had personal experience in the course of their daily activities.

Only 12 per cent of the users had experienced condom breakages, while only 2 per cent believed that condoms were harmful. However, 76 per cent would continue to use condoms primarily as protection against STDs and unwanted pregnancy. The remainder would stop using condoms because it is artificial and reduces enjoyment of sex. Interestingly, 56 per cent of the sex workers had asked their clients to use condoms, at least on one occasion, more than one-half of whom had agreed to do so for protection against STDs and AIDS.

However, 62 per cent of the sex workers reported that their clients liked the restrictions placed on them, 64 per cent said they would still go on to have sex with clients who refused to use condoms, and 44 per cent said they would charge more for clients who refused to use condoms. Partly because of protection against STDs, and partly because of the fear of AIDS, 12 per cent of the clients always provided their own condoms, 8 per cent usually did so, while 56 per cent did so occasionally, and 18 per cent had never done so.

Nearly all the sex workers were doing something to prevent unwanted pregnancies by taking the pill or using an IUD. The low level of fertility among the sex workers is an indication that the methods were working. Despite the high level of sexual networking and adoption of contraception, the sex workers did not foresee any obstacle in having the number of children they desired when they got married in future.

Conclusion

An investigation into commercial sex activities indicates that the commercial sex workers in Lagos were mostly migrants from the major regions of Nigeria. The reason for nearly all sex workers taking up the job is that it is lucrative and they can earn much more than in any other employment commensurate with their level of education and training. The majority of the sex workers did not see the occupation as a guaranteed high-income flow for a working lifetime but a means of raising enough capital which they would later plough into business ventures.

The commercial sex workers did not regard their occupation as a way of life but a stage in life. Although most commercial sex workers tend to be anonymous in the course of their daily activities, they could easily be recognized because of their way of life. They visit their home areas and show off their possessions among their relatives and friends.

The commercial sex workers were well aware of the dangers that their daily activities pose to their lives. One of the apprehensions of the commercial sex workers is that they stand the risk of being infected by their clients. They were doing something to guard against being infected by their clients. However, the AIDS epidemic has not really influenced the flow of women into the trade. Condoms are far more likely to be used and provided by clients of higher status than by the commercial sex workers. At present, protection against STDs was the main reason for the use of condoms by sex workers and their clients. STDs are widely recognized, and most commercial sex workers and their clients probably had personal experiences of STDs in the course of their daily activities. Condoms will be accepted by sex workers and their clients for protection against AIDS when the disease is in epidemic proportions in Nigeria and the campaign warning that it is becoming widespread is successful. The fact that the sex workers were asking for free condoms may well be the beginning of a recognition of the danger that the disease poses to their lives. However, a universal acceptance of condoms by sex workers will largely depend on an effective massive campaign about the use of condoms as protection against STDs and AIDS; their availability, cost, and supply. The chemists and the pharmaceutical stores have a major role to play in this regard, as they are currently doing, as the major sources of supply of contraceptives for family planning acceptors (Caldwell, Orubuloye, Caldwell, 1992). Intervention Programmes that will bring the family planning, STDs, and AIDS workers together will go a long way in promoting condom use. This may be a crucial factor in slowing or halting the AIDS epidemic and other coitally-related diseases.

REFERENCES

Caldwell, J. C., I. O. Orubuloye, and Pat Caldwell. 1992. 'Fertility Decline in Africa: A New Type of Transmission', *Population and Development Review*, 18 (2): 211–42.

Mann, Jonathan M., Daniel J. M. Tarantola, and Thomas W. Netter (eds). 1992. *AIDS in the World*, Cambridge MA: Harvard University Press.

Orubuloye, I. O., J. C. Caldwell, and Pat Caldwell. 1993. 'The Role of High-risk Occupations in the Spread of AIDS: Truck Drivers and Itinerant Market Women in Nigeria', *International Family Planning Perspective*, 19 (2): 43–8.

Orubuloye, I. O. 1994. 'Patterns of Sexual Behaviour of High Risk Groups and their Implications for STDs and HIV/AIDS Transmission in Nigeria', in R. G. Parker (ed.), *Conceiving Sexuality: Approaches to Sex Research in a Postmodern World*, London: Routledge.

Ransome-Kuti, Olikoye. 1992. 'Report to the meeting of Members of the National AIDS Committee and Media Executives', Lagos, Nigeria.

Shokunbi, W. A. 1991. Presentation. West African Research Group on Sexual Networking, STDs, and AIDS/HIV, Nigerian Institute of Social and Economic Research, Ibadan.

13 Sexual Relations Between Migrating Populations (Vietnamese with Mexican and Anglo) and HIV/STD Infections in Southern California

JOSEPH CARRIER, BANG NGUYEN, and SAMMY SU

Introduction

This chapter explores findings from a one-year ethnosexual field investigation conducted in 1992 by the author and his Vietnamese American colleagues on the relationship between the sexual behaviours of men of Vietnamese origin with their Vietnamese, Mexican, and Anglo American sex partners and HIV/STD infections in the County of Orange, located in Southern California. It provides an excellent example of some consequences of the sexual mixing of migrating populations and illustrates how these findings might assist health educators formulate meaningful programmes for the prevention and control of HIV/STD infections.

The chapter also presents historical ethnography on sexual behaviours in Vietnam, and surveys research findings of three limited studies of the sexual behaviours of Vietnamese Americans living in Los Angeles in 1988, in San Francisco in 1991, and in Orange County in the fall of 1992. Finally, a comparison will be made of the field research findings with the survey research findings to illustrate the limitations of survey research methodology in mapping out the sexual geography of populations like the Vietnamese where very little is known about their sexual behaviours.

The field research reported in this chapter was conducted by the author and his Vietnamese American colleagues Bang Nguyen and Sammy Su. Special acknowledgement is given Kim Khanh Mai who conducted several important focus groups of Vietnamese Americans. The authors would also like to thank the following Vietnamese Americans for their contributions to the field research: Sonny Phan, Dien Pham, Tuan Le, Anh Le, Thanh Phan, Nghia Tran, Tu Tran, Cuong Le, and Loc Nguyen. They would also like to acknowledge the support given by Lynda Doll and Kate McQueen at the Centers for Disease Control in Atlanta; Edwin Lopez, Esteban Inzunza, and Chuck Morrison who are assigned to the STD Control Unit in Orange County; Peter Burrell, Rick Greenwood, and Esther Murray at the Orange County Health Care Agency; and Pat Roemer, a special friend and ESL teacher of Vietnamese Americans in Orange County.

The Field Research: Mapping Out Sexual Behaviours[1]

A decision was made early on in the field research to use as large a variety of methods as possible to map out the diversity of Vietnamese American sexual behaviours in Orange and Los Angeles counties. Traditional ethnographic methods—such as in-depth interviews of selected respondents and participant observations—were the basic tools of the project. Additional data were generated by staff interviews of selected groups of Vietnamese students in 'English-as-second-language' (ESL) classes and in 'alcohol rehabilitation' classes using short questionnaires with open-ended items, and from historical interviews conducted by Disease Control Investigators of Vietnamese patients coming to the STD clinic over a period of several years.

Because of limited funding for field research and the likelihood that the male segment of the Vietnamese population was at higher risk of HIV/STD infections, a decision was also made to focus the study on Vietnamese male sexual behaviours. At the initiation of the project, all of the HIV-positive Vietnamese known by the Orange County Health Care Agency were men, and a large majority of the Vietnamese patients coming to the STD clinic were men.

The field research focused first on mapping same-sex and opposite-sex patterns of behaviour that put Vietnamese American men at special risk of HIV and other STD infections; and then on eliciting beliefs prevalent in the Orange County Vietnamese American community, the largest in the United States, related to the legitimacy of their engaging in the risky sexual behaviours identified. A comparative study was also conducted of the traditional Vietnamese patterns of sexual behaviour and the changes in sexual behaviour that occur as a result of living as refugees in the United States under new circumstances and as a result of acculturation.

As the study progressed, preliminary findings on the heterosexual behaviours of Vietnamese American men led to an extension of the field work to two Mexican cities located in northern Baja California: Tijuana and Ensenada. Observations were made of Vietnamese American men in pursuit of female sex partners in the 'red-light districts' of both cities.

Finally, in March 1994, some additional data on same-sex Vietnamese male sexual behaviours and on current HIV prevention programmes in Vietnam were collected by the senior author in Ho Chi Minh City.

[1] The field research project was part of a larger study funded by the Centers for Disease Control (CDC) and carried out in a cooperative agreement with the Orange County Health Care Agency (HCA). The two other parts of the larger study were a seroprevalence survey of HIV infection in several selected segments of the Vietnamese American population; and a standard knowledge, attitudes, beliefs, and behaviors (KABB) survey with respect to HIV/AIDS. To the detriment of the field research, the KABB survey consumed a large majority of the funds made available by CDC for the larger study. As will be noted in more detail below, money for field work was cut off prior to the completion of an important interview segment of the study.

Historical Ethnography of Vietnamese Sexual Behaviour

Few data were available on the sexual behaviours of Vietnamese people living in Vietnam or in the United States at the initiation of the Field Research Project in early 1992. Only three limited sources of information were found on Vietnamese sexual behaviours in Vietnam (Jacolliot, 1896; Hickey, 1964; Jamieson, 1986); and two in California (Flaskerud and Nyamathi, 1988; Murase, Sung, and Vuong, 1991).

At the turn of the century, a French Army urologist surgeon published detailed observations of sexual behaviours he had made in Vietnam and other French colonies. His observations, however, were highly coloured by European prejudices against people of colour and any kind of sexual behaviours other than the missionary position in vaginal intercourse. He nevertheless did establish the existence of same-sex anal intercourse and fellatio in Vietnam at the time of his observations; and that both male and female prostitutes were available to interested Vietnamese people and the French colonials (Jacolliot, 1896: 91–6).

In a field study of a Vietnamese village in south Vietnam in the late 1950s, an American anthropologist observed that although it is desirable for the ideal wife 'to be a virgin, it is not a prerequisite so long as she is not known as a woman of easy virtue' (Hickey, 1964: 100). He also observed polygyny and concubinage among married men in the village and concluded that 'affairs with other women of the village or relations with prostitutes in Tan An [a district capital] and My Tho [a province capital] may take place at any time, but generally a man takes a second wife or concubine only after ten or fifteen years of marriage' (Hickey, 1964: 112). It is interesting to note that in the summer of 1962, the government of the Republic of Vietnam in the south—under the leadership of a Catholic president, Ngo-Dinh-Diem—promulgated a law dealing with the 'Protection of Morality' (Republic of Vietnam, 1962). Article 7 of this law made both male and female prostitution illegal and punishable by fines and confinement. According to several of our respondents, however, it was never actively enforced.

In a relatively recent research article on the traditional family in Vietnam, an American scholar notes: 'If a married man had an affair with another woman, it might meet with some disapproval . . . but people often looked the other way. And in any event he could and usually would be forgiven, even (or perhaps especially) by his wife' (Jamieson, 1986: 116). With respect to the wife, however, he notes that:

A 'good woman' in traditional Vietnam was self-sacrificing, frugal, industrious, chaste, and totally devoted to her husband. She was 'bad' if she so much as glanced fondly at any man except her husband. The Vietnamese sometimes appeared to be prudes of the first order by the standards of most Western and many other Asian cultures. They were also second to none in having a double standard for judging the sexual behaviour of men and women. But the entire constellation of beliefs, attitudes, and norms regarding sexual behaviour may be seen to be intimately related to their over-riding concept of family and to have been enforced by the primary value of filial piety (*hiếu*) (Jamieson, 1986: 116–7).

The only data available on Vietnamese American sexuality was collected in California by two small surveys investigating the relationship between sexual behaviours and HIV infection. One survey, conducted by faculty members of the School of Nursing at UCLA in 1988 (Flaskerud and Nyamathi), collected a very limited amount of data on the sexual behaviours of Vietnamese women and their husbands coming to a Women, Infants, and Children (WIC) programme in Los Angeles. The focus of the study was on an AIDS education programme for Vietnamese women. The other survey, conducted by the Center for Southeast Asian Refugee Resettlement and the San Francisco Department of Public Health in the spring of 1991 (Murase, Sung, and Vuong, 1991), collected a limited amount of data on the sexual behaviours of a randomly selected sample of Vietnamese men and women living in the Tenderloin area of San Francisco. The study was mainly a KABB (knowledge, attitudes, beliefs, and behaviours) survey related to HIV infection and AIDS.

The major findings of the two surveys on sexual behaviour were as follows. The UCLA survey reported that 'a surprisingly large minority of respondents indicated that they had multiple sexual partners (24.7% of [74] males and 22.9% of [242] females)' (Flaskerud and Nyamathi, 1988: 636). The investigators note, however: 'Several questions still remain about the items on the questionnaire that attempted to measure drug use and sexual practices (Flaskerud and Nyamathi, 1988: 636).' They believe the responses to their questions on sexual behaviours may have been confounded by a lack of understanding as to what was meant by 'sexual intercourse'.

The San Francisco survey reported a much lower incidence of multiple sex partners by their small but randomly selected respondents (98 men and 107 women). No breakdown by gender is presented in their report; thus just the summary figure is available for both men and women: 12.7% of the respondents (26 of 205) reported having two or more sexual partners in the year prior to the interview; only 3.5% reported having five or more (Murase, Sung, and Vuong, 1991: 16–18). It is not possible to know who the sexual partners were of the respondents reporting more than one partner since the question about the number of sexual partners was not linked to questions dealing with their sexual practices.

Because the report does not break down the survey data by gender, a problem also exists with respect to the incidence of men having sex with female prostitutes and of men having sex with men. Assuming that only male respondents reported that they had had sexual relations with female prostitutes at some time during their life (that is, no female respondents had sex with female prostitutes), then the incidence is 9.1% of the male sample (9 of 98). And assuming that only male respondents reported that they had had sexual relations with homosexual men, then the incidence is 8.2% of the male sample (8 of 98); or with male prostitutes, then the incidence is 3.1% of the male sample (3 of 98). Male homosexuality in the sample may thus be as low as 3.1% or as high as 8.2%. One of the surprising findings of the survey is that close to 6% of the women (6 of 107) and 10% of the men (10 of 98) reported that at some time in their lives they had practised anal intercourse. We do not know, unfortunately, whether the anal intercourse prac-tised by the men was with the same sex or opposite sex.

The Vietnamese Americans of Orange County

More than 600,000 people of Vietnamese origin are estimated to be living in the United States at present (Bureau of the Census, 1990). Almost half of them (46.7%) reside in California. And the largest concentration of them in the United States and in California is in Orange County, where estimates range from 72,000 (the 1990 census estimate) to 140,000 (a Vietnamese community estimate reported by the Orange County Register, March 22, 1992). Within Orange County, over half of the Vietnamese population (41,254) is clustered in three towns: West-minster, Garden Grove, and Santa Ana.

'Little Saigon', located in Westminster and extending about a mile along Bolsa Avenue, is the focus of the Vietnamese community. It is composed of one large shopping mall, at least a dozen shopping centres, numerous restaurants and cafés, several discos and nightclubs, and offices for professional businesses. The mall and shopping centres serve as information hubs where Vietnamese newspapers are distributed and members of the community can congregate and never have to speak English.

Significant variations exist within the population of Vietnamese origin in Orange County (see Do, 1988). There are major differences, for example, in reli-gion (Mahayana Buddhist-Taoist-Confucianist ideology versus Christian), eth-nicity (ethnic Vietnamese versus ethnic Chinese), and time of arrival in the United States (from nineteen years ago to just arrived). There are also important differ-ences in family structure (broken versus intact families with a larger number of males (55%) risking escape from Vietnam than females), socioeconomic status, and education.

One major outcome of these variations is considerable differences in accultur-ation of people of Vietnamese origin to mainstream American culture. As is the case with other immigrant populations, those refugees arriving at an early age, and going through the American secondary school system, usually have the highest level of acculturation. Another noteworthy fact about the Vietnamese community in Orange County is the large number of its members returning to Vietnam for a visit. The Orange County Register (1992) reported that an estim-ated 12,000 visited Vietnam in 1991. Since then, the number returning to Vietnam has steadily increased. In 1992, an estimated 20,000 went back to visit their fam-ilies and, some say, to start up small businesses with friends and relatives living there. The number returning in 1993 was believed to be somewhere close to 30,000.

Chronology of Field Research

Given the limited information available on Vietnamese sexual behaviours in Vietnam and California and the limited time and money available for field research, contacts were made at the outset of the study with Vietnamese American respondents who were willing to provide basic knowledge about the heterosexual and homosexual scenes of immigrant Vietnamese living in southern California. Two Vietnamese staff members (Sammy Su and Kim Khanh-Mai) were assigned the task of getting information about heterosexual behaviours; two (Bang Nguyen and Tuan Le) were assigned the task of getting information about homosexual behaviours. On hearing about the project, several Vietnamese Americans volunteered to help (Tu Tran, Sonny Phan, Anh Le, Cuong Le, and Loc Nguyen). They worked diligently for many months without pay, assisting field research staff in their studies. All of the field research informants were informed about the nature and objectives of the study and their identities concealed by a coding system.

Initially, the most important set of informants on current Vietnamese American heterosexual behaviours in southern California were 43 Vietnamese American male students attending alcohol rehabilitation classes in Orange County. Ranging in age from 19 to 56 (average age 34), the majority were sexually active men with multiple female sex partners. Close to half (21 of 43) were married or had live-in girl friends; the remainder were single (12 of 43), divorced (7 of 43), or separated (2 of 43). Several of the students allowed field research staff to accompany them in pursuit of female sexual partners; and provided the staff with detailed information about their own ongoing sexual practices and the activities of female prostitutes sought out by Vietnamese American men in southern California and Mexico. Early in the study, all of them completed a brief questionnaire about their sex practices and agreed to be tested for HIV infection.

Two early findings from the first set of heterosexual informants—that many Vietnamese American men were actively engaged in seeking heterosexual encounters with prostitutes, and that a majority of these prostitutes were Mexican females working in Orange and Los Angeles counties and Tijuana and Ensenada, Mexico—led to the creation of a second data set on heterosexual behaviours from historical records: 65 interviews by Disease Control Investigators of Vietnamese people (63 men and 2 women) coming to the Special Diseases Clinic of the Orange County Health Care Agency in Santa Ana, California, from 1987 to the spring of 1992 to be treated for penicillin-resistant gonorrhoea (PPNG).

The first important group of informants on the homosexual behaviours of Vietnamese American men living in southern California was acquired through the services of a heterosexual field research project volunteer (Dien Pham) who cofounded the first Vietnamese chapter of the Parents and Friends of Lesbians and Gays (PFLAG) in the United States. He made it possible for the author to attend monthly Vietnamese PFLAG meetings at the Orange County Gay and Lesbian Center in Garden Grove and thereby get access to a network of approximately fifty homosexually identified Vietnamese American men living in southern California. As a result, Tuan Le, one of the gay co-founders of PFLAG, and Bang Nguyen, a gay activist graduate student at the University of California, Berkeley, were employed by the field research project to gather data on the social and sexual behaviours of gay and/or homosexually identified Vietnamese men and conduct some in-depth interviews of PFLAG members and their homosexual Vietnamese friends in southern California. Their employment by the field research project ended abruptly in August 1992 as a result of diversion of most of the study's funds from the CDC to the community survey component. By that time, Bang Nguyen had completed eleven in-depth interviews.

An additional set of informants—ten homosexually identified Vietnamese American men, ranging in age from 17 to 60, and one Anglo American man aged 35—provided the author with ongoing information about Vietnamese homosexuality in southern California and Vietnam. The author was able to socialize with several of the informants and thus view Vietnamese homosexual cruising, parties, and bar activities firsthand. Three of the Vietnamese American informants are HIV-positive but asymptomatic. They provided important information about their sexual practices and the way in which they may have been infected with HIV by their Anglo American sex partners.

By the spring of 1992, sufficient information had been gathered on Vietnamese sexuality to construct a questionnaire which would provide general information on Vietnamese beliefs and attitudes about same-sex and opposite-sex behaviours in southern California and Vietnam. The questionnaire was administered to several different groups of Vietnamese Americans living in Orange County. A preliminary brief version of the questionnaire was first completed by 43 Vietnamese American men attending alcohol rehabilitation classes. The final version was completed by 202 Vietnamese American ESL students (117 women and 85 men) at the end of March 1992; by 21 Vietnamese American patients (9 women and 12 men) coming to the Orange County Health Care Agency's Special Diseases Clinic during the spring and summer of 1992; and 10 Vietnamese American members of a focus group (5 women and 5 men) on June 24, 1992.

During the last four months of 1992, only the author remained as a part-time employee of the field research staff. This meant that two important project plans could not be carried out: in-depth interviews of several monolingual Vietnamese transvestite men who had recently immigrated to California from Vietnam, and HIV testing of a group of homosexually identified Vietnamese American men. With the assistance of volunteers from the PFLAG organization, however, two focus groups dealing with the attitudes and beliefs of Vietnamese Americans about male homosexuality were carried out in the fall of 1992; and the author was able to continue participant observations of the Vietnamese gay world until the end of December 1992.

Acculturation and Vietnamese American Sexual Behaviours

Recent research findings indicate that there is 'no single continuum of acculturation and assimilation . . . it is selective; and some ethnic traits, especially the maintenance of family ties, are sustained and surprisingly even strengthened from generation to generation (Keefe and Padilla, 1987: 189).' The most significant changes due to acculturation usually occur between immigrant parents and their US-born children. There is 'no gradual, consistent course of sociocultural change, but an initial burst of Americanization followed by a long-term process of settling into an ethnic community . . . a unique creation of the contact experience that contributes further to the ethnically plural society of the United States' (Keefe and Padilla, 1987: 8).

Although these findings were made in a long-term acculturation study of people of Mexican origin emigrating to the United States they may also accurately describe the experiences of Vietnamese Americans. A recent study of academic achievement in Indochinese (Laos, Cambodian, and Vietnamese) refugee families found, for example, that the family continues to be the central institution for maintaining cultural values and traditions from one generation to another. Based on 26 questions about values given to a random sample of 200 nuclear families and their 536 school-age children, the finding was that 'parents and children rated the perceived values in a similar fashion, providing empirical testimony that these parents had served their stewardship well. For the most part, the perspectives and values embedded in the cultural heritage of the Indochinese had been carried with them to the US . . . . The values formed a set of cultural givens with deep roots in the Confucian and Buddhist traditions of East and Southeast Asia' (Caplan, Choy, and Whitmore, 1992: 39).

Further, in a study of the acculturation of Vietnamese refugee adolescents and adults in Los Angeles, Heifetz (1990) found that 'adolescents were more acculturated to life in the United States than adults due to greater contact in school and more participation with day-to-day life and activities in the host community'. She also found that 'adolescents were encouraged by parents to adjust their behaviour in terms of perceived norms in the American culture, specifically at public school, but remain Vietnamese in the home' (Heifetz, 1990: 664); and that in Los Angeles, because most Vietnamese refugees were located in or adjacent to Latino neighbourhoods, 'the real acculturators or change agents were predominantly Latinos' (Heifetz, 1990: 502–3). It should be noted that 'Little Saigon' is also located adjacent to Latino neighbourhoods.

An important characteristic of Vietnamese refugees is that they 'are among the most youthful of all immigrant populations in the United States, with an average age of 26 years [in 1992] for all Southeast Asian refugees in the United States' (Gold, 1992: 64–5). Since most of them arrived prior to 1981, they have been resident in the United States for many years.[2] Their average age at arrival was extremely young and included a larger number of males (55%) than females.

Early age at arrival has meant that a relatively large segment of the Vietnamese-born refugee population has been educated in English in the secondary school

---

[2] The length of time most emigrants from Vietnam have lived in the United States varies from 19 years to a year or less since under the orderly departure program family members of Vietnamese Americans and former south Vietnamese government political detainees of the current communist government of Vietnam are still emigrating to the United States. The first wave of refugees began in April 1975.

systems in Orange County and elsewhere and has, as noted above, acculturated at a much faster rate than older members of the Vietnamese community.

One effect of this acculturation at an early age is that sexual socialization of Vietnamese American adolescents may be mostly with Anglo American, Latino, or other non-Vietnamese school friends and neighbours. A finding from previous field research on the homosexuality of men of Mexican origin in Orange County by Magaña and Carrier (1991) suggests that composition of friendship networks while growing up determines to a large extent whether adult sexual behaviours tilt towards or away from patterns based on the culture of origin. If this finding holds true for Vietnamese Americans, then, depending on the extent of their familiarity and attraction, we should expect highly acculturated sexually active young people of Vietnamese origin to prefer Anglo-American, Latino, or other non-Vietnamese people as sex partners and to incorporate some of their sexual practices into their sexual repertoires.

The sexual behaviours of Vietnamese people who emigrated to the United States at the age of puberty or older may thus continue to be more influenced by traditional Vietnamese beliefs and attitudes about sexuality learned in Vietnam than those that exist in the communities in which they now live in southern California. The available cross-cultural data suggest that significant differences continue to exist between the sexual behaviours of ethnic minority populations and mainstream middle-class white Anglo populations in the United States.

Beliefs and Attitudes about Heterosexual Behaviors

There is general consensus among Vietnamese American informants in Orange County that many Vietnamese men in Vietnam have sex with female prostitutes prior to marriage, and that some do afterwards. For young men in Vietnam, first sexual encounters with female prostitutes may be considered by older male members of the family to be an important learning experience and a rite of passage. And successful sexual contacts may be something to boast about to certain family members and friends: 'A man without a venereal disease is not a man at all' ('nam vô lậu, bất thành nhân').

There is also high agreement that Vietnamese men continue to have sex with female prostitutes in Orange County. A divergence of attitudes exists between Vietnamese American men and women, however, about the appropriateness of the behaviour; and their opinions differ about the proportion of men that have sex with prostitutes, and how frequently they do so before and after marriage.

The following discussion by the field research focus group illustrates current differences in beliefs and attitudes between Vietnamese American men and women about female prostitution.[3] The opening question was: 'Some Vietnamese

---

[3] The focus group met for three hours in June 1992. It was made up of ten urban middle-class Vietnamese originally from north, central, and south Vietnam and was divided equally between men and women. Their ages ranged between the mid-30s and mid-40s.

men use the services of female prostitutes in Vietnam and Orange County. What do Vietnamese people think about this kind of behaviour?'

A man responded to the opening question: 'It is acceptable among men'.

A woman countered: 'Do men really need this service? If so, please share your views with us?'

A second man answered her question: 'Each person has a different attitude about this—some are very content with one woman, others want more. Nothing wrong with this, it's just a need.'

Another woman asked: 'Would you condemn this behaviour?'

A third man replied: 'Morally, I do. But in terms of physiological and sexual need, no, I do not. The use of prostitutes is normal among Vietnamese men, especially young men just coming of age. A majority of them use their services—about 99 per cent—before getting married. Even after being married, many still use their services. Just something to break the monotony of sex in marriage.'

The woman then asked him: 'What if a Vietnamese woman had the same sex need, would you accept her doing the same thing?'

He replied: 'Well, this is just a traditional male view. But if she needs to do so she should be able to use the services of a male prostitute'.

Two other men in the focus group chimed in saying her question was controversial. Then one returned to the subject of male behaviour: 'Well, even though they had primary wives and additional secondary wives, my grandfathers and great uncles still visited houses of prostitution. No one said anything. Even among their wives, they accepted it as something natural. No questions were asked.'

She replied: 'Well, that was in old-fashioned society. Nowadays it's different. Would you accept this type of behaviour today?'

The third man answered her question: 'Present-day women are somewhat more equal with men and more liberal than older generations so when we visit prostitutes now we do so in a discreet manner. We do not share information about this behaviour with our wives.'

And a fourth man said: 'It is just a need, a physiological need for married men—one of curiosity for young, unmarried men. There's nothing immoral about this, a normal behaviour.'

A woman then asked: 'Don't you men worry about transmitting diseases? You should think about your wife and children and try to be monogamous.'

Before the men could make a reply another woman stated her belief: 'The sex drive of men is generally much stronger than that of women. It is acceptable for men to know about sex before they get married. But once married they should stop having sex with other women. Vietnamese men are selfish, because it's OK for them to go to brothels but not OK for their wives to do likewise.'

And still another woman generalized: 'Our view is influenced by Chinese social behaviour where men are more valued than women. Men can thus do practically anything they want, sexually, politically. It's acceptable, even expected, that men should have more than one wife.'

A man responded to their statements: 'Often when we visit brothels, it's just on the spur of the moment when we are out socializing with male friends. It's another form of male bonding. But we don't let this behaviour destroy our marriage.'

One of the women asked him: 'What if your wife did the same thing when she is out with her girlfriends? Would you accept this and not be concerned about her behaviour?'

Several men in the focus group pointed out to her that it had been a longstanding Vietnamese custom for men but not for women. One put it this way: 'It's a tradition for men to have more than one wife, and to visit prostitutes. But to let women do the same, it's not right! However, now that we are living in the United States it should be acceptable for us to see our wives have boyfriends, lovers.'

Another man pointed out that they were 'having conflicts with two different cultural points of view'.

And yet another man explained: 'Before 1975, it was uncommon in Vietnam to hear about a woman having extramarital affairs, let alone acceptance of them by her husband. But now, since I've been in the United States, I've heard about many families being broken up as a result of extramarital affairs by the wives as well as by the husbands. Some of my friends accepted, forgave, their wives for having affairs while they were still in Vietnam in re-education camps. They rationalized that their wives' misbehaviour was due to sex needs and loneliness.'

Two men then made essentially the same observation that Vietnamese men do feel a certain amount of guilt about their sexual encounters with prostitutes and so try to be discreet and hide it from their wives. They asked the women how they felt about this behaviour. The women in the focus group replied that it was not right either for men or women and stated their belief that most Vietnamese women have always been against female prostitution but have had to accept it as a fact of life. They have been forgiving, they said, because they believe that men have greater sex needs than women.

The focus group discussion ended with everyone agreeing that young Vietnamese men still use the services of prostitutes whether in Vietnam, Orange County, or Mexico. They also noted that though it is considered important for a Vietnamese woman to have a reputation for chastity prior to marriage, when a heterosexual couple become romantically involved and plan to marry—whether in Vietnam or Orange County—it is not unusual for sex to take place between them prior to marriage.

Risky Vietnamese American Opposite-Sex Behaviours

The field research data clearly indicate that, whether single or married, a sizeable number of adult Vietnamese men in Orange County continue the Vietnamese cultural tradition of having sexual intercourse with many different female sex partners; and that many of these sex partners are Mexican prostitutes. Participant observation and field interviews of sexually active young Vietnamese men revealed that clusters of Mexican female prostitutes operate in Orange and Los Angeles counties and in Tijuana and Ensenada, Mexico, specifically to service their sexual needs. Vietnamese men also go to bars, houses of prostitution, and massage parlours in southern California that provide Vietnamese, other Asian, Black, and Anglo American women, in addition to Mexican, but they appear to be few in number. There do not appear to be many Vietnamese American women working as prostitutes in southern California. Several informants suggested that this is related to the fact that so few Vietnamese women emigrating to the US were in the socioeconomic class from which prostitutes are usually recruited in Vietnam. Others suggested that even if they were, opportunities for other kinds of employment in the US would preclude most Vietnamese American women from having any financial need to play what is clearly a discredited role in Vietnamese society.

It is not clear how or why Mexican prostitutes have become one of the primary heterosexual targets of Vietnamese men. The consensus of informant opinion is that it is related to cost, physical attraction, easy availability, accessibility, and safety. Many young attractive Mexican women—who closely approximate the stature and size of Vietnamese women—are easily available as sex partners at relatively low cost in many different locations in Los Angeles and Orange counties and in Tijuana and Ensenada, Mexico. The relative safety of these heterosexual encounters has been historically proven to the Vietnamese male customers by the fact that over time the prostitutes have generally treated them fairly and honestly. None of the respondents believed that there was a high risk of being overcharged or robbed by Mexican prostitutes. When in Mexico, there is the additional safety factor that the Vietnamese men will not be harassed by the police since female prostitution is quasi-legal. And, as will be explained below, Mexican prostitutes specializing in Vietnamese customers operate relatively safely out of motels in southern California since non-Vietnamese undercover vice squad police officers would be immediately identifiable. Police Departments in Los Angeles and Orange counties apparently have few Vietnamese American sworn police officers.[4]

Clinical cases of Vietnamese men diagnosed as having penicillin-resistant gonorrhoea (PPNG) at the Special Diseases Clinic of the Orange County Health

---

[4] Law enforcement officials finally learned about this special category of commercial sex workers in the spring of 1994 (Anaheim Police Department, 1994). Based on a tip from 'a citizen regarding prostitution activity . . . in Anaheim' undercover investigators arrested eleven Mexican female commercial sex workers in May 1994 in the motel where they provided their services to 'Asian men.' 'Investigation revealed that the majority of the women had been recruited in Mexico to serve as prostitutes for a three month period.' They averaged 18 years old and the youngest was fourteen years old (ibid., page 1). Three of the eight were minors, 14 to 16 years old, who had been brought illegally to California under the pretense they would be working in factories. The four minors and two of the adult women arrested were examined by physicians in the Special Diseases Clinic at the Orange County Health Care Agency. Even though they claimed that most of their customers used condoms, they all had significant sexually transmitted diseases. One of the four juveniles, for example, had gonorrhea; another had chlamydia and a class III pap with dysplasia; the third had warts, gonorrhea, and a class II pap with metaplasia; and the fourth had chlamydia and a class II pap with papilloma virus changes.

Care Agency also document Mexican females as sexual targets. In fact there was an outbreak of PPNG in the county in 1987 and two-thirds of the patients (10 of 16) reported having been infected by female prostitutes either in Tijuana or Ensenada. Additionally, in January 1992, the author visited one of the most popular prostitute bars in Tijuana mentioned by PPNG patients and found that *all* of the bar's 65 patrons that evening were Vietnamese men. At present, there is a van transportation service between Little Saigon and Tijuana to take interested Vietnamese customers back and forth to bars; and Vietnamese men from as far away as San José in northern California go there. One male respondent reported that Vietnamese men have been going to prostitute bars in Tijuana since 1977. A female respondent said she had heard that 'any young Vietnamese man who has not had sexual experiences with Mexican prostitutes in Tijuana is considered square, nerdy, by his male friends'. Another male respondent mentioned that he had a nineteen year-old nephew who went to Mexico just about every weekend looking for sex.

Our field research observations of clusters of Mexican female prostitutes in Orange County were confirmed in a 1992 outbreak of PPNG among Vietnamese men. Interviews with several male patients conducted by disease control investigators revealed that they were most likely to be infected by Mexican female prostitutes operating out of a motel located only fifteen minutes away by car from Little Saigon. The field research staff had known about the motel and the Mexican prostitute operation there for several months. A State of California disease control investigator also confirmed our finding that the Mexican prostitutes at the motel *only* provide their services to Vietnamese men. Although originally from Mexico and fluent in Spanish, he was immediately mistakenly identified by the prostitutes as an undercover police officer. And even though he carefully explained his medical treatment mission and that he was not a police officer, the operation shut down straightaway and—we later learned—set up operations in another nearby motel.

An interesting fact about the Mexican female prostitute network is that both men and women in the Vietnamese community know about it. Approximately two-thirds of our ESL respondents, for example, (50 of 79 male and 50 of 74 female respondents) knew that Vietnamese men living in Orange County go to nightclubs in Tijuana to find sexual partners. And, according to one of our informants who assists new immigrants from Vietnam to find employment, shortly after arrival in Orange County many Vietnamese men quickly learn about the Mexican prostitute network.

Additional prostitute contacts are made by some Vietnamese men when they return to Vietnam to visit their families. Since they may stop over in Bangkok both going to, and coming back from Vietnam their sexual encounters may be with Thai as well as with Vietnamese prostitutes. Several male PPNG patients claim they were infected by Vietnamese prostitutes in Saigon. The acceptability of men going to prostitutes in Vietnam was illustrated recently by one of our respondents who, after a long absence, had returned from Orange County (without his

Vietnamese wife) to visit his middle-class family in a coastal town in central Vietnam. Even though they knew he was married, one of the first offers of hospitality by his brothers was a trip to a house of prostitution.

The results of the Orange County Health Care Agency's Knowledge, Beliefs, and Behaviours (KABB) community survey of a random sample of 532 Vietnamese Americans living in the vicinity of Little Saigon in the fall of 1992 (330 men and 202 women) provide some additional confirmation of the sexual contacts Vietnamese American men have with female prostitutes. Analysed according to two age groups, close to 60% of the men aged 18–35 (n = 193) and 94% of the men aged 36–45 (n = 137) said that they had had sexual encounters with women. Of those having sexual encounters with women, 17% of the younger group (20 of 115) and 10% of the older group (13 of 129) said that they had had sexual encounters with female prostitutes. In response to a question on whether any of these sexual encounters were with prostitutes in another country, 45% of the younger group (9 of 20) and 30% of the older group (4 of 13) replied in the affirmative. Two-thirds of the younger group (6 of 9) and three-quarters of the older group (3 of 4) said that they had had sexual contact with female prostitutes in Mexico; the remainder were in Vietnam.

Survey findings show an interesting difference in beliefs between Vietnamese men and women as to whether 'men have greater sexual needs than women': 52% of the women (106 of 202) agreed that they do, as compared to 39% of the men (129 of 330). Differences in felt need for sex by men and women is exemplified by responses to the question of whether 'sex before marriage is OK if the couple is planning to get married'. A much larger percentage of men (64%) agreed that it was OK than women (35%).

Opposite Sex Behaviors & HIV Infection

One potential risk of HIV transmission is sex between Vietnamese men and Mexican female prostitutes. Unfortunately, because so little information is available on the levels of HIV infection in either group, it is not possible at present to make any firm judgment about the magnitude of risk of HIV transmission. The available data suggest that although still relatively low, the levels of infection are higher in the Mexican prostitutes than in the Vietnamese American customers, thus the concern should be about the prostitutes transmitting the AIDS virus to their customers. However, judging from the generally low levels of HIV infection in Mexican prostitutes (believed to be around 1–2 per cent in Tijuana), the risk of Vietnamese men getting infected from their sexual encounters with female prostitutes exists but is not particularly high.

Another potential for HIV transmission exists in the sexual encounters between Vietnamese men and Thai and Vietnamese prostitutes during their trips back to Vietnam. Given the higher levels of HIV infection in Thai than in Mexican prostitutes, the Vietnamese men theoretically place themselves at higher risk of being infected by Thai prostitutes.[5] No information is available about the levels of infection in Vietnamese prostitutes in Vietnam. The belief is that they are still low at present, but may soon rise because of the increasing number of sex workers in Saigon and the large number of intravenous drug users who continue to share needles.[6] Judging from the KABB community survey, only a very small percentage of Vietnamese Americans—less than one half of one percent (2 of 531)—have a history of injecting drugs for non-medical purposes. Excessive use of alcohol appears to be a more serious drug abuse problem in the community and occurs more frequently among men than women. Close to 15% of the men surveyed (compared to 2.5% of the women) said that they had at least once 'used alcohol to the point where they did not remember what they did'.

Beliefs and Attitudes about Same-sex Behaviours

The field research data clearly indicate that the same-sex behaviours of Vietnamese American men in Orange County continue to be influenced by Vietnamese belief systems and attitudes about homosexuality and patterns of sexual behaviour that are Vietnamese in origin (that is, unique to Vietnam). The data also clearly indicate that the same-sex behaviours of some of these men change as a result of their acculturation to mainstream Anglo American culture, and coming into contact with the homosexual behaviours of other men of colour (Latinos, Blacks, and other Asians), as well as with Anglo American men. First, the effects of the Vietnamese heritage will be considered and then the changes that may occur with acculturation and non-Vietnamese sexual partners.

What seems of central importance to Vietnamese men having sex with men is the general denial of the existence of homosexuality at the community level, and the shame that ensues at the family level when a member is revealed to be involved in homosexual encounters. There appears to be a general belief in the Vietnamese

[5] Although it is no longer necessary for Vietnamese Americans to travel to Vietnam via Bangkok, some continue to do so to patronize female sex workers. In an interview in October 1994, for example, a Vietnamese American business man told the senior author that he always stopped off in Bangkok. On five different trips to Vietnam in the past twelve months, he had had sex with at least 15 different female sex workers during stopovers in Bangkok. He also revealed that he never uses condoms.

[6] Information gathered by the senior author during a visit to Saigon (now referred to as Ho Chi Minh City) in March 1994 indicates that sharing needles in intravenous drug use continues to be the major source of HIV infection in Vietnam: 'injecting drug users account for nearly ninety percent of all HIV infections. Most of the injecting drug users, and those with HIV infections, are concentrated in urban areas, especially Ho Chi Minh City (Vietnamese National AIDS Committee, 1993, p.15). Although they rank a distant second in number infected, the possibility of widespread HIV infection among commercial sex workers, however, is taken seriously by the National AIDS Committee of Vietnam: 'Sexually transmitted diseases have been documented and acknowledged as a serious public health problem in Vietnam for many years. In 1975, STD prevalence was estimated at eight percent, or about one million cases annually. At that time, the disease burden was correlated with an estimated 300,000 commercial sex workers, mostly in the south, 60% of whom were said to be infected' (ibid., p.19). Information about current HIV prevention programs in Vietnam are given by Koster (1993) and Schiffer (1993). It is clear that the Vietnamese government is trying to prevent the creation of a Bangkok-type international sex industry for tourists in Ho Chi Minh City.

community in Orange County that the homosexual behaviours of Vietnamese American men are mostly the result of their being seduced by Anglo American men. One of our heterosexual informants stated his belief this way: 'In Vietnam, homosexuality did not have a chance to develop because of Vietnamese culture and morals. . .Vietnamese society does not accept homosexuality.'

A recurrent theme in our interviews with Vietnamese men who have sex with men is the extreme homophobia that they feel exists in Vietnamese society and the stress that it has brought into their family relationships. Homophobia in the Vietnamese community of Orange County is perpetuated by widespread extremist conservative middle-class Anglo views about the evils of homosexuality and by the Vietnamese media. The following kind of article which appeared in *The Vietnamese Weekly Newspaper* in 1992, for example, 'Is homosexuality a disease?', reinforces cultural stereotypes held by many Vietnamese people about homosexuality: it is a mental disease; homosexual men are feminine (they 'walk like women, have soft hands, are talented in sewing, makeup, cooking, and singing'); and 'homosexuals' are perverted in their sexual practices. The most popular Vietnamese term for men who have sex with men, *Lại Cái*, also substantiates the association of feminine men with homosexuality in that it literally means 'half man, half woman'.

The existence of homophobia was further confirmed in March 1992 by our field research survey of 202 adult Vietnamese students attending ESL courses in Orange County (85 men and 117 women). In response to a question as to whether Vietnamese people have strong feelings against Vietnamese men if they have had sex (or are having sex) with other men, a large majority (90%) responded that they believed it to be true. A large majority (86%) also reported that they believed 'Vietnamese men who have sex with men can be easily identified because they are feminine'.

Individual beliefs held by Vietnamese men involved in homosexual behaviour may also reflect common societal beliefs and prejudices. The feminine male stereotype is perhaps held by many homosexually identified men in Vietnam; and is reported to be held by some recent arrivals in Orange County. A masculine gay-identified Vietnamese male informant reported, for example, that his recently arrived effeminate male homosexual cousin from Saigon initially refused to believe he (the informant) was also homosexual because he was not feminine.[7]

Another factor of importance to Vietnamese American male homosexuality is that Vietnamese families do not always pressure male members to marry at an early age. Although they are expected to get married and have children in their early twenties, Vietnamese men may be excused from this obligation if they are pursuing an education. In this sense the value of obtaining a good education is more important than getting married. A male in his twenties or thirties may

---

[7] Vietnamese people may be more accepting of cross-gender behaviour than masculine same-sex behaviour. In a recent interview (July 1994), for example, a male transvestite Vietnamese American respondent told the senior author that his family knew about and accepted his cross-dressing. He said, 'they can only understand how a female-like man would want to have sex with another man.'

suggest that he has no interest in girlfriends because he is busy studying. Judgments are thus not usually made by parents (or siblings) about the sexual orientation of the son (or brother) who shows little interest in women—so long as he is a student or advancing his career. The downside of this permissiveness is the secrecy with which the homosexual son (or brother) must manage his sexual relationships. We had a first-hand view of this problem when a young Vietnamese male respondent, a senior in high school, told his parents that he was HIV-seropositive and homosexual. Although he and his parents eventually made an accommodation, their initial homophobic reaction made him so desperate that he ran away from home and was gone for over a week before he let them know where he was.

Patterns of Male Same-sex Behaviours

In Vietnam sexual encounters between male adolescents may be facilitated by socially sanctioned close physical contacts considered 'normal' between males (such as holding hands and resting or sleeping close together in the same bed). Although adolescent boys know that homosexual exploration is not socially sanctioned, and therefore not to be disclosed, according to some of our informants it may also not be something to feel especially guilty about at that age.

An important aspect of this adolescent same-sex behaviour is that, in the view of most of our informants who had extensive homosexual encounters in their early youth while still in Vietnam, it appears to be restricted to mutual masturbation and fellatio. And in carrying out these sexual practices there does not appear to be any strongly developed sense of playing a masculine or feminine sexual role of the kind that is usually found in societies where anal intercourse is more prevalent and the ultimate objective of homosexual encounters (see, for example, Carrier and Magaña, 1991).

Two important unanswered questions about Vietnamese adolescent sexual behaviours thus arise. First, as a result of the cultural stereotype which equates effeminacy with homosexuality, do boys judged to be effeminate by their peers (or older men) become sexual targets and thus engage in a different set of sexual practices than do 'regular masculine' boys? Second, do they as a necessary consequence ultimately feel that over their life span they should only play the female sex role with other men? These questions remain unanswered.

One significant pattern suggested by our limited interview data is that as some homosexually involved adolescent males in Vietnam move into adulthood, and become aware of and comfortable with their homosexuality and the societal belief that equates it with feminine behaviour, they then restrict their sexual pleasures mostly to the passive role of fellating 'masculine' men. They may thus use their feminine behaviour to attract other males interested in homosexual encounters, and so become sexual targets. But their major focus appears to be on pleasing and meeting the sexual needs of their partners, whatever these may be—anal as well as oral sex. Their preference for one sexual technique over another generally becomes less important than the relational issue of meeting their partners' demands and needs.

Some of these young men move on to full cross-gender behaviour and present themselves in public as women. Indeed, to earn needed income, some also play the role of a female prostitute. For example, during the Vietnamese–American war, transvestite prostitutes congregated daily on the terrace of the Continental Hotel in Saigon (Carrier, 1994). They were reported to have disappeared from view after the communist takeover of South Vietnam in 1975, but recent reports from our informants returning from Saigon reveal that male transvestites can be seen on the streets once again and some are back earning an income as prostitutes.[8] Recently we have also observed Vietnamese male transvestites in Little Saigon and at private parties elsewhere in Orange and Los Angeles counties.

One lacuna in our field research data concerns information on the extent to which essentially *unacculturated* Vietnamese men who have sex with men are involved in anal intercourse in Vietnam or in Orange County. As previously noted, the San Francisco survey conducted in the spring of 1991 revealed that a small minority of adult men from Vietnam had at some time in their lives practised anal intercourse. However, since they were not asked whether it was carried out with a man or a woman, we do not know whether the interviewees responding affirmatively performed it homosexually or heterosexually. Again, our gay and homosexually identified informants of Vietnamese origin suggest that in Vietnam anal intercourse is not widely practised by men who have sex with men. The sex life histories of Vietnamese American men we interviewed (n = 15) reveal that those who have practised homosexual anal intercourse have incorporated it into their sexual repertoires as a result of sexual relationships with Anglo, Black, or Latino partners.

The sex life histories of the young Vietnamese American men we interviewed (n = 15) illustrate the effect of acculturation on sexual behaviour. The homosexual behaviours of those men highly acculturated are more similar to Anglo patterns of sexual behaviour than Vietnamese. One significant variation, however, may be the continuation of the Vietnamese-based homosexual pattern of usually letting the sexual partner take the lead in deciding which sexual techniques will be used in any given sexual encounter. This is why many Vietnamese American men may incorporate anal intercourse into their sexual repertoires: it is the preferred sexual technique of their Anglo American sex partners. It is of interest to note that the four young HIV-positive Vietnamese men we interviewed were sexually

[8] In March 1994, the senior author gathered some information about the 'homosexual scene' in Ho Chi Minh City (Carrier, 1994). Men continue to seek sexual encounters with men in many of the same locations observed during his previous visits in the 1960s and 1970s—like in the Eden movie theatre and in large downtown parks. One major difference is that transvestites now congregate in a bar, called Turtle Lake (Ho Con Rua), located near the center of the city. Masculine men interested sexually in other men also have a new meeting place, referred to as the Coconut Palm Cafe (Cay Dua Cafe), located about a mile from downtown. And there is now an annual transvestite event held during the last week of March at Long Hai beach, located about a two-hour drive south of Ho Chi Minh City. Although originally a transvestite celebration, it has now become, according to several respondents, a mecca for men having sex with other men.

active only with Anglo American men with whom they had played the receptive role in anal intercourse.

Two Tentative Categories: 'Gays' and 'Outsiders'

The field research data available at present suggest that men of Vietnamese origin involved in homosexual encounters can be sorted into at least two different categories: 'gays' and 'outsiders'. The two categories are not mutually exclusive since there may be some mixing of gays and outsiders, both social and sexual, from time to time. The two categories are nevertheless distinctive enough to be useful for explaining some of the existing networks of Vietnamese men who have sex with men. I will describe the major characteristics of both categories and the relative risks of HIV infection run by men in one and the other.

Vietnamese 'Gays'

Contrary to what we originally expected, there *is* an active friendship network of Vietnamese men who have sex with men in southern California who identify themselves as 'gay'. The gay network is composed mostly of middle-class, moderately acculturated, young men. They are bound together by being gay *and* Vietnamese. They want gay liberation, but they also want to retain their Vietnamese heritage. The network has two gay centres. The major one is located in Los Angeles and is presided over by the network's two young leaders in their late twenties—united in the summer of 1992 in the first gay Vietnamese marriage ceremony—who are also patrons of the group. The other centre, an extension of the major one, is located in southern Orange County and presided over by an older Vietnamese gay man in his late forties who is also a patron. Patrons are important for the maintenance of the network in that they provide a safe space— usually a house—and an ambiance where gay men can meet, eat, party, sleep, and get to know one another. The house-centres provide Vietnamese gay men with a refuge from the straight world and the families in which most of them live.

Some of the men who belong to the gay Vietnamese friendship network also belong to the Gay Asian Pacific Support Network (GAPSN) in Los Angeles. GAPSN meetings and social outings provide another vehicle for gay Vietnamese to meet and socialize with other Asian Americans and with each other in southern California.

An interesting aspect of the gay Vietnamese network is that it is more social in its orientation than sexual; that is, its members mainly come to form Vietnamese social support networks rather than simply to find sexual partners. Some of the social relationships formed may lead to dating, but they mostly represent a means of members getting to know each other. Many of the Vietnamese men making up the group arrived in the US prior to or around puberty and have been in the country for ten years or more. Their sexual histories are thus made up of the sexual experiences they had prior to leaving Vietnam plus the ones they have had since living in the US. Most of their American homosexual partners have been non-Vietnamese because their sexual socialization has mainly been with Anglo men. A surprisingly large number of their partners, however, have been Latinos, and to a lesser extent other Asians, African Americans and Native Americans. Many of the men in the network continue to have a majority of their sexual relationships with men found outside the network. Some, however, in an attempt to integrate their gay identity with their Vietnamese identity have become interested in moving from what they think of as a 'White phase' of their gay life into a 'Vietnamese phase' and are, therefore, also seeking Vietnamese sexual partners.

Another interesting aspect of the gay network is that there is a group tendency to speak primarily in Vietnamese. This is done as a courtesy for relatively newly arrived gay members who may have a limited understanding of English. Yet, it is also a group statement about Vietnamese identity and how this separates them from the Anglo gay world. English may be used but it is usually restricted to those occasions when younger Vietnamese present do not understand Vietnamese or for one-to-one conversations where ideas may be more easily expressed in English. At times they may also use a combination of English and Vietnamese ('Vietglish') to express themselves.

An explicit objective of the southern California Vietnamese gay network is outreach: providing support to all Vietnamese men who have sex with men—both to those who are gay identified and those who are still questioning their identity—in dealing with their coming out, self-image, families, homophobia in the Vietnamese community, loneliness, and isolation. With the assistance of an empathic straight Vietnamese (whose homosexual brother had committed suicide) and a supportive young Vietnamese woman (who is a cousin and close friend of a member), the network leaders organized the first Vietnamese chapter of a national organization called 'Parents and Friends of Lesbians and Gays' (PFLAG) in December 1991 at the Gay and Lesbian Center of Orange County located near Little Saigon in Garden Grove. Until recently, the Vietnamese PFLAG chapter held monthly rap meetings in Vietnamese for members and their family and friends; and sponsored occasional social outings where members could get to know each other better. In the spring of 1992, it also sponsored for the first time a 'gay booth' at the Vietnamese community's lunar new year 'Tet Fair' held in Little Saigon. 'Tet', which is family-oriented, is the most important annual Vietnamese celebration. PFLAG's major objectives at the 'Tet Fair' was to educate the Vietnamese community about the positive side of being homosexual and Vietnamese, the existence of their organization, the help it could provide families with homosexual members, and the sexual behaviours that lead to HIV infection and AIDS.[9]

[9.] Over time PFLAG lost its momentum and is currently inactive. A 'Gay Vietnamese Support Group' has taken its place and operates a telephone hot line. GAPSN continues to be a major organization for gay Vietnamese. And, as of Labor Day weekend 1993, there is also an annual Vietnamese Lesbian and Gay conference. In early May 1996, a major newspaper in Orange County presented a full

Vietnamese Homosexual 'Outsiders'

Given our limited field research data, all types of Vietnamese men who have sex with men but who do not belong to an established gay friendship circle are tentatively categorized as 'outsiders'. Some outsiders do not have a firm gay identity and are thus still questioning their sexual identity; others—some single, some married—have come out to themselves as being homosexual, or as being bisexual. But none have identified themselves as being heterosexual. This is not surprising given that there does not appear to be any cultural formulation—such as exists, for example, in the Mexican culture (see Magaña and Carrier, 1991)—which would allow a man of Vietnamese origin to participate in homosexual encounters and still think of himself as being heterosexual.

Outsider men can be sorted into two groups: those who are moderately to highly acculturated and those who are unacculturated. Most who are highly acculturated appear to prefer non-Asian sex partners. Highly acculturated Vietnamese men tend not to have many homosexual Vietnamese friends and to find their sexual partners mostly through institutions of the Anglo gay world, such as gay bars, baths, or gyms. An important subcategory is made up of 'loners', men who prefer to operate on the fringes of both the Anglo and Vietnamese gay worlds. They do not usually socialize with either Vietnamese or Anglo gay friendship circles. Four of our HIV-seropositive informants are loners. Two of them found their Anglo sex partners through a gay, predominantly Anglo, computer network.

Most unacculturated Vietnamese men who are sexually interested in men, on the other hand, are limited in finding sexual partners by their inability to speak English, by their lack of knowledge about the Anglo gay world, and by their social isolation in the Vietnamese community of Orange County. They do, however, know the Vietnamese ways of locating homosexual partners. Our field research reveals that they cluster in friendship circles and engage in the same type of cruising in Little Saigon that they did in Vietnam. Certain cafés, restaurants, and businesses (in shopping malls and centres) are favoured locations for finding Vietnamese men interested in homosexual encounters. One 'large' network of recently arrived Vietnamese men who seek sexual encounters with other men, for example, socialize on weekdays in a café located in a major Little Saigon mall. The network makes possible the sharing of information by newcomers about the homosexual world of Little Saigon and provides its members with access to relatively well-off older Vietnamese men who prefer younger Vietnamese men as sex partners. Since they may be part of a strong and interweaving social network of homosexual friends, the unacculturated Vietnamese men having access to Little Saigon circles of friends should probably be put into an as yet unnamed third group and neither categorized as 'outsiders' nor 'gays'.

page story about Vietnamese American homosexuality and noted that 'Vietnamese gays fight intense pressure from a traditional culture.' (The Orange County Register, May 2d, 1996, page 1 of Accent Section.) Gay leaders are quoted as saying that progress is being made in their fight against Vietnamese homophobia but only in small increments over time.

One interesting aspect of unacculturated Vietnamese homosexual behaviour that we have just begun to learn about is the role that older Vietnamese homosexual men may play as 'patrons' of relatively newly arrived young men who for a variety of reasons (including income) may be willing to participate in homosexual encounters. These patrons have a secure income and a place where they can entertain and carry out sexual encounters with their young friends. The 'private party' is the major vehicle used to bring members of the friendship circle together. Although our informants have told us of the existence of several patrons and their friendship networks, thus far we have met only one patron—a single man in his early fifties who owns a small factory. At a predominantly gay Vietnamese party of more than seventy-five guests, we met seven young and middle-aged transvestite Vietnamese men who are part of this friendship network.

In addition to the older homosexual men who act as patrons, we have observed some older businessmen in the Little Saigon mall who also seek sexual relations with the young unacculturated Vietnamese men who hang around the mall. Several of them had to operate carefully because they did not want their nearby family to know what they were up to. And some have 'bad' reputations with the younger men because they refused to pay them for sexual relations as is the custom. Stories also circulate about older Vietnamese owners of small businesses in Little Saigon hiring newly arrived young Vietnamese men and making sexual relations a condition of their continued employment.

Homosexual Behaviours and HIV Infection

A major question remains about the comparative frequency of anal intercourse by Vietnamese men in homosexual encounters in Vietnam versus California. If it indeed is not a highly preferred sexual practice in Vietnam, as appears to be the case, then we can expect unacculturated homosexual Vietnamese men to have the same set of preferences in California as they did in Vietnam, and thus to prefer fellatio over anal intercourse. If this turns out to be true, this means that Vietnamese men restricting their sexual encounters to other Vietnamese men in Orange County should be expected to be at relatively low risk of exposure to HIV, since not only would they be having sexual relations with a population having a low incidence of HIV infection, but would also be practising much lower HIV risk fellatio.

Acculturated gay Vietnamese men, on the other hand, would be at higher risk of HIV infection since their sexual partners (mostly gay Anglo and Latino men) have a much higher incidence of HIV infection and since there is a greater likelihood that they will be practising the highest risk sexual technique, receptive anal intercourse. The risk of HIV infection in the Vietnamese American population of men who have sex with men may be further enhanced by Vietnamese 'gays' who have a preference for anal sex, and have frequent anal intercourse with many different Vietnamese, as well as Anglo and Latino, sexual partners. It is the mixing of sexual partners from high risk and low risk groups that increases the likelihood of transmitting HIV from one group to the other. As Anderson and May (1992: 64) point out: 'The greatest uncertainty in assessing the rate of transmission centres on the prevailing patterns of sexual behaviour within and between communities.'

Discussion

Field research data on Vietnamese American sexual behaviours clearly indicate that the major risk of HIV transmission into the Vietnamese community in Orange County is related to the male segment of the population who have many sexual encounters with other men. Within that segment of the population, the greatest individual risk of HIV infection appears to be for highly sexually active acculturated men whose partner preference is for Anglo and/or Latino men with whom they play both sexual roles in anal intercourse. These individuals have the potential to spread the AIDS virus *within* the Vietnamese population of men who have sex with men if, when infected, they are also sexually active with Vietnamese partners with whom they play both sexual roles in anal intercourse. Unacculturated transvestite Vietnamese men may also put themselves at risk of HIV infection if they are highly sexually active with Latino or Anglo men. The level of their risk depends on the kind of sexual activity they practise, how often it takes place, and with how many different partners. None of these questions can be answered at this point in time. We need to know a great deal more about the attitudes of Vietnamese men towards anal intercourse both in Vietnam and California and how frequently it is practised.

Our study also indicates a potential for the spread of HIV into the heterosexual Vietnamese population through the sexual activity of Vietnamese men with non-Vietnamese female prostitutes in California and Mexico, and with Thai and Vietnamese prostitutes in Thailand and Vietnam. Studies of the association of HIV infections with infections from other sexually transmitted diseases among 1,006 female prostitutes in six cities of central Mexico found that although 'the prevalence of HIV-1 is low, the frequency of other STDs is high. Risk factors [were] identified as: low rate of condom use; [and] interrelation between HIV-1 and other STDs [which] is seen with genital ulcers and C. trachomatis infection (Valdespino *et al.*, 1991).' Among female prostitutes in Thailand, the median percentage infected with HIV in 1991 was reported to be 'rising steadily every 6 months, from 3.5% (range 0% to 44%) to 6.3% (range 0% to 42.7%) to 9.3% (range 0% to 67%)' (Ungchusak *et al.*, 1991).

Findings from the 1992 study of HIV seroprevalence in Vietnamese American men at six testing sites in Orange County showed that HIV infection exists at three of the six sites studied: the Health Care Agency's HIV Alternate Test Site (5 HIV+ out of 223 tested, 2.2%); a men's jail (1 HIV+ out of 122 tested, 0.8%); and a juvenile hall, a place for detension of minors (1 HIV+ out of 145 tested, 0.7%). No HIV-positive Vietnamese Americans were found at the other three sites: private labs (n = 284); alcohol treatment programmes (n = 67); and drug treatment programmes (n = 33). All five HIV-positive men found at the HCA Alternate Test Site were identified as men who have sex with men. The other two were found at blinded test sites (i.e. those places in which blood can be tested anonymously) so no risk factors are known. The overall HIV-seropositive rate of the study sample is 0.8%, 7 of 874 tested.

It should be noted that a critical effect of the high level of male homophobia that exists in the Vietnamese community may be an underreporting of AIDS cases and a reluctance by many men to be tested for HIV infection. The following conclusion made by Kitano (1988:4) about Asian people in general appears to accurately describe the beliefs and behaviors of the Vietnamese Americans living in Orange County: 'People do not want their families and community to know that they have AIDS because it means that their sexual preference may become known . . . They don't want to risk being rejected at a time when they are in need nor do they want to "shame" their families'. A hopeful sign for the future is that a group of Vietnamese individuals and organizations from southern California (Los Angeles and Orange counties) and northern California (San José and San Francisco) created a quarterly magazine in 1993, *Đối diện (Face to Face): The Voice of Vietnamese Lesbians and Gays*. Still in publication, the first issue was published in the summer of 1993. A major objective of the magazine is to try to rectify many of the misconceptions in the Vietnamese American communities about male and female homosexuality.

Given the high level of homophobia in the Vietnamese American community in Orange County, it is not surprising that *none* of the 532 male interviewees of the Orange County Health Care Agency's KABB Community Survey in the fall of 1992 reported ever having homosexual encounters. Given that the field research clearly documents the existence of both male and female homosexuality in Orange County it suggests that the design of the community survey dealing with sexual behaviours may have been seriously flawed. One wonders about the high percentage of 193 male and 202 female interviewees in the 18–35 age group (38 and 40 per cent respectively) who reported that they had had neither heterosexual nor homosexual contacts. This chapter has demonstrated the role of field study in raising such issues and points to the need for further study.

REFERENCES

Anaheim Police Department (1994), 'News Release: Prostitution Ring', 11 April.
Anderson, R. and May, R. (1992), 'Understanding the AIDS Pandemic', *Scientific American*, 266 (May).
Bureau of the Census (1990), 'US population census 1990', Summary tape file 1A, Washington, DC, US Department of Commerce, cited in *Morbidity and Mortality Weekly Report*, 7 February 1992, 41(5): 72.

Caplan, N., Choy, M. and Whitmore, J. (1992), 'Indochinese Refugee Families and Academic Achievement', *Scientific American*, 266 (February).

Carrier, J. (1994), 'Observations of Vietnamese Male Homosexuality in South Vietnam: 1962, 1965–67, 1972–73 and 1994', Unpublished fieldnotes.

—— and Magana, R. (1991), 'Use of Ethnosexual Data on Men of Mexican Origin for HIV/AIDS Prevention Programs', *Journal of Sex Research*, 28(2): 189–202.

Do, H. (1988), 'The Formation of a New Refugee Community: The Vietnamese Community in Orange County, California', Master's thesis, University of California, Santa Barbara.

Flaskerud, J. and Nyamathi, A. (1988), 'An AIDS education program for Vietnamese women', *New York State Journal of Medicine*, 88: 632–7.

Gellert, G., Maxwell, R., Higgins, K., Mai, K., Lowery R., and Doll, L. (1995), 'HIV/ AIDS Knowledge and High Risk Sexual Practices Among Southern California Vietnamese', *Genitourinary Medicine*, 71: 216–23.

Gold, S. (1992), *Refugee Communities: A Comparative Field Study*, Sage, Newbury Park.

Heifetz, J. (1990), 'The Acculturation of Vietnamese Refugee Adolescents and Adults in Los Angeles', PhD thesis, University of California, Los Angeles.

Hickey, G. (1964), *Village in Vietnam*, Yale Press, New Haven.

Jacolliot, L. (1896), *Untrodden Fields of Anthropology*, American Anthropological Society, New York.

Jamieson, N. (1986), 'The Traditional Family in Vietnam', in *The Vietnam Forum: A Review of Vietnamese Culture and Society*, Yale Center for International and Area Studies, Council on Southeast Asia Studies, 116–17.

Jew, S. (1991), 'AIDS among California Asian and Pacific Islander subgroups', *California HIV/AIDS Update*, 4 (9), September, 90–8), Office of AIDS, Department of Health Services, State of California.

Keefe, S. and Padilla, A. (1987), *Chicano Ethnicity*, University of New Mexico Press.

Kitano, K. (1988), 'Correlates of AIDS-Associated High-Risk Behavior among Chinese and Filipino Gay Men', Master's thesis, University of California, Berkeley.

Koster, P. (1993), *HIV/AIDS in Vietnam*, Occasional Paper 36, Third World Centre/ Development Studies, Catholic University of Nijmegen, The Netherlands.

Magaña, R. and Carrier, J. (1991), 'Mexican and Mexican American Male Sexual Behavior and Spread of AIDS in California', *Journal of Sex Research*, 28 (3): 425–41.

Murase, K., Sung, S., and Vuong, V. (1991), 'AIDS Knowledge, Attitudes, Beliefs and Behaviors in Southeast Asian Communities in San Francisco', The Center for Cross-Cultural Research and Social Work Practice, Department of Social Work Education, San Francisco State University.

Orange County Register (1992), 'Close-up: Return to Vietnam', in Section M, 22 March, 1992, *The Orange County Register*, Orange County, California.

Republic of Vietnam (1962), Law No. 12/62: 'Protection of Morality', 22 May.

Schiffer, J. (1993), 'HIV and AIDS Prevention in the Drug Users and Prostitutes of Ho Chi Minh City', Unpublished independent study project in Vietnam, Dartmouth College, New Hampshire, USA.

Ungchusak, K., *et al.* (1991), 'Trends of HIV Spreading in Thailand Detected by National Sentinel Serosurveillance', Paper presented at the Seventh International Conference on AIDS, Florence, 16–21 June, Abstract Book, M.C. 3246: 359, Ministry of Public Health, Thailand.

Valdespino, J., *et al.* (1991), 'Risk Factors Interrelated Between AIDS and STD among female prostitutes in Mexico', Paper presented at the Seventh International Conference on AIDS, Florence, 16–21 June, Abstract Book, M.C. 3226: 354, General Directorate of Epidemiology, Ministry of Health, Thailand.

Vietnamese National AIDS Committee (1993), 'Report of an External Review of the Vietnam National AIDS Control Programme 20 August–4 September 1993', Hanoi, Vietnam.

Vietnamese Weekly Newspaper (1992), 'Dong Tinh Luyen Ai Co Phai La Can Benh Hay Khong? [Is Homosexuality a Disease?]', 31 January, Orange County, California.

Index

252 *Index*

colonization
  and spread of sexually transmitted diseases
    41–2
  of Pacific Basin   23–4
commercial sex
  and loans/debt   207, 208, 210
  and social disparity   144
  and economic and social mobility   190–1
  and universally understood transactions
    144–5
  divorce and widowhood as pathway to   193
  in time of war   94
  reasons for male demand for   45
  types of client using   46
commercial sex workers (female)
  in Africa: and visits to home village   45;
    boyfriends of, risk of AIDS to   49; char-
    acteristics of   49; with AIDS, return to
    places of origin   45
  in Nigeria: and HIV prevalence   217; char-
    acteristics of   219;
  in Thailand   75, 77–85; among tribal people
    75; and gender-power relations in family/
    village   79; and recruitment process   83,
    195–8; characteristics of   78–9; spatial and
    occupational mobility of 198–211
concubinage   227
condom use   121, 135, 138, 148, 149, 216–24,
  236n.
Congo Free State, *see* Zaire
construction industries in urban Thailand
  72–3
Cook, J.   24, 33n.
Cortes, E.   160
Côte d'Ivoire   44, 48, 108, 110, 111, 115, 121
Coutinho, R. A.   160
Croatia   88, 92, 94, 97
cultural risk milieu
  definition of   16

DaGrossa, P. S.   185
Daniel, H.   55, 57, 59, 60, 161
Dararut, *see* Mattariganond, D.
David, N.   41, 112
Davies, P. M.   15, 17
Day, S.   181
D'Emilio, J.   8, 9, 11, 17
demographic anthropology
  and the study of AIDS   4, 10
development workers
  and public health programmes   146
Dewey, J.   29n.
DeWit, J.   15
deZalduondo, B. O.   89, 94, 144
DiClemente, R. J.   138
Diderot, Denis   32, 36
divorce   193–4, 218
Do, H.   229

domestic abuse   195
Douglas, M.   26
Dover, K. J.   29
drinking   137, 138, 139, 193

education
  and material aspirations, Nigeria   220
  and unemployment, Nigeria   219
  of girls in Thailand   189, 198
Elder, G.   14
Elias, N.   174
Ellifson, K. W.   160
Embree, J. F.   134n., 135
Enel, C.   44
Erlanger, S.   129, 132
'ethnic cleansing'   93
ethnoscape, definition of   143
explorers
  and sexual journeys   36

family
  and income from sex work   79, 152, 156, 188,
    190, 192, 196, 206, 221
  and gender-power relations   83
  as determinant of sexual relations, Nigeria
    216
  expulsion of lesbian and gay youths from,
    Brazil   147, 152, 159
Farmer, P.   4, 87
Feiden, P.   92
Fine, Michele   19
Flaskerud, J.   227, 228
Flowers, N.   63
Ford, C.   8
Ford, N.   127n., 129, 131, 136, 185, 194
Fordham, G.   137, 138
Foucault, M.   32n.
Fox, M. G.   129
Freedman, E.   8, 9, 11, 17
Fuller, T.   77

Gagnon, J.   4, 5, 13, 14, 16, 28
gay community/network
  and Vietnamese Americans   243–4
  emergence of in Brazil, and AIDS   66–8
  in Amsterdam, Thai participation in   176,
    178
gender roles/expectations   30, 83, 92, 132–4,
  168, 216, 227, 233–5, 237, 241
genocide   91
Ghana   44, 48, 49, 111
Gold, S.   232
Goldstein, S.   77
gonorrhoea   221, 236–7
Gotanegre, J. F.   109
Graham, D.   62
Gray, J.   189, 191, 194, 198
Green, E. C.   9